I07646I1

Collage:

Six Decidedly Fun & Eclectic Novellas

Written by
Dave Willert

Illustrated by
Doug Kuhl

"Collage: Six Decidedly Fun & Eclectic Novellas," by Dave WIllert.
ISBN 978-1-63868-114-4 (hardcover).

Published 2023 by Virtualbookworm.com Publishing Inc., P.O. Box 9949, College Station, TX 77842, US.

DEDICATION

TO BEGIN WITH, I WOULD LIKE TO **thank you** for picking-up this book! You see, this is a very *special book* to me because I wrote the stories in it over the course of more than *half a century*! It all began with '*The Foreign Exchange Student*,' which I first penned in 1969, when I was 15 years old, and ends with '*Cannon Manchester is Dead*,' which Doug Kuhl and I began writing in 2020. I am truly *honored* to share all six of these *completed* stories with you now! In fact, I believe that you are really in for a treat! Of course, I was inspired by a lot of great people before and during the writing of each story, so unapologetically I am pleased to announce that this will be by far the *longest book dedication* I have ever written! But before I begin thanking people, I would like to thank ***God***, for the guidance, help and encouragement I receive *every single day* of my life! There is not a word created that can adequately express my gratitude!

I'd like to start by thanking my nine brothers and sisters, ***Cathi, Robert, Chris, Linda, James, Stephanie, Jon, Kirra*** and ***Teresa***. Each one of them, in their own special way, contributed greatly toward making our mutual childhoods and youth so *fun* and full of *unforgettable memories*! Even today, I'm inspired, moved and entertained by many of those wonderful memories, *sometimes*, which inadvertently find their way into my stories! Along with my siblings, I would also like to thank my ***parents***, my ***Uncle Bud***, my ***Uncle Roy***, my ***grandparents***, my in-laws, ***Ernie and Betty***, my ***friends from childhood and youth***, my ***teachers***, my ***adulthood friends***, and my ***extended family members*** for the love, encouragement, fun, inspiration and especially the valuable *life lessons* I learned from them over the years whether they realized it or not! And a very special thanks to my ***former students and their families***, who inadvertently *inspired* me throughout my career! The concerts, tours, musicals, summer programs and competing shows that we created together over parts of five decades, using every bit of talent, imagination and energy we could muster, were simply *amazing* to be a part of!

My sincere gratitude to ***Walt Disney***, for the creativity and positiveness he shared through all of his creations! In particular, an always-evolving Disneyland, as well as an array of imaginatively fun TV shows and movies which went a long way toward making my childhood in the late1950s and 1960s, as well as that of millions of others, *so very magical*! Although this great man passed away in 1966, I am *still* inspired by him today!

Thanks to the many wonderful authors who have positively influenced my writing style over the years. They include ***A.A. Milne***, author of the delightful '*Winnie the Pooh*' stories; ***Robert Heinlein, Neil Gaiman, Ray Bradbury*** and ***Fritz Leiber***, four of my favorite fantasy and science-fiction novelists; as well as ***Jane Austin***, whose stories are so close to my heart, containing very human characters and plots, crisp and witty dialogue, and *always* wrapping things up with a *happy ending*! In addition, other gifted writers I owe debts of gratitude to include, ***Mark Twain, Charles Dickens, Arthur Conan Doyle, John Steinbeck, Raymond Chandler, Dashiell Hammett, Lewis Carroll, Edgar Allen Poe, Agatha Christie, and Kenneth Grahame.***

A great big thanks to ***Doug Kuhl***, who *co-wrote* the second story in this book, the very entertaining, '*Cannon Manchester is Dead*!' He also hand-drew a clever artistic black and white collage for *each* story (*preceding it in this book*), as well as *creating* the wonderful and very colorful tableau that proudly serves as this book's 'eclectic' cover! Is there *anything* this guy can't do?

A very warm hug goes to my son, ***Alex***, for the love and great experiences we have continuously shared ever since he was born! He has *always* been a great inspiration to me! Thanks also to he and his awesome wife, ***Katie***, for inspiring Margaret and I through their many exciting adventures! Most recently, their *adoption* of their two kittens, ***Sabrina and Binx***! Whenever we watch the four of them together, we can't help but smile. It's *heartwarming*!

Finally, I would like to thank my wife, ***Margaret***, for unselfishly sharing her life with me and making mine so much happier and more meaningful as a result! I thank her for always supporting and inspiring me through her never-ending compilation of knowledge, skills, talents, tenacity, creativity, friendship and love, *regardless* of whether the endeavor I have chosen leads to financial gain… which most of the time, *it doesn't*. To top it off, she meticulously shot and edited the picture of the exciting tableau that Doug created for this book's cover. In a word, she is *wonderful*!

INTRODUCTION

Collage: Six Decidedly Fun & Eclectic Novellas, is a unique collection of six original and *highly entertaining* stories I wrote, all suitable for preteen through adult readers. Although each one of these tales *began* as a grand idea for a complete 250-300 paged novel, as I worked on them, I soon realized that they fit *much better* in the shorter format of 50 to 90 pages. I was always excited about finishing these stories, but for years I unfortunately found myself unable to find the time due to being so busy. So sadly, they all sat *unfinished* for a very long time! That is until one magical day in 2020 during my retirement, I woke-up with the epiphany that *now* I finally had the time and inclination to *finish them*! I instantly grew *inspired* to immerse myself fully into resurrecting and completing *all six stories* simultaneously! Delightedly, I began working on them beginning in August of 2020, fully expecting this exciting process to take me no longer than a year to complete. Unfortunately, with *best-laid-plans*, things *don't always* turn out the way you expect them to? It was literally *two and a half years later* that these stories were finally completed, with this book not being published and released until April of 2023!

Although each story is very different from the others, there *are* a few stylistic similarities which bind them all together. These include *extreme possibilities* of the imagination, a *happy* or *hopeful ending*, and at least a *subtle sense of humor*. Despite the fact that each tale proved too long to be considered a short story and too short to be a novel, they all fit *perfectly* as **novellas**, or as I like to call them, *mini-novels*! Each one being the *perfect length* for the reader to complete in just an hour or two! So, welcome to a world of vibrant and diverse imagination and fun, which will clearly manifest itself through the reading of this book, ***Collage: Six Decidedly Fun & Eclectic Novellas***!

The first story is a fast-moving and exciting contemporary mystery-thriller, titled, '***Where is Mr. Madison?***' It was inspired by the classic novels created by mystery, crime and espionage writers from the latter half of the 20th century through today. Our story begins in Paris, France. Paul Madison, an American and son of the title character, along with his Parisian wife, Charisse, are both desperately searching for his father, who up until very recently… was *assumed dead*? The problem is, a number of *unsavory* characters are also searching for Mr. Madison? Apparently, *if* he is still alive, they intend to *permanently silence* him because of something very damaging to them that he knows? But if he *is* alive, *where is* Mr. Madison hiding, and what *exactly* does he know that is worth *killing* him over?

The second story is a humorous homage to all of the clever writers of the exciting '*Who Done It?*' *detective stories era* of the early to mid-twentieth century. In particular, Agatha Christie, Raymond Chandler and Dashiell Hammett, with just a *dash* of Arthur Conan Doyle. This story was initially born many years ago by way of an innocuous conversation at a movie theatre concession stand sometime in the middle 1980s. To pass the time as we waited in line for our popcorn and drinks, Doug Kuhl and I imagined a series of very catchy names like *Biff Berguhndy*, *Cannon Manchester*, *Muffy DuPont* and *Chet Freshcorn*, for characters in an imaginary tale we thought we *might* someday write. And then 35 years later, *voila*, '***Cannon Manchester is Dead!***' was born! This is a delightfully twisted tale (*with a striking dose of absurdity*), where the host of a swanky party inside his luxurious Hollywood mansion in 1950, an uncommonly wealthy man named *Cannon Manchester*, is murdered right in front of everyone in attendance! After being interviewed by private investigator, *Biff Burgundy*, *all* of the guests and staff at the party appear to have airtight alibis? So, *who* done it?

The third story in this collection may best be described as a quick-paced and fun science-fiction adventure, steadily fueled by a youthful teen romance, titled, '***The Foreign Exchange Student.***' I actually wrote the first draft of this fun and quirky tale as a six-week creative writing project for my English class in ninth grade (1969). A special thanks goes to my brother, Robert, for finding and returning that original (*and only copy*) of the manuscript to me in 2020. He was originally helping me to convert it into a play in the 1970s, and over the years, we both somehow forgot about it? In completing this story over 50 years later, I was *very careful* to keep the same small-town sweetness found in the original manuscript intact. This tale begins in the small California town of Masonville (*loosely modeled after my own childhood town of Glendora*) in 1962. Ninth grader, Thomas McAdams, falls for the new girl at Masonville Junior High, the beautiful and mysterious Della Seisman, and they get off to a *perfect* start! However, although this story may *begin* as a sweet tale of boy meets girl, hold on to your hats! It very quickly veers *wildly out of control*!

The fourth story in this collection is a fantastic journey of enlightenment and adventure, titled, '***Dr. Brighton's Secret,***' which I was inspired to write after attending several sessions of my son, Alex's, archeology class at UC Berkeley in 2009. This story involves a mysterious archeological dig that UC Berkeley grad student, Stan Kelly, accompanies famous archeologist Dr. Robert Brighton on. The *incredible* experiences they share take place in the San Gabriel Mountains of California, where they see and hear wondrous, even *unbelievable* things that are *not* fantasy, but *neither* can they be fully explained? As for the important *secret* that Dr. Brighton alone has learned? The single clue he *dangles* in front of the world with the inherent hope of leading it to discovering and understanding it, lies in the conundrum, '*And when your job is done, God will bring you home*?'

Next, a quirky and fun fantasy titled, '***The Adventures of Horace Black!***' In this wildly unpredictable tale, a retired man named Horace Black, suddenly finds himself trapped inside the *body and life* of a younger man named Horace Black, and is not allowed to return to his own body and life until he puts on a play (*homage*) to another man (*most definitely dead*) also named Horace Black, who arranged this whole body-switching thing in the first place! Understand? *You will*!

And finally, the sixth story in this collection is an exciting psychological-thriller, titled, '***Mind Over Mind***!' I wrote the first draft of this in 1984. I liked the main characters in this story so much that they '*starred*' in my first two published novels, *Dimensions: The Wheat Field*, in 2009 and *Dimensions II: The Plethora*, in 2010. To begin with, Alan and Mary Dunkirk were high school sweethearts beginning in 1971. Thirteen years in the future, we find them married and living happily in San Diego. And then one day, Mary notices that the project Alan is currently involved in with his former college professor and current friend, Joe Davis, is causing him to act increasingly more secretive? *Why*? In answer to that question, the mysterious project they are working on involves *time travel* into one's unique past, where the *conscious mind* controls the *subconscious mind* and all of its *memories*. This conceivably gives the person experiencing the mind journey the option of visiting their actual memories or *rewriting* them by *changing* any prior indiscretions that they may still find troubling… at least in their *own mind*. Alan Dunkirk is beyond intrigued! But is there a *dangerous compulsion* attached to his very determined desire to revisit his past?

In closing, let me just say that returning to and completing these six novellas and ultimately publishing them in this book, *surprisingly* proved to be one of the most fun and fulfilling artistic endeavors of my life! That is because through revisiting these six wonderful stories, in some cases *many years* after they were first started, I was blessed with the hard-earned feeling of *deep satisfaction* once I had actually *completed* them! I'm afraid *that* was something I honestly *never believed* would happen? But it *did*, and it was a labor of love, pure and simple. After spending so much time diligently working nearly every day, writing, rewriting, editing and finalizing each one of these six stories (*which were all started between 1969 and 2020*), I am so excited to finally have the opportunity of sharing this completed collection with you! This book is finally being published *not* because I expect to sell a million copies or garner prestigious awards, but because *I believe* that after working so long completing and polishing them, all six stories are now shiny and bright, and written *exactly* the way I envisioned them! With that in mind, I am very hopeful that they will bring you, your family and friends, many hours of good old-fashioned reading pleasure! In fact, as you read each story, it is my hope that you will be whisked away on a delightful and exciting adventure that may even *enlighten* you along the way? And once you have completed reading it, I hope you smile as it brings you to an *uplifting* and *satisfying* conclusion! Happy reading, my friends!

Dave Willert

Table of Contents

FBI
Moulin Rouge

"Where is Mr. Madison?"

(2012)

December 28

IT WAS FOUR O'CLOCK IN THE MORNING on a cold, cold night in December, when Paul Madison was rudely awakened by the shrill ringing of his telephone. Far from happily, he forced himself to turn over in bed and chaotically grab the receiver to end the ear-piercing torture. He mumbled a quick, "Hello," and then tried very hard to wake-up. Suddenly, his eyes grew wide and his face turned pale.

"When did it happen?" he asked anxiously.

He listened intently to the response.

"I'll take the first plane out," he declared.

As Paul hurriedly threw on some clothes, he felt numb. His father was *dead*! He had not seen him for two weeks, since they had both attended his *mother's funeral*, and not for a year and a half before that. They had *not* been on the best speaking terms ever since he had decided to study in Paris against his father's wishes almost six years ago. Now, the opportunity to make peace with him was *permanently* gone. He was going home to *bury* him.

"What's wrong?" the beautiful young Parisian girl sharing his bed sleepily asked with a start.

"I've got to fly back to Monterey, Charisse. My father has… *passed away*," Paul uttered slowly.

"Oh, how awful!" she whispered in shock. "Do you want me to go along with you?"

Paul smiled warmly at his wife. "Of course I do; but I'm afraid that I wouldn't be very good company."

Charisse nodded. She *understood.*

Paul was six feet tall, of average build and with handsome features accompanying his overgrown blonde hair and hazel eyes. Charisse stood just over five foot five, possessing a *beautiful* face and a seemingly never-ending stream of curly light-brown hair softly covering her head, effectively accenting her soft brown eyes. They were each 24 years old. Paul had come to Paris from California to study music when he was 18, and had instantly become enamored with art student, Charisse. Although his heart desperately wanted them to get married *then*, she had very sensibly convinced him to wait until after graduation. So, one week *after* receiving their diplomas, in a very small ceremony consisting only of Charisse, Paul, the minister and God… they were married. Paul's parents didn't know anything about it because Paul *wanted it* that way, while Charisse's parents… watched from *heaven*. They had both tragically died in their sleep several years before. Their unexpected deaths were sadly due to carbon-monoxide poisoning coming by way of a hidden leak in their old bedroom heater. The Paris apartment Paul and Charisse now shared, her family's former vacation home, was bequeathed to her in her parents' will. Living here always reminded her of the good times she had shared with them, as well as the generous nature they had always shown toward others. Charisse had invited her only brother, Peter, to attend the wedding, but he was predictably a *no-show*. No surprise there. She *rarely* ever saw him. In fact, Paul *still* hadn't met him? To pay their monthly expenses, Paul received a modest salary from his junior teaching post at the *American School of Modern Music* in Paris. Their income was then *supplemented* by the money that Charisse earned through giving personal guided tours of the *Louvre*. These would probably *not* turn-out to be their lifelong careers, but for now they had no complaints. They both loved living in Paris, although Paul *wasn't* thinking much about that at the moment.

"How did it happen?" Charisse asked in a whisper, her eyes tearing-up as she was blatantly reminded of the overwhelming pain that she, herself, had endured when first notified of her own parents' deaths. The pain had *never* really gone away.

Paul was tying his shoes. He wanted to answer Charisse's question, but he was still too mentally consumed by the shocking news of his father's death. It somehow seemed surreal to him right now? Both men had been so stubborn, each believing that it was *he* who held the higher ground. But each one of them *also* secretly believed that in time, they *would* find common ground. Yet, after all was said and done, the undeniable truth was startlingly simple. They had simply *run out of time*! His father, Roy Madison, was now *dead*, and their '*oh, so important*' disagreement seemed so very trivial by comparison. In fact, it seemed just plain *stupid*! "I was told it was an accident."

"Nothing more?" Charisse asked.

"Nothing more," Paul confirmed.

Charisse grew silent. She was certain there was *nothing* she could say now that would make her husband feel any better, and his somber mood only confirmed it.

In the next few minutes, Paul selected and threw some final items into his travel bag as well as closing his suitcase. Following this, Charisse joined him, offering a warm hug and a long kiss designed to last until his return. The two quietly said their goodbyes, and then Paul dejectedly walked out the door, slowly closing it behind him. Charisse watched him through the front window as he disappeared into a cab, which quickly drove off; completely out of sight within moments. This was *not* the way they had intended to celebrate the end of the year. It was all so sad now.

Paul was fortunate enough to catch the first available flight out of Paris to San Francisco, and as luck would have it, it was a *nonstop*! He was due to arrive in San Francisco at noon, California time. He had already decided that he would rent a car and drive the remainder of the way to his family's home in Monterey. Once on board the plane, although his entire row was empty, he opted to keep the inside seat he had been ticketed because it was next to the window. Soon after take-off, all of the shock and anxiety of the morning finally caught-up with him, causing him to zone-out deeply in his thoughts, eventually drifting off to sleep.

He was still half-asleep when he suddenly sensed that something was wrong? Although at first *disoriented*, he very quickly grew alert! Some man, was now sitting in the seat beside his, very subtly attempting to grab his travel bag? The bag was lodged beneath the seat in front of his, so with a quick thrust of his feet, Paul forcefully shoved it decidedly out of reach of the man. Immediately, he turned his attention toward the would-be thief. Obviously frazzled, the man instinctively covered his face while quickly getting up and walking off as if *nothing* had happened. Paul was up like a shot, and none too discreetly followed the man down the center aisle toward the rear of the plane. He had one thought in mind, and that was to find out *what the hell* this was all about? When the man finally reached a dead-end at the bathrooms, Paul *knew* that he had him! But as he approached him, the man abruptly turned around and viciously hit him squarely in the face with his fist! Paul reeled at the unexpected blow, and fell unconsciously to the ground. There were *no witnesses*, as all of the other passengers appeared to be asleep in their seats, while the few crew members assigned to this flight were *nowhere* to be seen? The offending man quietly walked away without incident.

Momentarily, Paul came-to, finding himself lying on his back at the rear of the plane with a man bending over him, carefully administering him with smelling salts. The man's expression looked to be *very official*. Paul gently brushed the smelling salts aside, tentatively touched his eye and *winced*, before slowly standing-up to face him.

"Hello. I am what you call in America, the *air marshal* on this flight. You are, Mr. Paul Madison?" the man gently asked in English with just a hint of a French accent. He was *staring* intently at Paul's driver's license which he had apparently already obtained, along with the wallet that encased it.

"Yes, sir," Paul was quick to respond.

"What happened?" the man asked, politely returning his license and wallet to him, and then handing him an icepack for his bruised and sore right eye.

"Thank you," Paul said gratefully. "I was following a man, and as soon as I caught-up to him, he *hit* me!" Paul replied tersely.

"The *name* please of the man you were following?" the marshal continued calmly.

"I have *no* idea?" Paul admitted.

"Then why were you following him?" the marshal asked in confusion.

"He was trying to *steal* my bag!" Paul announced, slightly irritated.

"Where is your bag now?" the marshal asked directly.

"Under the seat in front of mine, where I left it… I hope."

Immediately, the air marshal sent a nearby steward with Paul's ticket and seat number in hand to retrieve his bag.

"Why do you suppose this man would be after your bag? Random robbery?" the marshal calmly suggested with his eyes glued to Paul's.

"I'm sure I have *no idea*," Paul replied, gently dabbing his eye with the icepack, and acting as composed as possible, but unable to completely hide his annoyance. It was becoming increasingly more apparent to him that the air marshal *suspected him* of something very serious?

"You know of course, that covertly transporting dangerous drugs into other countries is illegal. *Even* in America," the marshal quipped.

Paul chuckled. "Yes, sir. I am quite aware of that."

A moment later, Paul's bag was placed in front of them.

"Although officially, I *don't* need to do this, I would prefer receiving your permission before searching your bag," the air marshal began politely. "Do I have it?"

"Of course. Go ahead and *search away*!" Paul gestured nonchalantly.

The marshal immediately unzipped the bag and began to reveal the contents one by one. First, he pulled out a laptop computer, followed by an empty notebook with two pens, a light jacket and finally a photo album. The marshal smiled. "Do you notice anything missing?"

"I don't believe so," Paul replied.

"Then my guess is that the thief was probably after your computer," he quickly shared. "You will pardon my honesty, but nothing else here appears to be of much *street value*."

Paul found his smile again.

The marshal also smiled, returned the items to the bag and gently handed it to Paul. "I don't wish to upset the other passengers with this, so I will discreetly search the plane for this man myself," he whispered. "But with *nothing* taken, this is really about assault and battery. What did this fellow look like?"

Paul paused a moment in thought. It had all happened so fast. "I… I'm not really sure?"

The air marshal grew very apologetic as he said, "Well, unfortunately, if you *can't* identify this man, have no witnesses and not a thing was taken, then there is really *nothing* that I can do!"

Paul stared back at him blankly as he disappointedly realized… he was *right*!

Charisse had gone back to bed immediately following Paul's surprise departure. She was having a nightmare about a *crashing jetliner*, when she awoke with a start! She quickly phoned Paul, but her call was never connected. She thought logically that of course, he was still in flight, probably sleeping. But that didn't stop her from feeling rattled until she checked the news on the Internet and found confirmation that *nothing* about any intercontinental plane crash had been reported. Finally, she sat down and exhaled.

It was so strange being home *without* Paul? They had never really been apart since before their wedding day, except for when he had attended his mother's funeral two weeks ago. She didn't like this feeling. With no real family but Paul to lean on, even as a native Parisian… she found herself feeling very much *alone*. Although Paul was currently on holiday from his teaching duties for the winter break, there was no such luck for her! Requests for private tours of the Louvre, in spite of the fact that they were *seasonably* expensive, had *not* slowed down one bit! She tried to keep herself free on most weekends to spend more time with Paul, but today, Saturday, the agency had just phoned her and said that she had now been scheduled for a 3:00 o'clock meet with a small group of Americans. It seems they had only just booked it, and very surprisingly had *requested her* by name? Although she couldn't help feeling a bit *flattered* about that, she was still half-inclined *not* to accept it, since this was supposed to be her day off.

But, she ultimately decided to take it, thinking that maybe the distraction would do her some good?

As Charisse sat around the apartment, she suddenly found herself growing deep in thought. All she could think about was how much she already missed Paul. She had always been attracted to him for so many different reasons. But now, after having been married to him for a year and a half, being apart… felt almost unbearable! The phone rang, effectively breaking her trance, and with frantic hope, Charisse eagerly answered. "Hello?" But then she did not utter another word for several minutes as her smile faded. It *wasn't* Paul. The voice on the phone obviously had a lot to say as she listened intently. Finally, Charisse replied softly, "Thank you. Goodbye," as she gently hung-up the phone. She looked to be very confused?

Paul's plane landed at the San Francisco International Airport right on time. Aside from his early dozing, he had not slept a wink during the entire flight. He had been much too concerned about the mysterious thief on the plane. As he prepared to disembark, he rubbed his right eye. Although he had intermittently held an ice pack on it for much of the flight, it was still noticeably sore and swollen. He tried hard to put the flight out of his mind as he clutched his carry-on bag very tightly, and followed the other passengers through the tunnel toward the terminal.

The first thing he did once arriving there, was to call Charisse. He had promised her he would do that, but in addition, he really *needed* to hear her calming voice right now. First, he tried their apartment, but she didn't pick-up. He followed that by immediately calling her cell, but it went straight to voicemail. Disappointed and discouraged, he shrugged his shoulders, slid his phone back inside his pocket, and began the long walk to Baggage Claim.

Once he'd successfully retrieved his suitcase and cleared Customs, he rented a bright blue Chevy Camaro, and was quickly speeding off toward Monterey on a perfectly *clear and blustery* San Francisco afternoon! Paul knew this airport well. He had flown out of it to his college in Paris and then back *into* it when he had come home to stay with his parents over Christmas and summer breaks. That is, up until completing his *final* semester of college, at which time, and against his father's continued objections, he had *opted* to stay in Paris and *secretly marry Charisse*. He wistfully laughed without smiling as he realized that for the first time in his life… he was going home to an *empty* house.

His cell phone rang. Thinking of Charisse, he answered it full of anticipation, "Hello?"

"Hello, Mr. Madison. I trust your flight was pleasant enough?"

"Who *is* this?"

The calm, male voice on the other end laughed out loud, "I'm hurt! Forgot me already? I'm your father's lawyer. I called you this morning about his *funeral arrangements*? Remember?"

Paul instantly calmed down. "Oh yes. I'm sorry. To tell you the truth, I haven't had much sleep, Mr.?"

"*Avery*. Douglas G. Avery."

"I should be home in a couple of hours," Paul suggested. "Maybe we could go over the arrangements then?"

"That's why I am calling you," the man replied apologetically. "Would you mind meeting me at my residence in Monterey? I'm feeling just a wee bit under the weather today."

"Not at all," Paul answered understandingly. "Where do you live?"

"Behind the Aquarium, near Cannery Row," he explained. "There's a rather old house there, mixed-in with some newer ones, that is *very oddly* painted orange with white trim. You can't miss it!" he chuckled. "The address is 789 Author Street."

Paul laughed. "Got it! I'll see you there."

"Goodbye, Mr. Madison."

Paul was only slightly annoyed that he had to meet Mr. Avery at a place *other* than his parents' house, but he quickly accepted the fact that he very clearly was *not* in control of things right now. Anyway, he appreciated the fact that the man would be helping him to successfully navigate this *nightmare*.

About half an hour later, he took a doubletake in his rearview mirror. He hadn't been paying much attention until now, but he could have sworn that the car directly behind him had been *following* him ever since he had left the airport? The car was *very hard* to miss! It was an old VW bug, probably from the 1960s, that looked to be randomly *hand painted* in swirls of bright yellow, orange, purple and red? The fact that it appeared to be following him, could of course, have been only a coincidence, but Paul needed to find out for sure? So, at the very next exit, he pulled-off the freeway and again, he intently watched his rearview mirror to see what the bug would do (*if anything*) in response? Just as he had suspected, it pulled off the exit *right behind him*! Quickly finding a gas station not too far away, Paul pulled in… and of course, the VW followed suit, parking just one bay over. This certainly *appeared* to be more than a coincidence, but he still couldn't be sure? So, he determinedly began walking toward the driver.

It was ten to three, Paris time, and Charisse was walking at a very comfortable pace, only moments from her scheduled meeting with the American group. Paul and her apartment sat so close to the Louvre, that she *never* even considered taking a taxi. She always told her clients to meet her at the back of the gallery, close to the tour group entrance, and then just as she was doing today, she would meet them there after a very short five-minute walk. As she turned the corner, she put on her best *Parisian* smile and prepared to meet her Americans. But disappointingly, there was *no one* there? She waited for a good ten minutes more before finally spying what she believed to be her *unfashionably late* American tour group approaching.

Two thirds of the trio consisted of two moderately tall men. One had thinning gray hair and a face that clearly showed a mature man in his early sixties, while the second one sported a head of thick curly red hair, looked to be in exceptionally good physical condition, and was probably in his late twenties or early thirties. The third member of the trio was a middle-aged woman of medium height and build, with a head of *short* bleach-blonde hair which she wore in an afro. Oddly enough, no member of this group appeared to understand the concept of *smiling*?

"Are you our tour guide?" the older man asked, without so much as an introduction.

But before Charisse could respond, the younger man chimed-in, "Maybe she doesn't speak very good English?"

The woman immediately directed some *garbled* English with a quasi-French accent at Charisse. It sounded so ridiculous that she almost laughed… but ultimately, she *didn't*. Through her almost daily experience of working with tourists from all over the world, she had quickly learned to *always* keep her composure, no matter *how bizarrely* they behaved. She smiled, unflustered, and said in very clear English, "Hello! My name is Charisse." Glancing quickly at a 'cheat sheet' she had brought with her, she added, "Are you the Smythe family?"

The three Americans nodded.

"It's swell to meet you, Charisse," the older man responded coolly with a forced smile. "This here's Chris, that's Brenda and I'm Cal."

Charisse smiled. In her business, no matter how *strange* a group of tourists turned out to be, the tour was only scheduled to last for three hours, and then she was home free! She was paid directly by the agency, so the *worst* thing that could happen today was that the Smythe family *wouldn't* tip her. "Would you care to begin our tour?"

"Sure," Cal, replied professionally. "But *first* we've got a few questions to ask you."

"Questions about the gallery?" Charisse asked curiously.

"Questions about *your husband*," Brenda aggressively corrected her, as all three tourists simultaneously flashed Charisse their *badges*.

"What is this all about?" Charisse suddenly lost her composure.

"We are from the American FBI," Cal explained calmly. "We called you this morning?"

"Oh, that was you?" Charisse replied, bewildered.

Cal looked very serious, as he replied, "Yep. As I told you on the phone, your husband's father, Roy Madison, is under criminal investigation."

Charisse looked befuddled. "Yes, I recall you saying that, but I'm a little confused? I was under the impression from my husband that his father had only just passed away as the result of an accident?" she blurted out in surprise.

"*Presumed dead*," Cal replied. "A body has *not* been found... as of yet."

Charisse gasped at the news. As soon as she had recovered, she said, "Well then, I don't suppose you would mind sharing with me what he is being investigated for?"

"It's about *state secrets*!" Chris boasted. But catching a stern look from Brenda, he quickly backed-off and immediately added, "Brenda will explain."

Turning toward her, Charisse asked with concern, "How does any of this pertain to my husband?"

"Well, *he* saw his father two weeks ago at his mother's funeral," Brenda shared. "The elder Mr. Madison could have easily passed information on to his son. Our fear is that Roy or Paul Madison is now preparing to *sell* that information to the *highest bidder*!"

"That's *ridiculous*!" Charisse completely lost her composure. "My husband has *not* been on good terms with his father for years! He didn't even tell him about our wedding a year and a half ago."

"Are you *sure* about that, Mrs. Madison?" Brenda asked mysteriously.

"Why would my husband lie to me?"

Suddenly, Brenda began aggressively digging through her handbag. Moments later she pulled out what appeared to be a letter, and handed it to Charisse. "Is *this* your husband's handwriting?"

Charisse took a moment, and then after thoroughly perusing the letter, she replied, "It certainly *looks* like it?" Then growing suspicious, she demanded, "Hey? *Where* did you get this?"

"Read the part I've highlighted first," Brenda bade her. "Then we'll talk."

Charisse began reading aloud,

"*Charisse and I are planning to come home in December, before Christmas, to visit. I know that she really looks forward to finally meeting you and Mom. Take care, and we will both see you soon. Love, Paul.*"

"How do I know this isn't a forgery?" Charisse demanded.

"*Ask* your husband!" Brenda dared her. "We came across this letter while searching through the senior Mr. Madison's desk in

Monterey. It sounds to me like the two of them were quite possibly planning to meet-up for a transfer of *state secrets*? Maybe your husband was *never* planning on telling you about this trip at all? Perhaps the letter was just a cover? Or even a *code* of some sort? In any case, it sounds very *incriminating* don't you think?"

Ignoring her question, Charisse challenged, "But what if I ask Paul about this and he denies ever knowing anything about it?"

"Well of course he'll *deny* it!" Brenda laughed mockingly. "He's no fool! And anyway, only his father would be able to confirm or deny its authenticity, and at the moment… *no one* seems to know anything about his whereabouts, or whether he's even *alive*?"

"I don't understand?" Charisse questioned softly. "Paul and I *don't* keep secrets from one another, and he has *never* suggested to me that we visit his parents? Do you suppose he was planning to surprise me?"

Brenda shook her head sadly. "I doubt it. Christmas has already come and gone, and December is not far behind. This letter must come as quite a shock to you."

"You're certain that he *never* discussed this with you at all?" Cal asked, with concern.

"Yes," Charisse whispered distractedly. "Quite certain."

"That *is curious*?" Chris commented thoughtfully. "Isn't it?"

Paul had nearly reached the VW bug, when the man pumping gas into it abruptly turned to face him with an expression of extreme surprise? He appeared to be in his early thirties, of medium height, and sported a fit but average build. His thick dark hair was loaded with gel and combed straight back, looking like he belonged in the 1950s? But in every other respect he looked pretty normal.

"Hi!" the man said confidently, but in definite surprise. "Can I help you?"

"Uh, yes," Paul replied slowly. "My name's Paul, and I was just… *admiring* your car," he said quickly.

"Oh? Really?" the man asked in surprise. "Well, my name's Alex, and do you want to *buy it*?" he asked with a humorous smile.

"No," Paul laughed. "It's just that it's so colorful, I was wondering if there was a story behind it?"

Alex laughed. "There *is*, but it's not much of one, I'm afraid. This car belongs to my baby sister, Laura. She fell in love with it at first sight, and bought it at some kind of a '*quasi-vintage car*' auction." Then he smiled while shaking his head. "The very first thing she noticed after buying it was how the paint on it was *oxidized* and even *peeling off?* So, as a class project, she asked her friends from Berkeley, to join her in painting it in multi-colored *psychedelic swirls*."

"*Why*?" Paul asked curiously.

With a distasteful expression, the man replied, "You know? To commemorate the *infamous* 1967 '*Summer of Love*,' in Haight-Ashbury!"

Paul laughed. "How fun!"

"If you say so," Alex smiled while rolling his eyes. "I'm taking her on a few errands and then back to school. Then I can finally *switch* this clown car for my Tesla!"

Paul chuckled, while inadvertently glancing inside the car, where sure enough, sitting in the front passenger seat was a young woman, undoubtedly named *Laura*, who looked to be in her early twenties. He thanked the man and returned to his car. Paul guessed that he was just feeling *spooked* because of what had happened to him on the plane. Five minutes later he was driving down the freeway headed toward Monterey with absolutely *no sign* of the psychedelic VW bug in his rearview mirror.

Douglas G. Avery had been in this business for decades. He was tall, slender and sported a wispy layer of graying hair on top of his balding head, accented nicely by a well-trimmed goatee of the same color. The middle initial 'G' in his name stood for *Gandalf*, the central wizard in the fantasy book and movies, '*The Lord of the Rings*.' His parents had both loved that story, so he had grown to accept his middle name with dignity and grace. The reason he officially used the first letter of his middle name between his first and last names had absolutely *nothing* to do with pleasing his long deceased parents however. It was simply because he thought it made his full name sound a lot more *professional*. But he drew the line at ever unveiling to anyone what name the letter 'G' actually stood for. That was because sharing his *real* middle name would undoubtedly lead to his friends thinking whimsically and consequently calling him *Gandalf* or *Wizard*! Unfortunately, a nickname like that could really stick and soon spread to everyone he knew, and then to everyone *they* knew, eventually making him a very well-known personality! In his business… it was much safer to *stay invisible.* He was sitting at his desk, a vintage, oak rolltop in his study with seemingly endless piles of folders all around him, quietly waiting for his client to arrive. There was a crisp knock on his front door. Avery sighed, and immediately rose to answer it.

"Good afternoon, Mr. Madison!" he said pleasantly, as he opened the door and motioned his guest inside, before closing it behind him. "I appreciate your taking the time to meet with me during these trying times," he added solemnly. "By the way, did you *win*?" he joked, motioning toward Paul's puffy right eye.

"As a matter of fact, *no*!" Paul admitted with half a smile.

"How did it happen?" Avery surprisingly showed a keen interest.

"Some guy on my flight tried to steal my carry-on bag when he thought I was asleep," Paul explained.

"Did he succeed?" Avery asked.

"No. But he left me this *presen*t to remember him by!" Paul smiled.

Avery smiled too. "I am actually very interested in hearing *more* about that story, Paul. Do you think we could discuss it a little later perhaps?" he asked eagerly.

"Sure," Paul replied obligingly.

"Great!" Avery responded as they shook hands. "But for now, if you will please follow me into the study."

Paul quickly walked down the short hallway. As he entered the room and perused it for the first time, judging by the numerous achievement plaques he saw decorating the walls, he ascertained that Mr. Avery must be a *pretty successful* lawyer! After Avery had taken a seat behind his desk and Paul sat facing him, they were both ready to begin their imminent conversation.

"Were you and my father good friends?" Paul began, in an effort to break the ice.

"Yes! We were *very good* friends," Avery responded. "Were the two of you also?"

Judging by his question, Paul reasoned that if Mr. Avery *had* been good friends with his father, he probably *knew* the answer to that one already! So, he ignored the question altogether. "My father was gone a lot while I was growing up," he shared, "but he always made sure to make the time he *did* spend with me feel very special. Being a financial consultant was a pretty time-consuming job I guess."

"You don't need to sell me on what a great guy your dad was. We worked together on and off for over *thirty years*!" Avery commented pleasantly.

"Did you help him with legal matters?" Paul asked the man curiously, in a matter-of-fact manner.

Mr. Avery's expression suddenly grew very serious, "No, Paul. To begin with, I am *not* really a lawyer. That's just my cover. Sorry about that."

Paul looked absolutely *stunned*!

"I work for the FBI," Mr. Avery smiled. "I deal with special projects."

"What type of *special projects*?" Paul stammered.

"Things that our government wants taken care of *quietly* and with as little fanfare as possible."

"I don't want to sound skeptical here, but do you have any proof that you *are* who you say you are?" Paul quickly regrouped, and politely asked.

Mr. Avery chuckled. "I like your style, Paul!" Then he proceeded to pull out and present his FBI badge and driver's license.

Paul took a good look at both items before asking him critically, "Couldn't both of these have been *forged*?"

"They *could* have been," Mr. Avery smiled, as he turned his computer around to show Paul some images. They all represented happy moments shared by Mr. Avery and Paul's father, and sometimes his mother. "I know," Avery sighed. "These pictures could have been *photoshopped* to add me into them, but they *weren't*! Your parents and I used to go out together, mostly while you were still a small child."

"Oh yeah? *Where* did you go?" Paul tested him.

Mr. Avery laughed good-naturedly. "Well, let's see? Oh yes! Your father loved watching the San Francisco Giants play, so we would catch a game together once in a while... especially when the Dodgers were in town."

"Yes, my father *did* love watching the Giants play... *especially* against the Dodgers," Paul chuckled. But then growing sterner, he suggested, "But you could have learned that through a simple investigation, right?"

Avery sighed loudly. "Sometimes, Paul, I believe that each of us needs to consider taking a big leap of faith when we aren't completely convinced of something, like the *authenticity* of my identity, for example. We've got to weigh the evidence carefully, decide whether or not to accept it... and then decidedly move forward based on what we believe to be the truth. Otherwise, we are forever in a state of paralyzing uncertainty. Now, I could spend hours telling you about your Little League games and your great love for music, even at a very young age, but I would much rather cut to the chase. Your father has disappeared, but he may very well *still be alive*!"

"*What*?" Paul exclaimed in shock.

"As head of this Special Projects unit of the FBI, I'm telling you that we are going to *find* your father, or at the very least *find out* what happened to him with or without your help. But I believe our chances for success will be exponentially better *with you* on board. So, do you believe that I am who I say I am... or not?"

Hope was all over Paul's face! "Yes, I believe you! I just need a moment to get over the shock that my father may still be alive? But what does his disappearance have to do with the FBI?"

Avery smiled. "Your father works for us."

"No," Paul laughed nervously. "He is a financial consultant, an *accountant*!"

Avery chuckled. "Well, he *does* use those skills on most of his assignments, but I'm afraid that he still works for the FBI, same as I do."

Paul was beside himself with confusion. "I don't understand? What's going on here?"

"Let me start from the beginning," Mr. Avery suggested calmly. "But please *don't* share this with anyone else! What I am about to tell you is *classified* information. It's the *foundation* behind a secret FBI investigation that's going on as we speak."

Paul nodded his head in agreement as he anxiously awaited the story.

"A couple of months ago while working on a routine audit, your father discovered that five million dollars had been *discreetly* moved from a secret political campaign fund to a number of blocked offshore accounts. Soon after he had reported this to his superiors, he was politely told that he must have made a *mistake*? Apparently the proof to back-up his claim was *not* where he told them it would be? When he checked his own computer to confirm this, sure enough, *all* of the information he had priorly discovered, even the things that he thought he had *saved*, had *mysteriously disappeared*?"

"Wow! That *is* odd? Did you investigate it?" Paul asked.

Avery grew solemn. "In a manner of speaking," he said cryptically. "We didn't want to tip-off the people involved by starting an *official* investigation, so your father continued to *unofficially* work on solving this mystery in *secret* instead."

"Well, what did he find out?" Paul asked anxiously.

"Unfortunately, *no one knows*?" Mr. Avery admitted disappointedly. "He *vanished* before he could share it with anyone."

"When *exactly* did my father disappear?" Paul asked intently.

Avery hesitated before answering. "I can't really say for certain, but I *can* tell you that I first became aware of it several days ago."

"*Several days ago*?" Paul repeated in alarm. "Then why didn't you just explain all of this to me over the phone? Why did you have to expedite my arrival here from Paris under *false* pretenses?" he demanded.

Mr. Avery sincerely embraced Paul eye-to-eye and calmly explained, "You were in danger, and I promised your father that I would protect you. Telling you that your father was *dead* seemed like the fastest way of getting you here."

"I was in *danger*?" Paul repeated in surprise.

"Somehow word quickly spread throughout the agency that your father had learned something *very important*! From there, the news, as it always does, soon spread to the undesirables."

"*Undesirables*?" Paul repeated in surprise. "Do you mean *spies* from other countries?"

"God, no! At least I hope not!" Mr. Avery exclaimed. "I believe *these* undesirables are Americans, and I also believe that they are looking for *you*!"

"For me? But why? Do you at least know who they are?" Paul asked with concern.

"Not a clue!" Avery admitted, shaking his head. "But we have recently learned through one of our sources that several purportedly *dangerous people* have begun adamantly searching for any and all members of your father's immediate family just as soon as he went missing. *That's* the reason we brought you in without delay!"

"Is that also why you chose to meet me here instead of at my parents' house? Are you afraid that their house may no longer be *safe*?" Paul asked uneasily.

"I would *guarantee* it!" Mr. Avery admitted solemnly.

"So, you think these people are looking to *abduct* me?" Paul asked incredulously.

"There's *no* doubt!"

Paul's mind was moving at a mile a minute. "Do you believe that the man who tried to steal my carry-on bag on the plane had anything at all to do with these people?" he asked.

Mr. Avery sighed, "*Definitely*! If your father *is* still alive, these folks will try anything to find him! They probably thought you were carrying a map or a letter that would have given away his location."

"At least no one over here knows I'm married," Paul sighed with relief.

"I'm afraid that's *not* quite true," Avery smiled. "Your parents and I watched your entire wedding ceremony right here via satellite from a hidden camera that was set-up by one of our agents. I actually think there are a number of people in the agency who probably know about your marriage."

Paul gasped. "Then Charisse could be in danger?"

"Only if anyone connected with the FBI who found out is *working* with the bad guys," Avery replied quickly. And then suddenly becoming much more concerned, he insisted, "But just to be safe, you should call Charisse. I mean *right now*!"

Charisse cried softly just as soon as she arrived home from work. She truly did not know what to think? She'd tried calling Paul, but once again she had listened to a recording that told her, '*This call cannot be completed as dialed.*' Probably some Franco-American conspiracy to raise the rates! And then at last, about 11:00 o'clock that night, just as she was preparing for bed, her phone rang.

"Hello?" she said in inadvertent desperation.

"Hi, Charisse, this is Paul. Are you all right?"

A rush of relief immediately flooded her face as Charisse was quick to reply, "Oh, Paul! It's so great to finally hear from you!" Then processing his question, she added in confusion, "Yes, *of course* I'm all right. Why wouldn't I be?"

The awkward silence that followed, in addition to not answering her question, made Charisse begin to feel very *nervous*. Paul's voice returned momentarily, but he surprisingly made *no* attempt to alleviate her anxiety? Instead, he cryptically whispered, "Go to our secret place in five minutes! And Charisse, *I love you*!" Then the phone went dead.

Although Charisse was very confused and shaken-up, even so, she knew *exactly* where Paul meant her to go. The problem was, she couldn't think of any way that he could be back in Paris so quickly? Then too, there were those three tenacious FBI agents? They had *strongly* advised her to call them the moment she heard from Paul or went out. Yet something deep in her gut just *didn't trust them*? So, she *didn't*!

It was very cold outside her apartment this time of year, so Charisse bundled herself up in her long, white winter coat before she left. Once she began walking down the sidewalk toward her destination, it didn't take much to realize almost immediately that she was being *followed*? She noticed a man across the street, dressed in a heavy brown coat, discreetly matching her stride for stride. Shaken-up by this, she gradually sped-up until she eventually found herself *running*!

About the time that she finally arrived at their secret meeting place, the *Moulin Rouge*, she appeared to have lost her stalker. She quietly sighed with relief as she headed toward the front door which she *hoped* was still unlocked. She had learned through friends who had worked here, that the Moulin Rouge was usually open while being cleaned each night after a performance, sometimes 'til the wee hours of the morning. But on nights like this one, when it appeared that there had *not* been a performance, select cleaners, set builders or dancers and choreographers were still often there until at least midnight tying up loose ends... although *not* always. She really hoped that tonight was one of those late nights for *somebody*!

"*Naughty girl*!" an irritated male voice suddenly broke the silence. "You were *supposed* to call us first before you went out anywhere... remember?"

Charisse turned around sharply to see Cal, the FBI man, oddly 'tut-tutting' and wagging his finger at her. "Let me guess," he began mockingly. "You got a call and are supposed to *meet* somebody here. But *who*?"

"You know it's against the law to tap people's phones without a warrant!" Charisse declared boldly.

"We didn't tap your phone, sweety," Chris said condescendingly, as he surprisingly stepped out of the shadows. "We just *followed* you here."

"That's right," Brenda added, as she too revealed herself. "Now, *who* called you and *why* did you come *here*?" she demanded bluntly.

Charisse realized for the first time, that these people *really meant business*! Regardless of the fact that they *might* actually be FBI agents, she was certain now that her instincts *weren't* wrong, and *she didn't trust them at all*!

"Alright boys, read Mrs. Madison her rights!" Brenda hollered. "Looks like we'll need to take her someplace *real quiet* to get our answers."

"You *can't* arrest me! You don't have any jurisdiction in France!" Charisse screamed frantically.

"Who needs *jurisdiction*?" Cal smiled contemptuously, giving Charisse an immediate chill.

She didn't bother to converse with them any further. Instead, Charisse raced toward the front door of the Moulin Rouge like her life depended on it! She was relieved beyond belief to find it unlocked as she ran inside! The first floor was only a blur as she hurriedly climbed the stairs to the main showroom on the second floor. She immediately heard people seemingly not too far behind her, entering the building, their anxious footsteps seeming to run around everywhere below her on the first floor. Making a quick decision, she ran to the stage. Feeling that her bulky coat might slow her down if she had to move quickly, she frantically removed it and slid it under a large settee that was set on the stage, before hastily deciding to also hide herself behind it! In the dim light, the set onstage looked very *eerie*, as everything including the backdrops were colored in a deep *blood red*! Hopefully, Charisse thought with a shudder, this was not some cruel *harbinger* of things to come? Suddenly it occurred to her that the inside of the Moulin Rouge seemed oddly void of anyone except for the FBI agents and herself? That very strange scenario begged the questions, if no one was here rehearsing or building sets tonight, then why had the front door been unlocked? And even more perplexing, by *whom*?

Minutes later, after thoroughly scouring the downstairs, the three FBI agents noisily arrived on the second floor.

"Where did she go?" Brenda *demanded*, out of breath from running so hard.

"Well, I would guess she either stopped here, or there are still three other floors she may have run up to?" Chris obediently offered.

Cal quickly became irritated. "*Shut up*, Chris! Tell us something we don't *already* know!" he bellowed.

"You only know because I just *told* you!" Chris angrily retorted.

"You two go up and check the upper three floors," Brenda ordered, ignoring their bickering. "Let me give this floor a good looking-over… *by myself*," she insisted bluntly. "Yell, if you find anything."

In a flash, the two men dashed upstairs, leaving Brenda alone on the second floor... *with Charisse*.

Brenda laughed, "I *know* you're here, Charisse. My intuition is *never* wrong. Just come out and we'll finish our little talk. Believe me, you're in no danger from me."

The mere fact that Brenda was saying, she was in '*no danger*,' completely assured Charisse that she most definitely *was*!

Brenda, very deliberately walked through the seats in the house, carefully inspecting each one for any clues, no matter how small, that Charisse had come in contact with them tonight while desperately searching for a place to hide. Finally satisfied that she was not hiding anywhere in the audience portion of the room, she decidedly turned around and began walking in the opposite direction, *toward the stage*. "We can be friends, Charisse," she pleaded, with a sardonic smile that was just dripping with *insincerity* as she ominously stepped up onto the stage for the first time. "I know some great places to shop in Paris. Doesn't that sound like fun?"

Brenda was getting closer to Charisse's hiding place with every step she took. Suddenly, Charisse felt her heart *stop*! Watching her through a small gap between the settee and an end-table, she spied the woman viciously grin in *her* direction? Perhaps she had noticed a part of her coat which she had *too hastily* hidden? Slowly and methodically the woman retrieved a small pistol from her purse. Pointing it directly toward the settee, she seemed almost impatient to use it? "Last chance, Charisse. If you don't show yourself *right now*, I will be forced to consider interrogating you with *this*! And if I'm not happy with your answers," suddenly becoming very angry, she yelled, "I will very likely turn into a *goddamn raving bitch*!"

Charisse felt like *screaming* in terror, but if she didn't want to be found-out, she knew she had to absorb the shock of that unexpected tirade, so somehow she managed to hold it together. Out of nowhere, she suddenly felt a very small hand gently *tapping* her leg? Her body *froze* in panic! But once again she knew better than to utter a sound. The hand on her leg followed its introduction by giving her leg a gentle pat. This, very thankfully, put her more at ease. Next, the hand gently guided her leg to a sizeable hole in the stage floor, evidently so that she would *understand* what her next move should be? In the absence of a better plan or of *any plan at all*, Charisse decided to trust and follow the silent instructions of her *mysterious* benefactor. Their timely escape was severely hampered however, by their need to be absolutely quiet and swift. But they somehow managed to navigate their way through a trap door on the stage, conveniently placed behind the settee, and down a number of steps on a rope ladder leading into a secret room. It was very dark, but her new 'friend' continued to pat her reassuringly as she carefully helped Charisse down the precarious ladder. As soon as she had reached the bottom, the stranger very quietly and methodically closed and locked the trap door and then huddled with her as they silently waited. Presently, they heard the sounds of the frustrated woman walking all over the stage, including *directly above them*, angrily pushing set pieces in a desperate search for Charisse? She was obviously *dumfounded* by her perceived disappearance? Following a lot of cursing, Charisse heard the woman angrily calling the two men down from the upper floors. As soon as they arrived, there was a long discussion which Charisse could not hear well enough to understand? Finally, there were the reassuring sounds of the three possible agents slowly walking down the stairs leading back to the first floor. But just as Charisse prepared to speak, a friendly hand immediately covered her mouth. A few moments later the scurry of feet returned!

"I told you she *wasn't* here!" a younger male voice shouted in frustration. "She probably escaped off the roof!"

"Off the roof? The roof?! Now just what do you think she is? A *damn bird*?" an older male voice retorted sarcastically.

"Shut-up!" a stern female voice ordered.

And then… *immediate silence*, which was soon followed by the welcoming sound of multiple feet running down the stairs and presumably out the front door. Shortly… it became apparent to Charisse that the three agents were *really* gone! And this time, *for good*! Even so, she and her new friend still waited a good long time before finally coming out of hiding. When they finally climbed out of the secret room, Charisse took a good look at her protector. She was a very attractive young woman with short brown hair who only stood about five foot three, with a very petite but *fit* physique.

Charisse had to smile at how confidently and effortlessly this woman had saved her from harm. The woman smiled graciously at Charisse as their eyes met for the first time.

"Hello, Charisse," she said softly in English, with a strong French accent. "My name is Gabriela. I was sent by a *mutual friend* to assist you," she offered warmly. "Come on! We must leave through the backdoor! There is little time to lose!"

"What do you mean by that?" Charisse asked in bewilderment.

"We must catch a cab to the airport right away!" the girl explained knowingly.

"*Why*?" Charisse's mind was completely boggled.

Handing her a passport, Gabriela replied, "Because *you're* flying to America!"

December 29

About noon the next day, Paul excitedly met Charisse at the San Francisco International Airport. Upon their joyous reunion, once Charisse had gotten past her initial *shock* at seeing the discoloration and swelling around Paul's right eye, it was as if they'd *never* been apart! She had already spoken with him on the phone much earlier while still in Paris, and as a result of her being told *not* to return to their apartment, he'd picked-up a few items she had requested. These items included a fresh set of clothes, which she had then *gladly* changed into in the airport bathroom. She had also assured him that she looked quite forward to shopping in Monterey or even San Francisco for *anything else* she might need, such as a few *more* changes of clothes and a pair of popular American tennis shoes! Soon the two departed the airport and were driving toward Monterey. Charisse had briefly shared her experiences dealing with the 'FBI agents' while she and Paul had walked together from the airport to the car. At the same time, Paul had shared with her the miraculous news that his father *might* still be alive! When Charisse responded to his news by sharing that the FBI agents had told her virtually the *same thing*; Paul felt exhilarated! It made the prospect of his father being alive seem all the more *plausible*! Now that they were driving, they wasted *no time* in continuing their conversation.

"Did you recently send your father a letter saying that we were coming to California this December to visit them?" Charisse asked him very straightforwardly.

"What?" Paul scoffed. "Of course not! You know very well that I would have discussed something like that with *you* first! Whatever gave you that idea?"

"It's just something those agents told me that I was very confused about. They also said that you would *deny it* if I asked you about it," Charisse shared uncomfortably.

Paul laughed. "Well, by *that* logic, I'm guilty no matter *how* I respond!" Growing more thoughtful he asked, "Did you *see* the letter?"

"Yes," she nodded anxiously. "They showed me a letter they *claimed* you had written and told me that they had confiscated it from your father's desk in Monterey. The letter confirmed our plans to visit them this December?"

"Did the handwriting look *exactly* like mine?" Paul asked inquisitively.

"I thought it did," Charisse confessed earnestly.

Paul grew more serious. "Well, first of all, that letter must be a great *forgery*, because I *never* wrote it! *Whoever* they are, they probably use that trick all the time to bend their target's sympathies toward them," he suggested. "I haven't written a letter since I sent one to Santa Claus asking for a Superman costume when I was *six-years-old*!" he laughed. "Nowadays, like most everyone else, I just send texts or emails."

"Of course, you do! Now why didn't I remember that?" Charisse exclaimed. "I'm so relieved!" Then her expression grew more serious as she asked, "Do you think I was a *target* then?"

"It sure sounds that way," Paul confirmed. "By the way, what makes you think that those people you escaped from were actually *with* the FBI?"

"I guess it was their official manner after first showing me their badges," she admitted honestly. "When they questioned me, they were just so smooth. It was as if they had interrogated hundreds of people before interrogating me?" Becoming more emotional, she added, "It wasn't until later, when they chased me into the Moulin Rouge, that I wasn't so sure? While I hid, that lady,

Brenda, actually pulled out a gun and *threatened* me if I didn't come out right then? Does that sound like something an FBI agent would do?"

Paul glanced at her sympathetically. "Not *ideally* of course, but honestly, who knows what FBI agents do under pressure?" Shaking his head, he added, "Well, unfortunately I guess the only thing we *can* believe right now with any amount of certainty regarding those people is that we really have *no idea at all* who they really were?" Then he added, "But why would they want to *terrorize you* for information about my father, which they must have *known* you didn't possess? Just the fact that you were *still* in Paris and initially *unafraid* of them should have told them right away that you had *no idea* what was going on?"

"I don't know?" Charisse replied apprehensively. "But I hope your Mr. Avery can shed a little light on that before something *awful* happens to us!"

"Me too," Paul agreed solemnly, as he gently squeezed her hand.

About two hours later, Paul parked his car in front of Mr. Avery's house and they quickly disembarked. When they reached his door, Charisse immediately rang the bell, Avery answered, and they were promptly escorted into his study where they were soon seated.

After Charisse and Mr. Avery had been properly introduced, he proceeded to hear all about her recent unsettling adventures with the 'FBI agents.' He frowned when she finally reached the conclusion of her story. "Well, Charisse," he said empathetically, "It seems that *you* are already tangled-up in this case."

"It certainly wasn't *my* idea!" Charisse declared. "I am obviously very happy to be here with Paul, but I still don't understand *why* I was whisked out of Paris without even being allowed to pack?"

"Well, after all that you went through, you must have known that going back to your apartment *wouldn't* have been a safe thing to do," Avery explained. "In addition, I believe that if we'd left you in Paris, it would have been only a matter of time before the bad guys would have figured out some slick and discreet way of *abducting* you."

"*Abducting me*?" Charisse repeated in shock. "But they said they only wanted me to answer some questions?"

"And yet, you *ran away*?" Avery responded thoughtfully. "You obviously did not trust them!"

"You're right there!" Charisse confessed.

"And *that's* why you're here, instead of *locked away* in a cold and dark basement somewhere in the backstreets of Paris," Avery shared seriously.

"I still don't understand why they were after *me* at all?" Charisse professed.

Mr. Avery calmly replied, "Don't feel singled-out, Charisse. They're after *all* of Roy Madison's family, and as Paul's wife, you *certainly* qualify."

Charisse didn't respond, but her face took on a very worried expression.

Noticing that, Paul turned to Mr. Avery and immediately changed the subject. "Have you heard any news since I was last here about this case… or *my father*?"

"Well, Paul, on those two fronts I just did receive an exciting *breakthrough* of sorts," Avery shared. "An agent of ours, who has been working undercover as part of the political group that sent the money to those five blocked bank accounts in the Cayman Islands, *intercepted* an encrypted message to five blocked *email* accounts. We strongly suspect that those email accounts more-than-likely belong to the *same* people they already sent the money to."

"What did the message say?" Paul asked quickly.

"If my translation is correct, it simply says, "*Hogmanay*.""

"Why, that's the Scottish New Year?" Charisse quickly added. "What significance could *that* possibly have?"

"Frankly, we have *no idea* at this point," Avery continued, "but the smartest minds in both the FBI and the CIA think a *big* event is being planned for that day. Probably something *horrific*!"

"Wow!" Paul exclaimed. "But why are you sharing that with us?"

"Because I believe that this event is *intimately intertwined* with your father's disappearance," Avery admitted. With a hopeful and sincere expression, he added, "So I would be very grateful if you both agreed to play an *active* role in this investigation for just a couple of days."

"You mean *risk* our lives?" Charisse declared in shock. "But Mr. Avery, we are *not* trained agents!"

"Precisely! That's why you'll fool our adversaries!" Avery shared confidently. "They will have no idea that you are both working for us. Perhaps they will even slip-up and enlighten us further on the significance of the word, *Hogmanay*?"

"That logic sounds *pretty iffy*!" Charisse retorted suspiciously. "What if we get killed in the process?"

"I don't believe that by helping us, you will increase your chances of experiencing an *untimely demise*," Avery replied calmly. "They obviously want you both *alive*."

"Why is that?" Paul asked curiously.

"To hold hostage and to get information from. Besides your dad, I'm certain that the two of you are their number one targets right now," he conjectured.

"If we agree to help you… do you think it will improve the chances that you'll be able to find my father?" Paul asked hopefully.

Avery thought for a short moment and then replied, "Yes, I honestly believe *it will*. Because the two of you can serve as *assets* which we can use to hopefully extract information from the plotters *without* them even knowing it!" Then immediately growing excited, he shared, "By the way, I've got a *big surprise* for you."

"What is it?" Paul asked curiously.

"*Your mother is alive*!"

Brenda, Cal and Chris, the self-proclaimed *FBI agents*, were comfortably lounging in a cheap Monterey motel room, having arrived only hours before from Paris. The motel was no doubt 'sarcastically' named, *The Elegant*! The single room they shared was small, with very shabby tan curtains covering the large 'picture window' by the door. The color of these curtains *unintentionally* matched the color of the walls? That was because although the walls had once been painted a stark white, over time and a whole lot of cigarette smoke, they had *morphed* into the same dingy shade of *tan* as the curtains. The 'cozy' room offered two double-beds with well-worn gray bedspreads, a small television set, a wet-bar with an old coffee-maker, a small table with four chairs, a small bathroom with a shower, but no tub, and a dusty green couch that they were currently *all* sitting on. The motel was located *far* from Cannery Row in a dodgy part of Monterey, and the room came complete with a serenade of loud and never-ending *street noise*. It wasn't glamorous, to be sure, but no one would *ever* think of looking for them there. Each of them was currently reading over the email they had received yesterday, as if to *double-check* that they all had the same information and were very clear on what it meant!

Brenda was the first to speak. "Even if Madison *has* told everybody in the FBI all that he knows... he *doesn't* know about any of this!" she declared. "How could he? We just found out ourselves?"

"You may be right, but we can't know that for *certain*, Brenda. Can we?" Cal shot back, sounding very nervous. "The sooner we take this guy out of circulation, the better for all of us."

"You mean *kill him*?" Chris interjected.

"*Not* my first choice," Cal grimaced at Chris. "First, we have to *find* him. Then, we squeeze out *everything* he knows and who he's told." After a short pause, he asked Brenda, "Do you think those two kids know anything at all?"

"Why ask me?" she laughed haughtily, and then deciding to grace him with an answer, she shared flippantly, "I really have *no* idea... but I strongly doubt it!" Suddenly growing inspired, she added, "You know what though? If we just *happened* to catch one or both of those kids, there would be absolutely *zero* chance that Madison would do anything that might jeopardize their lives. Wouldn't you agree?"

"Yeah, sure! So, what are we waiting for?" Chris suddenly grew very excited.

"Easy boy," she smiled. "Remember, tonight we're going fishing!"

"What are we going to catch?" Chris asked.

"We'll just have to *wait and see*," she smiled cryptically.

"Your mother has been hiding in a safehouse ever since your father caught wind of the fact that these guys were after him. He very wisely knew that they'd target her to get to him if she didn't disappear first," Avery shared. "So, we faked her death and she's been living there ever since."

"Is there any way we could see her *today*?" Paul asked hopefully.

"I wish I could advise that," Avery replied gently, "but I am very much afraid that these guys, whoever they are, are monitoring the two of you very closely. That's why I had you meet me here again. This is truly the *only place* I feel safe talking without fear of being overheard!"

"If we are under *constant* surveillance, then surely they must have watched us enter this house?" Charisse offered with concern. "So, they must *already know* that we are in touch with the FBI!"

Avery smiled. "Well, I certainly hope not. The sign over my door says, 'Douglas G. Avery, Attorney at Law,' and as far as anyone who wants to know, you two are coming here to discuss Roy's will and burial."

"Do you mean to say that your true identity as an FBI agent is kept *secret*?" Charisse asked in surprise.

"Well, it's kept secret to *most* people anyway, including the majority of agents inside the FBI. I work very hard at keeping myself *under* the radar," he explained.

Paul and Charisse nodded their understanding. "Is my mother doing well?" Paul implored.

"Oh yes. She's a real *trouper*," Avery smiled. "In fact, she was able to contact me not more than an hour ago by courier, with news that she had received an envelope this morning, *possibly* containing some very important papers." He paused momentarily and then added animatedly, "She strongly believes that the envelope may very well have come directly from *your father*!"

"Whoa! What made her think that?" Paul asked eagerly.

"She distinctly heard the *secret knock* at the front door that we developed to assure her that it was safe to open it. So, when she did, there was an envelope just sitting there on the mat in front of her. It was even *addressed* to her? She examined the handwriting and *swears* that it was Roy's!"

Charisse quickly responded, "But I was shown a letter by those three FBI agents…"

"Alleged agents," Avery interrupted calmly.

"Alright, *alleged* FBI agents," Charisse corrected herself. "A letter that they told me Paul had written to his father. And after looking it over, I could have sworn that it was *his* handwriting? Yet Paul assured me that the letter was definitely a *forgery*! Couldn't this letter be a decoy planted by the bad guys just to put the FBI on the wrong track?"

"Unfortunately, that is *always* a possibility, Charisse," Avery replied thoughtfully. "But since that packet was delivered to *her*, that would indicate to me that whoever sent it *knew* that Jocelyn was alive, and obviously *where* she was hiding. In reality, we actually have *no data* suggesting that anyone *outside* of a few agents in the FBI are aware of that?"

Charisse nodded.

Avery continued, "Jocelyn told me in her note that the papers are *encrypted* using some code she thinks she may have seen before? She can't break it though, so she doesn't think it's any code the FBI sees or uses regularly."

"How would she know that?" Charisse asked in surprise.

Avery laughed at her unbridled curiosity. "Because Jocelyn is *very* sharp! Over the years the FBI has used her from time to time to help us break difficult codes in encrypted messages like this one."

"My *mother* is an FBI agent too?" Paul shouted, flabbergasted.

Avery laughed. "Not an *agent*, Paul. I guess you could call her a part of our very specialized pool of *adjunct office help*."

Paul chuckled, and then suddenly grew very excited. "Well then let's go pick-up that envelope!"

"I told you, Paul, it's far too dangerous!" Avery began in earnest. "More than likely, the reason your mother *didn't* send those papers with a courier in the first place was because she feared that they might be intercepted. You see, if the bad guys ever got a hold of those papers, even if they couldn't crack the code, that would still *stop us* from ever getting the opportunity of reading them and learning what your father believes is so *timely* and *important*!" he fervently explained.

"Then have another one of your couriers pick it up and bring it back to you?" Charisse suggested simply.

Avery looked concerned. "All of my couriers have been to that house a number of times over the past couple of weeks already," he shared. "If by chance these plotters have been watching that house, and due to my sending the same couriers one time too many, they *suspect* any of them as being FBI, then our safehouse is compromised along with your mother's safety! So, I really hesitate to tempt fate."

"Then let *me* go!" Charisse offered, anxiously.

"It's too risky," Avery quickly shot back. "You're much too valuable of an asset to send out."

"But I am great at *disguises*?" Charisse said excitedly. "Make-up was a big part of my art training in Paris. They'll *never* know that it's me!"

"She *is* incredible," Paul confirmed hesitantly.

"And you can't really trust anyone else to do this, can you?" Charisse added slyly.

"As it is right now, aside from my usual couriers, the only people I trust are the two of you," Avery confessed.

"I'll go!" Paul immediately offered.

Mr. Avery smiled. "Thanks for volunteering, Paul, but unfortunately after that episode on the plane, without a *very* good disguise I'm afraid that *you* are simply too easily recognizable."

Accepting his defeat, Paul gently asked, "Are you *certain* you want to do this, Charisse? It sounds to me like if anything goes wrong, it could get *ugly* real fast!"

Charisse smiled at Paul, acknowledging his concern, but then replied stubbornly, "Yes, I *really* want to do this!"

Avery sighed and then grew serious. "Alright, Charisse. Tonight, as disguised and covertly as possible… we'll *send* you out!"

That night, under the cover of darkness, a young pizza deliveryman determinedly stepped out of his parked car and walked up to 314 Stonecrest Avenue in San Francisco. The house was located in a cul-de-sac between four other houses which appeared to be lived in, *but weren't*! As Mr. Avery had explained to Charisse, the FBI merely made it *look* that way, with lights turned on and off by timers inside the houses and cars parked on the driveways. In this way, the safehouse retained its secrecy, with no one passing by becoming suspicious that only *one* house in the cul-de-sac was occupied! This set-up was also a great way of sidestepping nosy neighbors! When he reached the door, he *didn't* push the doorbell, but chose instead to knock… that *special knock* he had learned only hours before. A few moments later, the door was quietly opened by a woman who graciously accepted the pizza and invited the boy inside before she carefully closed and locked the door. Then the woman politely ushered him toward a round oak kitchen table where they both proceeded to sit down.

"Hello," the boy quickly cut to the chase. "I am Charisse, wife of your son, Paul."

The woman, appearing to be in her early fifties, stood about five foot eight. She had medium-long and wavy dark hair, which fell down just past her shoulders. Judging by her smile, she also possessed a very warm persona. She immediately shook her head and said, "What a *great* disguise! No offense, but you look *pretty good* as a boy!"

Charisse laughed. "Thank you! That *was* the general idea!"

Jocelyn chuckled, but then stood up and walked over to embrace her! "Oh, Charisse! I have waited such a long time to meet you!"

The two women joyously hugged for the *first* time. Afterward, as they both sat down again, Charisse shared honestly, "Paul wanted to come and see you so very badly, but Mr. Avery thought it best that I come here alone. He said it would be less conspicuous."

"Disappointedly, I have to agree with him," Jocelyn admitted. "But you be sure to tell Paul how very much *I miss him,* won't you?"

"I will, Mrs. Madison… Jocelyn… mother…" Charisse grew a little confused as she asked, "How *exactly* would you like me to address you?"

Jocelyn laughed. “In any manner you wish, dear.”

“How about *Jocelyn*?” Charisse decided quickly. “That’s such a beautiful name?”

“Yes, that would be perfect!” she replied with a smile.

“Do you have any idea where your husband is now?” Charisse asked curiously. “Or if he is…”

“*Alive*?” Jocelyn solemnly completed her question. “Yes, I believe that Roy is very much alive. I have never doubted *that* for a moment. He’s been in this business a very long time, you see, and can be quite *elusive* when he needs to be,” she shared knowingly. “But as for *where* he is now, I really haven’t a clue?”

Charisse nodded, and then remembering why she had come, shared, “Mr. Avery told me that I was supposed to pick-up some papers that you believed were from your husband? He thought they *might* be very important.”

“Yes!” Jocelyn confirmed excitedly. “As you probably know, the papers were delivered to me early this morning. The only part of the delivery that was *not* in code was the front of the envelope which surprisingly had *my name* written across it? Oh, and there was also a hand-written note inside instructing me to deliver the packet to Mr. Avery as soon as possible,” she shared, while gently handing Charisse a standard-sized manilla envelope.

“Why doesn’t your husband just send Mr. Avery an email with this information on it? It sounds to me like that would be a whole lot easier than *this*?” Charisse mused aloud.

Jocelyn smiled. “You’re *new* to the spy game, aren’t you? The Internet is *not safe*, nor are phone calls, texts, mail, fax machines and all other known types of public communication. They are all wide-open to hacking in an ever-growing number of creative ways. Mr. Avery gleans a lot of information himself from those sources!”

“Oh!” Charisse gasped in surprise. “But how does a person’s enemies *know* when you are sending something out?” she asked honestly.

Jocelyn chuckled. “If it’s important to them, then *they know*! You would not believe how sophisticated, clever and technically savvy criminals are today! That’s why crime is a *multitrillion dollar* enterprise worldwide!” she shared intently. “That’s also why the *most secure* way of sending an important message, is also the *oldest*!"

Charisse nodded, and then perusing the contents of the envelope, asked very curiously, "What *exactly* do you think these papers say?"

"You *are* curious, aren't you?" Jocelyn laughed.

Charisse smiled. "Yes, I suppose I am."

"Well, these papers *probably* represent something very *timely* pertaining to this case. Otherwise, why would Roy risk capture or even *worse* by personally delivering them to me?" Jocelyn explained.

Just then, a high-pitched beep went off throughout the house!

"What is that?" Charisse asked in surprise.

"That was the sound of the house alarm being *turned off*!" Jocelyn shouted anxiously.

Suddenly, they both grew *terrified* as they heard a loud crashing sound and the spontaneous *ripping apart of wood*, as a very powerful battering ram was apparently making short work of the solid oak, steel-reinforced, previously triple-bolted, *front door*! It was so loud that their neighbors would have surely heard it... if they *had* any!

"Quick!" Jocelyn frantically whispered to Charisse. "Hide in here!"

"In the *closet*?" Charisse exclaimed in confusion.

"It has a false front!" Jocelyn rushed to explain. "*Whoever* is breaking into this house *must not* be allowed to get hold of these papers!"

Charisse, holding the envelope tightly against her chest, dashed inside the closet, quickly maneuvered her body behind the false front and secured the lock, while Jocelyn hurriedly closed the closet door and raced upstairs.

Within the next few minutes, Charisse heard the unmistakable sound of multiple footsteps running *just outside* her closet door. Next, she heard those same footsteps dashing up the stairs and then... her *heart fell* as she heard the gut-wrenching sound of Jocelyn's screams! Charisse could hardly bear it! But as much as she wanted to help her, she knew that Jocelyn would want her to stay and protect these papers at all costs. Finally, she heard the distinct decrescendo of footsteps leaving the house. Still, remembering what she had learned at the Moulin Rouge, Charisse remained *perfectly silent and still* for a long ten minutes. Breaking the silence in the house, she suddenly heard two voices conversing upstairs. From the sound of it, they were opening and closing *every closet door* on the floor! Before long, they had walked down the stairs and reached *her* closet door, which they abruptly opened! She distinctly heard someone meticulously tapping on all three walls. For a long moment, she was *terrified* that she had been found-out?

"I think this closet may have a *false front*?" a younger man's voice excitedly declared. "It sounds hollow behind this wall."

Charisse *stopped* breathing!

"Is there a latch or some button we can push to open it?" An older man's voice quickly suggested.

"None that I can find?" The younger man admitted disappointedly. "Hey, why don't we just *shoot it*? If we hear a scream, we'll *know* somebody's in there?"

Charisse was suddenly aware of a dreadful silence? She simply *could not believe* that the other man was actually *considering* the young man's insanely dangerous plan?

"You're joking, right? We *don't* want to hurt the guy?" The older man said hesitantly. "We just want to *interrogate* him."

"Don't worry," the younger man assured him. "I'll aim *low*!"

Charisse was *terrified*! She quickly deliberated whether or not to give herself up, when suddenly a gunshot shattered the silence and shockingly *blasted* through the closet's wall, perpendicular to the one she was hiding behind and to her right. It was all she could do to keep from *screaming*!

After a moment, the shooter's voice disappointedly admitted, "Well, I guess no one's behind *that* wall." Then suddenly growing more excited, he added, "Hey! Maybe I should shoot *all three* of the walls in *every* closet in this house? There's certainly room behind each one of the walls in *this* closet for somebody to hide?"

"*Stop*!" a loud female voice frantically yelled, as the woman raced into the house from outside. "What are you doing, goddamn it? *Everyone* in San Francisco probably heard that shot! Put that gun away, you *idiot*!"

"But I…" the young man began to explain.

"*Shut-up*!" The woman abruptly cut him off. "We want that courier *alive* and not bleeding and riddled with bullets! He's got to be around here somewhere, right? Just keep looking and try very hard *not to kill him*!"

Listening carefully, Charisse heard the footsteps leaving her closet and running upstairs. But she could not be sure that *everyone* was gone? Regardless, feeling as if her heart would *explode* at any moment, she forced herself to carefully pull out her depowered cellphone from her jeans pocket and turn it on. As she desperately prepared to punch Mr. Avery's number, her sweaty palms betrayed her! Her cellphone suddenly went *crashing* to the floor, creating a short banging sound as it hit! She was *terrified*, afraid to move even a muscle! But when she heard no sounds of footsteps or voices coming from anywhere in the house, she very slowly reached down to recover her phone. Silently her hand embraced it firmly this time, as she carefully called Mr. Avery. He quickly answered, and in very hushed tones she briefly explained her *precarious* predicament. He calmly acknowledged her situation and gently instructed her to turn-off and put away her cellphone to avoid the risk of them tracking it, or of it accidentally going off. Then he calmly instructed her to continue *silently* waiting. He assured her that someone would be there very soon. Not more than five minutes later, she heard the welcoming sound of multiple sirens blaring loudly outside on the street! They were *unmistakably* approaching the house, while in stark contrast, she heard the frenzied and panicked sounds of multiple footsteps *running away from the house* as fast as their feet would carry them! Moments later she heard the sound of a vehicle driving off! It was only a few minutes later that someone opened her closet door and clearly tapped the secret knock on the wall in front of her. With great apprehension, Charisse hesitantly unlocked and opened her false front. She *sighed* with relief the moment she saw Mr. Avery! Paul was nervously standing there beside him, looking *very* distraught as he saw the bullet hole in the inside closet wall.

"I'm so sorry!" Charisse cried, as she immediately ran to Paul's awaiting arms. "They *took* Jocelyn! I must have led them straight to her!"

"No, you *didn't*, Charisse!" Mr. Avery was quick to console her. "I'm sure that those people were staking-out this house long before you arrived."

"What makes you say that?" Paul asked, noticeably upset over this whole situation.

"The fact that they chose to break down the door and kidnap Jocelyn *only* after Charisse came by with a delivery. And I can assure you both that it was *not* the pizza they were hoping to get a hold of!" Avery looked as somber as they had ever seen him.

"What about my mother?" Paul asked desperately.

"Don't worry. I'm sure she's safe," Avery shared calmly. "Just be ready for the ransom demand."

"*Ransom demand*?" both Charisse and Paul gasped simultaneously.

"I'm certain that's why they took her, *with or without* those important documents they had hoped to intercept," Avery explained. "I just wish we knew for certain what became of those papers?"

"Do you mean *these* papers?" Charisse asked gently, removing the manila envelope from its hiding place under her jacket and presenting it to him.

"Yes! This is *wonderful*!" Avery proclaimed as his face lit up. "Thank goodness Jocelyn gave them to you *before* the break-in!"

"I believe that after we heard those people tearing down the front door, she gave herself up just to hide me. I think she believed that I was her *last chance* of getting those papers delivered," Charisse dejectedly explained, before finally losing control and gently sobbing into Paul's shoulder.

Avery nodded understandingly and said, "And I believe that she was *right*!"

Mr. Avery immediately instructed one of his agents to drive Paul and Charisse back to their hotel in Monterey. As soon as they arrived at the Spindrift, they hurriedly escaped to their room and ordered a late supper from room service. Charisse was still *horrified* at the memory of Jocelyn being kidnapped, and Paul had little luck calming her down. But thankfully, after dinner they both found themselves too exhausted to think about *anything*! So, regardless of their high levels of anxiety, they were both quick to fall asleep.

Meanwhile, it was well past midnight when Douglas G. Avery intently sat at the vintage desk in his den, carefully studying the documents he had received earlier from Charisse. Yes, they were encrypted, but just like Jocelyn, he had certainly *seen* this exact code before! He smiled. This was the encryption that he, himself, had developed many years before for secret correspondence between Roy and him! To his knowledge, no one else in the world knew or cared that this seemingly arbitrary code even existed! This convinced him that the message before him had, without a doubt, been written and sent by *Roy Madison*! It wasn't long before he had deciphered it in its entirety. He frowned. Now he understood what these plotters were up to. Unfortunately, the message left him with a few *critically* unanswered questions?

December 30

The next morning, as Paul first opened his eyes to daylight, he noticed that Charisse was *already* awake? She was quietly gazing out the window at the cold and overcast skies, while simultaneously listening to the hypnotic effect of the gentle ocean waves softly breaking. But her pained expression gave away the fact that she was *revisiting* her distressing experiences from the past night.

"Good morning, Charisse," Paul offered gently, not wishing to upset her further.

Turning around with a sad and distant expression, Charisse slowly replied, "Good morning, Paul."

"You're up so early?" he observed curiously.

Charisse's disheartened expression never changed as she replied, "Yes. I just *can't* seem to get over how selfless your mother acted last night in hiding me while giving herself up to those horrible kidnappers. I feel just *awful*!"

"Don't be so hard on yourself, Char," Paul tried hard to comfort her. "After all, you delivered those papers and I'm *certain* they will turn out to be pivotal in solving this case and getting my mom back!"

"I sure hope so," Charisse admitted. "But that *still* doesn't change the fact that your mother was *kidnapped* in the first place, does it? If I just hadn't insisted on going to see her last night, it would have been *her* hiding in that closet instead of me!"

"But if you *hadn't* gone to see her, she wouldn't have been able to *give you* the papers!" Paul insisted. "Face it, Char, all things considered, everything has turned out the best it could. I'm very confident of that!" Then he met her eyes and very gently said, "Don't worry. We'll get my mom back before you know it."

Charisse found her smile at last. "You are always so positive, Paul. You have been like that for as long as I have known you. How do you do it?"

Paul smiled wistfully. "Honestly? It's the best way I know of to deal with uncertainty. First, I believe that both of my parents are dead, then I receive genuine hope that they are both *alive*… but now, I have absolutely *no idea* what to think?" He paused a moment and added, "That's where hope and a smile come in," he said warmly. "They make every trial we face, regardless of the odds, somehow seem *possible*?"

Charisse hugged him like a loving mother hugs her child. Paul was alright. He just *needed* this moment of encouragement. As for Charisse… the *very same thing* applied.

After getting dressed, ordering room service and quietly sharing breakfast, they both agreed to call Mr. Avery to find out what he had gleaned (*if anything*) from reading the encrypted papers.

Just then, as if the walls of the room were secretly listening-in on their private conversation, the phone rang? Although the loud and strident ringing initially caused them both to jump, Paul quickly answered it.

"Hello?" he obviously heard a familiar voice. "As well as can be expected. We were just going to call you," he replied. Whatever the caller said next, really caught his attention. "We'll be right over!"

"What is it?" Charisse asked excitedly.

"Mr. Avery wants to speak with us," Paul whispered mysteriously. "He didn't want to discuss it over the phone."

"Well then *let's go*!" Charisse exclaimed with a new-found determination that seemed to invigorate every cell in her body.

Soon, the two of them had evacuated their hotel room and were headed for the parking garage. Moments later they were in their car, racing over to Mr. Avery's house. Once they arrived, it only took a few minutes before they found themselves once again, comfortably seated in his study… in *complete* anticipation.

Turning toward Charisse, with a very sincere and apologetic expression on his face, Avery started off by saying, "I'm so sorry, Charisse! I'm afraid I didn't do a very good job of predicting what would happen last night, did I. Thank goodness *you* weren't abducted too!"

"Thank you, Mr. Avery," Charisse replied appreciatively. "I still blame myself for Jocelyn's capture, but I also agree with what you said last night. You know, that they were just *waiting* for my delivery before knocking down the front door."

Avery nodded solemnly. "Whoever those guys were that turned off the alarm, broke down the door and took Jocelyn last night, they must have a very good *mole* in place in the FBI to have already *known* where she was being hidden and how to get her out!" he shared with concern. "Basically, Roy and I were the only agents who were privy to knowing where she was!" he declared.

"You said, '*basically*?' Did you share that information with anyone else?" Paul asked inquisitively.

"Just my peers and superiors at the FBI," he admitted. "That's normal protocol whenever hiding someone in a safehouse as a failsafe."

"Then the kidnappers *must* have learned where she was being hidden sometime during *that* spread of information?" Paul deduced.

"I was thinking that very same thing," Avery concluded sadly. "And unfortunately, that just about *confirms* that someone rather high up in the FBI is *definitely* involved in this!"

"Any idea who?" Paul asked.

"Disappointingly, still *no*," Avery replied slowly. "But at least we have a new place to start." Then he changed the subject and shared, "I read those papers last night."

"You actually *broke* the encryption so quickly?" Charisse asked excitedly.

Avery chuckled. "Don't be *too* impressed. It really wasn't very difficult," he admitted. "Roy and I had used that same obscure code a number of times before." He paused. "Those papers are without a doubt *from him*! I'm certain of it!"

"Well then, doesn't that imply that my father is *still alive*?" Paul blurted out hopefully.

Avery frowned gently. "Unfortunately, it only implies that he *was alive* at the time that he wrote those papers. We don't even know for certain that it was *him* who delivered them? He may have an accomplice?"

"But you *do* think he's still alive, right?" Paul asked, begging for confirmation.

"Yes, of course I do!" Avery smiled. "I only wish I knew where he was?"

"If you feel comfortable telling us," Paul asked intently. "What did the papers say?"

"*Everything* that Roy had learned about this case both before and after his disappearance!" Avery announced excitedly.

"Wow! What *exactly* was that?" Charisse pleaded.

Avery hesitated before speaking. "I know that I can trust you both, but you've still got to *swear* not to repeat this to anyone!" he demanded.

Both Charisse and Paul, eyes wide open, nodded their agreement.

"Well," Mr. Avery began, "those papers that Charisse gave me, said that these people, whoever they are, are definitely planning a major *political assassination*," Avery shared slowly. "And *soon*!"

"Where will it happen?" Paul asked quickly.

"*Washington D.C.*!" Avery exclaimed.

"Whoa!" Charisse spontaneously uttered in shock. "Who is the target?"

"We still don't know that?" Avery confessed disappointedly. "I can think of any number of politicians in D.C. who are among the *most hated people* in America today!"

"Well, do you at least have a lead about *when* this will happen?" Paul asked.

"Unfortunately... *no*!" Avery admitted disappointedly. "*That* information has not yet found its way to us. But I'm hoping that by leaving the two of you in the lion's den for just a bit longer, with any luck, we'll somehow discover that, and be able to *stop* this thing from happening!"

"We'll do our best to help, but *please* don't use Charisse as bait like you did last night," Paul insisted. "I nearly had a heart attack worrying about her!"

"Now wait a minute, Paul. We didn't *intentionally* use her as bait," Avery replied gently. "But yes, we always know that no matter how carefully we prepare, *every operation*, including last night's, carries a certain amount of risk."

"Risk or not, I'm *not afraid* anymore!" Charisse declared. "If it means getting Paul's mother back? I'll do almost anything!"

Avery laughed. "I *love* your spunk, Charisse!" Smiling, he said, "Today's *harrowing* assignment is for the two of you to visit the Monterey Aquarium."

"That doesn't sound too tough?" Paul remarked in surprise. "But why there?"

"Because the FBI *strongly* believes that you will be contacted by the kidnappers there," Avery explained. "We will be there too, of course, but *hopefully* we will be able to remain incognito. That is, unless there is some *absolute need* for us to intervene."

"But how will the kidnappers *know* that we'll be there?" Charisse asked, puzzled.

"We *told* them, so to speak," Avery smiled.

Both Paul and Charisse shockingly looked at him in disbelief?

Avery chuckled. "Actually, we put up a post from you on social media, Charisse. It said that you were '*excitedly* going to visit the Monterey Aquarium for the *very first time* today.'"

"And you're banking on the fact that they've *seen* that?" Paul asked dubiously.

"Without question!" Avery doubled-down. "I'm certain they were *all over it*! Perusing social media is a standard investigative technique used by the FBI, and now that we believe there to be a *strong connection* between the FBI and them, I would *bet this house* on it!"

"Okay. But how do you think they will contact us?" Charisse asked inquisitively. "In person, or by using some other more *discreet* method?"

"It's hard to say?" Avery confessed. "So far, their moves have been *anything* but predictable."

"So, what would you have us do?" Paul asked impishly. "*Hold up a sign*?"

Avery laughed, "I don't think *that* will be necessary." Then growing more serious, he added, "The *very first* thing I'd like the two of you to do once you arrive there is to split-up."

"*Split-up*? But why?" Charisse asked defiantly. "Wouldn't that be more dangerous for us?"

"Probably. But in that way, there will be *no witnesses* present to confirm or deny what either one of you talked about with them, making them more likely to approach you," Avery explained. "We also think that if you're *not together* when they contact you, they'll probably be more relaxed and more *likely* to say something they shouldn't!"

"Do you want us to wear wires then?" Charisse asked helpfully.

Avery smiled. "I'm afraid that what I *want* and what I *think* are currently sitting on opposite sides of the table. If they so much as caught an inkling that one or both of you were working with us, they would immediately *terminate* all contact, as well as probably killing your mother and the two of you to boot! Then with all ties to them severed, we might *never* find out how to stop this assassination!"

"Not to mention that *we'd both be dead*!" Charisse exclaimed.

Paul shuddered. "Do you believe that my mother is safe now?" he asked with great concern.

Avery nodded, and encouragingly replied, "Yes, I believe that she's safe and she'll *stay* that way just as long as you keep the channels open and play along by *their* rules." Then he added, "And guys?"

"Yes?" Paul and Charisse replied simultaneously, unsure of what to expect.

"If those kidnappers *are* FBI, they probably have access to all kinds of small high-tech gadgets including *lie detectors*. Pay very close attention! Their appearance will probably *not* resemble a traditional lie detector machine in any way, shape or size! The technology available to the FBI today is *unbelievable*!"

"Okay. But why are you telling us this?" Charisse asked, perplexed.

"Because the two of you seem like very *honest* people," Avery began. "Do me a favor. Practice hard on strengthening your abilities to *lie* in a believable way. That skill could save your lives as well as your mother's! Oh, and try not to get too nervous while answering any of their questions. That's a sure giveaway that you're *lying*!"

Although a bit shaken-up by what Mr. Avery had just shared with them, both Charisse and Paul nodded as they quietly accepted their roles. Avery then handed Paul a couple of tickets to the Monterey Aquarium… and they were off!

Although this was technically a 'working visit,' and Charisse had been experiencing a lot of stress and anxiety as recently as *fifteen minutes before*, when Mr. Avery had warned them about the deadly pitfalls of inadvertently 'giving themselves away,' she had apparently *forgotten* all about that! Instead, she soon found herself becoming completely *mesmerized* by everything she was seeing on this, her *very first* visit, to the vast Monterey Aquarium! In fact, she was actually quite determined to take-in the *whole* place in just one afternoon! Paul, as supportive of her excitement as he could be, had grown-up in Monterey and consequently had visited this Aquarium more times than he could count. For that reason (*along with the fact that Mr. Avery had asked that they split-up*), he left her to her fun, and sat down on a nearby bench.

"Good morning, Mr. Madison," a nondescript woman wearing dark sunglasses and a white scarf said to him in a calm and friendly voice. She had seemingly appeared out of nowhere and immediately sat down beside him.

"Good morning," Paul echoed back in surprise, as he turned to face her.

"You have a very *sweet* mother. It was so good of her to come back from the *dead* to join us," she said with a sarcastic smile. "If you ever want to see her again… *alive*… you had better follow my instructions to the letter."

Paul began to respond verbally, but was immediately *stopped* as she gently placed a gloved fingertip on his lips. Next, she demanded with a smile, "*Don't* talk! Just *nod* your head that you agree."

Just as she had requested, Paul nodded, and didn't say a word or dare to utter a sound from that point on.

"Good! Now, Paul. Answer *this* question," she demanded quietly.

Paul grew very anxious, even though he hadn't even heard the *question* yet?

"Is your father, Roy Madison, *alive*, and can you *contact* him?"

Although the question was pretty straightforward, he had *not* prepared to answer it or even *imagined* being asked? And the worst part, of course, was that *he didn't know the answer*? But he instinctively knew what answer *she* was hoping to hear!

The woman noticing his hesitancy, smiled with irritation and said sharply "You have *three* seconds to nod yes or no. If you don't, then maybe I'll just find Charisse and *torture* her a bit?"

Paul had *never* felt so nauseated and frightened at the same time!

"One, two…"

He nodded, *yes*!

She exhaled. "Good," the woman said. "That wasn't so hard, now was it! You will contact your father and convince him to exchange himself for his wife. This is *mandatory*! Do you agree?"

Paul once again nodded his consent.

"Now, don't tell *anyone* but Charisse about this meeting. If you do, then your mother *dies*!" the woman threatened. "Secondly, you will hear from me later today regarding when and where we will meet to '*do business.*' Do not share that location with anyone, or once again, your mother dies. Thirdly, you will bring your *father* to said location and exchange him for your mother. If you *don't* do this, then we will *kill all three* of you!" she said with a crazy smile. "Do you understand and agree to all three of these stipulations?"

Paul quickly nodded.

"Good *again*!" she facetiously said, like the owner of a dog, giving excessive praise to her animal for obediently *rolling over* on command! "I'll be contacting you *soon* at your hotel room. But not *too* soon," she laughed mockingly, making him feel very uncomfortable. "I wouldn't want to ruin what I hear is Charisse's first visit to this world-famous '*Monterey Aquarium*!'" Then, the woman gave Paul a friendly, but clearly *insincere* smile, and inconspicuously disappeared back into the crowd.

Paul remained seated on the bench for quite some time following that impromptu meeting with the woman. He had found that encounter to be nothing short of *terrifying*! In fact, in the aftermath, he felt spent and powerless, and didn't think that he even had the *strength* to stand up? Although he had known all along that meeting the kidnappers here in-person was always a very *slight* possibility, he had *never* expected it to *actually happen*? In his mind it made much more sense for them to contact Charisse or him in a more secretive way, via note or a phone call? Meeting them in-person, right here in the middle of all these people at the Aquarium, seemed to be *unbelievably reckless*! Surely this Aquarium had security cameras to record *every move* a person made? And there were FBI agents *everywhere*! Right? Or were there? Looking around, he didn't notice anyone who seemed to be watching him? No FBI agents, no police, *nobody*? Of course, he knew that Avery and his men were only here to observe… but they must have seen the woman talking to him? Why hadn't they had the *cojones* to just show themselves, arrest her, and then interrogate the *hell* out of her? As much as he tried to make sense of Mr. Avery's complacent behavior, he just *couldn't* make it jive for someone professing so strongly to be attempting to *prevent* a major political assassination from taking place *any day now*? Not to mention a man who had *assured* him several times that he cared greatly about getting his mother back safely? He felt himself suddenly growing angry and anxious with no apparent solution? So, taking a deep breath and slowly sighing, he decided to give Mr. Avery a *generous* benefit of the doubt. He admitted to himself that

Avery and the FBI *might* be on the level, and even have a plan that simply *didn't allow* for an arrest to be made at this time. But it seemed pretty clear that the kidnappers were *also aware* of this plan? That would certainly explain why the woman had felt so free to *threaten* and *harass* him without fear? *What* was going on?

Meanwhile, Charisse had taken a real interest in watching the live '*Octopus Dance Show*' that was being presented today. She had never before watched or even heard of anything quite so unusual? A *dancing octopus*? As she stood behind the glass, enjoying the show along with at least 100 other spectators, she suddenly felt odd, as though somebody were *watching* her? She intuitively turned to her left, and was immediately *shocked* to see 'Cal,' of the Paris FBI trio from *hell*, intensely staring at her, while slowly inching closer, like a lion *closing-in* on its prey. She frantically looked around for Paul, but then quickly remembered leaving him on a bench some time ago… along with her purse and *cell phone*! Not wishing to create a disturbance that might result in scaring off the kidnappers, she began to slowly move away from Cal toward the stairs that led up to the second level of the Aquarium. The next time she looked, she saw that he had *not* lost a step, but was in fact getting closer! To escape him, she raced up the stairs. As soon as she had reached the second level, she immediately headed for the very crowded '*Penguin Show*,' which was being presented across the floor from where she currently stood. Unfortunately, soon she spied Cal, who had just come up the stairs behind her, effectively *blocking* her escape route! In desperation, she spied a door marked, EMPLOYEES ONLY, at the far end of the floor! She slowly walked up to it, opened it and rushed inside, while quickly closing the door behind her! As she looked around, she found herself alone in a long, narrow and completely unfurnished strip of a room at the top of a stairwell, presumably leading down to the first floor. Just then, Cal rushed through the door and smiled victoriously at her. As she was about to sprint down the stairs, he said, "I wouldn't do that if I were you, girly. Chris is waiting for you at the bottom of that stairwell with a *stun-gun*."

"You're bluffing!" Charisse hotly retorted, hoping to stave off the inevitable. "This is a *staff stairwell*. How would he even know that I was on it?"

Cal condescendingly pointed toward his earpiece. "I *already* told him."

"What do you want with me, anyway?" Charisse suddenly lost her nerve.

"It doesn't matter," Cal grinned, realizing that Charisse's loss of confidence was his gain. "But it would be a whole lot safer for your mother-in-law if you came along with me *right now*."

"Have you *hurt* her?" Charisse demanded, with *fear* blatantly covering both her voice and face.

"Not *yet*," Cal laughed cruelly, as he finally caught up to her.

"*What* do you want with me?" Charisse repeated again anxiously.

"We want you and your mother-in-law to have a very *happy New Year* together!" Cal hissed mockingly, as he brutally grabbed Charisse's arm. He immediately attempted to drag her toward the door, but was met with some very unexpected and *fierce* resistance. This caused him to quickly lose his patience and snarl, "Now listen carefully, *sweetheart*! You're very quietly coming with me whether you like it or not!" He paused momentarily as a nasty grin slowly crossed his face. "If you don't, then someone very, very close to your husband might just have a sudden and tragic *accidental death* right here and now!"

Suddenly, a man wearing an *Aquarium Security* shirt burst through the partially open doorway and *aggressively* punched a very surprised Cal in the gut! Cal was hit so hard that he was very audibly gasping for breath, but he was somehow still able to make his escape through the now open door.

"Run down the stairs, Charisse! Go now!" the man ordered.

Charisse thought that she recognized the voice from somewhere, but she had *no idea* who the face belonged to? "*Who* are you? And how do you know *my name*?" she asked frantically.

"I'm a *friend*!" he smiled sympathetically.

She had *never* run so fast in her life! When she reached the bottom of the stairwell… *miraculously*, Paul was there waiting for her.

"Are you all right?" Paul demanded frantically.

"Yes! I was being chased by Cal… one of the 'FBI people' from Paris!" she explained. "But there was another man who *hit* him? I think he was part of the Aquarium security staff. That was how I was able to escape!"

"That was probably the same security guy who told me to wait for you here?" Paul suggested.

"Well, thank goodness he knew where I was!" she gasped. "Otherwise, *who knows* what would have happened to me?"

"I will *never* take my eyes off of you again for as long as I live!" Paul declared sincerely, hugging her tightly.

"Promise?" Charisse uttered softly.

After spending enough time to adequately calm themselves down following Charisse's very close call, the two immediately left the Aquarium to find solace somewhere as *far away* from it as they could possibly get! Curiously, as they passed through the exit doors, Paul found himself matter-of-factly handed a '*Monterey Aquarium Souvenir Program*' from an anonymous passerby with the words, "**Read Me**," neatly written across the front cover in black marker. Out of curiosity, he opened the program to the first page, and quickly noticed a note taped to it. It was signed DGA, which he easily identified as being *Douglas G. Avery*. He didn't let on that he was holding anything more than a program as he continued reading. On the note was written the street address of a nearby coffee house with the added words, "*Go there*!" It also instructed him to destroy the note just as soon after reading it as was *inconspicuously* possible. Paul could not help but smile. The note secretly taped inside the program *definitely* represented the closest he'd ever come in his life to playing a real live *secret agent*! But then he remembered that the criminals *had* his mother… and his moment of fancy quickly faded.

"Act naturally, Charisse. Just follow my lead, okay?" Paul discreetly whispered in her ear.

Charisse had no idea what was going on, but she played along *brilliantly*! She gently intertwined her fingers with his as they leisurely strolled hand in hand toward the coffee house, only minutes away from the Aquarium. Once they arrived, they quietly sat down at a table and were immediately visited by a waitress. She smiled and gave them a laminated paper menu. Discreetly attached to it was a short note from Mr. Avery, which read, '*You are on your own*! *Do not contact me again. Please give the menu back to the waitress and place your order. DGA*.' Both of them read it without reacting.

They nonchalantly ordered two coffees and a slice of lemon cake, while carrying on as if this were a spontaneous stop for coffee after a fun day out. The waitress (*whom they both assumed was an FBI agent*), calmly took their menu away and left. Five minutes later, she returned and served them. As they shared their cake and sipped their coffee, Paul pretended to be texting on his phone, as well as receiving messages from who he *hoped* they would believe to be his father. He and Charisse wore very serious expressions on their faces the entire time! They were only too aware that they were almost certainly being watched, although they could not actually identify *who* was doing the watching? Still, they intended to give the person or persons a very exciting show to hopefully back-up whatever they told them when they had their imminent meeting with them later. The toughest part to accept about everything that would happen to them from here on out, as Mr. Avery's note had confirmed, was that they would have to *go it alone*! Just as the woman at the Aquarium had threatened, 'Telling *anyone* but Charisse about their conversation would immediately result in his mother being killed!' Paul and Charisse didn't say it out loud, but both of them were quite certain that this was why Avery had sent them to this coffee house and had so abruptly broken-off all contact with them. Paul even seriously considered that Avery might have had some technology-based method of overhearing what the woman had said to him in the Aquarium to arrive at such a fast and *extreme* decision? And then it dawned on him; he was FBI. *Of course, he did*!

Following their impromptu stop for coffee, Charisse and Paul returned to their hotel room, where Paul immediately tore-up and flushed the note from the Monterey Aquarium program. As they quietly assessed their situation, frustratedly they didn't know exactly how to feel other than *overwhelmed*? Of course, they expected to be contacted by the kidnappers soon, but regardless of what happened as a result, they realized now that they were *definitely*, as Mr. Avery had so eloquently shared with them in his note… *on their own*! Everything about that difficult situation was causing them *great anxiety*, although they tried their best to hide it from each other. Suddenly, there came a firm knock on their door. Paul rushed to answer it, but when he opened the door… *no one* was in the hallway? However, looking down he unsettlingly saw a standard sized manila envelope labeled, *Paul Madison*. He quickly picked it up and brought it inside the room before closing the door. Once inside, he quickly ripped open the envelope to reveal a note, giving them the following instructions, '*Go to the bench outside of your hotel in five minutes with Charisse. Destroy this note immediately*!'

Charisse silently read the note as well, with a very curious look on her face. "Do you suppose they want to meet us?" she suggested. "Or do they just want us to *leave* our room?"

"Probably *both*," Paul replied solemnly. "Just remember *not* to say anything important once we come back here. Our room may get bugged."

"Who says it hasn't been *bugged already*?" Charise offered as an unpleasant alternative.

With that completely *non-reassuring* thought, Paul quickly tore-up and flushed his second note of the past several minutes. Moments later, they left the room and headed toward the front of the hotel. Upon arriving, they walked outside and sat down on the first bench they could find. Soon, a man dressed in a FedEx uniform with his head bowed low, passed by them. He looked very suspicious as he was conspicuously wearing a floppy straw hat which effectively obscured much of his face from their view. He very innocently dropped an envelope onto the bench between them before hastily making his retreat. Charisse impatiently tore the envelope open to reveal two tiny earbuds… *and* another note? This one instructed each of them to place an earbud inside one ear, which they quickly complied with. They immediately began hearing a now *familiar* woman's voice.

"Hello, Paul. Hello, Charisse."

"Can you *hear* us?" Paul asked in surprise, realizing that they did not have any visible microphones?

"Of course, I can!" the voice replied condescendingly. "I can hear every whisper that you make." Then after a pause, she laughed, "I think maybe I can even *hear your thoughts*?"

Both Paul and Charisse felt a *chill* at that suggestion.

"We are ready to make the exchange tonight," the voice declared calmly. "Paul, did you contact your father, and has he agreed to be exchanged for your mother?"

"I did, and he has," Paul lied, starting to inadvertently *sweat*. He realized that if the earbud he was wearing was also some sort of tiny high-tech lie detector machine that was instantly able to measure his level of anxiety, he might soon find himself *unmasked* for lying!

"Good," the voice replied, a little too calmly. "Remember Paul, if you are *lying*, then both you and Charisse will join your mother in *not living to see tomorrow morning*."

"I'm *not* lying!" Paul professed with an appropriate amount of passion, which thankfully alleviated his sweating.

There was a noticeable pause this time as the voice momentarily disappeared. Thirty anxious seconds later... it returned. "Okay, I believe you," it confirmed, causing both Paul and Charisse to silently sigh in relief. "Now, *don't* write these instructions down or share them with anyone else or we will be forced to *kill* your mother without hesitation. Don't worry, they're quite simple to remember. From your hotel, turn left and follow Cannery Row for several blocks until you can see the 'Monterey Canning Company building' to your left. The address is *711 Cannery Row*. Turn left, and a make a quick right, which will take you to a small street behind that building. Someone will meet you there and escort you to the site where the exchange will take place. *Do not* contact the police, and *don't even think about* bringing a cell phone or gun, wearing a wire or carrying a tracking device of *any* kind! If you are stupid enough to do any of those things, your mother and the two of you will *be killed*! And I personally guarantee that your deaths will *not* be quick or painless either, but as *grueling and hideous* as you can possibly imagine! And in answer to what you are probably thinking, *yes*! We *do* have scanners to check fully for all of those items I mentioned. The latest technology, as a matter of fact! So, if you want to live a little bit longer, I strongly suggest that you don't try to sneak any of those things in! Do we *understand* each other?"

"Perfectly," Paul replied calmly.

"But how do we know that you won't kill us once you have gotten your hands on Paul's father?" Charisse asked alertly.

"*You don't*!" the woman replied coldly. "But what other choice do you two have? I give you my word that we will *probably* give you a five-minute head-start following the exchange… unless, of course, I *change my mind*," she said darkly. "Be there at ten tonight!" The voice disappeared as quickly as it had arrived.

The next instruction on the note clearly told them to place the earbuds back inside the manilla envelope along with the note, leave them on the bench and walk away. They immediately did so. Moments later, when Charisse inadvertently turned around just as they were about to reenter their hotel, she saw that the envelope had *already* been retrieved. Preferring to remain *outside,* in case their room *had* been bugged, they very quickly turned around and began a carefree walk toward no place at all.

"I know that we aren't allowed to *officially* tell Mr. Avery about any of this," Charisse shared quietly, "but surely we should try to *secretly* notify him, don't you think? For our own safety?"

Paul hesitated for a moment, and then replied, "I understand how you feel, Charisse, but that woman *insisted* that she would kill my mother if we told anyone else about this meeting, and I don't think she was bluffing!" he shared intensely. Then changing the subject, in a much calmer voice he added, "And anyway, I know this will sound odd to you, but I think there's something *funny* about how Mr. Avery has been acting?"

"What do you mean by *that*?" Charisse asked in shock.

"To tell you the truth, I'm not really sure?" Paul confessed. "But don't you find it a little strange that when he sent you to the safehouse and both of us to the Aquarium, the kidnappers seemed to know *exactly* what our time schedules were? The other thing is that although you thankfully *escaped* some pretty hairy situations, where was the FBI during all of that? Why weren't they nearby *protecting* you? It just seems *very* odd? Don't you agree that something there feels not quite right?"

"That could all just be coincidental, couldn't it?" Charisse suggested nervously. "You don't really think Mr. Avery is working *with* the kidnappers, do you?"

After a slight pause, Paul replied, "I certainly *don't want* to believe that, but very honestly, I really don't know *what* to think, Charisse? I like Mr. Avery too. But I do *suspect* for some reason that he *may* be feeding the kidnappers information, and I don't just mean posting something in social media like he told us he did earlier today. I think he may be in more *direct contact* with them than that? What other explanation is there?"

"But surely he's one of the *good guys*!" Charisse insisted.

"And I'm *genuinely hoping* that's still true!" Paul declared. "But even *he* told us that someone rather *high up* in the FBI had to be involved with those kidnappers? Right? Maybe he's only *playing* with us, and it's actually *him*?"

Charisse was completely *shocked* and didn't know what to say?

"I know that what I'm saying may be a long shot, but shouldn't we be careful from here on out and distance ourselves from him, just in case?" Paul said understandingly.

"Okay," a noticeably disheartened Charisse agreed. "So, we *really are* on our own?"

"Yes. It would certainly appear that way," Paul confirmed, sharing her concern.

"We don't even have your father to trade like you told her we did?" Charisse *pointedly* reminded him with panic in her voice. "And even if we did, I doubt very much that you would want *both* of your parents in the hands of those awful people any more than I would!"

"You're right, Charisse! I *wouldn't*!" Paul shouted in exasperation, trying hard, but ultimately *failing* to control his overwhelming distress. Then looking at Charisse's shocked reaction, he suddenly felt *ashamed*! "I'm so sorry, Charisse!" he said gently as he hugged her tightly. "I truly didn't mean to yell at you. This is all just making me so crazy," he replied apologetically.

Charisse smiled softly. "It's okay, Paul."

Paul gave her a warm smile in return, but then inadvertently growing darker, he said, "You know? We don't have a *single* alternative to meeting them tonight that doesn't result in them *killing* my mother? So, all we can really do is follow their instructions and then *hope* for the best. Right? It's exactly as that woman said, '*What choice* do we have?'" That's when Paul, noticing how *deflated* Charisse had become since listening to his defeatist rant, suddenly produced a sincere and warm smile, took her hand in his and suggested eagerly, "Hey, maybe by the time we leave for this rendezvous we'll have already come up with a great plan? C'mon Charisse! We can do this!"

Charisse smiled back at him in a very believable way, although in her heart, which she tried so very hard to make positive, she *didn't* honestly believe they would come-up with *anything* at all! The two slowly turned around to go back to their hotel room. In her mind it was for nothing more than to quietly ponder their disquietingly hopeless situation… before the *final axe fell.*

That night at 9:45, Paul and Charisse, still feeling very anxious, walked out of their hotel and headed toward their meeting with the kidnappers. They still didn't know whether Paul's father was *alive* or *dead*? This certainly meant that they did *not* expect him to be joining them any time soon! They realized that this situation *could* ultimately create a big problem for them with the kidnappers? But, first things first. Initially they had to meet their escort and somehow *distract* him or her from noticing that their group was *one person short*! Otherwise, it was '*Game Over*' right from the start! In addition, no matter what happened tonight, they didn't want Jocelyn or themselves to be *hurt*! Knowing that they were possibly dealing with *hardcore criminals* made that thinking seem very *irrational* and *naïve*? But all the same, they were determined to get Jocelyn back, *alive*, and hope still seemed to be their *best* option! But at the same time, even if they were successfully escorted to the place they were supposed to make the trade, they had *no way* of knowing whether their efforts would actually achieve anything more than simply *getting them all killed*?

The Monterey Canning Company building was only a modest distance away from their hotel. It was just past the touristy shops and restaurants that had long since replaced the famous sardine canneries of John Steinbeck's gritty, but somehow charming, depression era *Cannery Row*. Aside from the hotels, most everything else looked closed-up for the night. Because the moon was covered with clouds, the farther away from the hotels they walked, the more the streetlamps became the only saving grace from total darkness. When they finally approached the Monterey Canning Company, it was surrounded by wooden barricades painted with alternating diagonal stripes of orange and white, with each one possessing a good-sized orange light blinking on the top of it. It appeared that the city was doing some extensive work on the water or sewer lines, as there were long and *mostly* covered trenches all around the area. The building itself was dark, and they saw absolutely no signs of life anywhere inside. Carefully maneuvering between barricades and trenches, they turned left as they had been directed to do. The tiny street behind the building where they were instructed to meet their escort, quickly came into view. Charisse, still feeling hopeless and scared, immediately turned to Paul for strength. His steeled hazel eyes met hers, clearly demonstrating the *courage* he'd managed to latch onto while simultaneously facing the fear of not knowing *what* would happen next?

"Be strong, Charisse," he shared warmly. "Everything is going to be just fine. You wait and see!"

As they turned right, they walked about fifteen feet behind the building before coming face to face with one of the kidnappers. Charisse immediately recognized him as the youngest one they called, 'Chris.'

Without emotion, Chris visually sized-up the two of them before firmly demanding, "Take off your coats and put your arms up in the air!"

They both immediately complied. Next, Chris waved a foot-long wand first over both coats and then in front of and behind each of them. For some reason, he spent considerably *more time* checking Charisse, and seemed to be enjoying every moment of it. Looking at her intently, not even attempting to hide his intense desire, he said with seedy undertones, "You look cold, honeybun. I can fix that. I mean I can *really* fix that if you'd like?"

"No, thank you," Charisse replied, extremely controlled, fighting off her initial rage at his repulsive inferences.

"*Your loss*," Chris replied nonchalantly with a disturbing grin. Apparently satisfied with his findings, while throwing them back their coats, he announced without emotion, "Okay, you two can put your coats back on. You're both clean." He followed that by carefully returning the wand to a specific location in the inside of his jacket.

As Charisse and Paul were putting on their coats, Paul abruptly turned toward Chris, and with restrained anger, intensely said, "Don't you *ever* speak to my wife like that again!"

Quickly pulling a pistol from his shoulder holster, Chris threateningly pointed the gun at Paul. Wearing an arrogant smile, he then flippantly declared, "You really don't have a say in *anything* I choose to do right now, do you, punk? So why don't you just shut your trap and do what I say! No sense trying to be a hero and ending up *dead*, now is it!"

"You just *remember* what I said!" Paul continued to glare at Chris. At that moment, he had absolutely *no fear* of him or his gun, whatsoever.

A hot flicker of rage suddenly flashed through Chris's dark eyes as he continued pointing the pistol at Paul, clearly *not caring* for his defiant words! As Charisse found herself terrified and holding her breath, the two men virtually *deadlocked* in an intense stare for a long fifteen seconds with neither one willing to break his focus! Finally, appearing to hear instructions coming through the earpiece he was likely wearing, Chris lowered his gun and laughed, "Take it easy, pal. I was only kidding around. Follow me!"

Paul was still *noticeably* angry, but after exhaling, Charisse quickly calmed him down and winked at him to let him know that their *first task was a success*! He gave Charisse a quick smile while Chris's back was turned and then *begrudgingly* adhered to the man's request by following him. After fifteen minutes or so of twisting and turning through a multitude of tiny streets and even *backtracking* several times, they at last found themselves at the doorstep of a very old and ramshackle two-story building. The entire structure looked so rotten and forgotten that it actually brought Poe's '*House of Usher*' to mind. The paint on the neglected building was long washed away by the elements, exposing the nails and decaying jagged-edged fragments of sun-bleached boards which now made-up the outside walls. They were covered almost entirely by many years of now faded contemptuous graffiti, like terminal sores on a diseased body in an ugly display of mismatched scribble and disrespect. Charisse frowned as she realized how terribly sad it was that what had once more than likely been an important part of the canneries or the people who worked them, was now only a dead, decrepit and long-abandoned building… a *haven* for these criminals!

"*Go in*!" Chris demanded.

They hesitantly forced themselves to go through the clearly *rotted* wooden doorway, where they immediately entered a dimly lit room that smelled strongly of mildew and urine. The meager light came from a small battery-operated camping lantern that had been *strategically* placed on a wobbly round table near the center of the room. Although the emitted light *did* make everyone in the room visible to one another; each body and face looked *shadowy and surreal*. Besides the cheap table, the room was limited to what had once been a beautiful couch that had been upholstered in fine red velvet, but was now only a tattered and broken shadow of its former self. It sat only a couple of feet in front of them, serving as home to hundreds of healthy-looking black water bugs which chaotically crawled over it at will. Soon they spied two other kidnappers.

"Welcome," the woman Charisse knew as Brenda, announced sarcastically. "We have your mother in the next room with Cal," she quickly said, gesturing with her right hand. Then her demeanor grew darker. "Now, I can't help noticing that you came here tonight *without* your father, Roy Madison?" Turning toward Chris, she angrily demanded, "Why didn't you ask them about that *before* you brought them here, Chris?"

"Sorry. I got busy," he replied feebly, with underlying fear. "It just slipped my mind?"

Brenda *shot* him a scathing glare, but quickly regained her composure. Turning to Paul, she smiled *way too big* as she very threateningly seethed, "That really *wasn't* very smart of you to come here with *nothing* to trade for your mother's life. I distinctly remember you promising to bring your father with you tonight?"

"I did agree to that," Paul carefully replied. "But before we bring him inside, we need some assurances from you."

"What kind of *assurances*?" Chris, who was now standing beside Brenda, asked saucily.

"We want assurances that you won't hurt either one of them before, during or after we make the switch," Charisse declared, without missing a beat.

"We don't have to make any more *deals* with you," a man who Charisse couldn't identify, but Paul somehow recognized as the *would-be thief* on his plane flight, said with disgust.

"Yeah, your mama wants to go home!" Cal yelled, from the next room. "Let's get on with this!"

"First things first," Paul declared. "What do you *really* want with my father?"

There was loud and derisive laughter as all of the kidnappers joined in.

"That's none of your business, *Junior*!" Brenda laughed. "We don't have to tell you anything!"

"Are you planning to *kill him*?" Charisse brazenly interjected.

"Well, that depends now, doesn't it," Brenda replied calmly, drilling her eyes into Charisse's.

"On *what*?" Charisse demanded.

"On whether or not he tells us *exactly* what it is we want to know."

"Are you people *really* with the FBI?" Charisse demanded.

Once again there was raucous and ridiculing laughter from the kidnappers.

"What do *you* think?" Brenda asked humorously.

"I think they're just wasting a lot of our time!" Paul's attacker from the plane declared angrily.

"Yeah? We *are* making a hostage switch here, aren't we?" Brenda suddenly grew very suspicious.

"Sure, we are," Paul replied boldly.

"Then *where* is Mr. Madison?" Brenda demanded.

"He's coming, just as soon as we give him the signal," Charisse lied.

"You're *lying*!" Brenda declared, ditching her patience like a pair of worn-out sneakers, as she pulled out her gun and determinedly pointed it at Charisse. "Now, *where is Mr. Madison*?" she requested softly but intensely.

"*She* doesn't know!" Paul shouted frantically. "Let her go, and point that gun at *me*!"

"Awww. Aren't you the *gallant* one!" Brenda said sarcastically. "But I don't think so!" Then growing noticeably sterner, she added, "If you tell me *exactly* where your father is and why he is not here now, then perhaps I might consider sparing your lives for just a little bit longer."

Paul and Charisse, both terrified by now, were apparently *out* of ideas as they nervously attempted to keep their composure!

Brenda slowly cocked back the hammer of her pistol which she continued to point at Charisse. "Someone had better tell me *quickly* where Roy Madison is, or poor Charisse will find herself in an *ungodly amount of pain* as I empty this gun, *one bullet each minute*, into a different part of her lovely *French* body!" she threatened with a terrifying smile.

"Yes, ma'am. He's *right here*!" the loud voice of a stranger suddenly passing through the front door and entering the room, *immediately* startled and grabbed everyone's complete attention! The stranger was a man of moderate height and build, with thick blonde hair and a closely trimmed moustache to match. True to his word, he held a pistol to the back of an older man who he implied was *Roy Madison*.

Paul immediately shared a faint smile with the man, and incredulously realized that it *was his father*!

"Who *are* you?" Brenda asked in distrust and shock, as she slowly moved her gun away from Charisse and turned it on the stranger.

The man chuckled. "Who do I look like?" he asked as if the answer were obvious. "The name is Bud Barbier," he announced. "I am a bounty hunter."

"But what are you doing here, *Bud*?" Chris demanded, clearly *mocking* his first name.

The man ignored Chris, and replied magnanimously, "What're we *all* doing here? I caught wind that you needed '*Mr.*

Roy Madison,' and were paying handsomely for his delivery. So, I collected him and *here he is*, all wrapped up with a bow!"

"But how did you know to meet us *here*?" Paul's attacker on the plane asked him suspiciously.

"Relax, fella," Bud laughed. "I knew these two young people were involved, so I've been following them ever since yesterday, and they led me straight to you! Now, if they'll be so kind as to leave us, I can collect my money. I believe you were offering *twenty thousand dollars*?"

"I want to *see* my mother first!" Paul demanded.

Brenda yelled to Cal to bring her in from the next room. As soon as the female hostage was within plain sight, she unexpectedly smiled broadly at both Paul and Charisse, like the *Cheshire Cat*.

"That is *not* the woman I met at the safehouse?" Charisse exclaimed in shock.

"*She's* not my mother?" Paul concurred.

Brenda did not flinch, as she instantly moved her pistol away from the stranger to *Roy Madison's head*! There sometimes comes a time in each of our lives when an urgent situation requires immediate action, without time for forethought or concern for one's own safety. *This* was one of them! Charisse didn't hesitate as she decidedly grabbed Brenda's right hand and *fiercely* struggled with her for control of the gun! Unfortunately, although Brenda had been completely surprised by Charisse's unexpected moxie, she was still able to fire off three rounds at Roy Madison before finally taking back control of the gun. Roy immediately collapsed to the floor with a groan.

"Dad!" Paul cried out in horror.

Brenda *smiled* at Paul's fearful reaction.

"Quick! *Behind* the couch!" Bud yelled.

Instantly Paul, dragging his father, and Charisse with the woman masquerading as his mother, hurriedly hid behind the couch for cover. Meanwhile, Bud was the last one to join them, but not before quickly *shooting out* the single lamp that provided the only light in the room. Suddenly, they were all immersed in *complete darkness*! Brenda quickly backed-up, pushed the table over and took cover behind it, while the rest of her gang hastily hid behind *anything* they could find!

"Hey, this *wasn't* part of the plan, Brenda?" Cal shouted.

"Shut-up, and help me *kill* the rest of these *witnesses*!" she ordered.

The other three kidnappers in the room were suddenly confused and paralyzed with uncertainty? But Brenda *knew* what she had to do! She began firing toward the couch with abandon, trying to obliterate *everyone* who was there! Although she emptied her gun, somehow she *narrowly* missed hitting anyone? Meanwhile, astutely getting Brenda's location from the light given off by her shots, Bud fired back at her, successfully *wounding her in the leg*! As she fell down screaming, dropping her now empty gun and writhing in pain, *utter chaos* ensued! Apparently *none* of the other kidnappers had changed their minds about joining in the gunfight, much less about even taking out their guns? And then only moments later, the kidnappers completely panicked when they heard the unmistakable sound of *Douglas Gandalf Avery's* voice, sternly shouting from outside, "*FBI.* You're all under arrest!"

Frenzied and lacking any workable escape plan, two of the kidnappers desperately ran through the darkness to a *secret door* in the floor and quickly disappeared. Bud Barbier astutely raced through that same door in fast pursuit! At least one other kidnapper immediately ran blindly through the building, hoping to find a place to hide! Moments later, a number of FBI agents *burst* through the door, bringing with them bright lanterns to cut-through the darkness! They seemingly ran *everywhere* throughout the house, unwilling to let even a single kidnapper escape!

Paul, along with Charisse, horrifically looked at his father, who was now lying silent and motionless on the floor. "Dad? Dad!" he screamed *hysterically*. Fortunately, a quick check of his vital signs told them that he was still alive! There was, however, a very concerning ever-increasing pool of blood forming on the floor beside him!

One of the FBI agents gently nudged Paul aside and began extensively checking Roy's body for wounds. He nodded reassuringly at Paul as he bandaged a single one, and shared, "The bullet that entered his right side above his hip was the *only* one to hit him! And luckily it appears to have *missed* all of his organs!"

"But I watched her shoot him *three* times from point blank range? She *couldn't* have missed those other two shots?" Charisse said incredulously.

"You're right! She *didn't*," the agent confirmed. "But those other two bullets were stopped by his vest."

"He was wearing a *bulletproof vest*?" Charisse exclaimed.

"Of course," the agent said. "The FBI always sends their agents out that way."

"Then why isn't he conscious?" Paul asked urgently.

"It appears that he *likely* hit his head on the wooden corner of this couch as he fell. See that *gash* just above his left eye?" the agent suggested with concern. "Although it's impossible to know the extent of that headwound without x-rays, I promise you that at least your father's *not* going to die of blood loss!"

Moments later, an ambulance arrived and Roy Madison was swiftly rushed off to the hospital. Paul and Charisse were *terribly* conflicted. Although they were, of course, very *thankful* that Avery's troops had arrived, they still felt very distraught over Roy's life or death condition! As if sensing this, one of the FBI agents thoughtfully called them over and calmly shared with them which hospital he would be taken to. He also explained that specialists at the hospital would have to find out what exactly was wrong with him first, before they could even hope to make a prognosis. The fact that he was unconscious, he said, made their job that much more difficult. He hesitantly went on to say that unfortunately, they *couldn't* rule out his experiencing a stroke or a heart attack in *addition* to being shot. Finally, he advised them to call the hospital first thing in the morning to find-out about his updated condition. Charisse and Paul gratefully thanked him for all of the information, although it had not been as *positive* as they'd hoped.

Before long, it appeared that everyone had left the crime scene except for Paul, Charisse and a few FBI agents who were still diligently taking blood and fingerprint samples from the house. Mr. Avery *did* stop by to tell them that they had caught all but one of the four kidnappers, and that Paul's mom was safe. But then he had to rush off without answering any of their pressing questions in order to monitor Roy's very concerning condition at the hospital.

As Paul and Charisse dismally walked outside, still *shell-shocked* and deeply concerned for Roy, Paul suddenly grabbed Charisse in a warm embrace and held her tightly for a very long moment. "Thank God you're *safe*!" he exclaimed. "How in the world were you able to react so quickly to that shooter? You may have *saved* my father's life?"

"I really wanted to! But that woman shot him anyway!" Charisse whispered disappointedly.

"But at least he is still *alive* and has a *chance*!" Paul said soothingly. "*You* gave him that, Charisse!" Paul was completely choked-up as he hugged her once again.

"I'm so happy to hear about Jocelyn being safe," Charisse began, after their hug had ended. "But *where* do you think she is now?"

"I really have no idea?" Paul admitted. "But I'm *sure* that its somewhere safe!" he smiled. Suddenly, his expression changed to surprise as he thought of something important. "Did that FBI agent just tell us that 'Dad was wearing one of *their* bulletproof vests?'"

"Yes, he did," Charisse agreed, not sure *where* he was going with that question.

"Wow! Don't you see, Charisse? Dad must have been working *with* the FBI tonight!" Paul exclaimed. Then growing thoughtful, he suggested, "Does that mean that what happened to us here was actually *part of their plan* all along?"

Before Charisse could even venture a guess, a male voice definitively answered Paul's question, "In a *roundabout* sort of way, *yes*, it does!" The voice belonged to Bud Barbier.

"Who exactly *are you*?" Paul asked the man in confusion.

It was then, unprompted, that Charisse joyfully flew into the man's arms! To put it mildly, Paul was taken *completely* by surprise?

"Paul? *This* is my brother!" she announced ecstatically. "He looks *nothing* like this normally. He is a *brilliant* master of disguise who taught me all I know!"

Paul smiled and hugged his newfound brother-in-law, before saying, "It's so great to finally meet you, *whoever* you are? What do you *actually* look like, anyway?"

"Like a *sumo wrestler*!" he began. "About six foot three, weighing five hundred pounds and wearing a *great big diaper*!" he laughed.

Paul laughed too, and then turning toward Charisse, he asked curiously, "If your brother looks so different now, then how did you know it was him?"

"Well, after I heard his voice earlier tonight, I *thought* he sounded very familiar?" she shared. "But as soon as he said that his name was 'Bud Barbier,' *my brother's name*, I began to think that his being my brother was really a *possibility*? And then when I looked into his eyes just now, *I knew*!"

Turning toward the man in confusion, Paul said, "But I thought your name was *Peter*?"

"*Oh, it is*," her brother admitted, "but my middle name, which also happens to be our mother's maiden name, is *Budig*. Years ago, as soon as my friends found out about that, they started calling me '*Bud*!' They thought that sounded *way cooler* than Peter," he winked, "and over the years that name has just sort of stuck!"

"But how did you ever get involved in this mess?" Paul asked.

Peter paused a moment, and then declared, "Well, the thing is, I am actually with *INTERPOL*," he replied seriously. "Our Mr. Avery, learning that I was Charisse's brother, recruited me one day before calling you."

"I am certainly glad that you arrived here when you did!" Paul confessed. "As that *psycho-woman* clearly proved with my father, she had absolutely *no trouble* trying to kill people. Especially *innocent* ones!"

Peter smiled warmly at Paul. "I know it will be hard, but try not to worry too much about your father, Paul," he said thoughtfully. "They'll have the best doctors in San Francisco working on him. And being so close to this case over these past few days, I truly believe that your family has come *much too far* for this to end badly."

Paul gratefully acknowledged Peter's gracious words through a warm smile of his own! "So, was 'bringing my father into the room' *your* appointed job in this adventure tonight?" Paul asked, anxious to change the subject.

"It was certainly an important *part* of it," Peter replied coyly, "but there was a *little more* to it."

Paul and Charisse were all ears.

"Because neither of you were wearing a tracking device, and Mr. Avery was afraid of using *any* electronic equipment for fear that the kidnappers might become aware of it and *kill* the pair of you, we decided to go old-school," he began. "I was assigned to *secretly follow you* to the location of the hostage exchange and then call Mr. Avery to let him know where it was. Finally, I was to bring your father, or a '*look-alike*' if we weren't able to find him, inside the building at gunpoint on his signal."

"Was it my father's idea to actually *participate* in this?" Paul asked.

"Yes," Peter replied. "He knew the dangers involved, being well aware that they wanted to kill him," he explained. And then smiling, he added, "But he just *couldn't wait* to see you!"

Paul smiled in a bittersweet sort of way.

"But I am so sorry we weren't there sooner!" Peter apologized. "This was never supposed to be a *life-threatening situation.* We thought that with the kidnappers surrounded, this would turn into a nice, quiet arrest, or I'm *certain* that Mr. Avery would never have allowed the two of you go through with it."

"Why *did it* take you guys so long to get here?" Paul asked curiously.

Peter smiled sheepishly. "Well, I hate to say it, but I'm obviously *not* as efficient at tracking as I thought I was," he admitted. "I did eventually get the job done, but with all of that slick backtracking you guys did on the way here, you *nearly* lost me!"

"Well, thank goodness you *found* us again!" Charisse shivered.

Paul looked at Peter very intently, and then puzzledly said, "Now that I think about it, you *do* seem rather *familiar* to me?"

Peter laughed. "I'm not surprised! That's probably because I was assigned to tail you *everywhere* you went ever since you first left Paris," he replied. "I might as well have been your *shadow*!"

Paul laughed, before he asked, "But where have we actually *met* over these past few days? I know that our paths must have crossed somewhere?"

Peter smiled. "They *certainly* have!" he confirmed. "I believe that we have *met* face to face a total of... *five times* since this whole thing started."

"Really?" Paul asked incredulously.

"I'm *afraid* so," Peter chuckled. "First, I was your cab driver in Paris, assigned to make sure that you made it safely to the airport. Secondly, I was the air marshal on your plane flight, who failed *miserably* by not finding out who gave you that shiner?" he said with disappointment.

"Well, you *did* give me an icepack," Paul quipped.

"Yes, there was *that*!" Peter smiled. "Next, I was the VW driver who was following you to Monterey in that *ridiculously painted* car, and tonight, I played a heavily disguised version of myself, Bud Barbier, world-class *bounty hunter*!"

"That's only *four*?" Charisse interjected.

"Oh, I'm sorry," Peter animatedly replied. "How could I have forgotten *this* one? I was also the Aquarium security man who told you to stand at the base of the stairwell and wait, while I went upstairs to get Charisse."

Suddenly Charisse grew very excited. "*You* were the man who saved me at the Aquarium?" she exclaimed.

Peter nodded.

"I *knew* your voice sounded familiar!"

"I didn't try to disguise it," Peter confessed. "I had hoped you would trust me when I told you to run down those stairs, and fortunately you *did*!"

"What about that young lady in your car who you *claimed* was your sister, *Laura*?" Paul asked firmly but playfully, with just a hint of a smile. "I know that you only have *one* sister, and her name is *Charisse*, so that was obviously a lie! Fess up! Who was she?"

Peter smiled broadly. "Okay. The girl's name *is* Laura, and she's *like* a sister to me, so, I didn't really lie to you, did I?" he laughed. Growing more serious, he added, "Alright, to be completely honest, she's actually one of Mr. Avery's assets who I have worked with before. I was asked to bring her to Monterey with me, driving her *clown car*! No wonder you grew suspicious that we had been following you! It must have been a *shock* and a *nightmare* seeing us driving that monstrosity in your rearview mirror!"

Paul laughed. "Was that auction story and the '*psychedelic painting*' of the car by her class even true?"

"*Every word*!" Peter proclaimed guardedly. "At least it was true *a few years ago* when she was a dumb college kid!" he admitted. "But she's an adult now, and she *still* drives that funky car!" he laughed.

Paul laughed too.

"Someone named *Gabriela* saved me from being abducted at the Moulin Rouge," Charisse added impishly. "Was that *you*, too?"

Peter laughed. "No. Even I can't make a disguise look *that good*!" Then turning to Charisse, he added warmly, "But I'm sure you know that I *would have* been there for you if I hadn't already been in Monterey watching over Paul."

"Then did you *hire* her to keep track of me?" Charisse asked curiously

"No," Peter replied mysteriously. "She *volunteered*."

"Well, who is she?" Charisse demanded.

"She is a professional dancer and gymnast who performs regularly at the Moulin Rouge," he shared calmly. "She knows that place like the back of her hand! But more importantly… she is *my fiancée*!" he exclaimed with excitement.

Charisse screamed with joy as she hugged him tightly, while Paul smiled and nodded approvingly.

"Congratulations, big brother! Do you know when the wedding will take place?" Charisse asked breathlessly.

"Just as soon as I can get a break from my job," he said, "and of course, both of you will be our '*guests of honor*!'" he assured them.

"We were a little disappointed that you didn't attend *our* wedding a year and a half ago," Charisse shared sadly. "But, now that we know you work for INTERPOL, it's perfectly understandable."

"*What do you mean*?" Peter exclaimed, clearly taking exception. "I *was* there!"

"Wait a minute," Paul asked in shock. "Were you *the minister*?"

"*Yes, I was*," Peter confirmed to gasps. "It was the only way that I could be there without blowing my cover in an important case I was working on at the time. And besides, I was assigned to set-up a hidden camera so that your parents could watch the whole thing from Monterey."

"So, it was *you* who set-up the camera that Mr. Avery told me about!" Peter accused him with a broad smile. "Well done!"

"Hey, wait a minute!" Charisse exclaimed, with feigned concern. "Are you even *qualified* to perform a wedding?"

"Of course, I am!" Peter vehemently insisted. "I took a comprehensive course on the *Internet*!"

Charisse and Paul burst out laughing, although Peter repeatedly assured them that their marriage *was* legal! Eventually, after much more laughter and even more hugging, the three parted ways. Peter went back to his hotel to sleep, while Paul and Charisse dashed off to catch a cab to *Monterey General Hospital*. That was where Roy Madison was probably at that very moment undergoing surgery for removal of the bullet embedded in his body, and who knew what else! It had been fun having that brief respite from reality while catching-up with Peter. In fact, it had been *perfect*! But unfortunately, Paul and Charisse's anxiety and fear quickly returned *in force*!

When they arrived at the hospital, *official* visiting hours had long since been over. However, after explaining that they were close family and Roy's situation was *dire*, the supervisor in charge took pity on them. She granted them special permission to spend the night in the 'waiting room.' They all agreed that *this* created the quickest way for them to be notified just as soon as Paul's father's prognosis was known. But when they entered the room, they immediately saw that it was *not* completely empty? They excitedly zeroed-in on the *one* other person who was there!

"*Mom*!" Paul frantically rushed to *embrace* her. Soon, Charisse also joined in the hug. It lasted a good long time, but Paul seemed oblivious to that, considering the lengthy and difficult period of time that he and his mother had spent apart. He could hardly believe how happy he was feeling at that moment!

As the monumental hug finally came to an end, and they each took a seat in the waiting room, Paul's mother gently asked Paul, "Have you heard the news about your father?"

"No," he replied anxiously. "What's his prognosis?"

"It's *excellent*!" she exclaimed, while smiling at both of them. "Following his surgery to remove the bullet, he was awake very briefly. Just long enough to smile at me and say, '*They will have to do a lot better than that if they expect to kill Roy Madison*!'"

Paul and Charisse laughed with relief. A *huge* worry was immediately lifted!

Following this, Charisse looked very curiously at Jocelyn and asked, "I don't mean to pry, but what *exactly* happened to you? I was so sure that you had been kidnapped at your safehouse?"

Jocelyn smiled. "Well Charisse, fortunately I too escaped. I had an FBI double staying with me for protection the entire time I was at that house," she shared. "Just as we had rehearsed, if the house were ever breached, we *each* were to hide in one of the closets built with false fronts. As a failsafe, and *only* if necessary, she would allow herself to be captured, *pretending* to be me. Unfortunately, I was unable to get to my upstairs closet in time, so my double, Gaelynn, made a ruckus in the upstairs bedroom at the other end of the house. *That* drew them to her, giving me the necessary time to reach and secure myself in the closet!"

"Thank goodness for that!" Charisse exclaimed.

"Yes," Jocelyn replied thoughtfully. "But to be honest, even though I understood that my double did *exactly* what she was trained to do under those circumstances, I still felt guilty that it *should have been me* who was taken."

Charisse gasped. "I felt the very same way about *you* being taken instead of me?"

Jocelyn gave her a hug and a warm smile, as she laughed, "I'm so glad that my only son married a girl who thinks *exactly* like I do!"

Charisse laughed.

"In any case," Jocelyn grew a little more serious, "I was *so relieved* to hear that Gaelynn had been recovered *unharmed*!"

Then she added apologetically, "But I am *so sorry* for needlessly worrying you two about my being kidnapped." Then she added humorously with a twinkle in her eye, "But *don't* blame me. It was all *Douglas Avery's* idea!"

They all laughed together once again… and it sure *felt good*!

"Oh Mom. You *can't believe* how happy I am to see you again!" Paul burst.

"I think I *can*," his mother smiled warmly at both of them.

"You know, Mom, I feel just terrible about that feud I had with Dad. It must have hurt both of you so much," Paul shared emotionally. "Do you think Dad will ever forgive me?"

"There's *nothing* to forgive," Jocelyn replied. "He understands the situation. You had *no way* of knowing that your father and I feared for your life the entire time you lived in Paris."

"But why?" Paul asked in shock.

"Because of your father's importance to the FBI," Jocelyn replied. "You would have been an easy target if anybody on the wrong side of the law or America's politics *ever* found out who you really were!"

"Is Dad really an *important man* in the FBI?" Paul asked, flabbergasted.

"Put it this way," she replied. "*Yes*!"

Paul laughed and then shared, "I suppose it was because I *didn't know* Dad was in the FBI that I never worried about bad things happening to me as a result?" Paul admitted.

"And we are *so happy* that you never had to!" Jocelyn confirmed. "Sometimes ignorance *is* bliss! Anyway, Douglas always had his agents keeping a keen eye on you while you were in Paris, and just as soon as we learned about Charisse… he kept a keen eye on *both of you*. He's your *Godfather* you know!"

Paul and Charisse immediately felt enlightened and *so grateful*, all in the very same miraculous moment.

"I was just thinking," Jocelyn shared, with a motherly air. "Now that Roy is officially out of danger, and since we can't see him until tomorrow, why don't we all head back to our hotel rooms and get a little shuteye? What do you say? We certainly don't want to be *yawning* when we see him tomorrow," she chuckled.

Paul didn't really want to leave the hospital, but he found himself *already* beginning to nod off.

Charisse felt the same apprehension about leaving that he did, but at the same time, she agreed with Jocelyn completely, and shared, "Your mother's *right*, Paul. The faster we get to sleep, the *sooner* we can visit your father in the morning!"

Paul begrudgingly agreed, and they all left for their respective hotels. But just as soon as Paul and Charisse arrived at the Spindrift, walking arm in arm toward their room, they were *surprisingly* met outside their door by Mr. Avery?

"Hello," he greeted them solemnly.

"What is it? Is my father still *okay*?" Paul asked frantically, quickly jumping to the worst possible conclusion.

"Relax! He's doing fine!" Avery immediately reassured him. "But I'm afraid we need your help, Paul."

"*My* help? *Why*?" Paul asked incredulously.

"Because even after making those arrests, we still *have not* confirmed the crux of what we need to know about this planned assassination, including the *target*, *location* and *time*!" Avery sounded genuinely worried. "Time is running out! This thing could happen at *any moment*!"

"Okay! What do you need me to do?" Paul asked with urgency.

"We need you to take a very good look at a final coded message we intercepted an hour ago to see if it's somehow *musically-related*? I've got several other agents working on deciphering the code using every angle they know, but unfortunately, *none* of them are qualified to even pretend that they understand music! And with *music* actually being a possibility, it seems that *you* are the only qualified person available to me at half past midnight!"

"Of course, I'll look at it!" Paul quickly found his second-wind and accepted the challenge, as he felt the driving sense of urgency in Mr. Avery's voice. "Do you have a piano keyboard and headphones I could use?"

"Already set-up in your room!" Avery shared.

Over the next few minutes, they all went inside the room, where Paul immediately sat down at the keyboard which Mr.

Avery had set-up in a far corner. Next, Avery laid out the coded message on the attached music stand. Paul quickly perused it, finding that the message simply appeared to be a random mix of 42 numbers and letters, which read like the *vin number* of a car, 'L*5K6R7S8M7Z65o6T5i32W1X51Y2P3Q2V1U21J23H2N*.' Aside from that, just like everyone else, Paul was unable to make any sense of it?

"How do you expect to decode *that*?" Charisse asked Paul incredulously. "You can't make words out of numbers?"

"There *may* be a message in there *somewhere*?" Avery speculated encouragingly.

"Well, if there is, I'll certainly do my best to find it!" Paul assured him.

"Do you want me to stay up with you?" Charisse asked helpfully. "Maybe I could help?"

Paul smiled at her. "I'm sure you could, and I *really* appreciate the offer! But after the long day and night *you've* had already, the best way to help me is by going straight to bed."

Charisse smiled back at him, and gave Paul a quick kiss before getting ready to retire for the night.

As Paul began his careful analysis of the coded message, Mr. Avery pulled-up a nearby chair and waited patiently. Although there was no concrete evidence to confirm that this message was in *any way musical*, Mr. Avery had discovered earlier tonight, and shared with Paul, that two of the men they had arrested *held music degrees* from university? So, there was definitely a *chance*? There was even a part of him that hoped his godson would be the one to *break* the code! He half-smiled as he considered that maybe Paul had inherited his mother's code-cracking gift? Wouldn't *that* be nice?

About an hour later, Paul had grown increasingly more frustrated as he had exhausted *every* clever idea that he had been able to come up with, and had absolutely *nothing* to show for it! And then, while attempting to find a new way of analyzing the message, he suddenly thought of something that Charisse had told him earlier, "*You can't make words out of numbers*?" He chuckled impishly, excitedly realizing that there *was* another possibility that was so simple he'd actually *missed it*! Looking at the code;

'L*5K6R7S8M7Z65o6T5i32W1X51Y2P3Q2V1U21J23H2N*,' he very carefully copied all of the *letters* in the message onto a separate piece of paper, and then arranged them in alphabetical order. He soon found that there were *no* duplicate letters, giving him a total of 19. But there were *26 letters* in the alphabet? That's when he discovered that the missing letters were the first seven; A, B, C, D, E, F and G. Excitedly, he realized that these letters corresponded *perfectly* to the seven basic notes of a musical scale! By then repeating the first note an octave higher and placing it at the end of the seven notes, this collection of letters immediately formed a *complete octave scale*, of eight pitches! Then looking only at the numbers, he copied down all 23 of them. Finding no 9 or 0, he was *ecstatic*! That meant that each of the numbers fell between 1 and 8, just like a *musical scale*! He quickly converted each number into *a note in the scale*, deciding on the key of C. Thus number 1 became 'C,' 2 became 'D,' 3 became 'E' and so on. Next, he prepared to play those notes on the keyboard in the *exact order* that they appeared in the coded message, choosing to give each one of them a random quarter-note value to start. The numbers read: 56787656532151232121232. He played the series of notes a number of times, thinking that it possibly sounded like a familiar tune, yet frustratingly, he found himself unable to place it? And then on his fourth time through, he suddenly *stopped* and gasped? His expression grew exuberant as he laughed out loud!

"What is it, Paul?" A thoroughly exhausted Mr. Avery exclaimed, suddenly growing alert.

"You were *right*! This message *is* musical! *Listen to this*!" Paul exclaimed softly, as he pulled the cord to his headphones out of the keyboard so that Mr. Avery could hear him play. Next, just as he had before, he played the numbers in the message as musical notes, but *this time* giving each one of them what he considered to be the correct duration.

Mr. Avery's jaw dropped as he softly uttered, "*Oh, my God*!"

December 31 ~ Epilogue

The next morning, after being contacted at 10:00 o'clock, at precisely 11:00 o'clock, Paul and Charisse met Mr. Avery at his house for the final time. He wanted to speak with them regarding the exciting developments that had transpired since last night. He had already brought Peter and Jocelyn up-to-date half an hour earlier. So, once they were both comfortably seated facing the man, who as always, was sitting relaxed behind the desk in his study, the very important meeting began.

"Thanks for coming to see me on such short notice," Avery affably began. "First of all, my news regarding your father, as you well know, is *fantastic*! He's awake and resting comfortably. In fact, he's probably gearing-up right now for our imminent *invasion* of his hospital room right after this meeting is concluded!" he laughed. "Secondly, I'm so excited to share my most up-to-date information regarding this case," he exclaimed. "Let me just say that I don't believe we could have done it without the two you!" Turning toward Paul, he added, "There's no question that your incredibly quick and clever decoding of that final message, which turned out to *not* be a typical message at all, but the song, '*Hail to the Chief*,' directly led to saving the life of the *President of the United States*!"

"Was *he* the target then?" Paul asked curiously.

"He was only *one of them*," Mr. Avery replied coyly.

"*What*?" Charisse gasped.

"I think you had better tell us the *whole* story," Paul urged him.

"Of course," Avery agreed amicably. "To begin with, in addition to not knowing *who* the target of this assassination plot was, I was really stumped about what *day* and *time,* as well as *where* this assassination attempt would actually take place? That is, until your *father* surprisingly met me here late yesterday afternoon. He reminded me that the very first clue I had received, *Hogmanay*, the Scottish New Year, is celebrated in Scotland on December thirty-first, *not* on January first, as it is here in America. Then he added that Scottish time is *five hours ahead* of Washington D.C. time, and that meant that Hogmanay actually began *yesterday*, on December thirtieth, at 7:00 p.m. and ends today, on December thirty-first, at 7:00 p.m., D.C. time. I knew this information was somehow important, but I didn't know how to use it? But after you had decoded the message, Paul, I realized that, 'Hail to the Chief,' *had* to be a *confirmation* to the plotters that the planned assassination attempt was moving forward as planned! I also knew by the title of the song, that the target *was our President*! With that in mind, next I discovered that the ending time of Hogmanay, 7:00 p.m. on December thirty-first, actually *coincided exactly* with an important televised speech the President was scheduled to deliver to the nation, outside, near the Washington Monument. And he was actually going to be *joined* by the president of Mexico and the prime ministers of both Great Britain and Canada. This was to be a formal proclamation to the world that these four great nations were in *complete solidarity*."

"So, you believed that all four of those leaders were the targets then?" Charisse asked dumbfounded.

"Oh yes! Without a doubt!" Avery replied firmly.

"But how could you possibly *confirm* that?" Paul asked inquisitively. "I'm sure you considered that the coded message I deciphered could have been *meant* for the FBI to intercept and decode in order to act as a *diversion*, while the plotters were actually planning an assassination *elsewhere*? Surely you *also* concluded that this event would have been an ideal target for any number of random *crazies* who the FBI *didn't* even have on their radar?"

"Yes, Paul. *Both* of those possibilities *were* considered, and could have *easily* been true," Avery confessed. Then smiling, he admitted, "But, in the end, I would have to say that we got *very lucky*. We had been continuously interviewing the three plotters *separately*, ever since they had been arrested, and not one of them so much as uttered a sound or changed their facial expression in response to any of our questions?" Avery smiled at Paul. "It was not until I returned to the interrogation rooms playing, '*Hail to the Chief*,' through the loudspeakers in each one of them and bragging to the plotters that we had cracked the case wide-open, that we *finally* got some cooperation!"

"You're kidding? You don't mean that they confessed what they had been up to and agreed to help you?" Charisse asked in surprise.

"Not *all* of them," Avery replied cryptically.

"Who then?" Paul urged.

"Well, when I went into the room of the youngest suspect…"

"Do you mean, *Chris*?" Charisse exclaimed in shock.

"That's right," Avery nodded. "After hearing '*Hail to the Chief*,' over and over again, and my telling him juicy tidbits of what we already knew to be true, he was quickly convinced that we *already knew everything*, so he agreed to tell us all he knew in exchange for *plea bargain* consideration."

"What did he tell you?" Paul demanded excitedly.

Mr. Avery smiled. "He confirmed *everything* we had guessed concerning the assassination and even more importantly, he told us *exactly* where we could pick-up the trigger man!"

"Wow! *Where* was the trigger man hiding?" Charisse asked.

"Ah! He was very patiently hiding in *plain sight*, as a veteran member of the 'official security crew' for all D.C. *Presidential events*," Avery began. "A job which he had been quietly inserted into by the people who had set this whole assassination plot in motion. As a highly decorated former Marine, getting him in was easy. He had already served as a valued part of the crew for the past *two years*!"

"They've been planning this assassination for that long?" Charisse asked in surprise.

"Maybe even longer," Mr. Avery calmly replied. "These high-level assassination attempts always take time to set-up."

"How was he planning to kill them?" Paul asked anxiously.

Avery continued, "We learned that his plan was to plant a bomb onstage, by discreetly hiding it inside one of the chairs the custodial crew would bring in. The bomb would have the strength to *kill everyone* in the general area! If the bomb was somehow discovered *prior* to the event and then disabled, his back-up plan involved a high-powered rifle, fired from a police helicopter! Fortunately, he was picked-up about three hours ago by the D.C. Police without incident."

"Did they find the bomb?" Paul asked urgently.

"Oh yes! The chair was already randomly set-up on the stage when it, along with the bomb, were located by bomb-sniffing dogs, and carefully deactivated."

"How *horrible* if that bomb had actually gone off and all of those world leaders had been *killed*!" Charisse exclaimed.

"That's *very* true!" Avery declared. "But much more concerning, a devastating incident like that could have very well proven to be the catalyst for another *World War*, which I *believe* was the goal of the group that ordered those hits all along!" Not wishing to dwell on this, he added, "Thank goodness we uncovered the plot in time!"

"Yes! *Thank goodness*!" Charisse repeated with a sigh.

"I am very curious though," Paul began. "That is, *if* you are allowed to share this information with us? What were the *names* of the people involved in this planned assassination? And were they *really* with the FBI?"

"That information is actually scheduled to be released to the press within the next hour or so, but I think the two of you have *earned* the right to have it *leaked* to you a little earlier," Avery smiled. "The ringleader was a *department head* in the FBI, same as your father and I are, which explains how she got Roy's information on the illegal transfer of funds so quickly. She is a woman named *Brenda Gates*," Avery offered. "Unfortunately, she's still at large, but I'm sure it's just a matter of time before we catch-up with her. She was apparently wounded in the leg last night by Charisse's brother, agent Barbier," he winked, "so I can almost guarantee that she's currently holed-up somewhere in Monterey, just trying to hide and heal. Her picture is posted *everywhere*, along with a handsome reward for her capture."

"I hope you catch her *soon*!" Charisse said nervously. "She *scares* me!"

"Don't worry, Charisse. *We will*!" Avery assured her, and then gently added, "Your brother told me how you grabbed her arm last night and tried to wrestle her gun away from her just before she was set to shoot Roy in the *head*!" He paused before saying, "In that split second, if you hadn't decided to do what you did, I'm quite certain that Roy would have *died instantly* from his head wounds."

Charisse looked embarrassed. "I *wasn't* trying to be a hero, believe me," she stuttered uncomfortably.

"I know," Avery replied understandingly. "But all the same, *you were*."

Paul held her hand tightly as she smiled back at him.

Avery smiled too, and then continued, "*Cal Spenser* was the previous department chief who Brenda replaced after he retired from the FBI a couple of years ago. *Chris Smeltzer* was quietly *terminated* from the agency almost three years ago. He was 'let go' for reportedly doing shabby work and then trying to cover it up, having real trouble respecting authority, acting compulsively with no regard for rules or common sense and using some *highly questionable* interrogation techniques during his interviews, including physical and verbal abuse. But being friends with Brenda, he was enticed to join the group by the *lure* of a two-million-dollar payday! *Louis Crane*, the man who accosted Paul on the plane, worked for the FBI, serving as Brenda's second in command. None of those four had a criminal record of any kind… *before this*. And finally, the trigger man had been a top sniper for the Marines, with an excellent understanding of explosives, before quietly changing careers for something more lucrative, and becoming a *hitman*! And as we only just discovered, he had been at the heart of a number of high-profile murders *this* decade, but *none* as big as this one would have been! His name is *Alvin Taylor*."

"But why did the plotters come to Monterey in the first place?" Paul asked curiously.

"Well, I should probably begin with a little backstory," Avery suggested. "It was the *crack* in their plot's imperative need for secrecy that was created the moment Roy discovered the illegal money transfer that immediately got them spooked!" he began. "This messy situation quickly escalated until it *dictated everything* that they did. Deleting the evidence didn't remove the fact that Roy had already reported it to his superiors. Immediately after realizing this, complaining of fatigue, Brenda and Louis requested *and* received two weeks of vacation time to *clean-up the mess* that Roy had created for them," he explained. "Then, they *specifically* came to Monterey because just as soon as you and Charisse flew-in from

Paris, that meant your father's *entire family* was going to be here! They hoped to stop the possibility of more leaks in just one fell swoop. The plotters were getting more and more desperate as they neared the finish line. They *had* to get this assassination done *before* anyone found out about the plan, and more importantly for them, before anyone found out about *their involvement in it*, so they would still have time to safely flee the country!"

"Not to change the subject, but *why* didn't you tell us that my mother was *never really kidnapped*?" Paul demanded. "She told us that was all *your* idea?"

Mr. Avery laughed nervously, and then replied, "Well, yes, I'm afraid that it *was*. But before you get too angry with me, I knew that your meeting with the kidnappers would come across much more *honestly* if you both actually believed that Jocelyn *had* been kidnapped," he expressed sincerely. "I strongly felt that there would be far less chance of you inadvertently giving yourselves away." Smiling, he added, "That was honestly *not* a knock on your *superb* acting skills, believe me!" he chuckled. "You've both performed *flawlessly* during this entire case!" Then he paused, and gently added, "I did it for your own safety. Truly!"

"Thanks," Charisse replied appreciatively. Then she added sheepishly, "You know, very honestly, Paul and I strongly suspected after what had happened to me at the safehouse and the Aquarium, that you were somehow *tipping off* the kidnappers and could *not* be trusted! But after you arrived to save us last night, I knew that we were wrong! Thank you for saving our lives."

"Of course!" he said. "And you are very welcome!"

"I've got to apologize too," Paul shared hesitantly, with a touch of embarrassment. "I just had it in my thick head that there were too many *coincidences* going on, so you must have somehow been leaking information to the kidnappers. Sorry for that."

Mr. Avery nodded appreciatively, but then he *chuckled*. "Well, of course there were *too many coincidences*, Paul! You two were *quite perceptive* to notice that! We have actually suspected Brenda and company of being involved in this plot ever since they first approached Charisse in Paris!"

"Then why didn't you *arrest* them or at least interrogate them?" Paul asked, aghast.

Mr. Avery replied solemnly, "The culture of the FBI is to catch people with their *hands in the cookie jar*. Arrests that are done prematurely, usually *don't* end well for us."

"But surely after the Aquarium trip you must have *known* that they were involved?" Paul continued.

"Yes, and no," Avery responded cryptically. "We knew that they were *involved somehow*, but we didn't yet know if they were major players or just some hired thugs who were 'taking care' of anyone who they identified as being possible *threats* to the success of their plan! We didn't know for sure what role they were playing and how deeply they were involved until your meeting with them last night."

"Wow!" Charisse exclaimed.

Mr. Avery smiled, "Here at the FBI, we *make things happen* to flush out the bad guys and learn the truth. We do *whatever* it takes, including setting-up stings and leaking information. This unfortunately can often involve deception, even to those innocent people like the two of you, who are on *our side*!"

"Then you *did* use me as bait?" Charisse gasped.

"Well, yes. A *couple* of times," Avery sheepishly admitted. "But we *always* had your back, Charisse! Believe me!"

A slight smile crept over her face as she admitted, "Thanks for having my back, Mr. Avery, but I could *never* do this for a living!"

Avery chuckled. "Now, do either of you have any other questions?"

"Well, one thing I never understood was why Brenda and her gang never wore masks or attempted to hide their faces?" Charisse admitted. "They even called each other by their *real* first names? We would easily have identified them in the end? Why didn't they seem at all concerned about that?"

"This is only my *opinion*, Charisse, but I'll bet that Brenda and her gang figured they'd hide behind their badges for as long as they could, making it completely *unnecessary* for them to use aliases. Aside from the shooter, they were all currently or previously FBI agents, so they probably figured that the police would *not question* anything they did!"

"I hate to ask you this," Paul said slowly. "But what about if their plot *had* been successful? What would have happened if their covers had been blown before they escaped to another country?"

"Well, Paul," Mr. Avery replied thoughtfully. "I can't speak for the rest of the gang, but I think I *can* speak for Brenda. Based on her behavior, I think there is little doubt that she is a fame seeking *sociopath*! I believe that whether they had escaped or not, she would have been *ecstatic* that everyone knew about her part in this murderous plot that had killed *four top leaders* of the free world! That would have caused her name to live on in the history books *forever*! She'd be even more infamous than *John Wilkes Booth*! As far as what she would have done with any hostages they had at the time? I *hate* to think about it! With Brenda Gates in charge, *God* only knows?"

"I'm so glad that we *never* had to find out!" Paul replied with a shiver.

"Me too," Charisse agreed.

"Of course this is only the beginning," Avery announced dramatically. "Now, the FBI and INTERPOL will very *aggressively* go after the actual political group and their allies who paid these guys to set-up this heinous assassination plot in the first place! Taking *them* down will obviously help us all to sleep a lot better at night."

"Will we eventually read about the conclusion of that story in the news?" Charisse asked.

"I sincerely *hope not*!" Avery laughed. "My job is to get things done as *quietly and efficiently* as possible." He stood-up, and with a huge smile, announced, "Thank you again for all that you did, and *now* let's go give your father a rousing *welcome back*, shall we?"

With that, the three of them embraced each other in pure, unadulterated *relief* that this whole frightening affair had *finally* reached a happy conclusion. And the best part was that Roy Madison had been found, and was in fact, *very much alive*! Soon they would be smiling and laughing with him at his bedside in the hospital!

With the closing of this case came freedom for Paul and Charisse to consider doing any number of wonderful things in the future, that *hopefully* didn't involve polititical assassination plots! Their possibilities seemed *endless*, and to be perfectly frank, the hardest part for them now would undoubtedly be making that *final* decision. But that could certainly wait. There seemed to be so very much more to celebrate *right now*! It was simply incredible to realize just how much things had changed in a single day, wasn't it? And after living the past few days in *hell*… well, Paul and Charisse were both so *incredibly grateful* that things had ultimately turned out the way they had. To them, life felt very, very hopeful, once again. And regardless of what challenges they faced in the future, they felt so very blessed to know that just like in *this* adventure, they'd be *facing them together*!

"Cannon Manchester is Dead!"

[2020]

ONE NIGHT IN JUNE OF 1950, eight people, including at least *one* member of the Hollywood elite… maybe more, depending upon the *liberalness* of your definition, were invited to meet at the swanky mansion of millionaire Cannon Manchester, for a dinner party. The biggest surprise of the night was *not* the lobster bisque, which had actually been made substituting the lobster for a very tasty Bavarian escargot. No, the *biggest surprise* was that someone had un-sportingly *murdered the host*!

"Hello. I'm *Biff Berguhndy.* I am the hardnosed private investigator, or *P.I.* to those of you who prefer snappy abbreviations, whose responsibility it was to *solve* this bewildering case? The truth is, everybody at the party had a pretty solid reason for disliking someone. But the question is, who had the *motive*, the *means* and the *opportunity* to murder Cannon Manchester? Let's unravel this whole crazy story step by step before presenting the surprising conclusion to this most exciting caper. For those of you who might be faint of heart… consider yourselves *duly warned*!"

This whole puzzling affair began when a former New York hoodlum named Cannon Manchester, moved to Hollywood, California. Cannon, aged 37, was a big man (*he weighed over 350 pounds and was just under six feet tall*) with big ideas that he believed would someday make him the toast of the town! But he soon realized that he had to *know* people first… the *right kind* of people. So, one day he decided to show-off the mansion that he had only just acquired by throwing a dinner party for a few of his well-to-do neighbors.

A little background on Cannon Manchester would include that his wealth had *not* been accumulated from 'old money.' The truth was that no one knew *exactly where* all of his wealth had come from? But then again, they didn't really care, did they. They just welcomed him with open arms into their elite and snobby little Hollywood society as part of the *new* money set.

Before moving to Hollywood, Cannon had loved playing the '*big man*' while living in New York City. He had achieved quite the status for being a '*man about town,*' by wearing a wardrobe of tasteful and fashionable suits, throwing around as much money as possible, and most importantly, through attending 'Broadway premieres' whenever he could, with a *buxom and beautiful lady* hanging from each arm. This never failed to get his picture plastered on the front page of the 'Entertainment Section' of the New York Times, as was *always* his goal. Unfortunately, during the last Broadway event he'd attended, unbeknownst to him, one of his ladies had shockingly turned out to be the *mob boss's daughter*! Needless to say, the 'boss' was *not* very happy about it! Consequently, not wishing to become part of the next new city skyscraper's *cement foundation*, Cannon Manchester accepted an offer he could not refuse, and quietly moved away from the East Coast, which he loved so dearly, to become a new resident of the West Coast.

He soon located a beautiful mansion in the Hollywood Hills that was said to have been formerly owned by actor *Clark Gable*, during his heyday. The generous size of the offer he presented to the owner? Well, let's just say that it *too* was an offer the man could *not* refuse!

The trouble for Cannon Manchester began right away that fateful morning on the very day of his party. It was then that he received a *death threat* delivered directly to his home in the friendly guise of a letter. His devoted butler, Mr. Hertz, presented the letter to him at breakfast at the start of that perfect California day. After silently reading it, Manchester, dressed in his monogrammed white robe with matching slippers that were curiously curled at the ends like those worn by the genies in, '*Tales from The Arabian Nights*,' (*just because he liked the way they looked on him*), grew anxious. Turning to his butler, uninterrupted he proceeded to expound on what appeared to be a very *urgent* topic, ending his robust soliloquy with, "*More pancakes*, please!" In all likelihood, *eating* was Manchester's panacea for dealing with all types of stress. Just *looking* at him confirmed that up to this point in his life, he must have had a *very stressful ride*! After Mr. Hertz had delivered the additional stack of pancakes, he timidly asked the question that had been bothering him ever since he had given Mr. Manchester the very disturbing letter, "More syrup, sir?"

The simple nod, yes… *confirmed it*!

Curiously, that evening proved to be *vastly* different from the bright sunny day that had preceded it. A storm was brewing. The clouds were dark, the wind was howling and there was a definite chill in the air. In two words, it was a *sinister night*! Even the stars were *hiding*! In spite of this, as planned, beginning at 7:00 o'clock, two by two, the 'crème de la crème' of Hollywood society proudly arrived at Cannon Manchester's party. They were soon seated around his elegant and obviously very *expensive* solid-marble dining room table. Cannon greeted his guests from the head of it, dressed in his spanking new black and white tuxedo, *accented* nicely by a pair of freshly-made alligator shoes. He had recently received them as a gift from a couple of his friends who had '*retired*' and taken-up residence in the furthest reaches of the Louisiana Bayou… at least until the law *stopped* looking for them.

Cannon's newest girlfriend, the famous cover girl, *Eve Engood*, was sitting alone at the other end of the table. She was feeling a bit left out, but as a professional model, she had learned early-on to *never* let anyone know when she felt anything other than what they expected! So *tonight*, she appeared to be happy and charming. Although in truth, she really didn't need to *fake it* because she actually *was* a lovely girl in every respect. The path to her presence at this party had all started when she had fallen 'head over heels' for Cannon Manchester's *immense* charms *(yes, even his charms were fat*) at a celebrity soiree in Beverly Hills. Soon after that event, she had ecstatically accepted his very tempting offer to move into his house and become his '*steady girl-friend.*' Aside from having such a perfect body and facial features, Eve was also a natural redhead with exceptionally long hair, which she wore *perfectly*! Tonight, she let it hang down freely, allowing it to dance sexily across her naked back and shoulders whenever she turned her head.

The invited guests were predictably seated as they had arrived, *in pairs*. To the left of Manchester sat *Miz Turrey*, a dark lady if there ever was one, and her date, the exceptionally thin but also exceptionally rich, *Mylo Girth*. Next, came the well-known Hollywood gossip columnist, *Cee Cee Cretz*, alias the wild '*Muffy Du Pont,*' former heiress to the vast *Du Pont fortune*. However, she had been disowned by her family a decade earlier for making the family blue by *painting the town red*! Beside her sat her very muscular and handsome date, *Chet Freshcorn*. To Manchester's right sat the ever-popular *Ace Lutt*, and her *fifteenth* different escort of the month, a very *unexceptional* man in every respect named *Van Nish*. Seated right beside him was the ultra-creative but equally unpredictable, *Miss Lott*, and her boyfriend, a highly excitable man who I've heard is very prone to violent outbursts, appropriately named, *Thomas (Tommy) Gunn*.

The hunchbacked butler, Mr. Hertz, served the delicious dinner assisted by two of Mr. Manchester's other household employees, the very efficient mother and daughter team of Biddy and Giddy McClinen. Both of these women appeared as scandalously dressed (*or undressed*) French maids, although in reality they each served a dual role for the household as maid *and* cook. Tonight however, rather than having one woman dress as a maid and the other as a cook, Cannon had boldly decided to have them *both* dress as French maids. He had done this solely because he believed that saying, 'scandalously dressed French *cooks*,' just didn't *sound* right? Meanwhile, Manchester quickly embraced his role as host with a vengeance! He told tantalizing tales of his *very naughty* past in New York City, which had his guests hanging on every word!

"How did you make all of that money, Mr. Manchester?" Miss Cretz asked him very bluntly with a *smirk*, as any good gossip columnist worth her salt would do. “I have heard a great number of *different stories* about that?”

Manchester laughed, and stayed just as charming as ever, not missing a beat as he replied, “Darling, I didn’t only *make* the money, but as you can see, the money has *made me*!” The entire table of people burst out laughing, and *that* my friends, was *exactly* how the dinner portion of the evening played out. After dinner, the buckled butler, Mr. Hertz, poured a bottle of *one hundred-year-old sherry* into beautiful crystal schooners for each guest before they left the table to mingle throughout the room.

Cannon Manchester was quickly cornered by Ace Lutt, who appeared to have a lot to talk with him about. However, I imagine those topics would probably *not* make appropriate after-dinner conversation for *classy* people like you or me. Meanwhile, Ace’s escort for the evening, Van Nish, slowly stroked the ‘*soft as a baby’s bottom*’ stubble of his barely visible goatee and frowned. Much to his chagrin, his wayward date, Miss Lutt, was very publicly making time with the *party’s host* as if *he* wasn’t even there? Although he was never one to lack confidence, he was beginning to feel like a juicy steak in a room full of *vegetarians*!

Miss Lott and her intimidating escort, Tommy Gunn, appeared to be deeply involved in a high-spirited duelogue, *not* to be confused with a ‘duologue.’ You see, a *duo*logue is simply defined as two people conversing together, while a *duel*ogue derives its meaning from the word, *duel*. Historically, the duelogue was accidentally invented by a young sister and brother named Beatrice and Bruno McAfee, in Newark, New Jersey, in the 1940s. They walked outside of their family’s apartment one day, and determinedly began to argue *over each other* for a good hour, without ever listening to a single word their sibling said? They argued (*without ever waiting for a response*) about everything imaginable, and to those listening and watching them, it was so unusual, it was *exciting*! As luck would have it, an out-of-work promoter who was sitting on a bench at the bus stop outside their apartment, watched the whole thing! As a result, a lightbulb went on in his head, and just like that, he became rich and famous as the creator of the ‘*The Duelogue League*!’ In fact, it quickly became the *hottest competitive sport in America*! Married couples throughout America were *especially* actively practicing it *every day*! In a nutshell, a duelogue is simply defined as a contest between two people where each one must continuously speak over the other one about anything at all, until someone (*the loser*) runs out of thoughts or breath! And *killing* or *maiming* your opponent in any way as a method of winning, is *absolutely forbidden*… as is tickling! Miss Lott and Tommy Gunn had apparently decided to continue honing their skills tonight and just as I had surmised, they were taking *this* practice *very seriously*! You see, they had dreams of someday going pro, and competing in an official '*Duelogue League Tournament*,' where the prize for winning was often in the *thousands of dollars*! So, they continued to talk over one another for pretty much the remainder of the party. This was nothing new for them, however. They had once practiced during a prizefight that had lasted hours after a knock-out punch had ended the fight, while all of the other spectators had departed to go out *drinking*! Miss Lott and Mr. Gunn only stopped *that* duelogue because they noticed that the lights had been completely turned out in the building. It was a simple matter of *integrity*. It seems that they both refused to continue competing if they *couldn't see* the anxiety-ridden, mind-numbing, sweat-soaked, tear-streaming, baby-sobbing, hope-depleted face of their *vanquished* opponent! Otherwise, *what the hell was the fun of winning*? Meanwhile, back at the party, Tommy kept fidgeting. This had always been a telltale sign of his that meant he was growing very impatient to do… *exactly* what he had come here to do!

Suddenly, outside the upstairs bathroom was heard the *ghastly* retching of someone *vomiting* uncontrollably? Apparently, the food and alcohol served at this evening's dinner had proven to be too rich for simple and mild-mannered Chet Freshcorn to handle. The awful sounds of his muscle-bound body expelling it, was *definitive proof*! His date, Miss Cretz, was absolutely *unconcerned* with his wellbeing however. She rapidly traversed amongst every conversation in the room, desperately searching for the best story to lead-off her upcoming newspaper column.

Cannon's girlfriend, Eve Engood, still without anyone to talk to, found a nice vacant corner of the room and sat down on a chair. Surprisingly, she pulled out a very popular Agatha Christie novel from her purse and began reading it. It looked as though she was really enjoying it too! It was an exciting story about a group of well-to-do people who were attending a '*high society dinner party*' on a dark and stormy night, very much like *this* one. When suddenly, out of nowhere... one of them was *mysteriously murdered*?

Finally, there was Miz Turrey, the '*dark lady*' as she was so often referred to (*more for her demeanor than her skin color which was not dark at all, but more a light shade of alabaster*), who seemed to be having an odd monologue in Russian with an audience of *one*; her overly-attentive date, Mylo Girth. However, as Mr. Girth continued gazing directly into Miss Turrey's eyes, he began reading an intense expression of *shock* as she stared off into the distance, appearing to be almost *hypnotized*? Her highly focused expression proved to be *so intense* in fact, that it made him feel extremely uncomfortable, eventually forcing him to anxiously walk away. But as usual, *nobody noticed.*

Suddenly, without warning, the room went *completely black*! This was immediately followed by a shocking flash of lightning and a crash of thunder, horrifically accompanied by the *blast* of a gunshot! Everybody screamed! When the lights came back up again just a few moments later, all eyes were transfixed on the Picasso painting that had been hanging so perfectly on the wall facing the entry doors. Now, appearing smack dab in the middle of it was a mysterious *bullet hole*, which to be very honest, actually made this uncommonly *bland* painting look all the more interesting? Curiously, there was absolutely *no* sign of a gun or a shooter? And fortuitously, no one had been hurt.

"What the devil just happened?" Manchester bellowed, as he arrogantly waddled toward the center of the room to address his guests. "This is a dinner party, *not* a shooting gallery! Just where does the person responsible for this *gauche* display think they are? On *Coney Island*?"

His guests laughed, but it was more a case of easing their tension caused by the *frightening* gunshot than their 'appreciation' of his *borderline* humor.

And then out of nowhere, Cannon Manchester suddenly grabbed his throat and exclaimed, "*Oh God*!" as all three hundred and fifty blubbery pounds of him unceremoniously collapsed to the floor! Immediately, Mr. Hertz, Manchester's trusted butler, rushed to his side and checked his pulse to shockingly discover... there was *none*?

"Cannon Manchester is *dead*!" the butler cried out in shock. "Quick! Call the ambulance to see if they can revive him!"

"Why don't you just give him a little mouth to mouth?" Miss Lutt suggested coyly.

"Because, dear lady, I don't want to *catch his lip rash*," the frightened butler replied defensively.

"I've had worse!" she shared nonchalantly, recalling a few lip rash *doozies* she had experienced (*for undisclosed reasons*) during the past year alone. "Okay, fine! I'll do it myself!" she announced assertively, as she easily pushed the crooked butler out of her way and commenced with some pretty heavy-duty *mouth to mouth*! The ambulance arrived ten minutes later and quickly whisked the body away.

Soon after that, *I arrived* on the scene. If you remember, I am *Biff Berguhndy*, the private investigator who the Hollywood Police Department's Homicide Division *always* calls-in when a possible murder occurs *after* six o'clock at night. That is on account of *this* is Hollywood, and most of their *regular* detectives are also actors, *daylighting* as cops in order to pay their bills until after they get '*discovered*!' Many of them have rehearsals or performances at local theatres or movie studios almost every night of the week. As a matter of fact, you can often hear *crickets*, and if you're not careful you may also find yourself colorfully sliding across the floor on a half-eaten jelly-doughnut, while traveling through the 'homicide detective' wing of the precinct at that time of night. That's why I serve such an indispensable role for them. You *could* call me the '*dark knight of the night*,' but Batman might object to that title. So, I suppose it's safer to stick with that *endearing* little nickname the detectives themselves created for me... *That rent-a-cop guy*!

As my job required, the very first thing I did once arriving at the scene was to round-up *everyone* who had been in attendance at the party. With that job completed, I politely asked them all to wait in the living room until I called them into the den to be interviewed.

I know that sounds pretty straightforward and simple, but *none* of those Hollywood prima donnas were used to ever being told what to do? *Much less doing it*! So, as you probably already guessed, it took me a lot longer than it would have taken for *normal* people like us to follow my instructions!

The first people I called-in were Mr. Manchester's household helpers, Biddy and Giddy McClinen. They were both rather short, with their heads covered by thick red hair that they wore in matching pixie cuts. Along with their sexy green French maid outfits, they also wore vibrant green berets atop their heads, reminding me for some reason of sexy *Irish elves*? Both women gave similar accounts of Manchester's death, yet it was easy for me to sense that they seemed quite nervous while talking to me? For the life of me, I couldn't understand why? This convinced me that they *could* be leaving something important out of their stories? I vowed to find out exactly what that something *was* the very next time I spoke with them. In addition, I noted that they both spoke with a thick Bronx accent, which inferred that they were both originally from New York City... *just like Cannon Manchester*? Or, I suppose it could also mean that they just watched too many gangster movies? Whether either one of those two possibilities meant anything important at this early juncture, I really *couldn't* say?

Next, I called in Miz Turrey and Mylo Girth. Miss Turrey was an attractive woman who looked to be in her mid-thirties, sporting long, dark, wavy hair. In addition, she was wearing a slinky black dress that just happened to be backless. The moment I laid eyes on her, I noticed that she was giving off a '*dark and mysterious aura*?' This aura followed her around very closely as she entered the room, much like the *dirt that follows Pigpen* of Peanuts fame, only *far sexier*! Mylo Girth, on the other hand, was a skinny runt of a man wearing an expensive *brown* suit made from the silk created by the finest silkworms in the world, the *mulberry silkworm, Bombyx miri*! In addition, the color of his suit matched the color of his hair *perfectly*! As impressive as that might sound, it was completely wasted on him because he was so very dull that *absolutely nothing* could have possibly helped! After getting less than helpful interviews from both of them, I asked Miss Turrey one final question.

"Did you *like* Cannon Manchester as a person?"

"I *didn't* know him, did I!" she replied with an obvious chip on her shoulder.

"Do you mean that you had never met him before coming to this party?" I sought clarity.

"I mean that I have *never met Cannon Manchester*, period!" she shouted angrily. "The man meant nothing to me, see! In fact, I didn't know anyone at this so-called party!"

"Not even your date, Mylo Girth?" I asked her in surprise.

She gave me a little half smile that was both irritated and mysterious as she intensely gazed into my eyes, and said, "Yes, I suppose I *do* know Mylo."

"How so?" I asked.

"He is taking my '*Russian Literature*' class, which I offer twice weekly in the lecture hall of the Hollywood Roosevelt Hotel. Unfortunately, the material in that course can be quite dull, boring and often forgettable. *He fits right in*!" she proclaimed with a laugh, unmasking a very sardonic sense of humor.

Having answered my question a little *more* completely than I would have preferred, Miss Turrey abruptly got up from her chair and left. Mylo Girth meanwhile, intentionally lagged behind and then very nervously approached me.

"Just one more thing, Mr. Berguhndy," he said.

"Yes, Mr. Girth?" I responded curiously.

"Just so you know, I was invited to this party due to my *prominent* place in Hollywood's financial circles," he shared. "But Miss Turrey was *not* invited at all! She merely came as my date," he explained quietly and unapologetically. "Mr. Manchester would *never* have invited her. From simple observation, if there was one thing he loved, it was silly, shy and sexy women… not *brooding bitches* like Miz Turrey," he added gently. "So, I hope you *aren't* considering her as a suspect?"

"I don't *have any suspects* at this time. I'm just collecting information," I replied frankly, while also trying to understand the motivation behind his heartfelt plea. "But tell me, if you hold such a low opinion of Miz Turrey, then why did you invite her to this party in the first place?"

Mylo looked shocked and quite obviously taken aback. "I *don't* hold a low opinion of her, Mr. Berguhndy!" he corrected me as defiantly as I had seen him. "The truth is, I am *deeply in love* with her!"

As Mylo Girth left the room, although I was feeling a bit confused by his final statement, I had to move on. Next, I called-in the butler, Mr. Hertz, professionally dressed in a perfect fitting black tuxedo that even possessed a little extra material on top to accommodate the '*hunchbackian*' shape of his shoulders and back. As soon as he sat down, I just knew that this man's position and knowledge of the deceased would undoubtedly provide me with a *treasure-trove* of pertinent information. After sharing what he had seen, while also demonstrating how 'beastly bad' he felt about his employer's untimely demise, I followed that up with a couple of questions designed to fill-in the holes I still had with his story.

"Mr. Hertz, After Mr. Manchester collapsed, I understand that *you* checked his vital signs, but did a *real doctor* also check to see if he was still alive?"

"I beg your pardon? I *am* a real doctor!" Hertz insisted, obviously offended. "I was a practicing doctor *prior* to taking this job, and I *swear* to you that I found Mr. Manchester to have absolutely *no pulse*!"

"Oh! Well then pardon me!" I smiled apologetically. Then I added, "How very interesting that you went from being a *doctor* to becoming a *butler*?"

"Yes, sir," he replied calmly. "Mr. Manchester paid me more than *twice* what I had been earning as a doctor in order to ensure my service."

"Did Mr. Manchester leave any type of will?" I asked.

"Yes, sir," he responded. "But you will have to take *that* up with his lawyer."

"Alright. *Who* exactly is that?" I asked.

"Why, that would be *me*!" Mr. Hertz laughed impishly. "You see, Mr. Berguhndy, I was a lawyer first before becoming a doctor, and *well before* I assumed the role of Mr. Manchester's butler."

"Have you had any *other* careers that might somehow be pertinent to this case?" I asked in order to save time.

"Let me think?" he began slowly. "I was an *exotic dancer*, an *airplane pilot*, as well as a *sous-chef at 'Sardi's,'* but Mr. Manchester had no need of any of those talents here, so… *no*!" he replied quite firmly.

"Who stands to inherit all of Mr. Manchester's property and wealth?" I asked.

"That would be his twin brother, Bannon," he replied with a slight frown.

"Hmm. I have actually heard a couple of rumors about him having a *mysterious twin*? But no one seems to have ever seen him?" I professed thoughtfully.

"Yes. *That* is true," Mr. Hertz confirmed. "Of course, aside from telling those closest to him of Bannon's existence, he *never* spoke of him again," Hertz replied, shaking his head sadly. "To tell you the truth, he was *terribly embarrassed* by him and the mere fact that the two of them were even *related*!" Motioning me over, so as not to be overheard, he whispered, "He told me that he was a bit of a *dandy*!"

Speaking in a *normal* voice, I asked, "Will you be notifying him of his brother's death?"

"Of course, sir. I will be calling him first thing in the morning," Mr. Hertz assured me. "He will need to make the arrangements for poor Mr. Manchester's funeral."

"What about the death threat that your former employer received this morning? What did the *note say*?" I asked intently.

Mr. Hertz regretfully shook his head. "I *didn't* read it, sir. I have absolutely *no idea*?"

"Then what makes you so certain that it was a *death threat* at all?" I asked incredulously.

"Because Mr. Manchester *told me* that it was, just before burning it and eating his second batch of pancakes."

"Ah… very good!" I said, with sudden understanding.

"Thank you, sir," he replied, and then with a very noticeable knot in his back, he stood up and walked out of the room. Although I was not really done exploring what appeared to be the many *cryptic kinks* that seemed to run counter to whom Mr. Hertz purported to be, it was growing late, so I decided to get back to him very soon, *if or when* I thought of any more pertinent questions to ask him.

Next, I called in Eve Engood, the deceased's girlfriend. The moment that stunning redhead entered the room, I suddenly could think of *nothing else*? The girl was truly a knockout! She was wearing a long black (*obviously designer*) gown that showcased very clearly why she was one of the top models in the industry! I mean, when you compared her to the ever-popular redheaded star of B-movies, Lucille Ball, she even made *her* look like *Bozo the clown*! After going through the normal chitchat in order to make her feel more comfortable, I got right to work.

"So, how did you feel about Cannon Manchester?" I asked her directly.

"Oh, I *loved* him," she replied sweetly. "I loved everything about him."

"How long had you two been an *item*?"

"For quite a *long* time. Ever since we'd first met, in fact," she proclaimed proudly.

"Oh? And when was that?" I asked casually.

"About two weeks ago," she replied.

I inadvertently chuckled. "*Two weeks* hardly sounds like a *long time*?" I remarked jokingly.

"Well, as they say, the length of someone's relationship doesn't matter nearly as much as the *length* of the person it's with," she replied mysteriously.

Although I had no idea what her last statement had actually meant… I was *afraid* to ask!

As if reading my mind, she clarified playfully, "I'm speaking of Cannon's *height*, Mr. Berguhndy. I am a firm believer that tall men, like Cannon or yourself… make the *best lovers*."

Her risqué remark *completely* covered me in a shroud of sophomoric embarrassment (*even though it was probably the truth*), and I could actually feel myself beginning to blush like a *ripe tomato*! But quickly remembering *who* I was and *what* I was here to do, I somehow held it together and just smiled like the professional I knew I could be. Fortunately, this mindset soon saw my bright red face *fade* to a dull shade of pink. Moving on quickly,

I asked, "Can you think of *anyone* who might have wanted to see Mr. Manchester *dead*?"

Miss Engood grew sullen for a few moments before gradually donning an angry face, and replying, "*Me*! If I ever caught him *cheating*!"

"Okay," I was taken a bit off-guard.

"Is poor Cannon's death officially thought to be from natural causes… or *murder*?" Miss Engood suddenly changed her demeanor and inquired sweetly.

"The coroner will undoubtedly let us know the answer to that very telling question the first thing tomorrow morning," I explained calmly.

"Then *why* are you interviewing me now as if *this* is already a murder investigation?" she pried aggressively.

The fact that Miss Engood was *seductively* standing only a few inches from my face, immediately caused me to grow *nervous*! Although standing next to an extremely beautiful woman *often* had this effect on me, it had *never* felt this intense before? "Because, Miss Engood," I replied calmly, "*this* is Hollywood. If Mr. Manchester's death *does* indeed turn out to be murder, I will then have *already* interviewed everyone at the crime scene *before* they are possessed to *change* their stories. Because if *that* happens, it will very obviously result in the police being inundated with more exciting but *false* renditions of what actually occurred here tonight. Such a situation would surely impede the integrity of the investigation!"

"But why would anyone want to *change* their story?" Miss Engood asked innocently, with her big blue eyes *piercing* my heart.

"To *sell* to the studios as a future movie deal, of course!" I explained. "That's how this town works. Honesty *does not* sell tickets!"

"Oh," she replied nonchalantly. Then she surprisingly stepped forward and gave me the sweetest little kiss right here on my forehead? "That's just a *down-payment*," she cooed coyly, before provocatively turning around and leaving the room.

Miss Engood's very unexpected little kiss on my forehead as well as her final remarks were just about as peculiar as finding a *goldfish in a snow cone*? But I couldn't dwell on that right now. I had to move on.

Cee Cee Cretz and Chet Freshcorn were the next guests I interviewed. Cee Cee, always the hardworking reporter, as I mentioned earlier, had lived the wild life of the '*rich and reckless*' during her youth as *Muffy Du Pont*, before being unceremoniously kicked out of the family and even *forced* to change her name! However, she was now happily living the life of a happy extravert with very little money to her name, but *plenty* of energy and the skill to always make herself the *center of attention*! Many viewed her behavior as being a bit eccentric or even weird, and it *was*! But that was because she was *still* 'Muffy Du Pont' at heart! Tonight, she was dressed in dark formalwear (*as mandated for this dinner party*), but obviously she *did not* have the clothing budget that she used to, although to be honest, she probably *wouldn't* have dressed any differently even if she *had*! Her long black gown was apparently made from some sort of *cheap cotton* that lacked the sheen of a more expensive fabric. In fact, her gown was the sort of garment you would find languishing on sale for months in a *Sears Catalog* due to being *just plain ugly*! Apparently this was exactly the type of '*head turner*' she had been searching for, and it *did* garner its share of, '*What the hell is she wearing*?' looks! To top things off, she wore a foot high hat on her head made from faux black and white animal fur, that strongly resembled a small curled-up animal, more precisely, a sleeping *baby skunk*! Chet Freshcorn, on the other hand, looked *perfect* in his traditional black Italian tailored tuxedo. Although neither of them offered me much information of substance, I immediately got the feeling that Miss Cretz was *exactly* as she appeared; a wild and crazy gossip columnist go-getter! But I also deduced that although Mr. Freshcorn *did* understandably seem a bit under the weather (*presumably due to his bout with food poisoning earlier in the evening*), I was completely convinced that he was actually the *polar opposite* to the naive simpleton that he appeared to be! I had no actual proof of that however? Let's just call it a hunch. But, if my hunch proved to be *correct*, I asked myself, '*What* could possibly be his motivation for putting on such a dramatic deception?' I took a note to have another conversation with Mr. Freshcorn very soon.

The next ones to enter the room were Ace Lutt and Van Nish. They were quite the perfect couple… *Not*! Ace was as flirtatious as a randy dog, while it seemed as though Nish wasn't even there? Or to put it bluntly, as though Nish *didn't matter a bit* even though he *was* there! I would describe Ace Lutt's attire as formalwear for 'the class*y* stripper!' I say this with the utmost respect because her strapless gown, although beautiful, left *nothing* to the imagination by exposing most of her buxom bosom. *Not* that it bothered me! Van Nish was wearing a black tuxedo, easily a size too large, which he had *probably* borrowed. But I hardly noticed him because I was too busy checking out *his date*! After Ace had gotten her fill of flirting with me and protruding her massively magnificent chest every time she spoke, I began the interview.

"So," I directed my question to both of them. "What made you accept Mr. Manchester's unexpected invitation to attend his party?"

"*That* invitation wasn't at all unexpected for me," Mr. Nish bragged. "In fact, I helped Mr. Manchester decide *who* to invite!"

"Oh! Are you in his employ?" I asked curiously.

"There's certainly no record of that. I mean *not officially*," he quickly replied. "We were just friends."

"By *friends*, do you mean you talked together often?" I asked logically.

Mr. Nish chuckled. "No. Mostly *he* did the talking… *I'm* much more of a do-er."

"Well, I was not surprised in the least by *my* invitation either!" Miss Lutt declared. "Mr. Manchester and I were fast becoming… *very close friends*, if you know what I mean."

"No. Exactly what *do you mean*?" I pressed her.

"I mean that the way I just *implied* it, is a far more respectable way of describing what we *really* were!" she smiled flirtatiously.

"You *deceitful and loose woman*!" Nish suddenly yelled at her. "I thought you had the hots for *me*?"

"The *hots*? For *you*? Are you kidding me?" she laughed haughtily. "I always prefer a man whose personality is *hot* like a firecracker. *Sizzling* first and always followed by a *pop*! But *you*?"

She hesitated, narrowing her eyes to show unabashed pity and disgust as she sneered, "Don't take this wrong, *lover*. But if you were a firecracker, you'd be a *very disappointing dud*!"

Miss Lutt's heinous and debilitating words could not have been more hurtful to Van Nish than if he had been *hissed at* by his beloved cat, *Brutus*! He quickly lowered his head, let out a small sob and ran off like the beaten man he was!

I felt sorry for the guy, I *really did*! Although it generally takes a lot to make a grown man cry… that apparently was *not* the case with Van Nish! What a *crybaby*! Still, I somehow felt bad for him? So bad in fact, that I didn't even try to stop him.

Realizing then that my curiosity had created one final question for Miss Lutt, I asked, "By the way, *where* did you get that very interesting first name?"

"I *earned* it!" she declared. "I *always* play my cards right, honey," she smiled mysteriously. "Remember, *Ace always wins*!"

If that was some sort of poker metaphor, I think I somehow missed the point? That is, if there truly was a *point* to catch at all? Regardless, after that, there was really no reason to continue our interview, so I allowed Miss Lutt to strut out of the room like a 'Playboy Bunny' (*a type of sexy model that is not created until 1960*)! After she left, I realized that I might have a couple more questions to ask her later if this case *did* turn-out to be murder! So, in the back of my mind I decided to meet again with her sometime in the very near future.

At long last, I called-in the two remaining party guests I had not yet interviewed; Miss Lott and Tommy Gunn. But they *never* showed? When I walked outside of the den to check the living room for myself… *it was empty*? I was clearly disappointed, but whether I liked it or not, my interviews for tonight had now been brought to an abrupt and *incomplete* end!

The next morning, I woke-up in my studio apartment off Hollywood Boulevard to the harsh ringing of my telephone unbearably torturing my ears! It was all the harsher this morning because I had consumed a whole *fifth of Scotch* last night and my head was naggingly reminding me of why I *shouldn't* have done that! I managed to pick-up the receiver and briefly chat with the coroner. After I'd hung up, I smiled. I was so relieved that I had interviewed those people last night. It seems that Cannon Manchester *had indeed been murdered*! Apparently, some form of poison had been found in his body which the coroner *could not* immediately identify? This in itself was *odd*, but in the murder business, something like this *does occasionally* happen. It had probably been covertly delivered to Manchester's meal sometime during last night's *soiree*. Based on what Biddy and Giddy McClinen had told me, that meal had consisted of lobster bisque (*as previously mentioned, with Bavarian escargot substituted for the lobster*), and Chateaubriand, served with an assortment of delicious vegetables. For dessert, they had enjoyed chocolate mousse, while the after-dinner drink was, of course, sherry. Just thinking about that delicious meal made every gland in my mouth *salivate*! As a result, just as soon as I got home last night, although normally all I make for dinner are *reservations*, I was inspired to prepare my own meal! Due to the excellent 'culinary arts training' I had received while working several summers of my youth at *Big Louie's Delicatessen*, I was able to prepare myself a slew of delicious sandwiches, *regardless* of what I had on hand to make them! So, since I hadn't shopped for fresh groceries since my last paycheck two weeks ago (*which was pretty much already spent*), my sandwiches consisted of peanut butter, strawberry jam, oatmeal, sardines and just a touch of Dijon mustard on stale rye bread, with the afore mentioned bottle of Scotch to wash it all down! *Delicious*! Yes! I am a man of *many* talents! But that's not important now. *Back* to the case.

No one came forward to report that anyone else had *died* after consuming that scrumptious meal at Cannon Manchester's mansion last night, although I already knew that Chet Freshcorn *had* experienced some severe intestinal problems directly after finishing his. However, he reportedly felt fine just an hour later? Based on that finding, I had to conclude that if Manchester *had* ingested the poison from his meal, then *his* meal had to have been *singled-out* and intentionally tainted with poison by one of his servants… or even a *guest*? Another reason I was beginning to feel that Manchester and Freshcorn had *not* consumed the same poison was because if Chet Freshcorn's ailment *was* caused by the very same poison as Manchester's... then *why* were their reactions to it so diametrically different? I mean, Freshcorn's 'upset stomach' was a far cry from Manchester's *complete deadness*? And another thing. There was a blackout and then a gunshot that created a *hole* in that Picasso painting? How in the hell did *that* fit-in with anything?

My meditation was abruptly cut short as I heard a gentle tapping at my door? I very cautiously opened it a crack, and was immediately both surprised and delighted to come face to face with *Miss Lott*, one of the two remaining party guests who had given me 'the slip' last night.

"Why hello, Miss Lott! May I call you by your first name, which I believe is Liza?" I asked her at the door as I undid the multiple locks with as much polite friendliness as my throbbing headache would allow.

"No, you *may not*!" she declared very sternly.

"Okay," I mumbled in both surprise and embarrassment.

"Good morning, Mr. Berguhndy!" she inexplicably transitioned from the extremely foul mood she had exhibited only moments before, to an energetically sweet, but oddly *seductive* persona? I was *confused as hell* as she slowly slinked her way past me into my apartment like some *sexy time-bomb* that I just knew could go off at *any moment*!

"I see you haven't begun decorating your little... *mansion* yet?" she said with friendly sarcasm.

I'm certain that she must have been poking fun at my very small apartment with its minimal furnishings. To be precise, those furnishings began with a small, square, wooden table and two mismatched wooden chairs. I used that table for eating, writing, playing cards, and more often than I'd care to admit, to *catch* my unconscious head whenever I become *stone drunk*! I also had a hotplate and small refrigerator, a dresser and a large fourposter brass bed that had once belonged to *Louis the Fourteenth*... or at least that's what the beautiful salesgirl told me. Finally, there was a tall stack of magazines in the far upper-right corner of the room that I had *dedicatedly* collected over the past fifteen years or so. They featured some of the most popular cover girls of each year in a wide variety of dress and *poses*! In addition, those classy pictures had been taken in some of the most magnificently scenic locations in the world! Although to be quite honest, most of the pictures looked suspiciously as if they had been shot in a photography studio in *front* of a backdrop of a *magnificently scenic location in the world*! But *that* didn't bother me one bit! You see, I *wasn't looking* at the background! The magazines also featured articles, although I'm not too sure that anyone *actually* read them? I *will* admit however, that whenever things got really dull around here, in order to quickly perk myself up, I truly enjoy turning to these articles… and *looking at the pictures*! Regardless of any obvious shortcomings, this place felt very cozy to me. It was home!

"Have a seat, Miss Lott, and make yourself comfortable," I said invitingly, not missing the fact that her behavior suggested to me that she could be manic-depressant or perhaps more seriously, a recent escapee from the *funny farm*! In addition to having to put-up with her rude and unpredictable behavior, I was still suffering from a horrendous hangover as well as an intense shock to my fashion sensibility that occurred the *moment* I horrifyingly discovered that I was wearing a very rumpled version of the *same* clothes I'd worn yesterday, complete with my badly scuffed shoes! Although I can't remember much about last night following dinner, the mere fact that I had *slept in my clothes* suggests that it must have been a real drunken bender; the kind that I used to experience every single night that I so much as *thought* about getting a real job!

"Thank you, Mr. Berguhndy. You may call me Liza," she said, *unsurprisingly* changing her mind about that! It also became very apparent to me that she was purposely displaying her *sexiest* voice, and *damn* if it didn't come across quite naturally?

"Okay, *Liza*," I hesitantly agreed, once I got past my confusion. "Your name suits you, so I'm told," I laughed pleasantly.

"Do you mean my *full* name? *Liza Lott*?" she asked curiously.

"Exactly!" I smiled impishly. "I hear you are quite the champ at '*bearing false witness*' in important court cases!"

"Why *thank you*, Detective!" she cooed excitedly. "It's not every day a girl receives such a *wonderful* compliment as that!"

Although I wanted so very badly to yell at her, '*That was not a compliment*,' I wisely decided against it, opting instead to let her think whatever the hell she was thinking inside that warped little brain of hers, while hoping that it was *not too* dangerous! "Did you stop by my apartment to be interviewed about last night's murder of Cannon Manchester?"

"Yes, I did!" she responded spiritedly.

"*Who* told you that I wanted to see you?" I asked her curiously.

"*Who didn't*!" she proclaimed angrily.

"Okay," I said, attempting to calm her down into some semblance of a normal human being. "What did you *see* at the party last night that might have some bearing on Mr. Manchester's murder?"

Well, Liza answered *that* question with gusto! *Several times* in fact, with each rendition of the events being made to sound even more exciting than the last? The confusing part was that although she had to be lying *most* of the time, was it possible that she was actually telling the truth *part* of the time?

"Miss Lott... Liza," I said, very gently. "Your stories *completely conflict* with one another? Do you know *which* of them, *if any*, are even remotely truthful?"

Liza shook her head sadly. "I've been accused of lying before."

"Oh? By whom?" I asked her curiously.

"By our country's first president, *Abraham Lincoln*!" she laughed.

"What?" I shockingly exclaimed. Miss Lott was not *only* a liar, but she was also horrendously bad at *historical facts*! I couldn't help but feel terribly discombobulated! And the nightmare did *not* end there! *Oh no*! Going a step further, Miss Lott had apparently saved her *best* for last! She abruptly began showcasing her *perfect* impersonation of an unbelievably cute six-year-old *Shirley Temple*, as she fanatically pranced around the room singing, '*Animal crackers in my soup*,' and shouting over and over again with an exaggeratedly protruding pout, "*Oh my goodness*!" After that, she immediately evolved into *Groucho Marx*, complete with a cigar she pulled out of her bosom, and told a terrible joke about a janitor jumping out of the closet yelling, '*Supplies*!'

Needless to say, I very politely *ended* her nightmarish performance and immediately brought the curtain down on that batty interview! The truth was, I really *didn't* want to find out what other bizarre personalities Miss Lott was capable of creating. Just thinking about that was just *too damned disturbing*! So, with no shortage of relief, I quickly escorted her out of my apartment, closed the door, and locked it several times (*you can never be too careful*), before finally collapsing on my bed, still fully dressed, to hopefully sleep off this darn hangover!

It was nearly 2:00 o'clock that afternoon when I finally left my hangover in the rearview mirror and felt sober enough to continue my investigation. But first, I took a much-needed shower and changed into my best detective-wear. That consisted of an old but still stylish tweed suit, a pair of newly shined brown wingtip shoes and my lucky brown fedora. After that, I left my apartment. I was soon driving the most *valuable* thing I owned; a shiny black 1941 Packard One-Twenty convertible! I had received it as payment in full for spending two long months of my life cracking a car-theft ring in San Francisco a couple of years back. It was a *beautiful* car that always served as a reminder that even a dope like me could sometimes leave with the girl… or in this case… the *car*! As an aside, I have often been told that I looked *great* driving it!

A mere fifteen minutes later, I arrived at the *Frolic Room*, the most famous bar in Hollywood, which also happened to possess a boatload of class! This bar had handled the afterparty following the Academy Awards ceremony at the neighboring Pantages Theatre last year. *All* of the biggest stars in the industry had attended! In addition to that, I heard that Sinatra and Garland were regulars whenever they were in town! In any case, word on the street had it that this was the habitual hangout for Tommy Gunn. After parking my car as close to the place as possible (*which was a full block away*), I crossed the street and confidently walked through the front door. I immediately smiled at my luck, as I quickly spotted Tommy, sitting alone at the bar on a red stool. He looked depressed as he sat there slowly sipping his ginger-ale. I also couldn't help noticing that he must have been feeling pretty cold, because he was wearing a long gray trench-coat *inside* the bar? Furthermore, the coat did not particularly go well with his highly unusual brown and white penny loafers? I must say, looking at the result was *hideous*! Regardless, I walked right up to the bar and sat down on the empty stool just to the right of him.

"Hello, Mr. Gunn," I said politely.

With a *terrified* expression on his face, he quickly turned to meet my eyes, stammering, "III dddiiidddnnn'''ttt dddooo iiittt!!!" Impressed, I was guessing that his *very percussive* style of speech probably sounded as much like a tommy gun as the *real one* that was barely peeking-out beneath his open trench-coat… *not* that I was in any hurry to find out!

"Take it easy, Tommy," I tried to calm the overtly panicked man. "You are *not* a suspect in Cannon Manchester's murder. I just stopped by to find out what you had possibly seen or heard last night that might help me to solve this case?"

Before Tommy had the chance to offer me his insight, a very pushy bartender wearing a nametag that clearly said, ***Death***, made his way to me. Judging by his appearance, I immediately *imagined* that his terrifyingly ugly face would perfectly mirror the extremely repugnant-looking '*fish-pig*' that I believed could hypothetically be created by the unnatural union between a *blobfish* and a *rabid warthog*! Through his complete lack of civility, I also suspected that he would have made an excellent entertainment director for *Al Capone*! Well, he *insisted* that I buy a drink, and the way that he said it didn't leave *any* room for discussion! I took one look at the matching tattoos on each of his muscular arms, proudly and vividly showcasing a *blood-covered fist*, and I won't lie. I began to *sweat*! This guy's expression (*or lack of one*) immediately told me that he was *not* one to be trifled with, especially by the likes of *me*! So, although I had no plans to drink while I was on the job, I ordered a Scotch on the rocks and donated it right back to him! He thanked me without smiling, and then waited until I coughed up two hard-earned bucks to more than cover the cost. Even though he *never* brought me back my change (*undoubtedly keeping it as a tip*), I didn't say a word. Instead, I exhaled a great big sigh of relief, grateful for the fact that although I'd lost my last couple of bucks, at least my *handsome mug* was still intact!

Meanwhile, Tommy obviously realized that his habit of speaking like a *machine gun* was genuinely difficult, if not *impossible*, for most intelligent human beings, living or dead, to understand. *Except* of course his *mother*, Anita, who was happily living out her golden years in an upscale trailer park in the God-fearing town of *Laurel, Nebraska*, where he had been both born and raised. Although he had *never* been an exceptional student in school, or had many friends, he *had* been *unanimously* selected by his senior high school class as being '*The Most Likely to Get Arrested*!'

In any case, he very thoughtfully wrote down everything he could remember about last night's party onto a stack of two-ply cocktail napkins. Just as soon as he had finished, I thanked him as I gratefully stuffed them deep inside my coat pocket. But then, surprisingly, he spent the next minute seemingly whispering sweet nothings into my ear. But in this case, those sweet nothings turned out to be *sweet somethings*! When he was done, he very curiously acted as if he'd completely forgotten that he had *ever* been talking to me or for that matter, that I even *existed*? Without so much as a nod goodbye, he abruptly turned away and spent every last bit of his focus on reacquainting himself with his ginger-ale?

I looked forward to reading the 'Great American Novel' that Tommy had written down on those cocktail napkins, I *really* did. But right now, I was even more excited about what he had just whispered into my ear! As closely as I could decipher it, he had told me that he was a part-time assassin who worked for New York City mob boss, *Lucky Cuomo*! Interestingly enough, that was the *very same man* who had successfully kicked Cannon Manchester out of New York City and *forced* him to resettle on the West Coast! Hmm? Even *more* importantly, he had told me that there was *another* assassin of Cuomo's at the party, but unfortunately, he was not privy to their identity?

After that, I *knew* that my next destination had to be returning to the scene of the crime. Specifically, to the living room of Cannon Manchester's mansion! It would be *there*, where I would hopefully uncover a clue to the identity of that second assassin. In any case, I planned to interrogate everyone at the mansion whether they liked it or not! That was because, as I had learned very early in my career, there was always the possibility that some important new information could *unintentionally* be revealed by catching people off-guard! My genius really *knows* no bounds!

When I arrived at the Manchester mansion, I was immediately met at the door by the obviously *bowed* butler, Mr. Hertz. Remembering my vow to interrogate him further, I asked him as nonchalantly as possible, "Where *is* everyone?"

First, he looked at me in great surprise, but that expression proved to be fleeting. Very quickly it changed into a severe look of *full-blown suspicion*? Just as I'd hoped, it was abundantly clear that he had *not* been expecting my visit! But he quickly recovered and replied, "Alright. If you *must* know, Miz Turrey is at a Russian tea room, Tommy Gunn is at the comic book store at the corner of Third and Vine, and Liza Lott is in a confessional."

"A *confessional*?" I asked in surprise.

"Oh yes, she simply *loves* it there!" Hertz shared whimsically. "She generally keeps talking until the priest runs out of the booth *screaming*!"

"Okay," I confirmed with a slight smile. "Is there anyone *else* whose whereabouts you might know?"

Mr. Hertz took a very deep breath, and then very awkwardly admitted, "Mr. Nish is on the *toidy*."

"Never mind," I groaned, with less patience than a burned down hospital. "Please take me in to interrogate everyone who *is* here."

"Aside from me, sir?" Mr. Hertz inquired.

"Aside from *you*!" I confirmed.

Mr. Hertz, the consummate professional, nodded and immediately escorted me into the living room. You can imagine my surprise when I first entered the room to see a tall and obese man sitting in a chair with his back turned to me, who looked to be the spitting image of *Cannon Manchester's backside*! But when the man stood-up and turned around to greet me, I was flabbergasted! I was now convinced beyond a doubt that I was looking at the *dead man himself*?

"*You're* Cannon Manchester!" I declared.

"No, I'm not!"

"Yes, you are!"

"Am not!"

"Are to!" I reiterated boldly.

"*I am?*"

"No, you're not!" I somehow said, in confusion.

"Yes, I am!"

"You are not!" I said, even *less* sure of myself.

"Are you very *certain* of that?" the man asked charmingly.

After realizing how cleverly the man had turned me around, I defeatedly uttered, "*No*."

The man laughed, and said, "Don't feel bad. I used to be an *expert arguer*! That was quite fun *rowing* with you, sir! No hard feelings? It was all in good fun, I assure you!" Then he jovially smiled, and announced, "*Bannon* Manchester, Cannon's identical twin brother, at your service!"

"You guys are *Cannon* and *Bannon*?"

"No, sir!" he winked. "We are *Bannon* and Cannon!"

To tell you the truth, I *wasn't* in the mood for any more jokes from him after the *humiliating defeat* his cleverness had just handed me on a platter! I thought that *I* was supposed to be the clever one? As retaliation, on a *worse* day, I could see myself *strangling* him and thoroughly enjoying it! But, I wisely decided that *one murder* was quite enough to worry about for now.

"You must be Mr. Berguhndy, the detective? Welcome!" The man said, thrusting out his right hand.

As I shook his tepid hand, I carefully looked him over, and suddenly realized that I had been completely wrong about his identity! I had embarrassingly made a *rookie mistake* by jumping to conclusions. Based on Cannon's photograph that I had seen in the newspaper, aside from their obviously similar body types, facial features and hair, surprisingly, these two men looked *completely different*? The first of three major differences that I immediately spotted was that unlike Cannon's clean-shaven face, this man sported a dark, thin moustache that was so finely trimmed it actually looked as though it could have been drawn-on with an eyebrow pencil? Secondly, unlike Cannon, this man *wore glasses*. And to top it all off, he looked and *acted* like an *Easter egg*, dressed in a French tailored pink and yellow suit! From everything I had already learned, Cannon would never have been caught *dead* wearing that! (*Pardon my very insensitive choice of words.*) As a matter of fact, I believe that Cannon would have likely viewed his brother's outfit as being a hideously gawky and unsophisticated ensemble worn only by a *dandy*! And I had to agree with that assessment! All of that aside, Bannon offered me a seat on his black and white settee, I politely sat down and he immediately joined me.

"Well, Mr. Berguhndy, what can I do for you?" Bannon smiled.

"As you probably know, I am investigating the untimely demise of your brother, Cannon. In that regard, I would like to... *look around* if you don't mind?" I said, using my most *official* detective-sounding voice, which fluctuated between the charm of Cary Grant and the manliness of John Wayne!

It was then that I spied Ace Lutt, who was wearing... *nothing*! Well, nothing but a sheer and skimpy bathrobe that was being held together by a transparent sash made of... *more* nothing! (*Or something that looked darn close to that.*) Her attire might have fit well in the story, 'The Emperor's New Clothes,' except for the fact that she would have definitely looked *underdressed*!

"Excuse me for barging in like this, straight from the bath, but I just heard a *sexy man's voice*, and I wanted to see whom it belonged to?" she whispered coyly. "Oh! I believe it was *yours*, Mr. Berguhndy!"

I admit that I was momentarily speechless as she *very slowly* removed the towel from around her *head*, and dropped her long blond hair down just past her waist, highlighting her obvious assets. I quickly pulled myself together and said, "Why thank you, Miss Lutt. Are you staying here at the house?"

That very *pointed* question would have *rattled* the best of them, but Ace didn't miss a beat. "No, I came by to help Bannon sort through some of Cannon's things. After all, I am *much more familiar* with them than he is."

"Well actually, I'm glad that you're here, Miss Lutt," I smiled. "You can answer a few questions for me, if you don't mind?"

"I don't mind at all!" she happily professed with a broad smile. "I'm always more than happy to help you '*guardians of goodness*' to find the truth!" she winked.

"Terrific!" I exclaimed, feeling myself beginning to grow *mesmerized* by her charm? "To begin with, where *exactly* do you remember standing last night when the shot was fired?"

Again, Ace was smoother than my chin at age ten. "I was standing right over here, talking to Mr. Manchester," she offered, moving to the far-left side of the room.

"Do you own a gun, Miss Lutt?" I asked her none too discretely.

"I do," she admitted calmly. "A brand-new Ruger .22 caliber semi-automatic pistol. They just came out last year, you know. I have *already* been known to have used it from time to time."

"Oh yeah? For what purpose?" I inquired intently.

"*Self-defense*, of course," she explained very matter-of-factly. "With all of the boys who are always *lusting* after my body, I must admit that there have been more than a few times when this '*baby*' has come in real handy, in a completely *legal* sense, of course."

"*Of course*," I agreed hesitantly. "Did you *shoot* your gun at the party last night?"

"As a matter of fact, I *did*," she confessed.

"When?" I pressed.

"When I was leaving, and one of those little boys from the party followed me outside and refused to take '*no*' for an answer," she calmly explained.

"But I believe that *I* was the last one to leave the mansion last night, and I *never* heard a gunshot?" I said in confusion.

Miss Lutt laughed. "That's because I used my *silencer* to avoid waking anybody up, *silly*! I *did* hit a nearby tree, though? I'd be happy to show you where the bullet's lodged, if you like?"

"Who was this *guy*?" I asked, ignoring the 'bullet' for the moment.

"Trust me. That's really *not* important," she smiled at me bewitchingly. "And anyway, I would rather *not* embarrass him," she admitted charitably. "After all, there was *no harm* done."

I nodded, and then said, "So, you *didn't* shoot that painting last night? Right?"

"*Of course not*!" Ace exclaimed in shock. "Check the painting if you don't believe me!" she insisted. "*Whoever* fired that shot had to be standing directly in front of the painting in order to place the bullet *cleanly* through the center of it, *not at an angle*, which is where *my* shot would have certainly entered the picture had I been the shooter!" Exhaling and growing calmer, she gently stroked my left cheek and adoringly looked into my eyes. Then she added with a meaningful smile, "As I said, I checked it out myself last night just before having that *delightful conversation* with you!"

I was floored! This lady really *knew* her stuff! "Alright, Miss Lutt," I said appreciatively. "Thank you for your help."

"The pleasure is *all* mine," she smiled with deep sincerity.

She immediately returned to her bath, while Bannon Manchester gladly obliged me by scampering from the room to stare at himself (*using multiple poses*) in the life-sized mirror (*with excellent lighting*) hanging temptingly in the hallway. Fortuitously, this allowed me to freely look around at anything in the house I wanted to, *unfettered*… and I did! I immediately left the sitting room and walked straight into the dining room. I walked over to the painting in question and studied it! It was Picasso's masterpiece of the very eccentric, and not particularly sexy, Gertrude Stein, the early 20th century writer. Next, I studied the bullet hole in the middle of it. I was impressed to find that just as Miss Lutt had suggested, the shooter would have to have been standing *directly in front of it* to have made such a perfect shot! But *why* was it done? And what did it *mean*? Was this person actually *trying* to shoot Cannon Manchester and somehow missed their aim? Or was this bullet hole in the painting just a *red herring*? I must have spent the next ten or fifteen minutes closely studying and restudying that painting on the wall with the hole in the middle of it, before suddenly realizing that aside from the bullet hole itself, this picture and room were surprisingly *useless* to me? To study it any further made about as much sense as *serving bacon at a Bar Mitzvah*!

At that point, there was only one course of action open to me that made any sense. *Leave the house pronto*! So, I did! Once outside, I remembered to check for the tree with a bullet lodged in it that Ace Lutt had *allegedly* put there last night. It didn't take me long to find it. The bullet had been shot into a mature oak tree less than ten feet beyond the front door. Just to be thorough, I decided to stop by the police station on my way home and ask them to check it for *size*. I had to confirm that it lined-up with the .22 that Miss Lutt had *claimed* to have shot it from. Then it was back to my Packard and off.

After briefly visiting with the police, I arrived at my apartment, and immediately felt *unsettled* at the shocking sight of my front door being *slightly ajar*? Once I succeeded in very slowly and discreetly pushing the door fully open, I was relieved to find the maid cleaning my room, as she was hired to do once a week. This was not the first time I had mistaken her normally scheduled visit for a criminal break-in. At least *this* time I hadn't *tackled her*!

Just as soon as the maid had left, I sat down at my table and began to read Mr. Gunn's cocktail napkins. Five minutes later, I was done. From what I could gather, just as he had shared with me at the bar, he and an *unknown* accomplice had been hired by Lucky Cuomo to kill Cannon Manchester on the night of the party. However, he swore on a stack of coasters that he had absolutely *nothing* to do with his death? He went on to say that Cuomo had already paid him a thousand dollars just to *be* at the party. But, why in the world was Tommy Gunn *invited* in the first place? Van Nish had bragged that he had helped with the guest list. Could there possibly be a *connection* between the two of them? I quickly called Mr. Nish and fortunately he answered right away. When I told him where I lived, he promised to meet me here in fifteen minutes. *Exactly* fifteen minutes later, there was a crisp knock at my door. I quickly opened it, and ushered the *very prompt* Mr. Nish into a chair at my mismatched two-seat table.

"Thanks for coming over on such short notice," I said cordially. "I was just wondering how certain people had made the guest list to Mr. Manchester's party?"

"Oh? Who are you speaking of *in particular*?" Nish asked politely.

"Tommy Gunn, for starters," I replied seriously.

Van Nish hemmed and hawed a bit before finally divulging his answer. "I didn't do nuthin' illegal!" he pleaded. "But some folks offered me money to put them on that list. Tommy Gunn and his girlfriend Liza Lott were two of them."

"There were *others*?" I asked in surprise.

"Yes," he replied awkwardly. "Mr. Manchester didn't really know anyone on this side of the country, so after inviting Mylo Girth, who he *knew* was one of the richest men in Hollywood, he asked me to fill-in the rest of the seats with *movers and shakers*," he admitted. "But he *didn't* specify the *method* I should use for selecting them? So, I held a 'Secret Auction' with two of the party invites going to the highest bidder. Chet Freshcorn and his date Cee Cee Cretz were the winners!"

"If the auction was secret, then how did anyone find out about it?" I asked curiously.

"Simple. I advertised it in the L.A. Times the week before," he replied.

"If you advertised it, then it *wasn't* really secret… was it?" I chuckled.

"No, you misunderstand," Mr. Nish laughed. "'*Secret*' is my professional name!" he declared proudly. "It sounds so *mysterious*, don't you think? I was just giving the heads-up to everyone that I was the one *hosting* the auction!"

"Does anyone actually *know* that your 'professional name' is *Secret*?" I asked in disbelief.

"Well, no," Mr. Nish admitted obliviously. "That was the *first* time I had ever used it. But I expect it will *catch-on* from here on out!"

His glaring lack of logic *defied* understanding? I couldn't help it. I *rolled* my eyes! "And *you* brought Ace Lutt to the party, but what was the *relationship* between Manchester and Mylo Girth?" I questioned.

"There really *wasn't* one," Mr. Nish confessed. "But Girth was rich, so Mr. Manchester wanted to talk with him about investing in his new company."

"*What* new company?" I asked him in surprise.

"Beats me?"

"*Beats Me*? Hmm? That is a very unusual name for a company?" I shared honestly.

"What? *No*! And you call yourself a *detective*?" Van scoffed while irritably throwing his hands into the air. Then surprisingly smiling, he offered, "I'm not certain of this, but his company *might* actually be called, *Cannon's Dot Com*."

"Okay, I'll bite. What was this company supposed to do?" I asked hesitantly.

"Well, since dots *are* the newest rage in decorating, I would venture that it was Cannon's company for creating all sizes of beautiful and decorative dots made from whatever materials the customer wanted, including gold or silver, 14 carat diamond clusters, horseshoes, goat hair, poison ivy or even your *old sneakers*! The sky's the limit!" Van shared excitedly.

"Wow! Really?" I responded in delight.

Van laughed very impishly, "*Of course not*! How ridiculous! I'm afraid I lied and *you* fell for it, *Mr. Detective Man*!"

Ignoring his rude comment, I moved on and asked, "What was *your* role in Mr. Manchester's activities?"

"I suppose I was his '*go-to man*' to help him get things done," Nish explained more calmly.

"Like the party?" I suggested.

"Exactly!" he confirmed.

"Did he pay you when you helped him out like that?" I asked.

"Not usually," Van began. "Well, actually *never*! But he *did* let me hang around his mansion sometimes. That was pay enough for me!"

"Is that where you met Ace Lutt?" I pressed.

"Yes," he replied. "I met her at the mansion a week ago in the pool room."

"Oh. You both play pool?" I speculated.

Van laughed derisively. "Are you for real? *No*, genius! We were playing in the *indoor swimming pool*!"

Feeling *very* disrespected now, I took a deep breath and exhaled before calmly suggesting, "Well wouldn't you logically call that the '*indoor swimming pool*,' instead of the '*pool room*?'"

"*I wouldn't*!" he very bluntly replied. "But it appears that squares like you *would*!" Mr. Nish laughed heartily once again at *my* expense.

I tried very hard to maintain a professional demeanor, but I was growing quite testy at being constantly ridiculed by Mr. Nish with *complete disregard* for even a semblance of manners? Finally, I asked, "Was there *anything* more?" I had honestly *reached my limit*! Although it probably was not the most professional thing to do, I had decided that anymore tomfoolery from *him* would result in my serving him a *big, fat, knuckle sandwich*!

"Well, I hate to admit it," he began hesitantly, "but Ace actually *shot* a gun at me while I was visiting her at the mansion a week ago, and she *barely* missed!" he shared animatedly. "But then a few days later, I think she realized her mistake when she agreed to go to the party with me."

I didn't immediately respond. Van had *finally* delivered an honest and respectful response? He must have grown tired of behaving like a *weisenheimer smart ass*, although the day was still young! Looking past his immature behavior, Van was one of those fortunate or unfortunate souls, depending on how you looked at him, who spent their entire life *basking* in the successes of other people, and happily allowing himself to be *used* by them. At Miss Lutt's interview last night when she had cruelly sized him up, it was not surprising at all to hear her tell him, "*Don't take this wrong, lover, but if you were a firecracker, you'd be a very disappointing dud*!" On the other hand, it must have been a great deal of fun for Van to hang-out at Cannon Manchester's mansion? He certainly appeared to *love* it there? As far as I was concerned, the genuinely happy feelings that he shared about it were proof positive that no matter how *irritating*, *low down, mouthy*, *immature*, *dimwitted*, *dishonest*, *worm-like*, or *completely worthless* a person was, creating an exciting diversion for their sad and empty existence sure beat thinking about what a loser they were *any* day of the week! I have occasionally subscribed to that *very same philosophy* myself!

Just as soon as Mr. Nish had made his departure, I began processing this new information, trying like crazy to make sense of it? But somehow I kept feeling as though I was carrying the football in a big game, just moments away from making the winning touchdown, when suddenly I found myself being *blocked* at the goal line by that huge and *butt-ugly* bartender named *Death*!

Suddenly, there came *another* knock at my door? I obviously had not been expecting anyone, so I cautiously approached the door and erring on the side of caution, shouted loudly in the voice of an uncouth ruffian, "*Who is it*?" Although I didn't own a gun, I certainly hoped that my loud and menacing voice would make whoever it was, *fear* that I did!

"It's me, Eve Engood," was the sweet and innocent response. "May I come in, please?"

I won't lie. I was surprised? I was *very surprised*? Just as soon as I'd unlocked my multiple locks and opened the door, Miss Engood immediately rushed inside the room, dressed in a tight, red dress, passionately threw her arms around me and planted a '*so good to see you*' kiss right here on my unsuspecting lips? As soon as I was able to untangle myself from her, I pointedly asked, "What was *that* for?"

"I told you that the last one was just a *down payment*," she smiled flirtatiously. "Remember?" Then she came on to me really strong when she brazenly announced, "I *like* you, Biff. You don't mind if I call you by your first name, do ya? Now that we're… *friends*?"

I didn't know exactly *what* her little game was, but due to her immense beauty and charm (*which were unfortunately already affecting me*), I'll bet sailors had a far easier time maneuvering their ships past those *deadly sirens*! "I prefer keeping things professional, if you don't mind," I replied calmly, knowing all the time that I was *lying*! "I've got to stay objective while I investigate this case. I'm sure you understand."

"Of course, I do," she smiled genuinely, while simultaneously pulling me down closely, I mean *very closely* beside her at the edge of my bed.

"Why specifically have you come to see me?" I asked, at once feeling lightheaded and nervous. I was suspicious? If there was one thing I *couldn't* stand, it was when a beautiful woman tried to seduce me with *no* apparent motive, because like every guy with half a brain knows from experience… *there is always a motive*!

"Okay," she confessed with honesty filling her great big eyes. "I really *need* your help! But… well… I'm actually a little nervous about telling you *why*?"

"You are?" I replied, suddenly feeling less nervous and more in the middle of my comfort zone. "How about a nice big glass of Scotch to help settle those nerves?" I asked with a debonair touch. She quickly nodded, and I got up to pour *two* glasses of the stuff because whenever someone in the room asks for a drink, it's never polite to make them *drink alone*!

When I returned, she was alluringly lying across my bed, looking more glamorous than Veronica Lake, Ingrid Bergman and *Jessica Rabbit* combined! She sat up to take the glass from me, and the two of us toasted life's sweet little surprises, which to my mind, certainly included *this visit*! "So, can you talk to me *now*?" I asked her gently.

"Yes, and thank you so much for the drink, Mr. Berguhndy. I think it is exactly what I needed," she admitted gratefully.

I smiled and thought, 'Here's to the relaxing power of *booze*!'

"My trouble really began just after our interview on the night of the murder," Miss Engood began to explain, and then she abruptly *stopped* herself for some reason?

"Is everything all right?" I asked her with concern.

"Oh yes," she shared hesitantly. "It's just that… well… I'm very sorry, Mr. Berguhndy, but could I trouble you to top-off my glass? I think I might need a wee bit more of this stuff to continue?"

"Already?" I chuckled in surprise and amusement. But then noticing that her glass was only a quarter full, I nodded understandingly. Next, I gently handed her my glass to hold for safe-keeping. I then walked over to the table, grabbed the bottle of Scotch and returned to the bed to more completely *fill* both of our glasses. After accomplishing that very simple task (*I was a pro at anything involving alcohol*), I put the bottle back on the table and then returned to the bed. I took my glass from Miss Engood, and once again *excitedly* sat down beside her. But this time, I was *not* feeling a bit nervous! "Please *continue* your story," I urged her with a confident smile.

"Okay," she agreed, looking very relaxed. "As I was saying, after our interview, I walked up to my bedroom and while preparing for bed, I very surprisingly found an envelope with a note on my writing table?"

"Wait! You *didn't* share a room with Cannon?" I asked her in dismay.

"Heavens no!" she exclaimed in horror. "How would that have looked to *other people*? I was brought up in a good Christian home. My first name is actually *not Eve* at all, but *Naïve*!"

"*Naïve Engood*?" I asked with a smirk.

"Yes," she admitted solemnly. "It is both a curse and a blessing for me to spend every waking moment of my life *trying* to live-up to that name!"

"About the *note*?" I gently reminded her.

"Oh yes!" she continued animatedly. "When I took the note out of the envelope, there was only *one* sentence? It said, '**Go away and never return, or *you will die*!**'"

"Wow! May I see that note, please?"

"Of course," she replied, pulling it from a small, strikingly *gorgeous* blue sequined purse which she had brought with her.

"That is one *beautiful* purse," I felt compelled to tell her.

"Why, thank you!" she replied appreciatively, with a stunning smile. "It was actually made using the same materials they use for mood rings."

"What in the world is a *mood ring*?" I asked her curiously.

"Well, at the moment it's just an *idea* that a couple of my friends have been toying with."

"What *kind* of idea?" I asked.

"It's actually quite fabulous!" she exclaimed. "They want to produce rings where the color of the stone in them or in my case, the *sequins* of the purse, actually *change color* depending upon the different *moods* of the person touching it," she explained. "They have discovered the meanings behind a whole slew of different colors! Unfortunately, they haven't found a backer to mass produce it yet. But a famous fortune teller told them that their idea will *absolutely* catch on by the year 1975!"

"Wow!" I exclaimed, most impressed. "Since you're holding the purse, what does the color *blue* indicate?"

"It indicates that I am very *calm* right now," she replied, rather sedately.

"Do you mind if I hold it for a moment too?" I asked, completely mesmerized by the magical qualities of her purse. "Let's see what it says about *me*?"

"Of course," she smiled, gently handing it to me. "That will be fun!"

Fifteen seconds later, as I firmly held the purse, it *miraculously* changed color once again. This time to a vibrant violet.

"What does the color, *violet* mean?" I asked excitedly.

"It means that you are *passionately in love*, and can barely contain yourself!" she shared with a laugh. "Should I be *concerned*?"

It was then, feeling hopelessly riddled with embarrassment (*like a proud piece of swiss cheese that humiliatingly smells like limburger*), that I seriously regretted the childish sense of wonder that had completely consumed me when I had first asked to take hold of that *accursed purse*! Unfortunately, it had allowed my romantic feelings for Eve to be unveiled, and myself *exposed*! Damn violet! It wasn't even a masculine color! I quickly changed the subject by hurriedly returning Eve's purse to her and accepting the note that she had been long holding out to share with me. I carefully examined it, and seeing as it had been *typed*, disappointedly realized that studying its 'handwriting,' as I had planned, was *now* completely out of the question. Looking at the paper a bit more closely however, the note *did* carry one distinct peculiarity. It had been typed using what I assumed to be Cannon Manchester's *personal bond*. This was evidenced by the fancy CM in the shape of a cannonball being shot from a traditional 19th century black cannon at the upper right corner of the page! I had to stop for a moment to *admire* the creativity which was evident in the design of such a fine logo! "Did you notice that this note had quite possibly been typed using Cannon Manchester's personal bond?" I asked excitedly.

"Yes," Miss Engood looked and sounded irritated. "That's *his* logo alright! But since it's a cannon, and I just abhor violence... I've decided *not* to like it!"

I didn't tell her this, but based on her negative reaction, I quickly realized that in general, images of shooting cannons were probably much more of a guy thing. Being a woman, she was probably much more into images of beautiful things. But that was way too easy. All she had to do was *look at herself in the mirror*! I politely returned the note to her and made sure to appreciate the tremendous excitement I felt as our fingers momentarily *touched* during the very brief exchange. And then suddenly without warning, I felt as if the room were *spinning* around me? It was that '*I'm about to faint*' feeling one gets after drinking one too many. But I knew that I was *nowhere near* my limit? *Give me a break*! I quickly turned to see how Miss Engood was doing and *shockingly* discovered that she had already passed-out ahead of me! But even in that unfortunate state, she still looked radiant, *seductively* lying across the bed like a *fallen angel*! I tried to get to the phone to call for help in case we had been *poisoned*? But it was *too late*! Moments later, I too slumped helplessly on the bed, completely *out* to the world!

When I awoke, it was *dark* in the room except for the dull light escaping the bathroom from a single overhead bulb that was dangling on a lone wire from the ceiling. I always kept that bulb on, in order to ward off *monsters*! I have been devotedly following this little ritual ever since I was a kid. That was of course, when I first discovered that it actually *worked*! It was obviously nighttime and I was feeling a little disoriented. Could you tell? As I gained more clarity, I noticed that the cheap electric clock on my dresser read 11:13 p.m. and *shockingly*, I also realized that I was lying in my bed under the covers, dressed only in my *skivvies*! I was even more distressed to discover that Naïve Engood was lying there beside me dressed only in *her* skivvies! I thought long and hard about what recent events might have rationally led up to this inconceivable situation? But I disappointingly drew a blank? About that time, Miss Engood opened her eyes.

"*Oh my God*! How did this happen?" she gasped, as she glared at me, completely horrified.

"It's not as it appears!" I insisted weakly.

"Honey, it's *exactly* as it appears! We are in *bed together*!" she exclaimed frantically. "If this news ever gets out, my modeling career as a '*squeaky-clean bombshell*' is over! Mr. Berguhndy! How *could* you?"

Feeling mortified at the prospect of being completely at fault for ruining Eve's stellar career, I quickly jumped out of bed, turned on the light and got back into my pants, which I found neatly folded on the floor beside me. I followed this by attempting to sing the first verse of '*Some Enchanted Evening*,' from the popular musical, '*South Pacific*.' I focused all of my attention on Eve, got most of the words right, and used my sometimes-passable baritone voice to hopefully '*enchant*' her toward a friendlier mindset, while simultaneously *subliminally* encouraging her to completely forget about this horrible nightmare! It *wasn't* logical thinking, I know, but I had seen it work well in movies a number of times! And frankly? I was *desperate, damnit*! Unfortunately, judging by her still highly irritated expression... It *wasn't working*! But before I had time to think-up another dumb idea, I found an envelope with a *note* lying at my feet on the floor? After removing the note from the envelope, I immediately noticed that this one was *also typed* on Cannon Manchester's personal bond? I picked it up and perused it quickly. Just like the previous note, this one got right to the point. I decided to read it aloud so that Miss Engood would realize that this situation was *definitely not* my fault!

"Miss Engood? I've found another note. Listen to this! '***I took pictures that will RUIN you both. Walk away from this case... or else!***' Whoever it was that typed this note, they must have *drugged* the scotch too," I loudly deduced, hoping with all my heart that she too would *deduce it*. "That's why we find ourselves in this *most embarrassing* predicament!"

I paused to let her reply, but still not getting a response, I quickly grew *frantic*! Dramatically turning my body toward hers and falling to my knees with my hands clasped together in front of me (*as in prayer*), I pleaded in desperation, "I swear that I'm *innocent* of all wrongdoing here! You've just got to *believe me*!"

But Miss Engood was having *none* of it? She didn't seem the least bit inclined to dedicate even one more iota of her attention toward my heartfelt disclaimer? In fact, she now appeared to be taking our delicate situation here *in stride*? To be honest... this change of heart took me *completely* by surprise? Perhaps she was thinking about the note I had just read to her? Or *maybe* she was realizing just how much she was head over heels in love with me? In any case, she remained deep in thought for a full minute before finally unveiling the fruits of her meditation.

"My mother would say that this person's '*bark is bigger than their bite*!'" she said crytically with a twinkle in her eyes.

"Would she?" I replied in great relief, as I unclasped my hands and stood up. I was instantly immersed in a delightful sense of euphoria! Yet I was also very curious about what *exactly* had caused this sudden civility? But I didn't make a big deal out of it, because just as my mother had drilled-in to me every time my alcoholic father was sober, '*Never question miracles*!' "Do you have any idea who may have sent this?" I asked her intently.

"I'm thinking that the *same* person sent both messages from Cannon's mansion, since *both* are typed on his personal bond!" she confidently explained.

"Great thinking!" I concurred encouragingly.

"So, I suggest that we look very carefully through every room in that mansion!" she declared. "There is probably something *very incriminating* hidden away there, wouldn't you agree?"

"Yes, I *would*!" I agreed loudly, very impressed by her stellar powers of deduction. Every good P.I. should possess that valuable skill if they hope to survive in this competitive 'dog eat dog' business! That is, unless their *partner* has it!

"I think we should sneak in there *tonight* while everyone is sleeping," she suggested strongly. "What do you think?"

"I'm with *you*!" I declared. "Why don't we get dressed and go there together?"

"Sounds like a plan!" she agreed. "But first, would you please get my purse for me, darling? It's right there beside you." she said mysteriously.

"Sure," I replied, very cautiously picking-up her purse by its zipper so as to avoid being embarrassed a *second* time by the unexpected color-changes of that *demonic handbag*! It sat beside a neatly folded pile of *her* clothes, right next to where my clothes had been. "Do you need your purse for any particular reason?" I asked, as I carefully dropped it into her awaiting hands.

"Yes!" she proclaimed eagerly, as she immediately pulled out an ordinary looking folded piece of paper and handed it to me. "When you open that up, you will find that it is the *floorplan* to the Manchester mansion. This should make our job much easier!"

"Wow! Where did you ever find *this*?" I asked in surprise, as I quickly unfolded it.

"I suppose I thought I *might* be needing it," she confessed slowly, "so I *accidentally* removed it from Cannon's desk."

"Have you suspected that there was something *criminal* going on there for a while then?" I asked animatedly.

"Oh yes! Ever since the night Cannon was *murdered*!" she admitted sadly.

"But that was only *last night*?" I said in surprise.

"I know!" she shared emotionally. "But it affected me so much, I shall *never* forget it!"

"Is that why it is so important for you to see this murder solved?" I gently asked.

Eve teared up a bit as she smiled at me. "*Yes*! Whoever did this terrible crime must *answer* for it!"

"Don't worry, Eve!" I proclaimed. "I *won't quit* until those responsible for this heinous murder are behind bars! I *promise*!"

Eve smiled a little broader, and then softly wiping her tears, she replied, "I know, Mr. Berguhndy! At first, I was so worried about my chances of *ever* solving this case. But now that I have *you* helping me, we're sure to *solve* it together in no time!"

For some reason, that simple and sincere compliment made me feel so happy that I could have kissed her! Well, to be honest, even if I had felt extremely sad or morose I *still* would have kissed her! In fact, even if she had contracted a terrible case of the *black plague*, where just *touching* her lips would have meant *certain death* for me of the most hideous variety, or if she had a *glaring pimple* at the tip of her perfect nose… not even *then* would I have been deterred from smooching those delicious ruby red lips! "Thanks!" I exclaimed, like a doting schoolboy experiencing his first crush. "I'll study this floorplan after we're finished getting dressed."

Miss Engood smiled warmly, and didn't even ask me to turn around as she gloriously burst out of bed like the *beautiful angel* of my dreams (*who just happened to be dressed in her underwear*)! She immediately began to dress, right there beside me? But being a gentleman of good breeding (*when I wanted to be*), I didn't *gawk* at her loveliness… I quickly turned away, and focused entirely (*well, mostly*) on getting myself dressed.

After a couple of minutes had passed, I felt two warm lips very tenderly caressing the back of my neck. I must admit… it felt *better* than when my old pug, Charlie, used to do it! When I finally turned around, I saw a priceless expression on her face, like the cat who had swallowed the canary and wanted *more*! I think her playfulness was one of the things I loved most about her. Did I just say *love*? We left the apartment, got into my Packard, and before long we found ourselves fast approaching Cannon Manchester's mansion! Oh, and there is something extremely important that I neglected to mention. When I handed Eve her purse and she touched it that last time, just as it had done for me… it turned *intensely violet*!

Once we arrived at the mansion, the plan was to split-up and find whatever we could find. Eve would take the top floor with all of the bedrooms full of sleeping people, while due to my *extensive* experience as an investigator, I of course would take the *bottom* floor. Actually, she had just *assigned* me the bottom floor without a word of explanation? But I am pretty sure that when she did, she was thinking *exactly* what I just said! Anyway, Miss Engood entered the house through the front door, since she still had the key that Cannon had given her. Bannon had agreed to let her stay until she found another place to live, so nothing would seem odd or out of place to anyone who chanced to see her entering the house so late. Once inside, she quietly opened the backdoor for me to sneak inside. I must admit, '*breaking and entering*' with Miss Engood felt great! In fact, I believe that just about *anything* with her would have felt great! Even mundane things such as… Wait a minute? *Nothing* could ever feel mundane with her!

I really had no idea what I was looking for, but whatever it was, it was going to blow this case *wide open*! That is… if I ever *found it*? It was nearly midnight and thankfully, just as I had hoped, there were no signs of anyone from the household being awake or downstairs. Still, just to be safe, I walked on tiptoes (*or 'on point' for all of the classical dance enthusiasts*), like a Julliard trained ballerina who had just been cast as the lead character in a Broadway play titled, *Cat Burglar*! Slowly and methodically, I began to check every room on the bottom floor for clues. I quickly found myself silently opening and closing doors and drawers, while looking for *anything* out of the ordinary? At first, the oddest thing I found was a 5x7 photograph of Cannon Manchester? There was absolutely *no doubt* in my mind that the picture was of him, but strangely, it had been juvenilely marked on with a dark felt pen, adding both a razor thin moustache and glasses. It was clear to me that this highly immature attempt at defacing the picture of Cannon was undoubtedly *Bannon's work*! I quickly ascertained that this pointless activity must have resulted either from his simply having a very *dull* day, or if we're talking sibling rivalry here, from the powerfully intense feeling of inferiority growing into *hatred* that Bannon undoubtedly harbored toward his much more successful twin! Although no one had told me, I imagined that Bannon was probably a world-class loafer, who always sponged off his living relatives… or in this case… his *dead* one!

I had nearly checked every door and drawer in every room on the bottom floor, when exhilaration suddenly consumed every part of my being! I finally discovered what it was I had been searching for! I came across a *locked door*? This find was highly unusual because unless certain people who lived here were kleptomaniacs or sleepwalkers, there didn't appear to be *any* rational explanation I could think of for this door to be locked? Another thing that struck me as odd was that unlike all of the other doors, the floorplan I was looking at *didn't show* what was behind this locked one? I wondered why? I immediately pulled a 'tool of the trade' from my pocket. I always carried this lock-picking marvel with me for opening just such a locked door. Very quietly I got to work. A few moments later, the lock clicked *unlocked* as I excitedly prepared to open the door! I slowly turned the knob and pulled. But to my horror, the hinges on the door *squeaked*, causing me to immediately stop what I was doing, and *panic*! Would it really have hurt them to put a little oil (*or WD-40 if it had been invented yet*) on those hinges once in a while? Fortunately, I was able to control my alarm by staying perfectly still for the next five minutes. I achieved this by focusing my mind *entirely* on the heavenly image of *Eve Engood*, dressed in a sexy red swimsuit, smiling at me with her great big *angelic eyes* as we both stood at the church altar about to be *married*! When I had finally become satisfied that there had been absolutely *no* sound of movement from anywhere in the house, I *begrudgingly* left my blushing bride at the altar and finished opening the door. What I saw next, *shocked the hell* out of me!

There were stairs, forbiddingly descending into darkness which *could* ultimately lead… to a *basement*? But, as you know, according to the floorplan of the house *no basement* was mentioned? Hmm? I immediately began to tread very carefully down the dark stairway, clutching the accompanying handrail very firmly, not daring to turn on a flashlight (*even if I had remembered to bring one*). Although it was pitch black down there, I could almost make out the shape of something extremely large at the bottom? Whatever it was, the locked door promised that it *had to be* very valuable? Perhaps it was a prototype of Ford's upcoming new car of the future, the *Edsel*, that one of my friends had told me about? But based on what he had said, the Edsel wouldn't be unveiled until 1957 or 58? Hmm? Maybe it was a *mechanical bull*! You know, the kind that you ride at county fairs? It actually sounded quite intriguing! Did I *actually* think that? I must have been feeling pretty brave because up until tonight, *coward* that I am, I had *never* had the guts to even *consider* riding one? Wait a second! I had it! Perhaps it was an impressive collection of brand-new *television sets*, all stacked together in the middle of the room? My God! A stash like that would be worth *thousands*? I have heard about how truly *magical* it felt to own and watch a television set every day, but personally, I have only enjoyed the occasional glance at one in a random store window, and *never* long enough to make any sense out of any of the shows I was watching? That's because I have *never* been rich enough to afford a television set of my own. Hey? Maybe I could *take* one of those for myself? They'd never miss *just one*? It wouldn't be like stealing, *exactly*, if no one knew about it? Right? As I completed my larceny-laced thoughts, I finally reached the bottom of the stairs and was *relieved* to find a solid concrete floor beneath my feet. Did I mention that I sometimes suffered from vertigo? Well, climbing down those stairs in the dark tonight was definitely *one of those sometimes*! And although no one could hear it, my vertigo was *always* accompanied by incessant mind-babbling (*also known as 'intellectual blabber'*) in order to distract me from my fear. I was just beginning to lose my dizziness, and was all set to begin exploring the room, when out of the darkness I suddenly felt the *crack* of a blunt object striking my head from behind! The impact initially hurt like hell, but very quickly I forgot all about that as it caused me to crumble and fall into what smelled like a fragrant pool of '*cabernet*,' where I soon lost all consciousness.

When I came-to, sometime later, aside from the sizeable headache I had acquired from being conked on the noggin (*the knot on the back of my head would clearly attest to that*), I found that I was very damp, and that dampness really *did* smell like expensive cabernet? I had thought I'd dreamt that aroma due to the fact that I was a 'hardcore, card-carrying alcoholic?' But by Jiminy, if my being soaked in cabernet didn't turn out to be *true*? It wasn't long before I also realized that I was snuggly tied-up in the darkness of that basement *next* to another person, or judging by their extremely large size, perhaps a *grizzly bear*? I assumed that the mysterious creature next to me was *also* tied-up since it sat on the floor, still as death. And unfortunately, *that* was yet another strong possibility! It was dark, and even though I couldn't see my neighbor, I considered talking to them. But alas, even if for some strange reason they *were* still alive, talking wouldn't work because as I quickly discovered, I had also been *gagged*! Feeling pretty tired of helplessly sitting there, I decided it was time for me to *escape*! So, I focused my inner-strength until I felt as powerful as *Superman*! Next, I confidently tried to wriggle out of the ropes as I had often been able to do in the past… but disappointingly, today my Superman must have accidentally put on *kryptonite underwear*, making all of my efforts to escape prove hopelessly futile! My abductor must have obviously been a sailor at some point in their life as evidenced by their skill at tying these impossible knots, and probably a Boy Scout before that! I felt completely helpless! No brilliant plans crossed the threshold of my mind like they do in the movies. Dejectedly, I escaped the unhappiness of my situation by dozing-off.

When I finally woke-up, what must have been hours later, at first I was surprised to see the blurry image of a very large and muscular person holding a flashlight over me? But then I excitedly felt them quickly removing my gag as well as untying my hands and legs. Suddenly, a powerful light appeared from the ceiling, completely *flooding* the room with brightness! It took a few seconds, but I soon found myself face to face with someone flashing their FBI badge at me? It was *Chet Freshcorn*? My second surprise was that on the floor beside me sat a very disheveled and tired looking *Cannon Manchester*? I looked around the room and immediately realized that it was intended to be a *wine cellar*, and judging by the aroma… one that stocked expensive bottles of *cabernet*! Suddenly, I was shocked to see, right there in the center of the room, a very large printing press? And based on the papers that had already passed through it… one that *printed money*!

"Hello, Mr. Berguhndy," Freshcorn smiled in a friendly sort of way. "You and Mr. Manchester here, were being held captive by a very bad man. Both of you might have eventually been killed, except for the fast thinking of Eve Engood. She called me fifteen minutes ago, just as soon as she discovered that you had gone missing."

"How did you ever find me?" I asked incredulously.

Freshcorn chuckled. "It was simple. I had attached a small 'tracking device' to your shoe!"

I was impressed! "When did you do that?" Chet Freshorn was intensely talking to someone on his walkie talkie, and apparently *didn't* hear my question. So, I turned to Mr. Manchester and asked, "Do *you* know who imprisoned us?"

I heard Cannon painfully clearing his throat beside me. "Yes, I do! It was my no-good brother *Bannon*," he explained hoarsely. "That *damn dandy*!"

With that, I fainted once again to the enchanting aroma of cabernet. Minutes later… the ambulance arrived.

The next time I awoke, I found myself lying in an uncomfortable hospital bed with my head bandaged. But aside from that… I *think* I was okay. I was dressed in a standard issue white hospital gown, while my clothes rested neatly on a nearby table; washed, pressed and ready for a fresh wearing. I understood that my clothes had probably been filthy, but I already missed that *mildly sweet scent* of cabernet that I had spent so much time with in the basement. In a strange way, having my clothes laundered felt as if it had been a huge betrayal of the memory of a '*fragrant*' old friend of mine, who had stood by me during my darkest hour! Looking around the room for the first time, I noticed that I had a couple of visitors. One was Chet Freshcorn, while the other… was *Eve Engood.*

"Hi, Mr. Berguhndy!" Freshcorn began, with what *appeared* to be his patented smile, although it *did not* seem the least bit insincere. "How're you feeling?"

"I've been *better*!" I quipped, forcing a smile. "But being here, sure beats being *dead*! Thanks for rescuing me!"

"Sure!" Freshcorn replied graciously. "And *thank you* for leading us to the solution of this case!"

I was stumped. "What are you talking about?"

"The FBI has been trying to find some airtight evidence of wrongdoing by New York City mob boss *Lucky Cuomo* for years!" Freshcorn explained. "The *proof* we found in your apartment, cocktail napkins written in Tommy Gunn's own hand, which described in detail how he had been hired by Cuomo to kill Cannon Manchester, was a *great* start! Incidentally, Mr. Gunn has agreed to turn state's evidence, in exchange for our *dismissing* all of his past indiscretions."

"You would *do* that?" I asked in amazement.

"In a heartbeat!" Freshcorn laughed. "Tommy Gunn has actually *never* killed a soul! He's just very good at *looking* like he would! It's a great deal for us!"

"So you have enough to *convict* Cuomo?" I asked excitedly.

"It *may* have been enough?" Freshcorn began. "But finding that printing press in the wine cellar that specialized in '*counterfeit money*,' complete with the printed one-hundred-dollar bills and a damning envelope full of more one-hundred-dollar bills that was *addressed to Cuomo himself*? Now *that* was all we needed to confirm that Bannon was printing money for him! That was the '*piece de resistance*!' Cuomo will be in prison for the next twenty years!"

"Great! But where is Bannon now?" I asked curiously.

"Oh, he's probably *long gone*," Freshcorn speculated. "I'll bet he's fled to some other country by now! My guess would be England. He would fit-in very nicely with all of those other *dandies* who live there!"

I couldn't help but laugh. And then suddenly I thought of a very baffling question. "So, what in the hell was Cannon Manchester doing down in the wine cellar with me… *alive*? Wasn't he supposed to be at the undertaker's being sized for a *triple-wide casket*?"

"Quite so," Freshcorn agreed. "But Bannon had a mysterious confederate at the party who drugged Cannon, causing him to only '*appear*' to be dead. Then he was picked up by a phony ambulance, while his death certificate was signed-off by a phony coroner. Finally, Bannon stashed him in the wine cellar until he could decide what to ultimately do with him."

"Who *was* this mysterious confederate?" I asked earnestly.

"Don't *know*, don't *care*!" Freshcorn replied firmly. "We got our man, and that's all that matters to the FBI."

"But how did Bannon get the printing press into the wine cellar, set it up, and get it working so quickly?" I asked him incredulously. "He had only been in that house for *one day*?"

"That's *not* exactly true!" Freshcorn chuckled. "Right after Cannon purchased the house a couple of months ago, the man that he hired to convert his basement into a wine cellar was in truth, *Bannon Manchester*!" he declared. "Apparently, he is a world class master of disguise and was *easily* able to fool even his own brother! He had secretly set-up the printing press in the basement *before* Cannon had even moved into the house, and then proceeded to *print money* to his heart's content ever since!" Freshcorn explained. "Then, he would send *inconspicuous* packets of bills to Lucky Cuomo in New York, as per their agreement. As you discovered, Although Bannon took wine bottles down there for appearances, he *always* kept the basement door *locked*, and refused to let anyone see how the wine cellar was coming along until he felt it was *completed*! Which of course, it *never would be*!"

"Wow! *That* is some story!" I exclaimed. "Congratulations on getting Cuomo and figuring this whole thing out," I complimented him robustly.

"Thank you, Mr. Berguhndy! But I couldn't have done it without my partner here," he said, graciously motioning his hand toward Miss Engood. And then smiling at me, he added, "And getting *you* involved in our investigation is the single largest reason we solved the case so quickly! That was hands down the *best* idea Eve has had as long as I have known her! Well, besides agreeing to secretly *marry me* last year!"

Okay! *This* is the part of the story where this '***major plot twist***' is supposed to take me completely off-guard. And it ***did***! "Hey Chet," I said in a weak voice, with an even weaker smile. "Do you mind if I speak with your wife privately for a moment? I just want to ask her about a couple of loose ends, if that would be all right?"

"Sure, buddy!" he chuckled. "After all, you two probably have a *lot* to talk about. I mean… you *shared* a bed together, now didn't you!"

As soon as he'd left the room, I gave Eve a very stern look as I said disapprovingly, "You played me for a fool, Miss Engood." And then I added sarcastically, "*Bravo*, on such a superb performance!"

"It *wasn't* like that," she replied gently with those soul-piercing blue eyes of hers. "The truth is, Chet convinced me to go undercover as Cannon's girlfriend to help with his investigation of Lucky Cuomo."

"So, you *did* share Cannon's bed!" I declared in shock.

"No, I *didn't*!" she laughed. "Cannon is a full-fledged *narcissist*. He has no interest in anybody but himself! The purpose of his girlfriends has always been just for show."

"Oh," I gasped in surprise. "So, then you really *are* a good Christian girl?"

She laughed. "I wouldn't go *that* far, but I try."

"I suppose it was *you* who spiked my drink and typed those two threatening notes?"

"Yes," she replied in surprise. "Was it really *that* obvious?" she chuckled. "But Chet took off your clothes and moved you under the covers," she confessed playfully. "It would have been *scandalous behavior* for an 'upstanding *married* woman,' like myself, to do *that*!"

"Is that also when he attached a tracking device to my shoe?" I asked curiously.

"Yes," she was once again surprised. "Drugging you and placing you in that '*undressed scenario*' was the only way Chet could think of to get your shoe away from you without giving away his *true* identity."

"I kind of figured that there was much more to that drugging than met the eye," I confessed. "In fact, I was reasonably sure that it had been *you* who had drugged me when I found both of our clothes folded-up so neatly there on the floor," I admitted. "*No criminal* would have ever bothered to do that."

"Then why didn't you *call me out on it* at the time?"

I smiled. "Because I was enjoying our adventure together way too much!" I confessed with heartfelt honesty. "I really *didn't* want to take the chance that bringing that up would make it all end prematurely," I admitted.

"It was very special for me too," she smiled like the angel she was. "And just so you know, I treasured *every moment of it*!"

"Eve?" I said gently. "You don't mind if I call you by your first name, do ya? Now that we're friends?"

"Not at all, *Biff*," she chuckled. "I only wish we were together now under different circumstances because I truly *am* attracted to you… and I *always* will be."

"You're not just saying that are you?" I asked with my voice cracking and my heart breaking.

"No," she confirmed. And then she kissed me. A long, *beautiful* kiss that in many stories would have marked the beginning of a magical love affair! But in this one… it sadly marked the *end*, even before anything had gotten a chance to begin.

All too soon, Eve gently pulled away from me. As our eyes met, I smiled at her while somehow feeling very sad at the same time? As much as I didn't want it to be, I suppose I realized at that moment that it was really *over* between us. Eve knew it too as she smiled at me in a *wistful* sort of way. Next, she very gently caressed my hand and met my despondent eyes with hers. There was really no need for a verbal goodbye. Her *eyes* said it all. Then she gently released my hand, blew me a slow and silent kiss… and disappeared through the door. I knew that I'd *never* see her again.

Later that day, after checking-out of the hospital and going home, while thinking about it, something just *didn't* seem to add-up about the solution to this case? I suppose my misgivings didn't matter much now that the FBI had closed it, but to me, somehow they did? And then, out of the blue, I received a very *surprising* telephone call? I didn't speak much, mostly just listened, but that was okay. You see, in every case I have ever solved throughout the years, there has *always* been a breakthrough which causes everything to suddenly come together, making the solution to the mystery seem perfectly obvious? *This phone call was it*! I inadvertently laughed to myself once the call was over, realizing that the reasons for all of my misgivings were actually *valid*! If I had not been so susceptible to the inherent charms of one particular sexy woman, I was certain that I would have solved this case much earlier! I had a few phone calls to make, and then this case would be solved the way it should have been solved in the first place. *Correctly*! Everything seemed so very clear to me now with absolutely *no* questions remaining! *Now* that I was no longer being *bamboozled* by Ace Lutt!

It was bright and beautiful in Southern California just two days later, when I asked a small group of carefully selected people to join me at the Manchester mansion. We assembled in the dining room where the faux murder of Cannon Manchester had taken place. I invited Mr. Manchester, Mr. Hertz, Biddy and Giddy McClinen, Ace Lutt and Miz Turrey to attend, and they were all there.

"The reason I have asked you all here, is to describe in detail what *actually* happened regarding Mr. Manchester's attempted murder and in the aftermath," I announced professionally.

"We've *already* heard that story from Chet Freshcorn and the FBI," Cannon whined. "Shouldn't we just put all of that behind us now and move on?"

Judging by the angry facial expressions with the accompanying *flood* of loud personal insults, and even a number of very crass *finger gestures*, it immediately became clear to me that almost everyone in the room *agreed* with Cannon. That is, everyone *except* for Miz Turrey.

"*Let the man speak*!" she proclaimed with the fierceness of a true Russian. "It is best that we all hear the truth!"

Everyone seemed to quickly accept that, or perhaps it was *more likely* they were *intimidated* by Miz Turrey! But regardless of the reason, the stage was now set, and with all eyes on me, I began my story.

"This caper was planned and executed to *perfection*!" I began. "But the target was *never* Cannon Manchester. It was *always* Lucky Cuomo. He was the only person on Earth who was keeping Cannon from returning to his beloved New York City. This all started when unbeknownst to each other, Tommy Gunn and Ace Lutt were both hired by Cuomo to *kill* Cannon Manchester. Cuomo is also the one who sent Cannon the death threat on the morning of the party. He wanted him to sweat, not knowing *who* the assassins were or *when* they would strike? And to make matters even worse, Ace Lutt was in reality, Cannon Manchester's *secret body guard*! Knowing this, Cuomo's plan was for her to take advantage of her position by *killing* Cannon at a time and place during the party when he least expected it. If she failed however, which was very unlikely given her stellar track record as a world class 'Ace of all tasks,' then and *only* then would Tommy Gunn be expected to step-up with his machine gun and *kill* Cannon and probably everyone else at the party, 'Tarantino-style' (*Tarantino is a writer and director in the future of ultra-violent movies*), to avoid leaving any witnesses! The problem was that although Ace was very much aware of Cannon's *love for only himself*, she still found that she liked him... *a lot*! Maybe even *loved* him? So, a little over a week before the party, she broke down and confessed Cuomo's whole terrible plan to him. But far from being upset upon hearing of the *murderous plot*, Cannon undoubtedly saw this as being much more of an *opportunity* to rid himself of Cuomo *forever*! Doing that would of course, immediately allow his own unobstructed return to New York City! So, later that day, Cannon, Mr. Hertz and Ace Lutt developed an ingenious plan to take down Lucky Cuomo once and for all!"

Cannon, Ace and Mr. Hertz listened politely to the story, but to this point, did not appear to have their feathers ruffled. (*Just an aside, in case you were wondering. 'People,' as a rule, don't have feathers to ruffle, as they are mammals. Although English men do frequently refer to women as 'birds.'*)

"Following that very scrumptious dinner," I continued, "only Chet Freshcorn got sick, which kept him a prisoner of the water closet for the better part of an hour. Was this random bad luck? Not at all! I believe that when Mr. Freshcorn entered Cannon's house, Ace *immediately* identified him as being an FBI agent, whom she had previously seen in action. So, she secretly sprinkled *his* dinner with a few soap flakes, which caused his temporary stomach ailment and got him out of the way in the process. When the time came, it was probably Cannon himself who flicked off the light switch, creating immediate darkness and pandemonium in the room. Just as soon as he did that, Ace quickly moved into position in front of the Picasso, and fired the famous '*shot heard around the room*,' directly through the center of it!"

"Now that's a *dirty lie*!" Ace vehemently insisted as she suddenly came alive. "Like I told you before, *my* bullet can be found outside in a tree!"

"I had the police check *that* bullet," I said confidently. "They confirmed that slug to definitely be from a .22 pistol, and I have little doubt that if we checked further, we *would* discover that it had indeed been fired from *your* gun, as you told me. But they *also* concluded that the slug in question had been lodged in the tree for at *least* a week? Scaring off an earlier suiter, Ace? *Van Nish* perhaps?"

Ace was quiet. She had *no* comeback.

"And remember that flash of lightening?" I pointedly asked her, feeling as though I was really on a roll.

She nodded, unsure of where I was going.

"Well," I said, feeling very self-assured. "It seems that someone at the party actually *saw you shoot the picture* during that very brief moment of illumination!"

"*Who* saw me?" Ace demanded.

I chuckled. "I think it's safe to say that whoever it was… they *wish to remain anonymous*!" Ace was immediately silent, so I continued my story. "The significance of that bullet hole in the picture *may* have been that it clearly told Cannon and Mr. Hertz where to be while the death scene was being played out," I conjectured. "A bullet hole through the *center* of the picture may have conceivably told them to be at the *center* of the room."

"That is sheer speculation!" Cannon angrily exclaimed, as he menacingly stood up to face me. "You *can't* prove a word of it!"

"I promised that I would detail how everything happened, *not* that I would *prove* anything," I smiled. "This is by no means an official inquest or a trial, Mr. Manchester. As far as the FBI is concerned, you were kidnapped and freed, while *Lucky Cuomo*, the man responsible for the attempt on your life as well as for counterfeiting, is now safely behind bars. In addition, your brother Bannon, his trusted accomplice, is thought to have probably fled the country. *Case closed*!" Turning toward everyone, I expounded, "You all have absolutely *nothing* to fear from me! In fact, you are all free to leave this room right now if you choose. But if you do… you'll miss the *surprise ending* of this story!"

Cannon sat back down and *nobody* left the room.

"I know that what I am about to tell you is *true*, because according to a number of witnesses at the party, both Mr. Manchester and Mr. Hertz quickly moved to the center of the room just as soon as the lights came back on."

"*Coincidence*!" Ace declared, losing much of her usual cool. "Why would they want to move to the center of the room anyway?"

I smiled knowingly. "Because that was where *you* were!"

"And just *what* do you mean by *that*?" Miss Lutt demanded defiantly.

"I believe that having all three of you meeting in the center of the room was more than likely the plan all along," I professed. "You knew that Chet Freshcorn was otherwise engaged, so as an FBI agent, he *wouldn't* be around to check Cannon's body. But you feared that somebody else, some *random* person at the party, a doctor perhaps, *might* spontaneously check and surprisingly discover that Cannon Manchester was *not* dead at all, but actually very much *alive and well*! *That* could not be allowed to happen! So, between you and Mr. Hertz, you effectively *blocked* everyone else at the party from getting anywhere *close* to Cannon's fallen body! Although I can't prove it, the gunshot and resulting hole in the Picasso," I continued, "was probably just a dramatic confirmation to Cannon and Hertz to go ahead with the plan. In any case, it certainly *heightened* the excitement of the death scene, don't you think?" Then I smiled, adding, "By the way, you must have really felt like laughing, Ace! While you were *presumably* giving Cannon mouth to mouth, no one else in the room had so much as a clue that it was actually the *longest* French kiss with a '*corpse*' you'd ever had in your life!"

"Not the *longest*!" Ace insisted mysteriously.

Not wishing to hear her *elaborate* on that macabre thought, I was relieved when another voice suddenly entered the fray.

"But I *was* poisoned!" Manchester insisted vehemently. "I know now that the ambulance and coroner were fakes, but Doctor Hertz checked my pulse and found none!"

"Ah yes, 'Doctor' Hertz," I said playfully. "Practiced medicine for ten years before becoming your butler. He practiced in a little town in the *Ozarks* without a license or *any* record of ever attending medical school or any other college for that matter!" Growing more relaxed, I shared, "No, anything that the good doctor has to say should *definitely* be taken with a grain of salt."

"*That* is my remedy for getting relief from headaches, you know!" Mr. Hertz proclaimed with excitement. "Just *one grain* of salt per hour."

I suddenly had a *brilliant* plan. "Something is still bothering me though," I calmly addressed everyone in the room. "I never did figure out *who* it was that hit me over the head when I was down in the wine cellar?"

There was absolute silence.

"But *whoever* it was, I must really compliment them," I shared with a smile.

"And *why* is that, sir?" Mr. Hertz apparently spoke for the entire group.

"Because the knots they tied on the ropes that bound me were i*mpossible* to break out of! That's no easy task, securely tying-up someone like me, who has so much professional experience *escaping*!" I explained with excessive admiration. "Yes! There is no doubt in my mind that the person who tied those stellar knots was most assuredly the *greatest knot expert* in the world!"

"Why, thank you, sir!" Mr. Hertz said, beaming from head to toe! "I was a Boy Scout and a sailor prior to becoming an exotic dancer, an airline pilot, a sous-chef at Sardi's, a lawyer and a doctor, before finally serving as Mr. Manchester's butler! The ability to tie a good knot has *always* been a strong part of my repertoire!"

You could have heard a pin drop. But I just smiled and said, "Thank you, Mr. Hertz, for filling-in that hole."

"You're very welcome, sir. Patching holes is *also* one of my specialties!" he replied, without the slightest sign of embarrassment, or the shocking realization that he had just been *tricked* into confessing.

Mr. Hertz was truly one of the most honest people I have ever met… and quite possibly the *dumbest*! But somehow I admired him, and so, I was *absolutely disinclined* to charge him with a crime. I believe that what he had done, he did out of fierce loyalty to his boss, *misguided* as that loyalty may have been. But, the bump on the back of my head was quickly going down, so heck! I found it in my heart to *forgive* him!

"*Is that it*?" Cannon asked sharply. "Off the record, I am *not* denying that what you shared with us today might bear some *slight* resemblance to the truth, but Mr. Berguhndy… I'm sorry to say that your little story lacks a *knockout punch*!"

"*Au contraire*!" I disagreed confidently. "For those of you who don't know the special guest from the dinner party who I have invited here, her name is Miz Turrey. It was only through her help that I was finally able to solve this case. She has a few things to say, and then this little soiree will come to an end."

"Hello," Miss Turrey said. "It was purely by chance that I happened to accept an invitation to accompany someone to that party. Once there however, when I *saw you*," she passionately declared, pointing directly at Cannon Manchester, "I was in complete shock! I immediately recognized you from twenty years ago, even though your *circumference* had grown so immensely and your name had changed since being that sweet, scrawny Russian boy."

Cannon's eyes and ears were hypnotically *glued* to her.

"You lived in Moscow, and your parents were killed by the Russian mafia, remember? I saw everything from a nearby hiding place. Then, you were taken against your will by a young Vladimir Petrov, to be raised by the mafia. As I learned a few years later, you and Petrov moved to America, where in order to fit-in, you both changed your names. You, to *Cannon Manchester* and he, to *Lucky Cuomo*! I eventually was able to leave Russia, also finding my way to America. Here, I longed every day for many *inconsolable* years that we would one day be reunited," Miz shared passionately. "Every night I cried myself to sleep, worrying about what terrible things might have already befallen you? Or if you were even *still* alive?"

"Who *are* you?" Cannon asked in surprise, irritation and arrogance (*in that order*). "An old acquaintance perhaps? A very distant family relative? A *crazy person*? I have *no* other immediate family members except for my twin brother, Bannon, and you most certainly are *not* him!" he laughed nervously.

"You are *correct*," Miz gently agreed, with her eyes still controlling Cannon's. "You have only *one* sibling, a twin. But that twin is *not* Bannon. That twin *is me*!"

Everyone in the room *gasped* in unison!

"There was *no* poison, no kidnapping and no Bannon Manchester, was there?" I declared. "*Look* at this photograph of you, Cannon," I demanded, as I thrust the picture of him that I had found in his den that fateful night that I had been *cabernet-ed* in the basement. "You *drew* the moustache and glasses on this photograph of yourself while you were planning your very effective facial transformation to Bannon just before you *faked* your own death! Am I right?"

Cannon was speechless as he listened to what he surely knew for a fact *was the truth*!

"Cannon and Bannon are *one and the same person* in this highly entertaining charade of yours," I announced confidently. "The *truth* is what you need to begin fixing all of those lies and deceitful acts you have created throughout your lifetime. And the truth is standing *right here*! Cannon, embrace your sister, Miz Turrey!"

Cannon Manchester immediately dropped the façade and excitedly shuffled over to embrace the awaiting arms of his long-lost twin sister Miz Turrey! Their reunion was *spectacular*! Everyone in the room cheered! This scene played-out very similarly to the endings of many movies from the 1980s (*in the not-too-distant future*), where all of the extras in the scene applauded emphatically for the main protagonists' happy outcome! A good example of this appears in a movie called, '*An Officer and a Gentleman*,' which may or may not be made in 1982. The only difference between the scene from *that* movie and the one we have just experienced, is that *no one actually applauded* in our scene, they only *cheered*. Although we could certainly make a case for it having been *implied*?

As soon as the newly reunited brother and sister finally broke their embrace, Miz looked at Cannon with those dark brooding Russian eyes and proclaimed, "Cannon Manchester, your birth name, as you know, is *Dimitri Turrey*. You must reinvent yourself by returning to that name, *our name*, when you return to New York City!"

"I am *returning* to New York City?" Cannon repeated in shock, surprise and glee… but mostly *glee*.

"Cannon Manchester is a counterfeiter, a liar and a cheat!" Miz proclaimed bluntly. "You must take this opportunity to become a *good* man as you once were… named *Dimitri Turrey*!"

"But with *what* money?" he asked in desperation. "All of *my* money is counterfeit! And even if for some *very good and perfectly legal reason* I wanted to make more money, *I can't*! The FBI has taken away my only printing press!"

"With *my* money," said the small voice of a skinny runt of a man with brown hair and a matching brown suit, who I *apologize* profusely for not introducing to you at the beginning of this scene. I simply *didn't* notice him? You might remember him from the party however, as *Mylo Girth*. Mylo proudly walked up to Miz Turrey and lovingly placed a scrawny arm around her. "You *won't* be needing that printing press any longer, Dimitri (*formerly known as, Cannon*)! Miz and I are to be married soon, making all of us *family*!" he motioned magnanimously toward Dimitri. "So, I will *buy* this house from you at a ridiculously inflated price using *real money*! Additionally, I will give you a sizeable monthly allowance for a few years *until* you get your life in order. With *that* money you shall change your life!"

"Why thank you, Mylo! I don't know what to say?" Dimitri stammered tongue-tied with excitement.

"Say, '*Cannon Manchester is dead*!'" Miz implored him. "Long live Dimitri Turrey!"

Dimitri *squealed* with delight! But then turning to Mylo, he asked very humbly, "May I bring my staff with me? They are the best and most loyal friends I have in the entire world! All of them have been with me for a good many years now, going all the way back to my happiest days in New York City."

"Of course you can," Mylo assured him kindly, as he took out a small pad of paper and a pen from his inside coat pocket, which unsurprisingly *matched* the coat's color *perfectly*! "Now then, what are the names of the people who you wish to bring with you?"

"Well, there are Biddy and Giddy McClinen, Ace Lutt and Mr. Hertz."

"What is your *first name*, Mr. Hertz?" Mylo asked.

"Miback."

"*Miback Hertz*?" he chuckled.

"You ain't whistlin' Dixie!" Mr. Hertz groaned.

Well, that about winds-up the exciting case of Cannon Manchester and his murder that *never actually happened*! All of the players in this story lived happily ever after as far as I know, with the exception of Lucky Cuomo. He keeps insisting from his new home in '***Sing Sing***,' that he's innocent, even as the FBI is finding more and more incriminating evidence that says *he's not*! And then there's the strange case of the newly retired quasi-criminal, Tommy Gunn, and his *truth-challenged* girlfriend, Liza Lott. The last I heard of them, they had finally stopped practicing, and entered an official 'Duelogue Competition,' sponsored by the *Holiday Inn Casino* in *Reno*, and *won*! Well actually, the Casino had held the competition outside, the two of them were the finalists and they kept going on so long that the competition was eventually called for darkness! So, according to league rules, they were *both* announced winners and split the ten thousand dollars prize money!

But I have *no idea* if they were actually happy about that or simply *irritated* that they were forced to stop prematurely before finding out *which of them was actually the loser*? And then there's Cee Cee Cretz (*alias Muffy Du Pont*) who *scooped* the sensational 'Cannon Manchester story' (*as it was explained to her by Chet Freshcorn*) and printed it in her weekly column! The success of the article she wrote in the Hollywood Gazette, proved to be so *intense* that it was soon reprinted and enjoyed by readers in almost *every country* worldwide! In fact, the article was seen as being such a splendid example of *sensationalist American journalism at its most blatant*, that it was actually nominated for a *Pulitzer Prize*! This stunning achievement was *not* missed by her family, as she was immediately given back her *Dupont* name, her title of *heiress*, and bestowed with a healthy monthly allowance in the hope that she would *stop* buying all of her clothes from the Sears discount rack! As for me… I still live in the same cozy apartment or *mansion* as Liza Lott calls it, drive the same beautiful Packard One-Twenty and pine for the same *perfect* woman who got away. But, at least I now do it as a full-fledged detective for the Hollywood Police Department's Homicide Division's *nightshift*! Not too shabby, if I do say so myself!

I have learned over the years that in everything we do, *win or lose*, there is always a payoff. We may not always *get* the one we were hoping for… but for me, there is always something very special waiting at the end of every case I solve. This time, although I didn't get the girl… *again*… I received the lasting memory of her *kiss*. That should be enough to keep me warm at night for a good long time, or at least until she gets that *divorce* I've been hoping for! Once she realizes that the name Eve *Berguhndy*, sounds a hell of a lot better than Eve *Freshcorn*, she'll come running back to me faster than you can say, "*Supermurgitroid*!"

But in the meantime, while I patiently await her return, maybe I'll watch my brand-new twelve-inch, black and white television set that I was able to buy with my *reward money* from Mylo Girth for helping to bring Miz Turrey and him together. I really am enjoying watching that Dick Tracy show and Jack Benny too! But even a television set is no substitute for holding and caressing the one you love… *forever*! And because of that, when my television set, along with everything else I own, eventually fails to distract me during the times that I miss Eve the most, I have one *final* plan.

In addition to the sweet memory of her kiss, I *also* possess the memories of our very short, but *magical* time together, carefully pressed and preserved in the 'Cinema of my Mind!' (*I am especially proud of creating that metaphor*!) Those memories have now surpassed even my Packard as being my most *valuable* possession! My plan is to embrace that fifth of Scotch, along with those happy memories to get me through even the darkest of nights and into the following day. And when that next day arrives, I plan on waking-up with *hope* in my heart that someday Eve will appear out of nowhere, kiss me for a long time and then promise to stay *forever*! Don't scoff! There's no harm in hoping is there? I have found that occasionally it *works*! One just needs to believe with all of their heart and tap their shoes together three times, or something like that. Right? Something else that will help is called '*positive thinking*,' and in a couple of years, this guy named *Norman Vincent Peale*, is going to write a best-selling book about its enormous power! In any case, I'll be seeing you soon in my next baffling mystery… with *Eve Engood* by my side! How's *that* for positive thinking! You know? I'm almost beginning to believe it myself? Yep, positive thinking is definitely the answer! In my mind, Eve Engood is *destined* to return to me. *Naïve* is the word!

"The Foreign Exchange Student"

(1969)

ONE SPECIAL MORNING AT 8:00 O'CLOCK, in the year 1962, Thomas McAdams, a tall, slender, sandy haired boy of fifteen was *abruptly* awakened by his alarm clock to his favorite school day of the week... *glorious Friday*! Thomas lived in a cozy, single story, ranch-style home on Tiller Lane with his parents and hyperactive eight-year-old brother named Ted. His brother's birth name was actually *Theodore,* but be warned... call him *that* at your *own peril*! The town they lived in was comfortably small, boasting only 5,631 residents...*exactly*! Located somewhere in the middle of California, between Los Angeles and San Francisco, this little haven was called Masonville. It was named after Eduardo Mason, the *not* so famous man who had originally owned all of the land that eventually became the site of this town. I hear that Mr. Mason also created some of the most delicious apple pies in the county at the town bakery (*operated by his wife*) anytime he grew bored with simply owning land.

Thomas yawned, turned off his alarm clock, and casually looked around to focus his eyes. With *those* important tasks behind him, he slowly pulled himself out of bed. Once up, he got dressed, combed his hair *just so*, and brushed his teeth before finally entering the kitchen and sitting down at the table for breakfast.

"It's so strange?" his mother told him warmly, while handing him a bowl of oatmeal. "I feed you more than the rest of us combined, and you *still* stay as thin as a lamppost?"

"Well, I'm sorry," Thomas said (*pretending that he had been deeply hurt*), "but if you *weren't* such a great cook, I *wouldn't* eat so much, would I!" His response, predictably inspired a little laugh from his mother, who secretly *reveled* in the compliment.

As the clock neared 8:45, Thomas hurriedly excused himself and rushed through the front door. He was dressed today in a well-worn pair of blue-jeans, matched with a long-sleeved red and white flannel shirt. Before too long, he neared the highly revered (*at least by the older alumni*) red-brick building that was known to all as *Masonville Junior High*!

Historically, as far as any former students coming out of MJH who had gone on to become extremely famous and successful, there had *almost* been one. His name was *Sheldon Bartlet*. Sheldon appeared to be a boy of average intelligence, but he was very lazy. He unfortunately lacked the drive to work hard at *anything* he didn't already excel at. This had predictably made him a very poor student. However, he was an outstanding athlete at MJH; hands down, the *best* the school had ever had! This made him a pretty big man on campus, *regardless* of his poor grades. He had attended Masonville Junior High, ending in 1947, and was personally responsible for three unforgettable years of *glorious athletic domination* in the local junior high sports leagues! In 1950, after *barely* graduating from high school, he was drafted by the Brooklyn Dodgers. Due to his enormous potential, he skipped their 'A League' and was immediately promoted to the Dodgers' 'AA team' in Fort Worth, Mobile. However, what should have been a stunning feather in Masonville's cap, quickly *disappeared* and turned into a sad and devastating end to the high hopes the town had uniformly held for the talented young man. He was unceremoniously *cut* from the Dodgers' AA team just one year later for basically not working hard enough! (*Something the teachers at MJH could have warned them about if they'd only asked.*) He *never* played professional baseball again, and was even rumored to have moved out of California altogether! Needless to say, the name, *Sheldon Bartlet*, was soon generally forgotten in the city of Masonville. Although, as a source of pride for the junior high, every new student was routinely taught about his *unbelievable* athletic exploits! His name also garnered occasional praise here at MJH whenever the mention of his past successes could be used *against* other schools in the county! As always, all's fair when you consider junior high school bragging rights… even the *infamous* name of Sheldon Bartlet!

But, even without a legitimate professional sports hero emanating from the school, Masonville Junior High was still quite proficient at educating happy children in grades seven through nine. In particular, Thomas was very excited about attending MJH this year because he very proudly sat at the top of the food chain as a *ninth grader*! In his short life, it just hadn't gotten any better than this!

As you have probably already guessed, Masonville Junior High was quite small compared to the much larger schools of its distant neighbors, Los Angeles and San Francisco, giving it a considerably smaller teaching staff. Unfortunately, this mandated that every student be assigned to only *one* teacher for *all* of their required courses. This disappointingly made MJH feel much more like an elementary school than a junior high! But regardless of that, *this* was how MJH had effectively operated ever since it had first opened its doors in 1892! The feeling of the school board seemed to be, '*What was good for MJH then, is good for it now*!' So, everybody just seemed to accept it as being one of those *immovable* traditions. To be honest, this arrangement would have actually worked out fine for Thomas, had his assigned teacher been fun and understanding, but unfortunately… *she was not*!

Luckily, within this very *basic* format, students *were* provided with a couple of courses outside of their regular assigned classroom. First, physical education was offered to every classroom of students at the school three times weekly and was taught by a very popular teacher named Mr. Tim Teltrab. Secondly, extracurricular creative arts classes were taught by members of the regular teaching staff *before* school twice weekly. The students were given a choice at the beginning of each semester of taking *drama*, *music*, *home economics*, *dance* or *art*. At the end of that semester, if they enjoyed the class they were in, they were allowed to repeat it for up to the maximum of all six semesters. These special classes did a lot for breaking-up the monotony of the long school week. Thomas absolutely *loved* his drama class!

Immediately noticing the frantic movement of the few remaining students around the locker area, Thomas quickly realized that he was *nearly late*! He must have run from his locker to his classroom in what he believed to be *faster* than any world-champion Olympian could have ever done it! But alas, by the time he'd finally seated himself behind his old wooden desk, the clock had already struck nine! His heart fell to his stomach as he quickly realized that he was indeed… *tardy*!

His teacher, *Miss Catherine Cornelia Cornwall*, a tiny, elderly woman who had served as a Catholic nun for a number of years and a reform school warden for a few years before that, *prior* to becoming a public-school teacher, was a stickler for making her students follow the rules! To her, being on time was certainly one of the *most sacred* rules of all! Sporting dyed *orange* hair and usually wearing a dowdy black dress, she was always quick-tempered, and *never* exhibited behavior that could even remotely be mistaken for being understanding or patient. Oddly enough, initially upon realizing that Thomas had arrived to her class late, she merely looked at him with only mild interest, without uttering even a single word? But then her mood abruptly changed as she determinedly marched up to his desk and screeched (*like the sound an angry parrot might make*), "Tardy again eh, Thomas?" He nodded guiltily, all the while wearing that same sickly expression he *always* sported whenever he was caught by Miss Cornwall for this very same offense. Surprisingly, she actually smiled back at him, but in a very *anticipatory* way? Then suddenly transforming that smile into the *horrific* face of a demon, she rudely grabbed his collar, and with the newfound strength of the monster she had become, she dragged him down the entire distance of the hallway to the principal's office! And you know what? Her hideously demented face showed that she had *greatly enjoyed doing it*!

After firmly seating Thomas down just outside of the principal's office in an unpainted and uncomfortable wooden chair (*that could have easily given a person splinters if they were not careful*), Miss Cornwall proceeded to step inside the principal's office for a private meeting. The principal, Mr. Herbert Zuffin, was short, a bit on the heavy side, and sported a head of thin, prematurely graying hair. It was difficult to guess his exact age, but he was 'probably' somewhere in his late forties or early fifties. To be fair, he was *not* a bad man at all. In fact, he always tried very hard in his position as principal to be '*impartial and understanding*' to every student, regardless of their prior *rap sheet*. Although this was indeed a very noble plan, *unfortunately*, due to a strong personality trait he had inherited from his mother, his most glaring weakness seemed to be his *inability* to deal effectively with *conflict* whenever his unusually high sense of empathy got the better of him. From the school's prevailing point of view, this behavior appeared to make him *less* than effective at efficiently dealing with disciplinary problems. But from his own point of view, *whatever* he decided to do about each student's school infraction, he *never* went to bed at night with regrets. Once Miss Cornwall had intensely reminded Mr. Zuffin that Thomas McAdams was a chronically tardy student (*as he was already quite aware*), she quickly glided out of his office wearing the triumphant smile of the conquering hero! To her way of thinking, Thomas should definitely be *paddled*, as the inevitable disciplinary consequence of his openly defiant rule-breaking actions! As already mentioned, Miss Cornwall was the first to admit that she was a 110% '*rule monger*!' She believed in issuing *harsh* punishments to all of her students who were caught red-handed breaking a rule, like Thomas McAdams was on a regular basis! In addition, she always did her best to enforce *every single rule* that the school issued, and then a few others that she believed should *also* be added to that list! She was disappointed however, that she was never invited to her students' disciplinary meetings, which she often referred to as their '*days of reckoning*!' She so wanted to watch those student 'criminals-in-training,' squirm like bugs, before ultimately getting *squashed*!

Principal Zuffin opened his office door following Miss Cornwall's abrupt departure. Solemnly ushering Thomas inside, he then sat him down (*where he always sat him down*) on another hard, unpainted, wooden chair facing his desk. Thomas looked at the wall behind the man, and twisted nervously in his chair as he viewed the *ominous paddle*! It was said to have already been used this year on many repeat offenders, although up to this point, he had somehow managed to *avoid it*!

"Hello, Mr. McAdams," Principal Zuffin said with a sigh, as he sat down. "What seems to be the trouble *this* time?"

Thomas, very 'sincerely' explained (*with a few embellishments*) that he had been late to class today due to some *unexpected difficulties* at home, conveniently leaving out the part about getting up and leaving the breakfast table late. He also shared (*with absolutely no disrespect intended*), that he believed Miss Cornwall, although a wonderful teacher, was once again making a mountain out of a molehill.

"Now, Mr. McAdams," Principal Zuffin shared weakly. "You have already been tardy quite often this year, have you not?" He included a 'pregnant pause' here as he attempted to create *fear* in the mind of his young student. However, he quickly realized by Thomas's *unfearful expression*, that he was actually coming up a *little short*. "Consequently, I believe that you leave me no other choice this time but to *punish you*!"

Thomas did not say a word, but gave the principal his most emotionally pathetic expression, as if this punishment would surely change his life forever… and definitely for the *worse*!

"No hard feelings now, son? You know that you're in the wrong, don't you?" Principal Zuffin, who as usual was *very* affected by Thomas's little performance, seemed to be silently *begging him* for permission to carry out his clear, but highly uncomfortable duty.

"Yes, sir," Thomas stifled his 'crocodile tears,' as he dutifully agreed with the principal.

"And this will never happen again… *ever*?" the principal pleaded.

"Oh no, sir! *Never*!" Thomas once again agreed, with a cherub-like expression, supporting the fact that he was beyond the shadow of a doubt portraying *absolute honesty*!

"Good boy, Thomas!" The principal praised him for producing the correct response, or at least the one that nervous principals, like himself, who find themselves in this very *uncomfortable* situation from time to time are *always* hoping for. "Now, for your *punishment*." He stopped for a long moment, apparently deep in thought, while continuing to be fascinated by Thomas' wide array of expressions. Although they were *all* pretty compelling, his *most* effective ones were definitely '*remorseful*' and '*pathetic*,' which each had the uncanny power of tugging at the principal's heart strings. "Well... let's just leave this as a *warning,* shall we?" Principal Zuffin said kindly but sternly, with an unmistakable sense of relief. "No punishment *this* time, but if this should ever happen *again*?"

Thomas's sincere and repentant expression immediately let the principal know that his understanding had been very much appreciated. After verbally thanking him, Thomas quietly left his office. Walking down the hallway, he couldn't help but smile. He calculated that this made *thirty-seven* straight times he had *not* been punished for being tardy this year! Who says that drama classes don't teach students valuable skills concerning human behavior, like how to '*talk yourself out of punishments*' which you very clearly deserve! Most importantly though, he hoped the school didn't so much as consider changing principals until *after* he had been promoted from junior high to high school. He couldn't help but feel that he and Mr. Zuffin had really *bonded* this year!

When he walked back into Miss Cornwall's classroom, her craze-ridden expression of surprise and disgust was all that Thomas needed to confirm that this was indeed turning out to be a *great Friday*! After sitting down at his desk however, he realized that *something* was different? He casually looked around and quickly grasped exactly where that odd feeling was coming from. The seat to his left, which was normally vacant, was now occupied by an '*Angel from Heaven*!' Describing her in more secular terms, she appeared to be a girl of average height, with long dark hair and blue eyes to boot! As a whole, she possessed extraordinary, even '*out of this world*' beauty! He vowed then and there that this was a girl he *had* to talk to right away! And somehow... he *did*!

"Excuse me," the new girl said gently during the morning break as she slowly approached Thomas outside of the classroom. "I couldn't help noticing that you were *staring* at me ever since you came back to class?"

'Aha!' Thomas thought to himself. 'She noticed that I was gone!' "*Staring*?" he replied very innocently. "Oh no! I just have a very rare medical condition where I sometimes *gaze* at nothing in particular without even being aware of it. Perhaps *that* was what you noticed?"

"Are you calling me *nothing in particular*?" she suggested humorously, in faux disgust.

"Oh, no! Of course not!" Thomas quickly tried to recover. "To tell you the truth… uh… I was just staring at your dandruff."

"But I'm quite sure that I don't have any *dandruff*," she replied humorously. "Are you certain that was it?"

"Naw," Thomas finally gave-up. "It's just that I've never seen you before, so naturally I wondered who you were?"

"Oh," she replied, not the least bit surprised. "My name is Della Seisman. I just moved here from Chicago."

"Wow!" Thomas was genuinely impressed because being from *any place* other than Masonville, California, was *truly exciting*! "I'm real glad to meet you!" he exclaimed with an oversized smile, strongly extending his right hand. "My name is Thomas McAdams."

Della seemed to get a real kick out of his *dynamic* introduction as she shook his hand and replied in kind, "I'm *real glad* to meet you too! But I think we had better get back to class now… don't you?"

"Right!" Thomas agreed, gently releasing her hand before adding (*with just a hint of anxiety*), "Do you think it would be okay if I walked you home from school today?"

"Of course! That sounds very nice," Della replied in complete surprise, with a sudden glint in her eye. "I'll meet you at the front of the school."

Thomas readily agreed to the plan, and the two teens quickly scurried back to class, just beating the bell as their morning break, much too quickly, came to an end.

The remainder of the morning dragged on as Thomas thought of nothing but Della. In the meantime, he looked forward to speaking with her again during class. However, as fate would have it, he did *not* find a single opportunity to do that during the entire morning, and he *suffered* greatly as a result! (*At least his 'heart' told him so.*)

When lunchtime arrived, Thomas had *planned* on sitting next to Della at a lunch table. But alas, once again his hopes and dreams were dashed when he found her sitting amongst a group of girls, continuously talking and laughing as groups of girls are prone to do. As much as Thomas was very fond of girls, he'd learned from experience that trying to speak with 'one specific girl' in a crowd of them, was very much like trying to catch 'one specific fish' in an *ocean* of them! So, he unhappily sat in another part of the room beside some of his buddies. Lunch seemed *longer* than usual as he silently sat at the lunch-table, trying not to be too conspicuous as he longingly stared across the room at Della. Happily, lunch eventually came to a merciful end, and the second half of the school day was upon them. Aside from sharing a few smiles, not having any additional contact with Della made this by far the *longest* second half of the school day he had experienced all year!

Finally, the 'end of the school day bell' rang, and he was *free* at last! Thomas wasted no time jumping out of his seat and racing toward his locker. When he got there however, he was met by a large, dark-haired fellow from his class whom he knew, but certainly had never cared for much, named *Joe Porter*. The reason Thomas disliked him so much, maybe even *despised* him, was because of his bullying tendencies toward his friends and him which had actually started way back in early elementary school! It's safe to say that there was absolutely *no love lost* between them.

"Hey," Joe began in his normal *thinly veiled* threatening manner. "Who's that girl you were talking with today?"

"What girl?" Thomas asked, playing it totally cool.

"You *know* who I mean," Joe snarled. "That *new* chick?"

"Oh *her*," Thomas said, trying not to sound the least bit interested. "She's just a girl who moved here from Chicago named Della Seisman." Then he added, "She's a friend of mine."

"Ah ha!" Joe's burly voice accused him, "She's yer new *girlfriend*, isn't she!"

"No, she's *just* a friend," Thomas corrected him calmly, while inadvertently growing agitated.

"*Good answer, punk*!" Joe hissed under his breath. Then, after giving Thomas a vicious glare, he thankfully walked off.

After a brief moment of deliberation, Thomas decided to dismiss this entire incident from his mind. He was in no way going to allow the nastiness of Joe Porter to ruin his afternoon. So, after opening his locker and putting away the books that he would *not* be needing over the weekend, he rushed off to meet Della.

"What kept you?" she asked inquisitively, without even a hint of irritation or impatience.

"Oh, nothing," Thomas replied with a great big smile. "I just had to say *goodbye* to *Miss Cornwall*!"

Della laughed. She knew *that* wasn't true!

"Are you ready to go?" Thomas asked eagerly.

"Absolutely," she replied.

"Uh, which way do we turn?" he laughed.

"Oh yeah!" she chuckled. "Well, to tell you the truth, I'm not too sure myself what my address is? We only just moved-in, you see. But it's *that* way," she laughed, pointing to her left. "Somewhere on Tanner Street. But don't worry, I'll know the house by sight."

"Oh! I know where Tanner Street is!" Thomas replied excitedly. "It's only a few streets over from *my* street!" Then he added, "Maybe we'll be seeing more of each other?"

"*Maybe*," Della responded sweetly.

Following that, they began walking side by side. After a few moments of *awkward* silence (*that usually comes with not knowing each other very well*), Thomas asked, "So, who all is in your family?"

"Just my aunt and me," Della replied sweetly. "I don't have any brothers or sisters, and both of my parents died in an accident two years ago."

"Oh, I'm so sorry!" Thomas responded quickly, feeling terrible.

Della smiled sweetly, "There's no need to feel sorry for me. Everything is *fine* now," she assured him, as she took his hand and squeezed it. "It wasn't anyone's fault, it just happened. Anyway, I've since dealt with it and have been living quite happily with my aunt."

Thomas didn't pry into the exact circumstances of the accident that had sadly claimed the lives of her parents. He could only imagine how *painful* that must have felt at the time, and probably *still did*! He really appreciated her understanding words after he had misspoken… but he appreciated that *little squeeze* she gave his hand even more! "Do you and your aunt plan on staying in Masonville very long?" he asked.

"We're planning on staying here through the end of this school year at least," she shared. "It's only been one day of course, but I really like going to this school. It's very… quaint."

"Oh yeah?" Thomas responded curiously. Absolutely *clueless* as to what she had meant. "How is Masonville Junior High *quaint*?"

"Well," Della stammered. "What I *meant* to say was that England's schools are *much* different."

"Wow, you lived in *England*?" Thomas asked excitedly.

"Yes," she answered carefully. "That's actually where I'm from, before we moved to Chicago, that is."

"But you *don't* have an English accent?" Thomas observed astutely.

"Where I lived, *all* of the people had the very same accent or *lack* of one that I have," Della explained with a smile.

"Wow! You're from a part of England where they *don't* have an accent!" he exclaimed, as if he had just discovered something incredibly important. "That makes you pretty special in my book!"

"Why, thank you, Thomas," Della blushed (*obviously positively affected by the compliment*), "No one has *ever* told me that before. You're so sweet!"

Thomas didn't respond verbally, but his shy smile immediately told Della that he had appreciated her response *greatly*. A few minutes later, they arrived at her house.

"Well, I guess I'll be seeing you," Thomas fumbled for words, obviously sad about parting so soon.

Della's response was equally awkward as she hesitantly replied, "Okay… bye."

"Uh, wait. Will you go to the movies with me tomorrow afternoon?" Thomas blurted out.

Della *suddenly* smiled. "I'd love to! If I can? I'll have to ask my aunt about it first."

"It's a *matinee*," Thomas added, trying hard to strengthen his case. "We'll be back long before dark… and anyway, tomorrow's *Saturday*!"

Della laughed, definitely appreciating all of his efforts. "I'll call you later today, okay? Your number is in the phonebook, right?"

Thomas nodded, they shared a warm smile and then traveled their separate ways; Della into her house, while Thomas began his short journey home. During his entire walk, all he could think about was the new girl, *Della*, and their upcoming date tomorrow!

A few minutes later, as Thomas walked into his house, *everything* immediately returned to normal. His younger brother, Ted, was determinedly playing with his army men, which were scattered all over the spacious living room floor and even on top of the furniture. His playing came complete with all of the sound effects and dialogue that should always accompany such an *exciting* epic battle as the one he was creating. His mother, meanwhile, was busily preparing dinner with wonderful aromas already beginning to seep out from the kitchen. The only sound he truly missed was that of his father, who was usually reading the paper about this time, hemming and hawing at every story he read. Thomas asked his mother where his father was and she quickly shared that he was in Los Angeles for a business meeting and would not be back until tomorrow. Being in advertising, he was gone quite a lot, Thomas thought. And although he understood his absence, he was *still* disappointed. He liked sharing his afternoons with his dad when he was home. He always listened to him and made him feel very special. He was also very generous about '*lending him money*' when the need arose… like *now*! But he quickly got over his father's absence as he formulated a new plan… or at least a *new target*!

"Mom, may I borrow a few dollars from you?" he asked using his sweetest face and voice.

"Don't you mean, 'May I *have* a few dollars?" she laughed.

"You *know* I'll pay you back just as soon as I get a job," Thomas replied in his most believable performance of the day.

"Of course, you will!" his mother winked. "But you know that I'd give you the money anyway, right?" she smiled at him. "After all, you are *one of my favorite sons*!" After getting four crisp dollar bills from her purse and handing them to him, she asked curiously, "What do you need this money for, anyway?"

"Well," he began slowly and thoughtfully, "I just thought I would take this girl to the matinee tomorrow."

"*What girl*?" his mother surprisingly reacted very sharply. "It's not that *Maggie O'Claren* is it?" she asked suspiciously.

Thomas laughed. "No, Mom. And Maggie isn't *really crazy*! She is just one of my friends from drama class who likes to *shock* people!"

His mother chuckled. "Oh! Okay. I must say, she certainly played a very believable *lunatic* the last time I saw her!"

Thomas chuckled. "That's because her goal is to be in *movies* someday! I guess she just *never* stops practicing!"

His mother smiled. "Well, then I really do wish her luck!"

Thomas smiled back at her, and then growing more serious, he shared, "But anyway, the girl I want to go to the matinee with is named, Della Seisman. She's really nice and just moved into Masonville a few days ago."

"You mean to tell me that you've only just met this girl and already you want to take her to the *movies*?" his mom humorously feigned shock. "*That* was certainly quick?"

"I know," Thomas smiled. "But she's a *special* girl, Mom." Then his face grew thoughtful as he added warmly, "Just like *you* are."

His mother smiled broadly. "Well then, I can't wait to meet her myself very soon!"

Just then, the strident ringing of the telephone broke what had been a calm and peaceful mood. Thomas immediately dashed toward the other side of the spacious kitchen to answer it. However, moments before he could reach it, Ted (*of playing with army men fame*), had already traveled all the way from the living room to beat him to it! After picking-up the receiver and saying, "Hello?" in his most *professional* voice, Ted playfully yelled to his brother, "Thomas, *te-le-phone*," in spite of the fact that Thomas was standing *right there beside him*!

Thomas humorously rolled his eyes at his brother's antics and even smiled as he grabbed the phone from him. He thought excitedly that it must have been fate that just as soon as he and his mother had finished talking about her, here was Della *already* calling him!

"Hello?" Thomas spoke warmly into the receiver.

"Hello *jerk*!" came a brisk and angry male voice. "Now you listen here, punk! Stay away from Della Seisman, or *you'll regret it*! This is your first warning and there *won't be no second one*!"

Before Thomas even had the chance of offering a reply, the person calling slammed their receiver down… and the line went *dead*. Thomas slowly hung-up the phone, thinking hard about the disturbing threat he had just received. Had it only been some jealous kid making idle threats… or something *worse*? This dark train of thought soon gave rise to curiosity, as the phone rang once again.

Very *cautiously* this time, Thomas slowly brought the receiver to his ear, ready for *anything*. "Hello?" he asked, hesitantly.

"Hi!" replied a perky female voice.

"Della?" Thomas confirmed with relief.

"Of course!" the friendly voice shared. "I just called to let you know that I *can* go with you to the matinee tomorrow!"

"That's *great* news!" Thomas replied ecstatically. "I'll come by your house tomorrow at eleven, if that's okay?"

"That would be *perfect*!" Della agreed. "I'm really looking forward to it!"

"So am I!" Thomas shared, trying hard to contain his excitement. "Bye, Della."

"Bye, Thomas."

Both receivers hung up at *exactly* the same instant, which according to some people is a very good omen for both of their futures together, as Thomas's smile seemed to confirm. But curiously, he felt something else too. The strange sensation that *everything* was not quite as it seemed? Perhaps his feelings of uncertainty were centered around that *first* phone call? Whatever it was, he was definitely *not* going to let it put a damper on his day as he continued looking forward to his upcoming date with Della.

After doing his homework, having dinner and watching a little television, Thomas was ready for bed. It was relatively early for a Friday night, but honestly, he just wanted to fall asleep as fast as he could and wake-up to Saturday morning! He changed into his blue and white striped pajamas, turned out the light and quickly crawled into bed. But as he was lying there, he suddenly became aware of a faint *scratching* sound just outside his window? With thoughts of dangerous intruders trying to break into his house, he slowly climbed out of bed, tepidly walked over to the window, and very *alertly* looked around outside before finally building-up the courage to open it. His eyes immediately focused on his next-door neighbor's tree, with a long, thin branch which had apparently been blowing in the wind, and for some strange reason was *scratching* his window? The odd part of it was, there had often been winds blowing outside his house, even harder than this one, but the branch in question had *never* done this before? Then, upon closer examination, he noticed that the branch appeared to have been *purposely bent*, as if someone had *intentionally* wanted it to scratch his window tonight? Hah! Now his mind was just making things up! He carefully unbent the branch as best he could, closed and locked his window and crawled back into bed. Soon, he fell asleep, where he dreamt of robbers, muggers, zombies and just plain villains, while still somehow experiencing a sound sleep. The simple truth of the matter was, *all* of the bad dreams in the world would *never* be able to take away that warm and happy smile of anticipation from his face, no matter how hard they tried!

It was a sunny and cheery Saturday morning at 9:00 o'clock when Thomas's alarm clock did a *wonderful* job of waking him up, whether he *wanted* it to or not! His first instinct was to go right back to sleep, as was his usual routine on Saturday mornings. But the unmistakable sound of his brother's raucous laughter at the 'hilarious' Saturday morning animated television show he was watching in the living room (*probably either 'Alvin' or 'Bugs Bunny'*), was quite a *deterrent*! And then, at that *exact* moment, he shockingly remembered *why* he had deliberately set his alarm to go off this Saturday morning in the first place! He was supposed to take *Della to the movies*! That thought not only struck him, but it struck him like a ton of bricks!

He wasted no time in getting cleaned-up and then dressed. For his clothes, he selected his favorite combination. It was a clean pair of blue jeans with a blue striped, button-down dress shirt which was accented nicely by the tan, pullover sweater-vest he had received from his Grandma Betty for his fifteenth birthday. He had actually accumulated a number of compliments when wearing this outfit (*even if most of them were from his mother and grandma*). Ten minutes later, after a quick breakfast of cornflakes and orange juice, Thomas excitedly left his house on a mission!

He was very much aware that it was way too early to meet Della at her house, so he walked over to Masonville's one and only city park (*uncreatively named, 'Masonville City Park'*) which was not far away from it. It was a lovely place, featuring lots of healthy grass and flowers as well as a baseball field and an area for families to barbeque. He sat on a bench there for a while admiring all of the natural beauty around him. And then he spied some *beautiful* flowers that were growing nearby. 'What a *perfect* gift to give Della on our *first date*!' he thought excitedly. So, he bent down and carefully reached over a short little fence which surrounded them, and decided to pick a few, in spite of the fact that a posted sign (*which he had not read*) very clearly said, '*Don't Pick the Flowers*!' He had only picked a couple of them, before an alert policeman ran over to him and effectively convinced him (*with a stern look*) that what he was doing was actually a *very bad idea*! He further explained that there were *laws* and even *fines* levied against people who knowingly *picked these flowers*! But then, after hearing Thomas's heart-filled reason for doing it, as well as taking a good look at his *innocent-looking face*, the policeman quickly decided that he more than likely had *never heard* about that law and was just doing what young men do for their best girls, while of course, factoring-in his *obvious immaturity*. So, no ticket or fine was issued, and he was even allowed to keep both flowers he had already picked; a couple of vibrant red ones. However, the officer did leave him with a few *pointed* words of advice. Meeting his eyes kindly, he gently asked Thomas to 'please try to exercise a little more *common-sense* the next time, and be sure to *read the signs*!' With no shortage of chagrin, Thomas wholeheartedly agreed with what the policeman had said, quickly acknowledging that his picking the flowers was *definitely not* his best decision of the day! Then, with a sigh, after mentally thanking his drama class once again for teaching him to make 'timely facial expressions' to keep him from getting in trouble, he returned to the bench and sat.

Soon, according to Thomas's watch, he felt he could safely head over to Della's house without appearing to be *too* anxious. So, that's exactly what he did! Ten minutes later, after initially becoming distracted by the sight of a couple of very '*cool looking*' hotrods parked on the street, he finally reached her house. Unfortunately, Della was *not* waiting for him outside as he had hoped? So, very courageously, he walked up to her front door and knocked.

A few moments later, a small woman with short brown hair and an impish face, wearing a bright yellow dress (*who Thomas guessed to be in her late thirties or early forties*) answered the door with a severe look of suspicion. Due to that obvious *parental expression*, Thomas confidently had her pegged as being Della's aunt.

"Hello," Thomas said politely. "Is Della in?"

"Is Della *in what*?" responded the woman with a hearty laugh accompanied by triumphantly throwing her fist into the air (*apparently denoting victory*). But then, alertly seeing the boy's sudden look of confusion, she explained sheepishly, "Sorry. That was *supposed* to be a funny joke."

Remembering his good manners, Thomas forced a smile and produced a loud *guffaw*, purely for the woman's benefit. He was undoubtedly 'over-doing it,' but the woman seemed to genuinely appreciate his efforts, anyway.

"Jokes aren't so easy to tell, are they?" the woman admitted, with a wink. "I guess I'll just have to keep working at it!" And then growing very excited, she asked, "Are those two *beautiful* flowers for *me*?"

Confused and *not* knowing what to say, Thomas finally nodded affirmatively, and very uncomfortably handed them over to her.

"Thank you!" the woman said appreciatively. "I'll just go inside and put these in some water!" Then without explanation, she slammed the front-door *in his face*?

A shocked Thomas just *stood there* with his mouth gaping?

A few moments later, the door flew open to reveal the woman, now smiling, throwing her arms up in the air, exclaiming, "*Ta da*! Was *that* funny?"

Thomas couldn't help but chuckle. "Oh yes," he replied charitably. "But is Della *coming out*?"

The woman didn't say a word, but immediately ran back inside the house, politely closing the door behind her. Moments later, the door reopened, and Della stepped through it, looking absolutely *beautiful* in her cute purple and flower print dress. After saying 'goodbye' to her aunt, they began their walk to the movie theatre, which was located at the center of town.

"The two flowers you gave my aunt were *beautiful*!" she said sincerely.

"Thanks," Thomas replied uncomfortably. "But, they weren't really for her. They were supposed to be for *you*."

"I know that," Della laughed, "and so did *she*! She was just *trying* to be funny!"

Thomas laughed.

"She believes that *joking* is the best way to break the ice with people she doesn't know very well."

"That actually makes sense!" Thomas replied encouragingly, with a grin. "Has she been working at it very long?"

"*Oh yes*!" she laughed. "But I'll bet you'll agree with me that she still doesn't *quite* have the hang of it!"

Both kids laughed, and once their laughter had subsided, they simply smiled at each other and continued their very pleasant walk together.

"I know you haven't been here very long, but how do you like living in Masonville so far?" Thomas asked, attempting to keep the conversation going.

Della was quiet for a moment, and then replied hesitantly, "I *like* it… I just wish I knew more about it? Chicago, where I lived before, is such a *famous* city!"

"Don't you mean *infamous*?" Thomas smiled. "Those gangsters like Al Capone and Baby Face Nelson ruled that town for years!"

Della laughed. "Yes, I guess they did! But assuming that there are *no gangsters* in Masonville, what is this town *most famous* for?"

"Being a place that *no one's ever heard of*!" Thomas offered humorously.

Della giggled. "Anything else?"

"Well?" Thomas shared, after having a genuinely difficult time coming-up with *anything* exceptional to say about Masonville. "We usually do pretty well in the '*Apple Pie Competition*' at the County Fair."

"Really? Wow! That *is* something to be proud of!" Della grinned. "I believe it's very difficult to find *anything* tastier! I look forward to trying a piece of Masonville's apple pie very soon!"

Thomas beamed! "It *is* pretty yummy!" he declared. For once, he felt genuinely proud of his little town and its county-wide contribution to scrumptious eating! He smiled at Della for giving him this special moment and he had to agree; there wasn't *anything* in town or maybe even the *world*, more delicious than a great big slice of that apple pie! The two walked in happy silence the rest of the way to the movie theatre with visions of apple pie tantalizingly filling their heads.

Once they arrived at the majestic and ever-popular *Masonville Theatre*, there were already a lot of kids and younger teens impatiently standing in line ahead of them. So, they patiently waited their turn, and when they reached the window, although Della politely volunteered to pay for her own ticket, Thomas, insisted on purchasing *both of them*, for fifty-cents each! After entering the lobby, they stopped by the snack-bar, where Della insisted on paying for two cokes, while Thomas bought the popcorn.

"Thanks for buying the cokes," Thomas said appreciatively. "You didn't have to do that, you know?"

"I know," Della replied. "But I *wanted* to. Thanks for buying the popcorn, Thomas!"

"Sure," Thomas said, and then he proudly escorted Della inside the theatre, where they quickly decided on two seats near the center.

"I am really enjoying this!" Della declared. "It's so much fun!"

"Do you mean that '*going to the movies*' is fun?" Thomas sought clarification.

"Yes," she smiled. "But especially coming here with *you*."

As the theatre grew dark, Thomas smiled broadly at Della's last remark. As much as he wanted to more deeply *explore* that thought with her, the movie began and any hope of further conversation with Della was dashed, at least for now. As they watched the movie, something about a *magic sword*, Thomas found that he spent much more time watching *her* than he did the film! But regardless, he *didn't* feel cheated out of the price of his ticket. The second movie of the double-feature was *very* unusual, but fun. It was about an old woman who became a world-famous chef with the help of her *magical parrot* named Mikey!

After the second film had ended and it was time to leave the theatre, Thomas excitedly turned to Della and asked, "Well, how did you like the movies?"

"I *loved* them!" she exclaimed. "They were both great! The second one even made me *hungry*!" she laughed.

Thomas smiled impishly. "They have double-features here *every* Saturday afternoon, you know. *Maybe*… we can go *again* sometime?"

"That would be very nice," Della smiled.

Just then, Thomas got beaned by a crumpled-up candy box thrown from well across the theatre.

"Ow!" he shouted in annoyance as he rubbed the back of his head.

"Are you okay?" Della quickly turned to him and asked with concern.

"Yeah," Thomas replied, slightly embarrassed. "I'll bet it was just some stupid kid throwing that candy box at me as a joke."

"Not a very *funny* joke," Della observed.

"Definitely *not* one for your aunt's collection!" Thomas added, with a chuckle.

"Nope!" Della quickly joined in.

Soon they left the theatre, along with the monsoon of other young moviegoers. They waited patiently outside for the crowd to disperse before finally heading for the sidewalk. As they walked, Thomas wanted so badly to hold her hand, but quickly decided that it might appear rude of him to do that without her permission. So, he gathered together the necessary courage and nervously asked, "Would you mind if I held your hand?"

Della smiled at him in warm amusement and replied, "Did you *really* have to ask me?"

"I wanted to be sure it was okay with you first," Thomas admitted. "I would really hate to make you feel uncomfortable."

"You are such a *sweet boy*!" Della smiled, not so much as a compliment, but curiously, *analytically*?

"Thank you," Thomas replied, gently taking her hand in his, completely oblivious to the odd tone in her voice.

"Have you ever dreamed of traveling far away?" Della suddenly asked him.

"Well," he replied (*still preoccupied with holding her hand*), "someday I do hope to see more of the world outside of Masonville."

"You do?" she asked excitedly.

"Oh yes!" Thomas declared. "Once I finish school, traveling the world sounds like it would be a real adventure!"

"Do you *like* adventures?" Della asked him pointedly.

Thomas thought for a moment before replying, "I can't remember *ever* actually having one?" he laughed. "But I believe that I *would* like it if I someday got the chance."

"Perhaps you'll get that chance *sooner* than you think?" Della suggested mysteriously.

But before Thomas could respond, he very alertly veered sharply to his left, lightly brushing Della's head with his, as he just did get out of the way of a low-flying apple core! The renegade missile had been on target to make *direct contact* with his head!

"Who threw that?" Thomas yelled, clearly expressing both shock and anger to anyone who could hear him. And then momentarily letting go of her hand, he abruptly turned toward Della and added very apologetically, "I'm so sorry that I bumped your head!"

"Oh, that's okay," she assured him. Then she asked curiously, "Who do you think threw that?"

"I've got a pretty good idea of who it *might* be," he shared, with his voice much more under control. "But I really don't want to think about that right now." Then greedily retaking her hand in his, he shared with a mysterious smile, "I'd much rather think about something else."

Della had no idea what he was referring to as 'something else,' but she had no trouble smiling back at him as they continued their leisurely walk home. Thankfully, they had no further disruptions along the way. Suddenly, Della realized that Thomas had taken her on a completely different route than the one they had taken to the theatre? This route ended-up at '*Masonville's Pie and Ice Cream Parlor*?' Like the city park, this was not a terribly creative name for the establishment, but to kids, if you had the words, '*ice cream*' appearing anywhere in the title… that was *all* you needed!

"So, *this* is what you meant by '*something else*?'" Della exclaimed in jubilant surprise. "But what are we doing here?"

Smiling broadly, Thomas replied, "Well, after talking together earlier and hearing you say that you felt hungry, I thought you *might* like to share a little snack here with me?"

"You guessed correctly!" Della laughed.

They quickly walked inside and were immediately led to a table beside the window by a friendly waitress named Stella. When she asked for their order, Thomas quite predictably ordered them each a hearty slice of '*Masonville's famous Blue-Ribbon Apple Pie ala mode*!' As soon as their generously filled plates arrived, both kids lost no time devouring their treats as if there was no tomorrow!

"What inspired you to bring me to such a perfect place? This apple pie tastes even *better* than you said it would! It's simply *delicious*!" Della gushed, and then joked with a smile, "You didn't even feel the need to *ask me first* before ordering it!"

Thomas returned her smile and replied confidently, "Well, after you agreed to hold my hand, I pretty much had you pegged as someone who appreciated the *finer things* in life."

Both of them laughed heartily at Thomas's little joke, although Della's eyes were far away, strangely full of a certain look denoting… *confirmation*! Thomas didn't notice *that* however. He was too busy having a wonderful time! But sadly, it wasn't long before they finished eating. To be honest? Neither one of them left so much as *a crumb* on their plate! Thomas used the last of his money to pay the bill and the tip, and then he silently thanked his mother's generosity for making this *perfect* date possible! And then once again, they found themselves walking together along the sidewalk. This time however, they actually *were* heading back toward Della's house.

"Thomas?" Della asked sweetly.

"Yes, Della?"

"I never really explained to you how my parents died. Would it be all right if I told you now?"

Thomas was genuinely surprised by her question? After having such a wonderful time together, a very serious topic like *that one* didn't really seem to belong in their conversation? In fact, it seemed to be coming from the outermost part of left field? Maybe even the *bleachers*? Truth be told, it also made him feel a little uncomfortable, but he quickly replied, "Of course. As long as you really *want* to share that with me?"

"I do," she responded sincerely. "I think I would feel much better with you knowing."

"Okay," Thomas agreed warmly.

Della smiled. "To begin with, my parents both worked for the same English school that I attended," she began. "They came over here from England a couple of years ago, as they did *every* year, to seek out some possible exchange students to attend it. But soon after arriving, they were tragically killed in a freak car accident. *That's it*! So, to honor their memories, I decided to come here myself… as an *exchange* student."

"And I'm so happy that you did," Thomas replied gently. "Although I am very sorry for the reason."

"Thank you, Thomas," Della replied gratefully. Then her demeanor suddenly grew a little anxious as she added, "There's something *else* that's actually very important to me that I *meant* to speak with you about earlier… before *losing* my nerve," she laughed uncomfortably. "We can discuss it now if you promise to at least *try* to believe me?"

"Of course! You *know* I'll believe you!" he replied encouragingly. "You can tell me *anything*."

Della sighed in relief. "That's what I'd *hoped* you'd say," she smiled. "Okay, here goes. I'm not actually from around here."

"I know," Thomas chuckled. "You already told me that you're from England."

"Yes, I did! And that is *completely* true!" Della assured him with a strained expression slowly appearing across her face. "But I'm not from the *country* of England... I'm from the *planet* England."

"What?!" Thomas was very quickly caught between shock and laughter, but unfortunately, he found himself leaning a lot more heavily toward *shock*!

"You see, Thomas, I'm just like every other foreign exchange student on this planet, with the very *minor* exception that I'm *not* from Earth."

Thomas was now seeing a completely different side of Della that he had never imagined was even possible? Over these past couple of days, she had seemed so normal, never acting overly dramatic or shocking like his drama friend, *Maggie O'Claren*. In direct contrast, she had been very much down to Earth... *until now*! So, he was having real trouble deciding if she was joking, or was *100% certifiably insane*?

"Please believe me, Thomas! I'm *not* making any of this up. I swear to you!" Della was almost in tears as she exhibited what he believed to be a deep sincerity.

He had to admit that her performance was far superior to *anything* he had seen in his drama class over the past years. And it was ultimately *this*, more than anything else, that finally convinced him that she *must* be telling the truth! "Alright," Thomas replied calmly. "Let's just say that what you've said is *somehow* true. Why are you telling *me*?"

Della smiled appreciatively as she pulled herself together. "I'm telling you because I *like* you, Thomas. And I want our relationship to be honest," she added earnestly.

Thomas suddenly felt ecstatic as he heard the words, '*like*' and '*relationship*,' gently fall from her lips. He was sincerely touched. By this time, they had arrived at the front of her house, but Della *wasn't* ready to go in, nor was Thomas ready to let her. "Why don't you tell me more about your planet?" he suggested eagerly.

Della smiled happily, "Okay. England is a planet far beyond your solar system, but in the same galaxy. On my planet, although we may look exactly like you and breathe the same type of air, we are *far more advanced* in many ways."

In *which* ways?" Thomas asked curiously.

"Well?" Della thought for a moment. "For example, I can travel to your planet from mine in complete safety and comfort in less time than it takes you to walk to school."

"Wow! That's incredible!" Thomas exclaimed. And then with a distorted face, clearly revealing his confusion, he asked, "But of all the towns and cities on Earth, what could have possibly *possessed* you to choose *Masonville*?"

Della laughed. "To tell you the truth, originally *I didn't*! As I told you, I first went to live in Chicago with my aunt, but I found the school there to be, as you suggested, *a bit too exciting* for my taste!" she smiled. Growing more serious, she added, "That's why we came here. Masonville has a *sweetness* about it that we were searching for on Earth. So, ultimately, we decided to give it a try."

"A *sweetness*?" Thomas asked in surprise.

"Yes. Most of the people I've met here seem nice, Masonville's lifestyle is easy-going and unrushed," she explained calmly, "but most of all, after living in Chicago, this town seems *refreshingly* naïve."

"*Naïve*?" Thomas said with confusion.

Once again, Della laughed. "Yes, Thomas. From our studies of Earth, there seemed to be a lot of dissatisfaction in many of your larger cities that turned into anger and violence, so we decided to investigate its smaller towns to find a *gentler* way of life. Although no place is without some dissatisfaction, Masonville just seemed to focus more on the positives, so that led us here!"

"But how did you learn so much about Earth and its people while being so far away?" Thomas asked.

Della broke into happy laughter. "Thomas, many years ago my planet was in the exact same stage of growth that yours is in *now*! We understand Earth *very well*. As a matter of fact, we have the interest and the means to study *all* of the inhabited planets for lightyears around. Earth was one of the few planets we found that was somewhat civilized, and where the inhabitants looked *strikingly* similar to us! So, for a number of years now, foreign exchange students, like me, have been sent here to live amongst you for a short while. We then take what we learn about your school curriculum and civilization and share it with our planet's leaders, who update our official knowledge of Earth, accordingly."

"But *why* do you even bother?" Thomas asked incredulously. "You said that your planet was already so much *more advanced* than Earth?"

"That's just it. We *aren't* more advanced in *every* way," Della conceded mysteriously. "Our greatest differences are what we are trying to study the most."

"How is it that you speak our language so perfectly if you are from another planet?" Thomas asked curiously. "Does the planet England speak *English* just like we do?"

Della chuckled. "No, Thomas," she replied with a smile. "Over the years our people have created a language that is actually a combination of *all* known languages. So, we can speak to anyone, anywhere, whose language is *familiar* to us, with complete and mutual comprehension."

Thomas was speechless! He realized that as unbelievable as that sounded, if he was to trust Della, and he really *wanted* to, then everything she was telling him *had* to be the truth? But it was all so fantastic? In fact, probably the *most troubling* thing for him to accept right now was the fact that this girl named Della Seisman, whom he *thought* he was beginning to know, he *didn't* really know at all?

"Thomas," she said, waking him from his self-induced trance, "I am *not* a lot different from you, really. And I like you very much. I think in many ways… you are perfect."

With that last word, she had once again claimed Thomas's *full* attention! "*Perfect?*" he repeated with excitement.

"Yes! You are *perfect* to be a *foreign exchange student* on England, while I am one here on Earth!" she shared joyously.

"*What*?!" Thomas exclaimed in surprise and fierce disappointment. He hadn't known where Della's astonishing story would ultimately end-up, but he had just assumed that it would be someplace where the two of them would at least be *together*? "I don't want to go to your planet! I like it here!" he soundly rejected her offer.

Della frowned understandingly at him and calmly replied, "Well, I like it on *my* planet too, but sometimes a little change in our lives is good for us."

"Not when it's *billions* of miles away!" Thomas passionately insisted.

"But remember, Thomas," she explained gently, "you would only be there as a visitor for a short time, while I am here. You would be returned home in no time!"

"I'm *not* going!" Thomas insisted hotly.

"You do understand that in order for me to be an exchange student *here*, I must exchange places with someone suitable from Earth?" she added gently, gazing pleadingly into his eyes.

"*Suitable*? Is that all I am to you? I understand *completely* what you're asking me to do, and the answer is *still, no*!" Thomas replied flatly. "I'm going to stay right here and that's final! Try to get some other chump to go!" He then softened his tone as he shared, "Before you told me any of this, I had thought you were such a nice girl. Someone who I would love to be friends with. Maybe even *more* than friends? But I couldn't have been more wrong! I'm nothing more to you than a *ticket* allowing you to spend time on Earth!"

Della suddenly looked very sad, causing Thomas to immediately begin to feel sorry for her. But even so, he felt *completely* justified in his blistering assessment of her insane offer. The fact was that today after unexpectedly talking with what appeared to be *two completely different girls* with the same name, the same body, and the same voice, he now found himself wondering who the *real Della Seisman* really was?

"Okay then," Della sighed dejectedly, as she had apparently resigned herself to accepting Thomas's decision. "*Don't* go to England as a foreign exchange student, but just know that you'll be missing out on the *chance of a lifetime*!"

Thomas shrugged his shoulders as if to say, '*Who cares*,' and then… their conversation abruptly *stopped*. Finally, after a very uncomfortable pause, Thomas opted to speak first. "I'm sorry if I upset you, Della. That's just how I feel about it. No hard feelings?"

Della smiled sweetly and replied, "No, of course not. I respect your honesty." After a short pause, she added, "But won't you come inside to visit with my aunt and me for a few minutes?"

Thomas grew a little suspicious, but after looking at the beautiful girl with the very hopeful expression on her face, he reluctantly replied, "Okay." Della immediately opened the door and politely motioned for him to enter the house ahead of her. Once inside, he heard the sharp sound of the door closing behind them, causing him to momentarily *second guess* his decision? But he kept walking away from the front door anyway. He really *needed* to believe that he could trust Della, and he saw this as the quickest way of achieving that.

Della soon joined Thomas in the sitting room, where she offered him and he accepted a seat on a stunningly vibrant *neon blue* sofa. She quickly seated herself on a white wingback chair that was set directly across from it. As Thomas glanced around the room, he was quick to notice that it had been very nicely furnished with popular furniture that he had recently seen advertised in magazines and on television! In fact, if those ads and commercials were to be believed, these were some of the *most popular* styles and colors of 1962 America!

"Your aunt has *great taste* in furniture," Thomas commented politely.

"Thank you!" her aunt smiled appreciatively as she unexpectedly entered the room from behind him, and joined Thomas on the couch. "I try to keep this house as up-to-date as possible."

"Did you study decorating then?" Thomas inquired politely.

"Oh no! I just *watch* a lot of television," she admitted with a wink.

"Auntie," Della interjected. "You met Thomas this morning, didn't you?"

"Oh yes! Of course," she replied (*with a twinkle in her eye*), "but it was only at the front door." Turning directly toward Thomas, she added with a smile, "I look forward to conversing with you properly!"

"Me too," Thomas replied.

"You may call me Jacqueline, if you wish," Della's aunt suggested as she met his eyes.

"Alright," Thomas agreed. "Hello, *Jacqueline*! You know, that's the name of our First Lady!"

"I know," she responded proudly. "That's *why* I chose it."

"Auntie, Thomas has decided *not* to accept our invitation to visit England," Della shared disappointedly.

"Oh! That is unfortunate," her Aunt Jacqueline responded gloomily. "Why don't you want to visit England, Thomas?"

"Are you afraid of having trouble making friends on a different planet?" Della asked with empathy.

"Maybe a little bit," he replied sincerely, "but that's *not* the main reason."

"Are you afraid of leaving your parents and everybody else behind with *no explanation*?" her aunt pressed him.

"Well, partially," he readily admitted. "They'd be devastated! They'd probably think that I'd been kidnapped... or *worse*!"

"Now don't worry about that," she calmly consoled him. "We have foolproof methods of making sure that *never* happens!"

That surely sounded better to Thomas, but he still responded by shaking his head, an emphatic, *no*!

"Alright then, what *is* your main reason for not accepting our offer?" Della finally asked.

"Well, to tell you the truth, it just came so quickly and unexpectedly," he replied honestly. "I haven't had any time to even think about it?"

"Would you like to '*think about it*' for a week before we ask you again?" Della's Aunt Jacqueline asked hopefully.

Thomas quickly considered her offer and decided that it sounded fair. It still allowed him to say *no,* at the end of a week if he so chose, and in addition, it guaranteed him *seven more days with Della*! "You've got yourself a deal!" he agreed.

"*Alright*!" Della exclaimed.

Almost immediately there came a very rude and persistent knocking at the front door. With an honest expression of, '*Who* could that be?' Della immediately rose from her chair and walked over to answer it.

"Hello?" she uttered in surprise as she opened it. "I remember seeing you at school, but I'm sorry… I never learned your name?"

"Yeah? Well, Hi!" replied a husky boy with dark hair and a grating voice. "The name is Joe Porter, and I stopped by to ask if you'd go to the movies with me next week? Here are some roses I brung ya," he added, handing her an *actual* branch from a rose bush with a few fully blossomed flowers on it.

"Th… Thanks," Della forced a smile as she politely accepted the branch, while very carefully avoiding the thorns. "But I'm afraid that I *can't* go out with you, Joe," she said regretfully. "I'm already going out with someone else."

"*Thomas McAdams*?" he growled.

"Y… Yes," she stammered, suddenly feeling a bit uneasy.

"I *warned* him!" Joe bellowed, as he quickly became livid. "Where is he?" Without waiting for a response, he abruptly steered past Della and hastily entered the living room, where he *immediately* spied Thomas and Aunt Jacqueline looking very concerned, as they sat together on the sofa. Ignoring both Della and her aunt, Joe determinedly approached Thomas, and demanded, "Get up you *loser*, so we can *fight*!"

"Forget it!" Thomas surprised himself by his confident response. "I *don't* fight in front of women. And anyway, it wouldn't settle anything."

Although Joe *appeared* to calm down a bit, Thomas *wasn't* completely convinced? Beneath what he believed to be a show of *false serenity* in the eyes of the formerly angry boy, he believed was a great deal of *molten anger*, just waiting to *erupt*! "Didn't my phone call or scratching on your window last night teach you anything at all, punk?" Joe sneered with threatening undertones.

"I guess not," Thomas replied with cool confidence. "I suppose the candy box and apple core that were thrown at me today were also '*gifts*' from you?"

Joe laughed without smiling. "You got it! Now you *stay away* from my girl, *or else*!"

"*Your girl*?" Thomas repeated in shock.

"*Your girl*?" both Della and her aunt screamed *simultaneously*, while looking at each other in bewilderment.

"Yeah," Joe announced proudly. "I never had me a real live girl of my own, and now I want one!" He abruptly turned toward Della and proclaimed to her (*with about as much tenderness as a Doberman Pincer*), "And *you're* it!" Then he angrily faced Thomas with an infuriated expression that defied sanity, and seethed, "Now I'm gonna *really* teach you to stay away from my girl!"

Joe's insane level of rage caught Thomas *completely* by surprise, as he quickly realized that there was absolutely *no chance* he'd be able to fast-talk his way out of this one! As the husky boy raced toward him, Thomas did the first thing that came to mind… *he ran away*! He spied a door directly in his path, and not caring where it led as long as it was away from *him*, he quickly opened it, ran inside, and immediately slammed the door shut behind him! The room he'd entered was a very neatly made-up bedroom painted bright yellow and green, but he had *no time* to admire it further, as Joe *crashed* through the door right behind him, mumbling every obscenity known to man! Once again, Thomas opened the door directly in front of him and ran straight through it, while *also* once again slamming the door behind him (*hoping to slow Joe down*). This time he had walked into a hallway which featured *five* different doors? With Joe only moments away from catching him, he chose to enter the door that was closest to him on the left. Looking around, he immediately recognized this book-filled room as being a library. Unfortunately, aside from the door he had entered from, there appeared to be *no other exit*! So, he quickly hid in a far corner, hoping beyond hope that if Joe came in… he would somehow *not* see him. Alas, this had apparently been wishful thinking as only moments later, Joe stormed into the room and easily spotted him within seconds!

"Is that the *best* you can do?" Joe was almost salivating as he had found his prey so easily. "Now you die!"

I know that Joe's eloquent words, '*Now you die*,' would generally be interpreted as a simple metaphor for expressing the passing of dislike from the lips of hateful bullies to the ears of genuinely nice people (*like Thomas*), and in most cases should certainly *not* be taken literally. But in *this* case, there was absolutely *nothing metaphorical about it*! Thomas felt uncontrollable shivers of intense fear chaotically shooting up and down his young spine! Still, he was determined to escape the thorough thrashing he would undoubtedly receive at the hands of Joe Porter if he *didn't* do something miraculous… like *now*! Just as soon as Joe moved a step toward him, Thomas picked up a random book from the shelves, which happened to be a first edition hardback copy (*published just a few years earlier*) of Robert Heinlein's science-fiction classic, '*Have Spacesuit Will Travel*,' and immediately wound-up to throw it. Joe was decidedly caught off-guard by Thomas's *feeble* attempt to defend himself, but he quickly adjusted. Just as Thomas threw the book at him, Joe '*cleverly*' stepped aside to avoid contact (*as Thomas had hoped he would*). That minor movement created *exactly* enough space for young Thomas's wiry body to dart past the much larger boy and escape through the door!

Finding himself alone in the hallway once again, Thomas felt disoriented from all of his running around? He was uncertain *which door* led back to the living room, on to the front door and finally *outside to safety*? With Joe undoubtedly right behind him, he was *incredibly relieved* to momentarily hear Della's sweet voice, like an oasis in the desert.

"Come in *here*!" she frantically urged him. "You can hide in that large crate over there!"

Thomas was more than happy to oblige, as he quickly did exactly what Della had suggested, and hid in a crate in a room across the hall! After a long moment of waiting, he heard no sign of Joe, which made him inadvertently sigh with relief. "Is the coast clear?" he whispered to Della, who was also in the room.

"*Stay* in the crate!" was the only response he received from her.

To tell you the truth, Thomas didn't actually understand *why* she had said that? Was it a warning that Joe was still nearby, or what? Growing impatient, he was just about ready to climb out, when all of a sudden he heard an unusually *high-pitched whizzing* sound all around him, and was *instantly* thrown tight against the back of the crate!

When he finally caught hold of his senses, Thomas found himself still lying in the large brown crate, about the size of a wooden box that had been built to house an extra-large refrigerator, *hurling through space* at a super-fantastic speed! The crazy thing was that he felt perfectly comfortable inside? He soon discovered that there was some *invisible force* that curiously did not keep him from moving around within the crate, yet it prevented him from falling out or being indiscriminately thrown about? Also, somehow the air that he breathed and the comfortable temperature that was all around him stayed remarkably intact? The bottom of the crate also felt comfortably padded, although curiously, to look at it, all one saw were hard wooden slats? As he laid there, he attempted to gaze out into space from the curiously *non-covered* top-side of the crate, but the stars and planets moved by him so quickly, he found that it made him dizzy? He had *never* experienced anything even *remotely* similar to this in his entire life! How could he have? Basically except for a fifteen-minute space flight by astronaut Alan Shepard last year and a recent five hour long orbiting of the Earth by astronaut John Glenn, he had absolutely *no* real knowledge of space travel? Maybe manned spaceships regularly hurtling through space *didn't* exactly seem like fantasy anymore, but they still felt like a thing of the *far distant future*… especially when that spaceship was traveling *billions* of miles away and happened to be in the form of an *uncovered crate*! He knew that he was heading toward a mysterious planet in another solar system and that thought alone was *mind-numbing*! There was no doubt that this was all *truly fantastic*… but at the same time… he was *furious*! How had he allowed Della (*the girl he 'sort of loved')* to lure him into this trap? Then all at once he became genuinely frightened! Where was he going? What would it be like there? What would happen to him once he arrived? As Franklin Delano Roosevelt, a revered former President of the United States had once said, "*The only thing we have to fear is fear itself.*" Although this may have been true back when he had said it, this was ***1962***, and the unknowns attached to Thomas's future destination were things that *no* famous lines from former presidents could help him with now! So, choosing the way of the ostrich (*burying his head in the sand to ignore this unpleasant* *situation and hoping that it would just go away)*, he made himself comfortable, closed his eyes, and tried to relax as best he could for the remainder of the flight.

In no time at all, Thomas felt his crate quickly but smoothly slowing down. In the next moment, he felt a very slight bounce as it landed. Then, very tentatively, he stepped out of the crate and onto a platform which towered about 20 feet above the ground. Looking around, he immediately realized with surprise that he and the crate were the *only things* on this platform? Below him were a lot of men and women diligently working in front of a variety of complex-looking machines. Everything seemed to be enclosed in what appeared to be a very large building, similar in its openness to an airplane hangar? He wondered how his crate had gotten into such a closed-up building in the first place? But he inadvertently stopped thinking about that just as soon as he saw something even *stranger*? He simply could not believe his eyes? He watched the ordinary-looking white walls throughout the building's interior, appear to be rhythmically *breathing in and out*? He seriously wondered if the fact that there were *no pictures* attached to any of those walls meant that unlike Earth, walls here were *living creatures*? Where exactly was he?

And then, thankfully, in answer to his last question, from twenty feet below, a vibrant voice announced, "*Welcome to England*! You are now in one of our 'Import-Export Buildings,' where people both arrive and depart all day long. You must be the boy our exchange student on Earth told us about. Come on down, Thomas."

Thomas forced a smile as he finally identified the location of the man who was speaking to him. But looking around anxiously, he *couldn't* find any stairs, escalator or elevator leading down from the platform to the floor? This seemed to create a *huge* problem for him?

As soon as the man realized his dilemma, he shouted to Thomas, "Jump!"

"*Jump*?" Thomas asked incredulously.

The man chuckled. "*Everyone* who is inside this building, including yourself," he smiled, "for the entire duration that they are in it are automatically equipped with *reduced gravity* when they jump. This allows each of us to efficiently travel up to elevated platforms or down from them with ease, comfort, and in complete safety."

Thomas hesitantly looked down from the ramp and his legs began to buckle. As he saw it, following the man's instructions would require a huge 'leap of faith,' *literally*! So, finding the courage (*or the insanity*) somewhere… closing his eyes… he *jumped*! He immediately found himself screaming with delight like a small child being tossed into the air and then being gently caught by their parent, effectively experiencing the thrill of *weightlessness*! As he opened his eyes, he grinned from ear to ear as he gently floated down to the floor. As soon as he'd reached the bottom, he pinched himself to make sure that he was awake? Confirming that he was, he then faced the man belonging to the voice. The man was of medium height and build, with a darker skin tone than his own, wearing a white lab coat and sporting a great big smile. He immediately greeted Thomas in a friendly but nonchalant manner, as if floating down from a 20-foot-high platform was normal? But of course here, it *apparently* was?

"Hello!" the man greeted Thomas with a friendly, yet professional smile.

"Hello," Thomas replied hesitantly. "I didn't really *mean* to come to England. Is there any way I could return to Earth right away?"

"Oh my!" the man responded in bewilderment, appearing to grow very concerned. "Don't you *want* to visit England first? Not even for a little while?"

"Well," Thomas replied, remembering his manners and trying hard not to offend the man, "I'm very sorry, but my parents and brother on Earth have all been captured by an evil wizard, and they need someone to free them immediately with a magic sword!" he shared dramatically (*borrowing a little from the first movie he and Della had watched at the matinee*). He then added disappointedly, "I'm afraid that I'm the *only* one who can wield that sword, so I suppose I had better go back home right away! I'm so sorry for the mix-up."

"Oh, is *that* all!" the man surprisingly exhaled in relief. "Our exchange student on Earth is top-notch. I'll have her take care of that little problem for you right away."

"*Never mind*!" Thomas exclaimed loudly, as he quickly stopped the man from taking action. Then speaking with complete sarcasm, he added, "I just remembered that my eight-year-old brother, Ted, chased away that evil wizard using a battalion of his bravest toy soldiers just after breakfast this morning."

"Splendid! Then everything's fine now, isn't it!" The man announced excitedly (*oblivious to Thomas' sarcasm*). "So, I guess you'll be staying with us for a while after all?"

"It certainly looks that way," Thomas disappointedly agreed, dejectedly resigning himself to his fate. "By the way," he asked very curiously. "Why do all of the walls in this building breathe in and out?" Then he added with apprehension, "Are they *alive*?"

The man laughed. "No, Thomas! They are certainly *not* alive! But in answer to your first question, the long explanation involves the understanding of *PPT*, or '*Perpetual Power Technology*,' created by England's ancestors a long time ago, which I'm afraid *I don't* fully understand myself? But the *short answer* is that the walls effortlessly and efficiently create *all* of the power necessary to run everything in this building, as well as the power needed to launch and receive spacecrafts like the one you just arrived in," the man explained knowingly. "Believe me, it's much easier to just accept *that* explanation than wasting another moment trying to understand the other one!"

Thomas was overwhelmed. "Wow!"

The man smiled. "Would you be interested in seeing where you'll be staying?"

"I *would*, actually," Thomas perked-up, surprisingly feeling just a little bit excited.

"Outstanding!" the man replied happily. "Please follow me."

The man quickly led Thomas through a myriad of doors, each one leading to a different room. Each room was filled with breathing walls and a variety of machines which were closely attended to by their operators. But eventually, they left all of that behind them and reached a very large picture window. Looking through it, Thomas finally saw what England looked like *outside*!

Pointing excitedly at a high-rise building, not too far from where they now stood, the man announced, "*There's* your hotel, Thomas! The *Eternal Sunshine*! Isn't she a beauty?"

Thomas had to admit that the building was indeed beautiful! A tall and sleek structure that *appeared* to be constructed of reflective metal and glass, ascending many stories into the sky. The place had a bit of an *odd* name? But, as William Shakespeare had famously said, '*What's in a name*?' Then again, prolific writer or not, to his knowledge William Shakespeare had *never* lived on the *planet* England! As he gazed across the horizon, except for the red sun, curiously this planet didn't *really* seem much different from Earth? There was however one *major difference* that was not too difficult to recognize. This planet had *far superior scientific knowlege*, as demonstrated by all of the technology used in getting him here in the first place! It was truly fantastic!

"Shall we check you in?" the man offered helpfully.

"Sure!" Thomas replied with enthusiasm.

The very next thing the man did was to take a small black box from the inside pocket of his lab coat, push a button and *voila*! They were instantly standing in the first-floor lobby of the Eternal Sunshine Hotel.

"*What* did you just do? How did we get here?" Thomas asked incredulously.

The man laughed. "It's just a matter of science, Thomas. We adjust the time and space continuum to cater to our wishes. It makes life so much *more* efficient."

"Is that how I traveled through space so quickly to get here?" Thomas queried.

The man smiled. "Basically… with just a few other little *modifications* we have picked-up over the years."

Suddenly, Thomas had a flash of brilliance. "Hey! Do you suppose that anyone on Earth who watched me blasting off has *reported it* to the authorities? My departure must have created quite a stir in town, eh?" Thomas suggested intently.

"No," the man gently replied with a smile.

"No? But *why not*?" Thomas asked in shock.

"Because you and your craft were completely invisible and undetectable from take-off, up until the time you left the Earth's atmosphere," the man calmly explained. "I believe your scientists on Earth would call that, 'going out under the radar.'"

"But how is that even possible?" Thomas exclaimed.

"A little scientific knowledge we once came across," the man winked.

Thomas didn't know what to say? So, as his father had so wisely taught him many years before… when in doubt… *don't say anything*!

Next, they traveled up an ordinary elevator, walked out into an ordinary hallway where the man gave him an ordinary key, which opened the door to his ordinary room, and then said, "If you need anything else, anything at all… just ask."

But before Thomas had the chance to ask the plethora of questions that he had amassed since his arrival to this planet, the man had *completely vanished*? Once he had gotten past the momentary shock of watching someone suddenly *disappear* before his very eyes, he carefully perused his room. Much of it reassuringly reminded him of what a nice hotel room might look like back home. But very oddly, it appeared to be well lit, with *no* visible sign of light-fixtures anywhere? Looking around further, he was again surprised to find absolutely *no* on and off switches or electric sockets? And then, *shockingly*, he realized that the light in the room was actually *coming from the walls*? In fact, the walls were *glowing*? He very hesitantly touched one of them and was immediately surprised to discover that if the wall *was* just one big lightbulb, as he had reasoned it was, it was *not* even warm to touch? In fact, to be perfectly honest, it felt *like an ordinary wall*? And if that wasn't enough, when he entered the bathroom, it looked *vastly different* from what he was used to? To begin with, there was *no toilet*? He was not only dumfounded by this, but also *horrified*! Were these people *crazy*? What would he possibly do when *nature called*? And another thing. While there *was* a sink and an attached cabinet with all of the regularly needed toiletries, the apparent shower was merely a large chain-link cage with enough room to stand in, but showing absolutely *no* visible controls? He immediately voiced his frustration by yelling in exasperation, "How does this *stupid* bathroom work?"

There was an immediate knock at his door. When Thomas opened it, a *different* smiling man in a white lab coat entered.

The man gazed kindly at Thomas, as if empathizing with his anxiety. "These bathrooms are a bit tricky for most of our exchange students to initially understand and navigate," he explained calmly. "So, let me just show you." Immediately he led Thomas back into the bathroom. "There is *no* toilet because it is completely *unnecessary* here. You see, the air on our planet automatically dissolves all of our liquid and solid body waste internally, odorlessly sending it out of our bodies as a gas and into the atmosphere, where it is then destroyed by the rays of our red sun. You will never have the urge to defecate or urinate again as long as you live on this planet. In addition, to be more efficient, our air *naturally* supplies our bodies with all of the hydration it needs to survive comfortably. Therefore, the drinking of water is fine… but *completely* unnecessary." The man stopped just in case Thomas had any questions, but hearing none… he continued. "The shower automatically turns-on every time you step inside and turns-off once you leave. It completely cleans you from head to toe, along with freshening up your clothes. In addition, you will have *no need* to ever use soap or shampoo while taking a shower here."

Although Thomas was extremely surprised to hear about the absence of soap and shampoo while taking a shower, something *else* the man had said bothered him *even more*! "Do you mean to tell me that we are expected to take our showers *with our clothes on*?" he asked incredulously.

The man chuckled at Thomas's reaction. "This is always the hardest thing for our exchange students to accept," he shared. And then smiling, he confirmed, "But *yes*!"

"What about controlling the hot and cold temperatures of the water?" Thomas exclaimed. "How do I do that?"

"Once inside, you just tell the shower to get hotter or colder if you wish," the man explained. "But generally speaking, I have always found these showers to be at the *perfect* temperature!"

"What temperature is that?" Thomas asked.

"I really *couldn't* say? Everyone's preference tends to be a little different," the man explained knowingly.

"You mean to tell me that the shower just *knows* the temperature that I would want the water to be at?" Thomas asked in disbelief.

"Please step inside," the man gently urged him in response to his question.

"No!"

"Don't be afraid, Thomas," the man smiled good-naturedly. "Stepping inside is the quickest way for you to learn how to use this shower."

Begrudgingly, Thomas agreed to try it. He slowly stepped inside the chain link cage and immediately felt a soothing mist penetrating his clothes and covering his entire body! A minute later, the mist stopped just as soon as he had stepped out, *completely refreshed…* and *dry*? In addition, as he looked at himself in the mirror above the sink, he immediately noticed that his hair, which he'd fastidiously combed this morning, *still* mysteriously looked the same as it had *before* he had stepped inside the shower cage? He could have sworn that he had made a point of going through the motions of washing his hair in the shower, *regardless* of the fact that there was no visible shampoo to use?

As if reading his mind, the man chuckled, "It's *not* magic, Thomas. This shower has a memory feature which ensures that you will step-out looking exactly the same as you did when you stepped in… only *cleaner*."

Thomas couldn't believe it. "That's incredible!" he raved. "That was the greatest shower experience I've *ever* had!" Then growing thoughtful, he asked, "But do we have to shower with our clothes *on*?"

The man laughed once again. "You certainly don't *have to*, but this allows you to wear the same clothes indefinitely without ever having to wash them. It's *highly* efficient!"

Thomas smiled, but he was actually thinking about how much more he enjoyed putting on *different* clothes each day, even though they had to be washed in the traditional manner, usually after each wearing. 'Some things, even though they were less efficient,' he thought, 'were just part of who he was!'

"And finally," the man shared, "I should probably tell you about that telephone on the table over there."

Thomas had noticed it when he'd first looked around the room, but he hadn't really given it much thought. One would expect to find a telephone in a hotel room back home. And then it dawned on him… this was *definitely not* back home!

"That telephone allows you to listen-in on your loved ones, hopefully reassuring you that they are doing well," explained the man. "Most of our other exchange students have found using this to be a very effective way of keeping them from getting too homesick while they are away."

"Thank you for taking the time to explain everything to me," Thomas shared graciously. And then suddenly noticing that the phone had *no dial*, he quickly asked, "But how do I dial the numbers of the people I wish to hear?"

The man very patiently replied, "Just ask."

"What?" Thomas clearly recalled hearing that very same instruction from the first man, which had resulted in no more sense *that* time than it did *this* time? "Would you mind *elaborating* on that?"

"Not at all," the man smiled. "Simply say the name of the person you wish to connect with… the phone will ring… pick it up… and then you will hear them speaking."

"That sounds simple enough," Thomas laughed, but then he excitedly asked, "Do we also have the ability to *speak with them*?"

"Unfortunately, *not*!" the man replied firmly, with a patented but *sincerely* empathetic expression on his face. "The Powers felt that speaking with your loved ones might potentially be a serious obstacle to each student's ability to successfully acclimate to this school and planet."

"*The Powers*?" Thomas asked curiously.

"The *leaders* of the school," the man explained. "Do you have any other questions, Thomas?"

"No, but thanks again for helping me out," he shared gratefully.

"Of course," the man replied. "And should you have any further questions…"

"*Just ask*?" Thomas ended his sentence with an impish smile.

"Exactly!" the man confirmed. "Ta-ta for now!" Then taking out a small black box from his coat pocket which was *identical* to the box taken out by the first man, he pushed a button and instantly disappeared.

This high-tech magic would have surely shocked and possibly even *terrified* Thomas just a few hours ago while he was still living on Earth, but *here*… he found himself actually getting used to it? So, he decided to try-out his one-way *intragalactic telephone*. "I want to call *my family*!" he declared loudly. A moment later, the phone rang. He excitedly picked up the telephone receiver, put it to his ear and listened. There was no phone ringing on the other end, but he instantly heard his family talking anyway. He listened very intently.

"So, what do *you* think about it, Ernie?" his mother asked.

"Well, Ruth," his father quickly responded, "I suppose that if Thomas *wants* to be an exchange-student in England, as we have apparently already agreed to on this paperwork with our signatures on it, it's okay by me. The only part of this I don't understand is *why* he didn't remind us about the date of his departure? On the other hand, maybe he did? Silly me! I seem to have completely forgotten all about this whole thing? It's just that I would have liked to have said *goodbye* to him?"

His mother quickly replied, "Well, you know how impetuous these teenagers can be… *especially* Thomas!" she laughed. "He was probably just so excited about going, that saying 'goodbye' simply slipped his mind."

"You're probably right," his father concurred, "But it certainly helped us to understand everything better when that sweet Della Seisman came by the house earlier today to explain it all to us."

"Yes, and just as she told us, this is a 'once in a lifetime opportunity' for Thomas!" his mother confirmed. "It's too bad the students aren't allowed to call or write though?"

"Yes, but as Della explained," his father replied knowingly, "it really makes them *appreciate* their families that much more when they return home."

"But who will I play with?" Ted asked, with great concern.

Then there was *complete silence*, so Thomas hung up the phone. He saw clearly now that just as Della's aunt had told him, concerning parents becoming suspicious of their child's sudden disappearance, '*We have foolproof ways of making sure that never happens*.' Hearing his parents converse had certainly *confirmed that*! He sighed as he realized that his parents trusted him so much that they were easily taken-in by this lie. The hardest part of that phone call however, was hearing his little brother. He already missed him terribly, even if he could be a *brat*. Thomas laughed as he realized that in truth, Ted acted *exactly* like he had at that age!

Next, he excitedly decided to call Della. He really didn't like thinking badly of her, and this was perhaps his final opportunity to reconcile what he perceived to be her *betrayal* of his trust. "I wish to call *Della Seisman*," he declared, and just like before, the phone rang. He immediately picked-up the receiver and excitedly held it close to his ear.

"Well, Della," a woman's voice (*who had to be her aunt*) began. "I'm going to bed."

"So early? Okay," Della replied. "Goodnight, Auntie."

"Aren't *you* ready to turn-in yet?" she asked curiously. "You have certainly had a very full day!"

Della laughed. "Yes, I have, but a very *productive* one too! I still have a little homework to do before I go to bed."

"Okay," her aunt replied sweetly. "Don't stay up too late though."

"I won't!" she assured her with a laugh. "Masonville is such an interesting place, isn't it, Auntie?"

"It certainly is!" her Aunt Jacqueline agreed.

"I'm so glad that we moved here!" Della proclaimed.

"So am I," her aunt replied cheerfully.

And then just like the end of his first phone call, there was *total silence*. This time however, Thomas *slammed* the receiver down in disgust! "I just can't believe it!" he seethed. "She sends me here against my will, and then just talks about her *nice day*? Not a word about *me*?"

Although he was feeling very angry right now, Thomas logically decided that the best way for him to keep from becoming obsessed with that phone call was to simply *stop* thinking about it and get a good night's sleep. Perhaps he'd feel better in the morning? So, he quickly proceeded to change into the blue and white striped pajamas which were neatly folded in a drawer for him, followed by going into the bathroom to clean-up. But when he returned to his room and looked out the window, he shockingly realized that it was *not dark* outside? This seemed very curious since he *did* feel tired? Shouldn't it be nighttime? His curiosity and confusion eventually got the better of him as he exclaimed, "Why is it still light outside?"

Immediately, there was a crisp knock at his door. Thomas quickly answered it.

"Hello, Thomas," yet a *third* different man dressed in a white lab coat addressed him. "The planet England *does not* rotate around our red sun, so on this part of our world… the sun is always shining."

"Doesn't that create *enormous* problems for sleeping?" Thomas blurted out, still seeing light that was *bright* as day pouring through his window. "Why, this window doesn't even have any curtains to *block-out* the sunlight? And how do I *turn-off* the light coming from the walls?"

The man smiled. "Don't worry, Thomas," he assured him. "Crawl into bed and you will see what happens."

This time, Thomas had *no intention* of arguing, but did exactly as the man suggested. To be honest, the bed *did* feel very comfortable. Moments later, he fell fast asleep. The man in the lab coat smiled understandingly, and closed the door… before disappearing.

When Thomas awoke, it was dark. This surprised him greatly after yesterday's '*always sunny*' explanation? However, just as soon as he climbed out of bed, the wall lights came on and sunlight further filled the room through his window? Aha! He quickly surmised that something from the bed had triggered the blackout in the room just as soon as (*or soon after*) he had crawled into it, and *lifted it* just as soon as he had climbed back out! Although he could *not* be certain of his diagnosis, he really didn't want to start-off his day by listening to any more 'smiling men in white lab coats' to confirm it. So… he *never* asked the question out loud.

He walked over to his window and predictably noticed that the red sun was still shining just as brightly as it had when he'd first entered the room yesterday. It seemed impossible, and yet it was obviously true? This planet *did not* rotate around its sun? He had to throw out *everything* he had previously learned in school about a planet's *need* to rotate around its sun or soon finding itself in the dreadful position of being *burned-up* when the gravitational pull of the fiery mass naturally dragged the poor planet to its *doom*! *Whatever* the explanation, this situation was obviously an *exception* to that rule? And exception or not, there was still a part of him that just *couldn't* accept this reality, and believed instead that he was currently *experiencing the impossible*!

Thomas proceeded to dress and primp, and then he was ready for the next thing on his agenda… *whatever that was*? At that exact moment, there came a knock on his door? He was quick to answer it, and came face to face with yet a *fourth* man in a white lab coat.

"Are you hungry?" the smiling man asked him.

"I *am*, actually," Thomas confessed.

"Eggs and bacon okay?" the man offered.

"Yes!" Thomas replied enthusiastically. "That sounds great!"

Immediately, the man handed him a small cup filled with clear liquid. "Drink up!"

Thomas briefly wore a confused expression on his face, but momentarily did as he was instructed. After accepting the cup, he drank the liquid down. Suddenly, his hunger vanished, and he felt completely satisfied? He was simply overwhelmed by the deliciousness of the '*liquid meal*?' "That tasted great!" he beamed. "Was that *really* eggs and bacon?" he asked the man suspiciously as he returned the empty cup to him.

"It was *our version* of it," the man smiled proudly. Then, taking out a small black box from his lab coat… well, you know… *he disappeared.*

Thomas closed his door, and sat down on a chair to properly take-in the incredible things he had already experienced today. But before he had time to get comfortable, he once again heard a knock on his door? When he opened it, *this time* he was greeted by a smiling young man about his own age. The teen was thin, and sported a head of very short white hair. He was also a couple of inches taller than Thomas.

"Hello, Thomas. My name is Lon," he introduced himself with a friendly air. "I have come to *accompany* you to school!"

"Hi, Lon," Thomas replied politely. Initially he felt genuinely *appalled* at the prospect of wasting his time on another planet by *going to school*! But then remembering that he *was* a foreign exchange '*student*'... he quickly adjusted his attitude.

"Let's go!" Thomas smiled back at Lon. Then following him out of the room, he quietly closed the door behind him.

They walked together to the elevator and took it down a couple of floors. Next, Lon led him into a large, open room filled with brown recliner chairs that each featured three buttons (*blue, red and green*) on the top of the right armrest.

"Have a seat," Lon directed him politely, and Thomas immediately complied. "When I give you the word, push the *red* button."

Thomas nodded, although he had absolutely *no idea* what to expect?

A moment later, Lon turned to him and excitedly said, "*Now*!"

Thomas pushed the red button, and *immediately* a strange sensation fell over him? He felt as if he were falling into a trance? His chair seemed to be spinning, but somehow he *never* felt dizzy? In a few moments they both miraculously arrived in another room? It appeared to be a classroom with a large and beautiful machine made of shiny bronze metal placed in front of a well-behaved group of young teenagers. All of the teens looked to be about his same age, sitting in identical '*reclining brown chairs*,' apparently waiting for class to begin.

This was all fine and dandy of course, but the thing he noticed that shocked him to the core, was the *complete absence of a floor* beneath them? There was not so much as a *ledge*? When he looked down, he saw only perpetual nothingness that he could only imagine led straight to the planet England's version of *China* on the other side of the world! Feeling sick and dizzy, Thomas immediately thought that he must be suffering from *vertigo*, just like Jimmy Stewart did in the Alfred Hitchcock movie by the same name! But fortunately, as he ceased looking down, the ill effects quickly wore off. Trying hard not to look too terrified, he asked a boy sitting next to him, “Excuse me, but why is there no floor beneath us?”

With a hefty dose of disbelief, the boy replied, “You mean to tell me that you really *don’t know*?”

Following Thomas’s lengthy explanation (*which included the fact that he was new here*), the other boy immediately understood his dilemma. “Oh, you’re the *new kid* from Earth?” he correctly surmised, almost compassionately… but *not* quite. “They haven’t had floors in these ‘Learning Centers’ for years! They used to say it was because floors created distractions for students from becoming focused. But now, ever since they’ve switched to ‘modern schools,’ I’d guess that the main reason there is no floor in this room is because it’s so much *easier* to keep clean!”

Thomas immediately checked to make sure that the boy *wasn’t* joking, and as soon as he had confirmed the sincere expression on his face, he graciously thanked him for sharing such a *definitive* answer to his question… whether it made any *sense* to him or not? Now he wondered what the boy had meant by ‘*modern schools*?’ Immediately, *that* question was answered! The large beautiful bronze machine at the front of the classroom suddenly *glowed*, and a smiling blue head *shockingly* popped-up from the top and center of it! Although Thomas knew better, aside from the blue color, that head looked and behaved exactly like a *human being*? It was the head of a clean-shaven middle-aged man, who sported a full-head of the most curious colored *lime green* hair he had ever seen? This ‘*man*’ looked to be kind, but at the same time he demanded respect! It *had* to be a robot, but completely unsimilar in appearance to *anything* he had ever seen in science-fiction movies or comic books back home? However, there was little doubt that this magnificent creature held the class’s *complete* attention!

“All present I compute,” the robot began in a very pleasant voice, featuring an obvious English accent, like the one commonly heard on *Earth*!

‘Now why would he use *that* accent?’ Thomas wondered.

"Today's lesson will involve the planet Earth, and we presently have a foreign exchange student with us from that very planet! Let's all welcome him to England!"

That explained his accent alright! But as soon as the robot had *introduced him* to the class, it immediately left Thomas feeling like the '*center of attention*!' A very *uncomfortable* place he generally tried to avoid. Every student in the room was looking directly at him and applauding. He appreciated the gesture, but did his very best to evade all of the odd stares coming his way from the ocean of unfamiliar faces.

As soon as the applause had stopped, the robot said pleasantly, "Please put on your headphones." Thankfully, this quickly took the focus *off* of Thomas. However, although he searched all around his chair, he found absolutely *no sign* of headphones anywhere? Everyone else in the room just seemed to reach over the right side of their chairs and *there they were*! Finally, a boy sitting to Thomas's left was kind enough to whisper, "Push the *green* button, dummy!" Thomas was grateful for that very timely advice. He proceeded to do as the boy had suggested, which thankfully produced a pair of headphones on a tray to his right! He gratefully picked them up and put them on.

A few seconds passed before the entire impressive bronze body of the robot in front of them began to glow even *brighter*! Simultaneously, a three-dimensional image of what appeared to be the miniaturized *rings of Saturn*, in shades of shiny metallic colors, spun around faster and faster in front of each individual student, effectively holding them spellbound! Along with these amazing visuals could be heard, for lack of a better description, *music from Heaven*! Thomas was listening to the most beautiful and inspiring music he had *ever* heard in his life! It sounded like angels singing to the perfect accompaniment of a heavenly orchestra! Next, out of nowhere, he smelled a nostalgic fragrance that intensely reminded him of pine trees in the mountains and Christmastime. As he continued to watch the exciting 'rings of Saturn' in front of him, and listen to the delightful 'music from Heaven,' as well as enjoying the pleasing fragrance, next Thomas began to feel his chair recline even more. In addition to reclining, it also gently rocked forward and backwards, simultaneously massaging him from head to toe. There was such a *determined* stimulation of their senses going on, that the students' young brains could not consciously handle it? It all made them so very relaxed… and *sleepy*? It wasn't long before they all grew overwhelmingly fatigued, and fell fast asleep. *Now* the modern school course could begin!

Through their dreaming, Thomas and all of the other students learned firsthand about some of the *best* things on Earth throughout the ages. There were simply too many marvelous things presented to remember! This list included, but was in no way *confined* to, experiencing the four unique seasons of the year complete with the weather that traditionally came along with each one, the wonderful feelings one experienced when falling in love, the warm and exciting feeling of friendship, a sample of some of the Earth's unique fragrances, railroads, listening to a symphonic orchestra, watching clouds, the different array of restaurants and foods, riding horses, swimming or boating in oceans, lakes and rivers, eating sweet candy and desserts, going outside and experiencing different temperatures on different days, square dancing, running through a waving field of wheat, driving a car, riding a bicycle, spending time with your family and friends, cavemen searching for food, submarines, the ballet, people being entertained and laughing, different sporting events, the many live creatures both large and small including dinosaurs that roamed the Earth throughout the ages, an array of different clothing throughout world, exciting, diverse and beautiful music, dance, art and theatre, yodeling, surfing, reading a great book, watching or performing a live musical, preparing a meal and taking-in the delightful aromas it creates, Christmas and other holidays around the world, visiting a museum, airplanes, mountain ranges, medieval castles, animation, Disneyland, movies, television and other '*exciting*' things which were all common to parts of the Earth in either past and/or present times. But the *best* part was that he experienced all of these breathtaking things *in his mind* while he was sleeping! He also observed the jobs that many people on Earth worked at, as well as what varied types of entertainment they enjoyed. But as he watched all of this, an *unforeseen* affect was that he found himself *missing* his life on Earth something terrible!

When Thomas and the other students finally woke-up, the robot teacher officially declared that school was "over for the day!" Thomas had loved this '*learning through dreaming*' experience! When he slept through class at Masonville Junior High, it was always Miss Cornwall screaming at him, "*Down to Mr. Zuffin's office with you, Thomas McAdams*!" But here, the sleeping was structured and educational. Why couldn't they do this at home? But then again… he couldn't help hearing a tiny little voice inside his head suggesting that maybe, just maybe… this type of learning was *missing something*?

"Hey!" Lon was shouting at him. "*School's over*, Thomas. This is no time for daydreaming! Put your headphones away and then push your *blue* button."

With a sheepish grin, Thomas gave Lon a knowing nod and then swiftly put his headphones back on the tray, where they immediately disappeared inside his recliner. Then he pushed his blue button. Soon, he experienced the same spinning sensation that he had known while first arriving at school. Then just like that, Lon and he arrived at the *recliner-chair parking lot*, where they had departed from earlier today. After climbing out of their chairs, Lon immediately escorted Thomas up to his room, smiled and said, 'goodbye,' and then left the room, closing the door behind him.

Thomas had absolutely *no idea* what time it was, and although there must have been some structured system of time on this planet, he did *not* seem to be getting any closer to understanding what it was? Apparently, the full day and night were always bright with sunshine, you ate (*or in this case, drank*) whenever you wanted to, and went to bed when you felt tired. He imagined that both Della and her Aunt Jacqueline must have initially struggled when changing from the highly structured but fantastic life here, to a far more basic, yet surprisingly *more complicated* life on Earth. He asked himself, 'Are there *ever* any problems on this planet?' Again, something about life here just seemed to be… *incomplete*?

In his mind, he was going through quite a big change adapting to life here on the planet England. He admitted to himself that before coming here, throughout the short lifetime he'd already spent on Earth, he had experienced both happy *and* unhappy days.

He *knew* that Earth wasn't anywhere near perfect, what with the everyday nuisance of dealing with people's unpredictable moods and behavior, the varying weather conditions, *very concerning* local and world events, and a myriad of *divergent* opinions from people he knew on *every* topic imaginable! But maybe all of that *nuisance* wasn't really so bad? Maybe that was how life was *intended* to be? He continued to wish that he were *there now*. He missed his family, and perhaps *not* that surprisingly... he *especially* missed Della! Although this planet was technologically *amazing* compared to his own far less advanced planet of Earth, and nearly perfect in so many different ways... from what he'd seen so far, everyone here seemed to be trained to think and act in the *very same way*?

Suddenly, Thomas realized that he was growing hungry again? So, as he had been conditioned to do, he yelled out to the room, "I'm hungry!"

Almost immediately, there came a firm knock on his door. When he opened it, there stood *yet another* smiling man in a white lab coat. Although this man was *very* tall, he was no more threatening than the others. "I have brought you a *roast beef dinner* with all of the trimmings," the man said, smiling down at the much shorter Thomas. "Is that acceptable?"

"Sure," Thomas replied, a little *less* enthusiastically than the last time.

The man proceeded to produce a cup, just like the one he had been offered at breakfast, and once again it was filled with a clear liquid. Thomas graciously accepted the cup and drank it down. He immediately felt *full*, while his senses seemed to be telling him that he had just consumed a great big roast beef dinner. Yet the truth was... *he had not*?

"That tasted really good," Thomas confessed to the man, returning his now *empty* cup to him. "But could I have a *real* roast beef dinner with all of the trimmings? The kind they serve on Earth?"

The man's friendly demeanor instantly changed to one of confusion, as he replied, "You have just consumed *our version* of a roast beef dinner. We have *no other*." He then took out a small black box from his lab coat, and... well, you know the rest!

'When it came right down to it, for all of its flash… everything around here was actually *quite predictable*?' Thomas thought to himself. Although the liquid meal had satisfied his hunger, he really *missed* holding, eating and tasting his food slowly over a dinner table conversation with his *family*. And he *loved* the variety of different ways food could be prepared, seasoned and cooked on Earth. This planet's idea of meal time made him feel more like a solitary lab rat, or perhaps a caged animal at the zoo? It was during this stress-filled moment that Thomas firmly made-up his mind to *return home* as soon as possible! He had absolutely no idea *how* he was going to *make that happen* of course? But somehow he knew he'd think of something. He just *had to*! On top of everything else, he couldn't believe how lonely he was feeling? As if in answer to that most pressing problem, he suddenly heard what sounded to him like loud teenage voices in the hallway just outside his room? This was followed by a very firm knock on his door!

He opened it, and was delighted to find a group of his new classmates uncomfortably (*yet excitedly*) standing outside his door in the hallway.

"Ahem." Lon, his earlier guide to and from school noisily cleared his throat before saying, "We just stopped by to see if you might want to do something with us… say, something that young people do on Earth for *fun*?"

"Are you asking me this because of today's lesson at school?" Thomas asked suspiciously.

"Yes!" a thin, blonde girl in the group giggled. "What we saw has made us all so very curious?"

"Okay," Thomas shared agreeably. "Well, what questions do you have?"

"What is it *really* like living on Earth?" a shorter boy with huge smile excitedly asked him.

Thomas explained as honestly as he could how his life in Masonville had been. He told his extremely captive audience all about school, homework, house and yard work, movies, dates, and everything else he could remember, including his teacher, *Miss Cornwall*! But when he began to explain examples of some *less common* alternative forms of weekend entertainment… *that's* when the kids really started growing excited!

"I know I would probably just *hate* living on your planet!" a thoughtful girl with long dark hair, surprisingly wearing a very *adultlike* expression confessed honestly. "Life there sounds so very backward compared to living here?" Then suddenly changing her expression to a child's look of whimsy, she continued, "But I believe that '*TPing of houses*' you do sounds *most* intriguing!"

"Oh, *it is*!" Thomas immediately agreed with a *devilish* gleam beginning to manifest itself in his eyes. "In fact, how would you guys like to *try it*?"

"Impossible!" another boy, a large athletic looking one sporting a thick head of red hair with a sparsely sprouted moustache and a goatee to match, quickly responded. "It's *never* dark here like it is on your planet."

"Anyway," Lon added logically, "we hardly ever go to the '*out of doors,*' and no one else does either! So, who would even *know* that we'd created the mess in the first place? And *who* would clean it up?"

Thomas chose to ignore Lon's contributions, although they seemed to make *perfect sense*. He continued instead, quickly devising his *own* plan. Although the way his idea was developing in his mind seemed very exciting to him, he was *banking* on the fact that The Powers would view their results as being *decidedly deviant*! "We wouldn't go to the out of doors like they do on Earth. Instead, we'd sneak into someone's room in *this* hotel, who had forgotten to lock their door," Thomas explained calmly. "And then, while they were sleeping… we'd very quietly *decorate* their room with *toilet paper*!"

"But in addition to the laws and social mores prohibiting such behavior, there *isn't* any toilet paper here on the planet?" the first girl, who was thin with blonde hair, shared disappointedly. "Well, except for what they keep in the Galaxy Museum of course. But they only have six rolls there which were brought here from Earth many years ago. That paper is considered to be so valuable that it's always kept under a glass case with *state-of-the-art* alarms all around it!"

"Why is that?" Thomas asked in surprise.

"Because they *don't* manufacture toilet paper on this planet anymore," Lon explained logically. "As you know, we've had no need for it ever since they got rid of all toilets on the planet when our scientists learned to *chemically* rid the body of *all* waste," he continued. "Therefore, the toilet paper from Earth, although completely obsolete here, is still considered a unique item *worthy* of being showcased in the museum for all to see."

"Well, why doesn't someone from your planet just bring *more* toilet-paper over from Earth then?" Thomas asked logically. "I'm sure they could get as much as they wanted to?"

Lon laughed. "You miss the point, Thomas. If they brought *more* toilet-paper from Earth, then the rolls the museum already has would *cease* to be special, and *no one* would care about seeing them anymore!"

Thomas smiled at Lon's thorough understanding of the Galaxy Museum's philosophy. They had a real need to keep toilet-paper *rare* on this planet to maintain the public's interest in their display. But they were achieving this goal through *artificial* means? For all of this planet's technological brilliance, Thomas was amazed that Lon or the others in this group didn't *question* that logic as being dishonest? On the other hand, maybe *here*, for some weird reason, it *wasn't*? In any case, he declared, "Well then, I guess we'll just have to *borrow* that 'unique item' from the Galaxy Museum… won't we!"

Although the other kids didn't seem to fully understand *why* Thomas was laughing, that didn't stop them from quickly catching his impish spirit and laughing right along with him.

"Come on!" The blonde girl whispered excitedly, sounding very empowered. "Let's grab that toilet paper and get started!"

Thomas laughed at her obvious eagerness. "Okay, let's go!" He quickly closed his door behind him, and joined the rest of the group in the hallway.

The group of kids, led by Lon, took the elevator down to the first floor and briskly walked out the front door of the hotel to the outside, or as Lon had referred to it previously, the '*out of doors*.' The air was breathable and the red sun didn't make it too uncomfortably hot, but for some reason very few people were traveling the sidewalks to and from the different buildings? Thomas recalled Lon mentioning this apparent phenomenon earlier. He guessed that it was probably because most adults used those same little black boxes the men in the white lab coats used to instantly travel from place to place instead of walking. But he couldn't help thinking that it was their loss. Their way might prove to be more *efficient*, which seemed to be of utmost importance on this planet. But to tell you the truth, he rather enjoyed walking outside! It just felt so natural? He was *glad* that Earth didn't have all of these advanced technologies that had immersed everyone's life here so completely. 'No matter how many new ways of making lives easier and more efficient you had, it was still impossible to improve on *natural* perfection!' he reasoned. Concentrating on the outside now and looking around, he realized that the buildings looked almost exactly like some of the ones he'd seen in the larger cities back home? 'Perhaps,' he also considered, 'even with all of their advancements here… down deep, folks on the planet England weren't really much different from the people of Earth?' "So, where *is* the Galaxy Museum?" Thomas asked the group, just as soon as they had reached the sidewalk.

"It's not far from here," Lon spoke for the group. "It's in that building across the street."

Suddenly, as Thomas perused the road they were about to cross, he noticed with surprise that there weren't *any* cars, trucks, motorcycles or *anything else* traveling on it? It looked absolutely deserted? "Hey, Lon," he asked as they walked. "Why aren't there any motorized vehicles on this road?"

Lon laughed. "*Motorized vehicles*? Thomas, England no longer has *any need* of them or these roads!" he exclaimed. "The roads on this planet were used a very long time ago during what we now call our '*Basic Age*' for everyday travel. But now that motorized vehicles have become obsolete, the roads only remain as a testament, reminding us every day of how very far we have advanced since then!"

Thomas nodded with a smile. He understood… sort of… but *not really*? So, to save himself a lot of time dwelling on a concept that he might *never* understand, he simply reminded himself that this was *definitely* a different culture from his own… and left it at that.

When they arrived at the entrance to the Galaxy Museum, located on the second floor of the MEMORIES BUILDING, at first no one had a plan for procuring the toilet-paper? But suddenly, a short, redheaded girl with pleasingly animated facial features who had been completely quiet up to this point, jumped up and excitedly declared, “Wait here everybody! I’ll be back with the toilet paper in just a few minutes!” Then she rushed off to another part of the museum. Everybody waited in hyper-anticipation to see if the girl actually *could* get a hold of those precious articles? Of course, at the same time, they couldn’t help wondering *how* she intended to do it? Five minutes later she returned.

“I told you I could *get them*!” the girl declared proudly in a loud whisper, carrying an oversized bag containing six authentic rolls of *toilet paper*!

“How did you ever do it?” the blonde girl asked in amazement.

The short red-headed girl beamed with pride as she replied, “I just informed the guards that I had to take these rolls to the manager’s office for cleaning.”

Thomas bewilderedly asked, “If this toilet paper is so valuable, then why did the guards just let you *take them all away* with such a flimsy excuse as that one?”

“Because I’m the *manager’s daughter*!” she laughed.

Thomas and the others quietly laughed too as they left the museum and quickly headed back toward the hotel. Once they arrived there, while being *extremely careful* to shield the bag of toilet-paper from everyone else’s suspicious eyes, they all nonchalantly headed toward Thomas’s room to select their target. It was not until they found themselves safely inside the confines of that room that they finally relaxed. That is, all except for Lon, who appeared to be on an all-important mission? He mysteriously walked over to a corner of the room and *magically* waved his hand across a paisley design in the wallpaper. Immediately, there appeared the gentle sound of a chime.

“What did you just do?” Thomas pointedly asked Lon, with a very perplexed expression on his face. Curiously, *no one else* in the room seemed to be even the least bit surprised by what Lon had done?

“I turned off the ‘Just Ask’ unit so that no one would overhear our plans,” Lon explained calmly.

"Do you mean to say that people have been *listening-in on me*?" Thomas exclaimed in shock.

"Relax, Thomas," Lon assured him with a smile. "It's nothing sinister. The '*Just Ask*' unit is automatically turned on in the room whenever an exchange student first arrives. It's so that the hotel staff will be able to more efficiently respond to their needs." Then smiling, he added, "Kind of like the *baby monitors* we hear you have on Earth!"

Everyone laughed *(including Thomas)*. With all of the preliminaries now behind them, as they *had* the toilet-paper and were *not* being overheard, they began to discuss their ultimate plan. Thomas obviously didn't know anybody in the building, so he left the room selection completely up to the rest of the group to decide. After a short discussion that included a number of *very unlikely* suggestions, they finally agreed on the idea of *randomly* selecting their target by trying *all* of the doors on Thomas's floor, which consisted entirely of foreign exchange students (*him*) and single staff members from the school, until they finally found one that was unlocked. Although this plan sounded a bit… no, it sounded *very* simplistic, and maybe even a bit *dangerous*, compared to the other suggestions, it was *brilliant*!

"What if the lights are still *on* in the room and there is a *very awake person* there when we open it?" the athletic redheaded boy asked with concern.

"Then we'll just say, 'Oops, sorry, *wrong* door!'" Thomas laughed, as everyone else quickly joined in.

Now united and determined, the group of eager future mischief makers very *quietly* walked out of Thomas's room. Trying very hard to act completely normal, they hoped to avoid drawing any attention to themselves that might *jeopardize* their most important mission! They quickly split-up, and carefully searched the entire floor for that *one* elusive room where the door was *not* locked, its lights were out and *no one* was awake inside. Although they found several promising unlocked doors within the first few minutes, they disappointingly discovered that when they opened them, they led to rooms with their lights still on, and their tenant *very much awake*! Finally, it was Lon who discovered an unlocked door… *where the lights were out*! Quietly opening the door there was only a nightlight on, which revealed a very shadowy version of a man with a bushy black beard lying fast asleep in his bed. Everyone but Thomas vaguely recalled seeing him *occasionally* at school, but no one had any idea what his *name* or *position* might be? Although his snoring was overpowering, that actually was a *good thing*. It proved to be a great way for them to monitor that he was still asleep while they worked.

Cautiously, without uttering a sound, everyone jammed inside the room and went about the business of distributing the rolls of toilet-paper. Since Thomas was the only *expert* in in the field of TPing, *he* began the decorating process. He very clearly demonstrated to everyone else just how fast and easy it was to unroll toilet-paper, tear off the number of tissues desired and gently lay it down someplace! Then taking turns, everyone in the group used-up every last paper on the rolls to cover the room *gloriously and completely*! They left the room as quickly and silently as they had entered it. The pride of a job well done was clearly evident on *each* of their young faces as well as the initial *excitement* of doing this for the *very first time*!

"This felt so much like being home, I simply *can't* believe it?" Thomas whispered excitedly to Lon, once everyone was safely outside in the hallway.

"How can that be?" Lon asked him incredulously.

Thomas quietly laughed. "I'm not talking about your planet's amazing technology, red sun, empty roads, liquid food or anything like that. I'm talking about how you all get so *excited* about doing something like this together! You act just like the kids on Earth do!"

Suddenly, the door to the room they had only just finished 'decorating,' *burst open*! The bearded man appeared and angrily shouted, "Stay right where you are, you *brats*!"

Some of the kids in the group tried to run, but all of the exits were immediately blocked by a regiment of eerily *smiling men* in white lab coats!

"What seems to be the problem, sir?" one of the white-coated men gently asked the bearded man.

"While I was sleeping, these... *kids* snuck into my room and placed some sort of flimsy paper material over everything, including *me*!" he bellowed angrily.

"Is this true?" a confident man in a white lab coat, who by his assertiveness appeared to be their leader, asked the group of young teens with *extreme* concern.

"*It certainly is*!" Thomas announced, to the shock of all of his cohorts.

"Hey! Wasn't this supposed to be a *secret*?" Lon whispered to Thomas in surprise.

"Yes. But just like on Earth, *sometimes* you get caught!" Thomas grinned. Lon grinned right back.

The kids were immediately made to return to the scene of the crime, carefully roll the toilet paper back onto their spools (*as best they could*), and apologize *profusely* to the bearded man. The *good* that immediately came out of this adventure was that the bearded man vowed *never again* to sleep with his door unlocked! But not surprisingly, he *neglected* to thank the teens for teaching him such a *valuable* lesson.

Just as soon as they had completed these tasks, and the toilet paper had been taken to a security office to be held as evidence (*as not one of the teens had yet apprised the security staff of where the odd paper had actually come from*), the kids were roughly herded into a large office. Here, they were very surprised to see that *same* man with the bushy black beard, intensely *scowling* at them! He was now wearing a cherry red lab coat, sat behind a desk on a padded swivel-chair, and impatiently awaited the *delinquents*' arrival. He was looking very cross, as though he had just been awakened from a very sound sleep, which of course... *he had*! Disappointingly, aside from the comfortable chair that the man was sitting in, there were no other chairs or benches to sit on *anywhere* in the room? This situation made for a lot of very uncomfortable standing for all of the kids. Since Thomas had a lot of experience '*getting in trouble*,' he logically thought that this was probably being done *intentionally* by the man for some psychological reasons intended to keep everyone off-balance and scared! Although he understood this, he smiled as he considered that part of this harsh reaction to what they had done could also be attributed to a *poorly developed sense of humor* in this planet's adults! It was then that he read the nameplate on the man's desk. Shockingly, the name of the man in the red coat was *Mr. Cornelius Cornwall*! 'Did *every school* in the galaxy have one rude and ill-tempered person working for them with *that last name*?' he wondered. For everyone's sake, he hoped it was only *one per planet*!

"What was this little '*adventure*' all about?" Mr. Cornwall immediately asked the group in a controlled but threatening manner. "The other Powers and I are *not pleased*!"

Thomas's young partners in crime gasped and looked terrified, just as soon as they discovered that the man was a school *Power*!

"It was *my* idea, sir," Thomas quickly cut to the chase. "It's something that teenagers do on Earth for fun."

"And what was that *strange* paper you were using?" the man demanded, quite obviously *oblivious*.

"Just a type of paper that *everyone* uses on Earth every day," Thomas shared cryptically. Then preparing himself for a strong reaction, he added, "It's called *toilet paper*. We borrowed it from a display in the Galaxy Museum because we couldn't think of anywhere else to find some?"

"*What*?" Mr. Cornelius Cornwall's face quickly grew as red as the shade of his coat. Standing up with authority he bellowed, "Every item in the Galaxy Museum is *rare* and *priceless*, and you *dare* to steal and possibly ruin such artifacts for a practical joke?"

Thomas nodded, and with a smile he said, "I thought it sounded fun!"

"*Fun*?" Mr. Cornwall's face was about to explode with anger. "Why, if any of you were my child, I would have you brought before the Powers and *kazumped*!"

All of the other teenagers in the room held their breath in horror! But they almost immediately sighed with relief as they were ultimately released and sent home with only a *warning*... while Thomas alone, was made to *stay*! As the other culprits left the room, each in their own way gave Thomas a subtle '*thank you*,' mostly with a smile, for providing them with the most fun and excitement they had *ever had* in their entire young lives! But their expressions also showed great concern for him, as they all wondered and feared what his final fate might be? Just as soon as they had left, Thomas was shuttled away from that room to another one, which *thankfully* had a chair for him to sit in. And it was even *padded*? To many people, this would probably appear to be inconsequential. But to Thomas, it clearly demonstrated that *someone* on this planet held respect for everyone! Including *practical joke-doers* like himself! This time, the person he faced behind the desk was a woman. She was probably in her mid-thirties, with long dark hair and wearing a very kind expression on her face. She was dressed in a lab coat that was colored *purple*.

"Hello, Thomas," she began with a friendly air.

"Hello, ma'am," he replied hesitantly.

"You have had quite an *eventful* second day since arriving here," she noted with a sincere smile, while carefully perusing a report that she held in her hand. "As a result, I'm afraid that most of 'The Powers' want you immediately returned home for being such a *corrupting influence* on our youth. On Earth, I believe they call that *expulsion*."

Thomas feigned great sadness as he nodded his understanding.

"But before you go, I really wanted to speak with you," she said without the least bit of animosity.

"Are you *in-charge* around here?" Thomas asked her curiously.

"You *could* say that," she smiled. "I am what you probably know on Earth as the '*school principal*.'"

Thomas gasped! "Am I in a *lot of trouble* then? Am I going to be *kazumped*?" he asked in *horror*.

The principal laughed. "No, Thomas," she smiled. "I don't think your offense quite merits *that* punishment."

"Well, what does *kazumped* even mean?" Thomas asked with concern.

"On Earth you would call that '*getting paddled*!'" she replied.

Thomas let out a great big sigh of relief, as he realized that he had come *this close* to getting paddled on *both* planets, billions of miles apart, in the span of only *three days*!

The principal smiled. "I just wanted to find out what it was that inspired you to lead the other kids on such an *unusual* activity as that one, which you must have *known* would be received poorly by Mr. Cornwall and the other Powers?"

"Well, to begin with, we didn't know that Mr. Cornwall was a *Power*?" Thomas shared honestly. "We just chose a room at *random*, and unfortunately, it was his!"

The principal smiled understandingly.

Thomas went on to share with her how he had been sent to England *against* his will and was having real trouble acclimating. But curiously, he added, "*None* of that was the reason I went with my classmates on that TPing adventure though."

"No?" she responded with surprise. "What then?"

"I told those kids about how some of my friends and me would 'toilet-paper' houses on Earth once in a while for fun, and they got *very excited* about doing it! So, we *all* figured out a plan together," he admitted. "But the whole thing was just for fun! We never meant any harm to the man in the room, or even to the toilet-paper."

The principal chuckled under her breath. "*Was* it fun?" she asked him curiously.

"Yes, it was!" Thomas confessed with a grin. "It made me feel unbelievably happy! The way I *used* to feel when I did things like that with my friends at home… while I was still living on Earth," he added nostalgically.

The principal nodded understandingly, and then said, "I *know* it was fun. You know what Thomas? I used to TP houses when I was a teen too!" she confessed.

"*You did*?" he replied in shock and disbelief.

She laughed again. "Of course! I am *originally* from Earth! I came here as an exchange student some years ago, and liked it so much that I simply stayed and made England *my home*."

"Wow!" Thomas exclaimed.

"I know that it was Della who recruited you to come here," the woman shared, "but please try not to be *too* hard on her. I just think she was very excited to share with you what her planet was like. This may have caused her to become a *bit* overzealous, but I'm sure she meant well."

"You *know* Della Seisman?" Thomas asked in shock.

"Oh yes! She is one of the brightest and kindest students I have ever had the pleasure of working with at this school," she raved.

"So that's really her?" Thomas asked expectantly.

"Yes, that's *really* her," the principal confirmed gently.

Thomas was *elated*!

"And were you also aware that it was her parents who originally founded this school and took regular trips to Earth to recruit exchange students?"

Thomas immediately remembered Della sharing the unpleasant memory of how her parents had both been tragically *killed* in an automobile accident on Earth while on a recruiting mission. "Yes, Della told me about that," he replied. "Were they part of 'The Powers' then?"

"Oh yes! They were *founding members* of this school's *Powers*!" the woman confirmed. "They were both such remarkable people, and I think Della learned very well from both of their *wonderful* examples."

Thomas suddenly felt enlightened! And he missed Della something awful? The truth was… he couldn't wait to see her again!

As if reading his mind, the woman said, "We are preparing to send you back to Earth in just a few minutes, Thomas. But *first*, I would like to thank you for what you have shared with these good people in your very short time here."

"*Shared*?" Thomas asked in surprise.

"Yes," she smiled. "You have shared the wonderful gift of being *creatively spontaneous*," she explained. "Unfortunately, that can sometimes be very misunderstood in England's highly efficient society and mistaken for *trouble-making*. In fact, it is probably one of the main concepts that the good people of England, especially their leaders, seem to have a very difficult time *understanding or valuing*."

"Is that because everyone here is taught to *think the same way*?" Thomas asked.

The principal chuckled. "Uh… no. There is plenty of *divergent thinking* going on all over this planet!" she insisted. "You should hear the politicians argue before elections! It's as *divergent* as I'm sure you've ever seen!" she laughed. Growing more serious, she added, "But as I said before, *creative spontaneity* does seem to be something that is more lacking on this planet than it should be. However, thanks to the fact that some of our students took part in a '*creatively spontaneous adventure*,' this experience should lead their class to *many* exciting official and unofficial discussions that will hopefully eventually spill over to their families and friends! After what happened tonight, I *know* they will have a lot to talk about for a *good long* time!" she assured him.

"But I thought education here was all about, '*learning while you slept*?'" Thomas said puzzledly. "There were absolutely *no* student discussions or interactions of any kind during my one day of class in your Learning Center? Everything happened while we slept in big easy-chairs… *without a floor*!" he recalled uncomfortably.

The woman laughed heartily. "Thomas! We have classrooms, write reports and take tests, just like students in Earth schools do. Please don't judge our schools by just one day. We only use the Learning Center about once every two weeks to *introduce* a new topic. The actual classrooms look very much like yours do. Complete with desks... and a *floor*."

Thomas laughed. "Wow! It's just way too easy to jump to conclusions, isn't it?"

"It is," she agreed. "That's why I wanted to speak with you," she explained understandingly, "and I'm *so glad* I did." She rose from her desk and slowly walked toward him with her arms outstretched. "Good luck in the future, Thomas. Remember, your creative mind is a *gift*, not a curse… no matter *what* anyone else may tell you!"

"You are certainly a wise person," he said with a smile.

"That's why I'm the *principal*!" she laughed.

Thomas got up from his chair and embraced her in a much-needed hug. He had learned more from her during this single *impromptu* conversation than he had learned from everyone else on this planet *combined*! But he had to chuckle because just like at MJH, he had gotten himself into trouble here, which had *led* to his punishment. And just like at MJH, his punishment had turned out to be *exactly what he had wanted it to be*! Almost like he had manipulated it? *Almost*? In any case, he was going home! He smiled.

Suddenly, without warning, another person entered the room.

"*Mr. Teltrab*?" Thomas exclaimed in shock. "What are *you* doing here?"

"I *live* here!" he laughed. "I actually came by to see my *wife*, the principal. When I saw *you* in here talking with her, I thought I might drop-in on your meeting to say, Hi!"

The principal chuckled.

"Are you, *Mrs. Teltrab*?" Thomas intently asked the woman in shock.

"No, Thomas. I'm Mrs. Bartlet... *Sheldon's* wife.

Completely shocked, but even more excited, Thomas abruptly turned back toward Mr. Teltrab and exclaimed, "Are you *the* Sheldon Bartlet? The all-time leader in *every* category for all of Masonville Junior High's sports teams?"

Mr. Teltrab laughed, and then explained, "I *used* to be, Thomas. But on Earth, I officially changed my name to *Tim Teltrab* over ten years ago. Tim is actually my middle name and *Teltrab* spelled backwards... is *Bartlet*."

"But *why* would you do that?" Thomas asked, completely confounded.

"Because," Mr. Teltrab explained, "I was too embarrassed to be Sheldon Bartlet anymore. The fact is, I didn't have *any idea* what I should do after failing so miserably with the Dodgers? I felt like a complete failure!"

"Then what *did* you do?" Thomas asked him anxiously.

Mr. Teltrab smiled. "Well, as luck would have it, after I had been cut by the Dodgers, it was only a couple of weeks later that I was fortunate enough to meet your principal, Linda, at a local dance. She shared with me what it was like living on England. One thing led to another, and soon I was here on England, giving it a try! After a while, I found that I was truly happy here. And a few years later, Linda and I were married!"

"But you *teach* us every day at Masonville Junior High?" Thomas insisted, perplexed. "How can you *possibly* live simultaneously here *and* on Earth?"

The principal, who had been following their conversation closely, chuckled, "Thomas, as you well know, it *doesn't* take very long to travel between our two planets. Sheldon simply goes to work on Earth, and comes home to England after he's done."

"Wow!" Thomas reacted in amazement. "But why do you *bother* coming back to Earth when your life is *here*?"

"My life is on *both* planets," Mr. Teltrab gently corrected him.

"As is mine," the principal added. "We spend a *lot* of time on Earth together doing all of the wonderful things that we love to do there. Things like going out to eat, bowling, or to the movies," she shared happily. "We also regularly visit our families and friends who live there!"

Thomas suddenly had a very curious question. "How many of the people on Earth do you figure were once '*foreign exchange students*' here on England?"

The principal smiled. "I don't know exactly, Thomas, but I'm sure there have been *quite a few*!"

"Yes! And they could be *anybody*? Teachers, parents, classmates? Maybe even *Miss Cornwall*?" Mr. Teltrab teased.

Thomas looked shocked!

Mr. Teltrab laughed. "No! *She's* never set foot on this planet, but I think you've met her brother, *Mr. Cornelius Cornwall*, the former foreign exchange student from Earth, many years ago!"

Thomas laughed out loud! *Now*, he understood why the two Cornwalls not only shared the same last name, but that *terrible temperament*! Suddenly thinking of something very concerning, Thomas said, "Mr. Teltrab?"

"Yes, Thomas?" he responded.

"Do you think that by using my ability to talk myself out of punishments every time I'm tardy at school, *I'm cheating*?"

Mr. Teltrab grew thoughtful. "No. But I have to wonder *why* a bright boy like you wastes so much of your time and effort avoiding punishments for being excessively tardy?"

"Well, what *should* I do then?" Thomas asked curiously.

"*Don't be tardy*!" Mr. Teltrab replied simply with a laugh. "You have already proven that you can talk yourself *out* of punishments. Now prove to yourself that you can *be on time*!

When you are an adult, *that skill* will always be highly valued. Unfortunately, I learned that the hard way."

Thomas smiled. "Thank you for that *great* advice, Mr. Teltrab.

"You're very welcome. You'll see that most of the time doing the *right* thing feels much better than getting away with doing the *wrong* thing."

The principal smiled, "Yes, Thomas. Sheldon's right! But don't forget that there will probably come times in your life when you will feel a great compulsion to do what you believe to be the *right thing*, which to many others, may be considered the *wrong thing*! And *that*, may lead you to *breaking a rule*. But don't worry. You'll know in your heart that it was the *best* thing for *you* to do at the time, and that's what counts!"

Thomas smiled. "Thank you for your understanding."

Suddenly the principal feigned severe sternness as she warned, "Well, I advise you to *take it* while you can, because I may *not* be quite as understanding if you ever decided to *toilet-paper my house*!"

The three of them spontaneously laughed together for a good long time. This was by far Thomas's favorite memory of the very short time he'd spent here on the *planet England*.

Flying through space on his return trip to Earth, was an exciting *blur*. But this time, Thomas could look out at the fantastic galaxy in front of him *without* feeling dizzy! He made sure to watch the incredible sights outside his 'flying crate' for the entire duration of his short trip, and even took detailed mental notes of what he saw. There is certainly a *lot* to see when one is focused on it! Before too long, he felt his crate slowing down and eventually coming to a gentle stop. He slowly climbed out and looked all around him. He immediately recognized the craft's landing spot as being the same room he had taken-off from in Della's house. But she *wasn't* there to meet him? In fact, the uncanny quiet in the house suggested to him that *no one* was there at all? He had so much to tell her, especially after talking with Mr. Teltrab (*alias Sheldon Bartlet*) and the principal. He understood things so much better now! He wanted so badly to tell her that. But deep down, he also realized that a reunion between the two of them now, would undoubtedly be *very awkward* given his quick departure from England. Della was probably terribly embarrassed for sending him up there in the first place since his visit had turned into such a *fiasco* for everyone. He really understood *why* she wasn't here, but he felt extremely disappointed just the same. So, hanging his head and his heart, he proceeded to walk out through the front door and begin his lonely trek home.

Just as soon as he arrived home and opened the front door, his family was there to greet him with a *strangely exaggerated* look of empathy covering all of their faces? His mother tightly wrapped her arms around him and whispered softly, "I'm so sorry they canceled your invitation to be a foreign exchange student, Thomas. Better luck next year." His dad was equally sympathetic, but without saying a word. Ted, however, smiled broadly and even gave Thomas a big hug, showing that he was very happy indeed that his *favorite* playmate had returned!

Thomas did *not* respond verbally to any of them, which was probably the best thing he could have done under the circumstances. Instead, he simply gave each of them a *warm* smile, letting them know how much he appreciated their concern for him, before slowly turning away and walking to his room. '*The Powers* are certainly very talented,' he thought with a grin. 'They miraculously covered for me when I unexpectedly *left* Earth, and then once again when I unexpectedly *returned*! Those people on the planet England are way more advanced than we are,' he thought, 'except like the principal said, when it comes to *appreciating* teenagers *spontaneously* having fun!' he laughed to himself. He had arrived home on Sunday, so he dreaded going back to school tomorrow on Monday. Not because he had any particular problem with school, but due to his keen sense of *foreboding* that tomorrow he would discover an *empty* seat in the classroom where Della used to sit… and that he would *never* see her again! That was quite a bitter pill for him to swallow.

For Thomas, the remainder of the day and night were uneventful. In fact, he found himself once again going to bed early. As he slipped under the covers, he thought about how Della was now *gone*, making it pointless for him to even attempt calling her. He *was* a little curious to know what had happened to Joe Porter?

But he sighed as he realized that he would probably hear all about that tomorrow from the big mouth of the *bully* himself! He thought about Lon and the other kids who were part of the *infamous* toilet papering adventure billions of miles away on the planet England! It all made him smile now. How odd? He had wanted to get home so badly… yet *without* Della… it didn't seem to matter as much to him? Weariness soon overtook his consciousness, and a moment later he fell fast asleep.

He was awakened in the middle of the night by the now familiar, yet still *unsettling* sound of his neighbor's tree branch sporadically hitting his window. Just as he had done the last time this had happened, Thomas got out of bed and walked toward the window. But this time he didn't hesitate to open it and slowly look around outside. There was no one to be seen anywhere? So, he quickly unbent the offending branch. But then, just before closing the window, he spied an envelope carefully taped to the outside of it, with *his name* boldly written across the front? The printing was very neat, and he had an overwhelming hunch (*and hope*) that it had been written by Della! So, he determinedly peeled it off the window and opened the envelope to reveal a short letter. He excitedly began silently reading:

Dear Thomas,
I'm so sorry about tricking you into going to my planet. I shouldn't have done that, and I know now that as a result, I was responsible for all of the trouble you experienced there. Will you ever forgive me? Anyway, I did save you from fighting Joe Porter, didn't I? But even if I hadn't, I believe that you would have found a way to win, because that's just who you are!

When The Powers contacted me to let me know that they were sending you back home, Aunt Jacqueline and I decided that we had better return to 'our' real home as well. I was afraid that my being here when you returned might cause you additional pain. In any case, I am afraid to face you after what I did to you. If I could turn back time, I would. But that's something the scientists on my planet have not 'yet' perfected.

Thomas, even after knowing you for only a short while, I know that you are a wonderful person, full of life and goodness. I would really have preferred staying on Earth, with the chance of getting to know you better... but it's obviously too late for that now. I'm sorry with all of my heart that things turned out the way they did, and I will never forget you!

All of my love,
Della

P.S.
If you should ever need to talk to me... just ask!

"*Just ask*?" Thomas repeated aloud, baffled. "Hey? That's what I did while I was on England?" Reading the letter had made Thomas grow very sad until he reached that *glimmer of hope* at the end. "I want to speak with Della Seisman *right now*!" he announced forcefully to the room with hopeful anticipation, even though he *knew* that there was no reasonable way for her to speak with him from billions of miles away? Even the *high-tech* telephones on England would not permit that! But, that didn't stop him from believing that *anything was possible* if you wanted it badly enough!

"*Here I am*!" Della suddenly announced, with a hopeful little smile from just outside his open window.

Thomas simply *could not* believe it, although he was certainly willing to try! "Is that *really* you?" he asked excitedly, wanting the answer to be '*yes*,' more than anything.

"Of course, it is!" Della laughed softly. "May I come in? It's very cold out here."

"Sure!" Thomas excitedly helped her through the open window and inside his room. He then gently closed the window behind her. Once Della was inside, he couldn't help but stare incredulously at her with a *big dumb smil*e on his face.

"Are you staring at my *dandruff* again?" she laughed softly.

Thomas chuckled. "No, I'm just so happy to see you."

"Do you mind if I hug you?" she asked sweetly.

"Do you really have to ask me that?" he smiled bigger. Moments later they found themselves locked in a very warm embrace which finally ended with the tiniest of kisses.

"Do you forgive me?" Della implored him.

"You *know* I do!" Thomas exclaimed with a huge smile.

"Thomas? I have something important to show you!" she said excitedly, mysteriously removing something from her purse and carefully placing it into her right hand, where her fingers immediately hid it from view.

His eyes were instantly glued to her hand, completely full of curiosity?

Slowly opening her hand, she revealed two slightly wilted *red flowers* with very short stems. "When you *indirectly* gave these to me yesterday," she smiled, "it meant so much to me that I've kept them with me *every moment* since you left!" Meeting his eyes with deep affection she added, "I just *couldn't* seem to stop thinking about you, Thomas!" Gently picking up one of the flowers with her free hand and handing it to him, she added, "I think we should *share* this beautiful gift. Don't you?"

Thomas's heart was *full*. Gladly accepting the flower and placing it into his pajama pocket, he replied, "Yes, I do. I shall *always* treasure this!"

Della smiled and sighing with relief, she gently returned the remaining flower to her purse. "I guess I'd better go home now."

"To *England*?" Thomas blurted out in horror.

"No, silly," she laughed. "To my home on Tanner Street! It's very late and we've both got school tomorrow morning, remember?"

Thomas smiled. "So… you *will* be staying in Masonville after all?" he gently suggested with anticipation completely engulfing his every word. "At least for a while?"

Della kissed Thomas on the lips, this time for a little longer. "Yes! Oh yes! Now that you have forgiven me, I've decided to stay here *forever*… or at least until the end of the school year," she assured him with a smile. And then after a slight pause, she nervously admitted, “Well, actually my aunt and I decided to stay in Masonville *earlier* tonight, but I had to know for *sure* how you felt about me after hearing about your *misadventures* on England before we made it official.”

“What do you mean by ‘*making it official*?’” Thomas asked curiously.

“Well, we would need to contact The Powers in the morning, and now… that’s *exactly* what we’re going to do!”

“I’m so glad!” Thomas was bursting at the seams with excitement. But then he frowned and said, “I thought you were only allowed to stay here if someone *suitable* from Earth was sent back to England to take your place?”

Della smiled broadly. “You’re right. And that *could* have been quite a problem, but luckily my aunt and I solved it.”

“How?” Thomas asked curiously.

“We convinced *Joe Porter* to go to England!”

“*What*?” Thomas responded incredulously. “When did you do that?”

“Soon after you left here,” she confessed. “After we explained to him that he never had to change his clothes, and he got to eat whatever he wanted to at any hour of the day or night, he was *sold*!”

“But the food there is all *clear liquid*?” Thomas objected.

“Does it fill you up and taste great?” she asked him.

“Yes,” Thomas replied hesitantly.

“Then I don’t imagine *he will care*!” Della laughed, with Thomas quickly joining in. “We promised him he could go just as soon as you came back.”

“Then my being sent home didn’t mess anything up for you?” Thomas asked nervously.

“Of course not! You *must* know how incredibly happy I am about the way things have turned out!” Della beamed.

“But what about Joe’s quick temper and his bullying?” Thomas asked with concern. “Won’t those cause a big problem on England? Especially in school?”

“Joe talked with my aunt for a long time and he actually told her that he *hated* that part of him. So, my aunt promised him that

The Powers would see to it that he was secretly helped with that problem."

"Can they really *do that*?" Thomas asked with surprise.

"Oh yes! You'd be surprised how much they can help him deal better with others *without him* even knowing that he's being helped," Della shared.

"*Solitary confinement*?" Thomas asked impishly.

Della laughed. "No. They have much *kinder* methods than that."

"When does he leave?" Thomas asked.

"He's *already* there!" she smiled.

"Does he *like it* on England?" Thomas asked curiously.

"The report I got was that he doesn't *ever* want to leave!" Della exclaimed.

"Then we're all set!" Thomas declared happily.

"All set for *what*?" Della asked in surprise.

"For going to next Saturday's matinee at the movie theatre!" Thomas smiled.

"Yes!" Della laughed.

Thomas laughed too. "I'm so happy that you've decided to stay."

"So am I," Della shared, with her bright eyes beginning to tear-up.

"You know what, Della? You were absolutely right!" Thomas shared seriously. "Going to England *was* a '*once in a lifetime*' experience for me, and I am so glad that I did it, even if only for a short while. I had wonderful talks with your principal, Mrs. Bartlet, and her husband, who is *actually* our P.E. teacher here in Masonville. Those talks really helped me to understand everything so much better! I think I would even like to try visiting England once again sometime in the future? That is, *if* The Powers will ever forgive me for all of the trouble I caused them on my *last* visit!" he chuckled. "My *one* stipulation however, is that *you* have got to be there with me!"

"That would be a *given*!" Della laughed. "Someone's got to keep you *out of trouble*!" Suddenly, becoming more serious, Della asked him, "What was the most important thing you learned from your short stay on England?"

"Well, strangely enough, even with all of the fantastic wonders of your planet's technology, the most important thing I learned… was just how very much *I missed you*!" Thomas admitted with a warm smile.

Della beamed, "I missed *you* too! Welcome home, Thomas!" With that, they hugged tightly, and both kids wished it would last *forever*!

When their embrace finally broke, Thomas was happier than the *happiest person* on Earth *or* on England, for that matter! After quickly putting on some shoes and getting coats for both Della and him, he very quietly led her out of his bedroom, through the front door, and just as *slowly* as possible… he walked her home. He made sure to hold her hand tightly *every step of the way*, and he *didn't* even ask her permission! As they walked together, hand in hand through the cold and dark night, it wasn't too cold or too dark to miss the warm smiles they offered each other, making them both want to stretch-out this beautiful moment for as long as possible! When they eventually arrived at Della's house, Thomas even said, "Hello," to her Aunt Jacquelyn as he was leaving. He also found himself *honestly* laughing heartily at the very funny joke she told him. Something about '*Noah having a tough time fishing because he only had two worms*?' She had *finally* done it! After that, Thomas had the most *satisfying* walk home in the middle of the night that he had *ever* known! And beginning tomorrow, he planned on taking Mr. Teltrab's great advice by committing himself *fully* to arriving at school *on time*! Just then, he reached into his pocket and pulled out the red flower that Della had given him, causing him to smile, and immediately think of her. Needless to say, as good as their time together was tonight, he *knew* that the time they shared tomorrow and each day after… would be *even better*!

"Dr. Brighton's Secret"

[2013]

"HAVE YOU EVER KNOWN SOMEONE who learned something so wonderful that it immediately brought them joy beyond their wildest dreams? And then you were *crushed* the moment you learned that the person would *not* share their secret with you or anyone else? My fellow archeologists and friends, my name is Dr. Stanley Kelly. I am here to speak to you about the greatest archaeologist I have ever had the pleasure of working with… *Dr. Robert Brighton*! *He* had such a wondrous secret. Sadly, he passed away last year, before anyone could convince him to share it. But before he died, he did leave us with this fascinating conundrum to solve in order to better understand the reason for his immense joy; '*And when your job is done, God will bring you home*?' Those thought-provoking words which he shared at our annual archaeologists' convention last year, have since become his *epitaph*, as he very unexpectedly passed away only months later. I was there at that convention along with several hundred other archaeologists from all over the world. I must admit that having spent a great deal of time with Dr. Brighton, I *was* able to string a few theories together as to the possible meaning behind those cryptic words. But the other archaeologists who were present, if their facial expressions were to be believed, *did not* seem to have even a spark of understanding? So, I was encouraged to speak with you tonight to share my thoughts, in hopes that they will rally you to join the important quest that I am currently on; the search for discovering and understanding *Dr. Brighton's secret*? I am certain *that* is what he would have wanted us to do. So, let's begin! What do you suppose Dr. Brighton *really* meant by those puzzling words, 'And when your job is done, God will bring you home?' There is of course the obvious. Perhaps he was letting us know that once we died, God would bring us back home… to *heaven*. But that sounds a bit simplistic, doesn't it? The Robert Brighton I knew was a brilliant individual who *never* shared such a pedestrian thought in his life! Instead as a rule, he uttered striking and profound hypotheses as often as he drank a cup of tea, which in *my* experience, was pretty often! So don't you agree that it's possible, even *probable* that he had something far more remarkable in mind when he uttered those words?"

"Robert Brighton was a brilliant but often reclusive man who showed little or even *no need* for human friendship, wouldn't you agree? I am *ashamed* to admit that this was *my* first impression of him too. But after working very closely with the man on his second expedition to the San Gabriel Mountains, I would have to respectfully *disagree* with that terribly flawed assessment, and humbly admit that I was *wrong*. In truth, I found Dr. Brighton to be insightful, very honest and caring, humorous… and even a bit *quirky*, but most of all, he was the *best friend* I ever had! But the *opposite* of that description is what I believe he encouraged most other people to believe. In that way, he never risked having them enter into his personal life, which he very clearly believed he *needed* to keep for himself as his own private corner of the universe. Call that behavior shy or reclusive if you will, but that was just who I believe the *true* Dr. Robert Brighton was."

"For those of you who were fortunate enough to attend his final archaeology convention last year, didn't you find it a bit odd that Dr. Brighton brought up *God*? He was after all, a learned man of science and as such had conceivably never before, judging by his many papers I have read, discussed his personal spiritual beliefs or carefully *weaved* them throughout his speech at an archaeology convention as he did there? But I tell you, during his last year of life, Dr. Robert Brighton not only *believed* in God, he believed that he was *communicating* with him on a daily basis! Was the man crazy? Of course not! He was merely doing what most of us are *afraid* to publicly admit; that combining the knowledge of science with one's faith in God, in many cases might very well be a viable way of finding and explaining the truth? Dr. Brighton was a traditional archaeologist you say. His work dealt only with life and relics from years past you say. He *never* proved to be a religious zealot in any way you say. I would have agreed wholeheartedly with all three of those statements *before* his second trip to the San Gabriel Mountains. But something happened up there that made him dramatically *rethink* his beliefs?"

"There was definitely something *very different* about the man once he returned to Berkeley following that expedition? For starters, he ceased being so punctual, so rule oriented and so... *perfect*. He even began wearing a wristwatch and carrying a cell phone; two things that he had *never* done as long as I had known him? He seemed to be so much happier and more relaxed, while at the same time, he carried a mysterious and wonderful secret with him which he *fiercely refused* to discuss with anyone? When I sometimes twisted his arm and got him to talk about some of his many expeditions, achievements or accolades, *not one* of them seemed to matter to him anymore? That is, *except* for his final trip to the San Gabriel Mountains."

(*Two Years Earlier*)

Dr. Robert Brighton woke-up at 8:00 o'clock sharp on that bright Saturday morning in February, just as he woke-up *every* morning. He smiled meaningfully as he took-in that perfect sunny day through his bedroom window. He stood just a shade under six feet tall, had a trim body, sported a head full of coarse black hair with graying temples, and possessed traditionally *handsome* facial features, including a striking pair of *piercing* blue eyes. In short, Robert Brighton was a fit and handsome man of fifty, who easily looked younger than his years. Because he was often perceived as being so good-looking, whenever he was complimented for it, he always attributed it to his Medieval English ancestors who according to him, *all* happened to be sheepherders, pig farmers and collectors of *dung*. Although this odd response was generally greeted by awkward silence or even a few raised eyebrows, that is probably because to the people listening, bringing *sheepherders*, *pig farmers* and *collectors of dung* into the conversation *didn't* really explain anything at all about his good looks? In fact, it seemed rather *absurd*? But he really didn't care. Without wishing to offend anyone, he just wanted people to stop wasting his time as well as their own by talking about something as mundane as *his looks*! And then again… maybe in his own way, he was simply *making a joke*? I suppose we'll never know for sure, will we? In any case, Dr. Brighton stayed in reasonably good shape by working-out at a local gym three times a week, always eating healthy meals, and drinking lots of tea. His favorite pastime, unsurprisingly, *was his work*! He was an archaeologist by trade, who lived in Berkeley, California, as he had most of his adult life. Although he did not officially teach at UC Berkeley, the University often hired him to give lectures to their archaeology classes on his findings from recent expeditions.

After showering and performing his usual toiletry tasks, he sat down at his kitchen counter with a nice cup of tea (*Earl Grey to be exact*). He did not have any particular plans for the day, but was actually quite satisfied sipping his tea and sitting at his breakfast bar… *alone*. The single-story bungalow which he owned and lived in had probably been built in the late 1940s. The house was constructed almost entirely of wood, but as you would expect from a very *thorough* man such as Dr. Brighton, it was termite-free and *always* very well maintained. The entire interior of the house had been painted white, a perfect backdrop to showcase each of the many eclectic pieces of colorful furniture decorating every room; much of it, antiques he had collected over the years from vintage shops and flea markets. The greatest feature of his house however, was the *whole* which covered a full *two acres* of land. It had served as an *apiary* by its former tenants, but with the bees gone, it was now considered to be the *largest residential backyard* in Berkeley!

Suddenly his doorbell rang. Without even a hint of emotion, Dr. Brighton calmly rose from his stool and slowly walked the short distance to the front door to answer it.

"Dr. Brighton?" A tall and lanky young man with thick brown hair, probably in his early twenties, smiled eagerly as Brighton slowly opened the door.

"Yes?" Dr. Brighton replied *inquisitively*, with his head slightly tilted to one side, not attempting to hide his curiosity in the least.

"Hello! My name is Stan Kelly," the visitor shared politely as he shook hands with him. "I am a graduate student, majoring in archaeology at UC Berkeley, and I was *hoping* to speak with you this morning if that would be all right?"

"Of course, Stan," Brighton replied politely as he motioned the young man inside. He proceeded to lead his guest into the kitchen and then offered him the stool beside his own, just before he himself sat down. Then, after his visitor waved off a cup of tea, Brighton nodded and immediately took a short sip of his own before officially igniting the start of their conversation.

"So, what can I do for you?" Dr. Brighton asked casually.

Sidestepping that most important question, Stan replied, "Thanks for seeing me. I apologize for surprising you like this. I would have called first, but your phone number *doesn't* seem to be listed in the Berkeley directory?"

"Oh? How very curious?" Brighton shared impishly. "Don't worry about that, Stan," he added. "I probably *wouldn't* have answered your call anyway."

Due to Dr. Brighton's peculiar little smile, Stan couldn't decide whether he was joking or being serious, so not wishing to take the risk of offending him, he took the safer of two possible routes by *not* reacting to his comment at all, but just *continuing* to smile. With their small-talk *obviously* completed, he decided to finally answer Dr. Brighton's original question. He began very hesitantly, "I'm, uh, looking for a job, and was hoping to assist you on one of your upcoming digs?"

"Oh?" Brighton eyed him curiously.

"Yes. I need to get some practical archaeology experience under my belt. You have quite the stellar reputation, and I know that an experience with you would be the best training I could *ever* hope to get!"

"Thank you, Stan!" Brighton replied graciously. "If you would just leave your name and number on that pad over there by the telephone, I promise to consider you *if and when* I may find need of your services."

Stan looked deflated. “Wouldn’t you at least like to hear about my credentials?” he pleaded, a little *too* desperately.

“Have you *ever* been on a professional dig before?” Brighton asked him gently.

“No, sir.”

“Then I’m sorry to say that regardless of whatever ‘great things’ you may have accomplished prior to today, you *haven’t got* the necessary credentials to go on one of my digs,” the man politely assessed, without even a hint of emotion.

“Please, Dr. Brighton. If you would just give me a chance?”

“You want *me* to give *you* a chance?” Brighten asked in feigned shock.

“Yes, sir,” Stan replied hesitantly.

“Would you give *me* a chance to kiss your sweetheart?”

“What?” Stan asked in shock.

“How about my brushing *your* teeth for you using *my* toothbrush?”

“No, of course not! That’s personal stuff!” Stan blurted out.

Dr. Brighton smiled kindly and said, “Yes, Stan. And to me, so are my *digs*.”

Stan could not help but smile back. “I understand, sir.”

“And will you please *stop* calling me, ‘*sir*?’” Brighton feigned disgust. “My name is *Robert*!”

“But the respect thing,” Stan insisted. “I certainly wouldn’t want to be disrespectful to you, sir.”

“If you call me, ‘sir,’ one more time, I’ll *fire* you!” Brighton declared firmly.

“You mean… *I’m hired*?” Stan asked incredulously.

“Just as long as you get my *name right*!” Brighton chuckled.”

Stan was immediately overcome with joy. “Thank you, si… Robert!” he exclaimed, as he shook his hand vigorously. “I swear I will be your righthand man! You just wait and see!”

“I believe I’ll be needing *both* of your hands,” Brighton smiled. “When can you start?”

“Excuse me?”

“You haven’t seen my backyard yet, have you,” Brighton said warily. “*Lots* to catalog out there, Stan!”

"I can start tomorrow morning if you like?" the young man declared excitedly. "I just need to tell my wife."

"Great! Be here tomorrow morning at 9:00 o'clock sharp!" Brighton insisted. "I will pay you professional wages, but I expect professional work. Can I count on you?"

"Yes, si... Robert. *You can*!"

Brighton laughed out loud. "Okay, tomorrow then."

"Tomorrow morning at 9:00 o'clock *sharp*!" Stan assured him. "And thank you. I can really use this job."

"I *know* you can," Brighton nodded understandingly.

"Just a hunch?" Stan asked curiously.

"Oh no, Stan. *Observation*," he responded thoughtfully. "Your eyes *told me that* the moment you first walked through the door. I'll bet you *don't* have a lying bone in your entire body!"

"Really? Well, thanks!" Stan said in surprise. And then growing more animated, he exclaimed, "I am so excited to be working with you, Robert!" as he robustly shook the man's hand once again and rushed out the front door, *both* in one humorously awkward movement!

Brighton laughed as he closed the door. His life had never been exceptionally predictable, but spontaneously hiring an assistant? He didn't actually need any help right now. But on the other hand, he *hadn't* lied. There truly was a lot of cataloging left to do in the backyard, and he welcomed the help. Besides… there was something *special* about this young man that he liked? He couldn't quite put a finger on it, but he just *knew* that he had done right by hiring him.

"You'll *never* guess what happened to me today!" Stan shared eagerly, as he briskly walked through the front door of the small apartment he shared with Stephanie, his wife of two years.

"You finally decided to drop out of school and *get a job*?" Stephanie replied facetiously.

"Close," he laughed. "I didn't drop out of school… but I *did* get a part-time job!"

"A part-time job?" she gasped excitedly. "Well, we can certainly use the extra money. What is it?"

"I'm the new archeologist's assistant… for Dr. Brighton!"

"*Dr. Robert Brighton*?" she shrieked in disbelief.

"Yes! Can you believe it? I feel so lucky!" Stan shared modestly.

"Luck had *nothing* to do with it, I'm sure," she replied, gently kissing her husband's forehead. "If Robert Brighton hired you, then he must have had a *very good* reason for doing it! I'm so happy for you, Stan! When do you start?"

"Tomorrow morning at 9:00 o'clock… *sharp*!" he chuckled.

Stephanie smiled, for she too had heard about Dr. Brighton's unusual zest for punctuality. Then she hugged her husband very tightly. "This could be the break we have been waiting for?"

That afternoon, following his meeting with Stan, Dr. Brighton was outside, finishing-up the cataloging of some of the more important *minor* artifacts that he and his team had uncovered on their very productive last dig. In truth, that excavation had surprisingly resulted in a treasure trove of historically interesting and even *valuable* items being discovered. Everything of greatest importance had already been cataloged and shipped-off to one of the major museums in California or New York, so now he was studying and cleaning everything else. Suddenly he came across a small, ordinary looking rock composed entirely of granite, which had been carved and sanded into the surprising shape of a square? But more importantly, it featured the unusual addition of what appeared to be a *Christian cross*, perfectly chiseled into the middle of one of the sides? He had found this curious artifact during his last exploratory journey into the San Gabriel Mountains. Of all the things they had uncovered, *this* was by far the most baffling? Based on the type of tools that were likely prevalent up there at the time of its creation, and the unusual square shape, as well as the skill level required to so expertly chisel the cross, he had the artifact roughly dated around 1200 A.D., give or take a hundred years. But Christianity was not known to have reached the shores of California until 1769, when twenty-one Roman Catholic missions sprang-up along its coastline? So, what was this *cross* doing there? Or was it merely some random ornament that had survived for over eight hundred years, that curiously had *nothing* to do with the Christian religion at all? Because he had these very important *unanswered* questions, Dr. Brighton had chosen not to catalog and send this unusual find to a museum. He was perfectly aware that it probably would have garnered a great deal of interest, but he *had* to know the truth behind its origin first. Although Robert Brighton had never been a particularly religious or spiritual man, there was just something about this artifact that captured his full attention? When he gazed upon it, it enticed him with the prospect that whatever this was… it was just the *tip of an iceberg*!

His phone rang right on cue as Dr. Brighton completed his thoughts.

"Hello?" he answered politely. He listened for a while before responding quietly, "Are you sure?" After listening further (*but this time for only a few seconds*), without changing his noncommittal tone of voice, he replied, "Thank you very much for sharing that with me." And then he gently hung up the phone.

That phone call, although sounding completely mundane in nature, had *actually* affected Robert Brighton greatly. He slowly walked over and sat down on the couch in the living room with a very thoughtful expression illuminating his face. Momentarily, he closed his eyes while very slowly breathing in and out. After five minutes of this calming meditation, he opened them once again and his face grew a barely noticeable smile. He knew beyond the shadow of a doubt *exactly* what he had to do next. He got up from the couch and slowly walked straight back to the telephone.

That night, Stan's head was overrun by a plethora of disquieting questions? Questions like how he was supposed to correctly catalog an *unlimited number* of valuable artifacts? And then he wondered what *other* important jobs he would be expected to do? He realized that he had very little *practical* experience in archeology… but Dr. Brighton had obviously known that, right? Even so, what if he arrived at his house tomorrow morning at 9:00 o'clock sharp and proved to be *completely useless*? He took a deep and calming breath. Next, he wondered *why* Dr. Brighton had chosen to hire him in the first place? Robert Brighton was a very intelligent man who *must* have clearly understood from his interview that he was a *raving rookie*! Was it pity? Of course not! It just *couldn't* have been? In any case, he *was* hired, so there was really no use worrying about the job until after he started doing it. At long last, he grew a very slight smile as he reclined in bed beside his beautiful sleeping wife. He strongly sensed that tomorrow morning his life would begin traveling a decidedly different path than the one he had journeyed thus far. He also accepted the fact that due to his *glaring* lack of experience he would definitely need a little time to learn the skills of a working archaeologist at an acceptable level. That's why he also knew that working in Dr. Brighton's backyard, cataloging artifacts *before* going on a dig was actually a godsend! By the time they went out on an expedition, he'd be more than ready! Stan was very much aware that it had been nothing short of *miraculous* that he had ever landed a job working for Dr. Robert Brighton in the first place! To be honest, he had *never* really expected to? He had just gone to see him on some crazy *whim*? So, he decided that no matter how frightened he was about exposing all of the archaeological knowledge and skills that he *didn't possess*, this fear was more than offset by the tremendous excitement he felt pondering the avalanche of knowledge and skills he was *going to learn* as a result!

At 8:59 the next morning, a very calm Robert Brighton, having just finished his breakfast, was quietly anticipating the arrival of his new assistant. As if confirming his sixth sense, the doorbell rang, causing him to smile.

"Good morning, *Robert*!" Stan excitedly greeted the man as Brighton opened the door for him.

"Good morning to you, Stan! Well done!" Dr. Brighton laughed. "You have just passed your *first* test with flying colors!" He quickly ushered the young man through the front door and into the main room, before taking him outside into his *immense* backyard.

Upon his first viewing of the yard, Stan was floored! He found himself feeling an all-encompassing sense of *awe* as he perused the countless rows of racks, protected from the elements by a gigantic awning that was capable of *completely* covering the racks on all sides as well as the top, thus keeping everything inside safe from high winds as well as being *waterproof*! But with no impending danger of inclement weather, the sides were currently left open. These racks were filled with the mysterious 'treasures' that Dr. Brighton had accumulated, but still needed to catalog. As impressive as that sight was, and the thought of cataloging all of those individual items was certainly daunting; there was still *three times* that much empty rack space left in the yard just waiting for the *next* load of artifacts to arrive!

Upon reading Stan's *hopeless* expression, Dr. Brighton let out a small chuckle. "Don't worry about any of this today, Stan. There's been a *slight* change of plan. We won't be cataloging any of these artifacts right now after all."

Stan looked surprised. "Oh? Then what *will* we be doing?"

Dr. Brighton smiled mysteriously as he replied, "We will be getting ourselves ready to travel to the San Gabriel Mountains for a *five-day dig* beginning *tomorrow*. Do you have a good pair of hiking boots and a sleeping bag?"

Shocked but excited, while still trying to comprehend the full scope of Dr. Brighton's words, Stan managed to reply, "Uh, yes. I've got a single tent as well."

"That's perfect!" Dr. Brighton replied encouragingly, without commenting on Stan's obvious hesitation. "Along with that tent and sleeping bag, pack a medium-sized suitcase with your clothes and personal items for a five-day trip. I'll take care of the food and archaeological equipment. Just be *sure* that you're back here by 9:00 o'clock sharp tomorrow morning!"

"But remember what you told me yesterday?" Stan hesitantly shared, suddenly feeling very nervous. "You said that I *wasn't ready* to go on a dig yet because I lacked the experience?"

Dr. Brighton laughed softly and met his eyes warmly. "Well, how are you supposed to ever get any experience, if no one gives you a chance? For a go-getter like I believe *you* are, what better way to gain that experience than by acknowledging your *rookie status*, but coming along anyway!"

Although Stan first looked at Dr. Brighton in utter shock, he quickly changed that expression to a smile of *relief.*

"You're going away to the mountains for a week?" Stephanie anxiously reiterated what her husband had just shared with her.

"What about your studies and teaching at the University?" she asked him with more than a mild amount of concern.

Stan smiled at her. "Already taken care of! My *first* professional dig, and it's actually going to be with a world-famous archeologist like Dr. Robert Brighton! I really can't wait!"

Now it was Stephanie's turn to smile. "You sound like a little boy getting ready for his *first* trip to Disneyland!"

Stan laughed. "It sort of *feels* that way too? And do you know what? Dr. Brighton doesn't seem the least bit concerned that I've never done one of these digs before?" Then quickly growing apprehensive, he asked gently, "Are you *sure* you will be okay here without me?"

Stephanie put on a facetious expression of irritation as she humorously replied, "You'll be gone for a whole five days? Uh… I *think* I can manage that!" She followed that with a smile and a kiss which were in *no way* facetious.

The following morning at precisely 9:00 o'clock, Stan arrived at Dr. Brighton's house… only *something* felt very odd? Of course, he was very excited about going on this dig, but he was certain there was *something else* going on which felt completely beyond his control? This strange feeling tenaciously nagged at him even when he wasn't thinking about it? Trying hard to put it out of his mind, he gently pressed the doorbell. Dr. Brighton momentarily answered the door and ushered him inside, along with his efficiently packed suitcase, bedroll and tent. Brighton smiled as he perused the evidence of Stan's expert packing. His own items for the trip were also fastidiously packed as one would expect, understanding his apparent *obsessive-compulsive* nature. *They* had already been set neatly in the backyard right next to the spot where he told Stan to place his things.

"Are you ready for this adventure, Stan?" Dr. Brighton asked cheerfully as they walked back inside the house.

"*More* than ready!" Stan replied with a child's whimsy. "Will we be driving?"

Brighton chuckled. "Not likely! Where we are going there are *no* roads and it's quite treacherous terrain to handle on foot!" he declared. Then meeting Stan's eyes, he shared, "There's no sense worrying about *any* of that, so we'll be traveling by *helicopter*!"

Stan couldn't help feeling excited and it showed!

"But first we'll need to wait for the rest of the team to get here. They were a little *late* arriving before our last dig too, but this group does excellent work so I will probably once again *ignore* their lack of punctuality," he winked playfully.

Stan didn't say anything, but Dr. Brighton had neglected to mention this to him yesterday, although he had *guessed* from the beginning that there would probably be others going with them. He was growing increasingly more certain that this would *not* be his only surprise this trip. He let slip a gentle smile as he embraced the fact that regardless of whatever else might happen, he was going on his very first *professional dig*!

Moments later there was a firm knock at the front door. Curiously, whoever it was *did not* appear to believe in using the doorbell? But Dr. Brighton only smiled as he threw open the door and watched four very friendly and relaxed-looking people enter the room. There were two men and two women, probably all in their early thirties, unceremoniously dressed for a casual California dig in tan shorts and colorful tee shirts. They smiled and greeted both Dr. Brighton and Stan with the word, "*Behne*," as they happily shook hands with them the moment they entered the room. After that *unusual* greeting, Stan guessed that more than likely they were all of some Native American descent, especially when you combined that greeting with the straight black hair and high cheek bones that they all sported. Dr. Brighton soon *confirmed* his hypothesis when he introduced Brennan and his wife Kirra, and Glen and his wife Teresa to him, as all being members of the *Shoshone* tribe. He went on to explain that this tribe was one of the first to inhabit the San Gabriel Mountains, and '*Behne*' meant '*Hello*' in their native language. 'No wonder Dr. Brighton had ignored their punctuality!' Stan thought, as he smiled at his own insightfulness.

For the next fifteen minutes or so, everyone chatted freely, offering Stan a perfect opportunity to learn a little bit about each one of these interesting strangers before they left on the trip. To begin with, he discovered that Brennan and Kirra were both educated and trained archeologists, earning their Masters degrees from UC Berkeley, while Glen and Teresa had done their studies, and earned their advanced degrees from Stanford. The latter pair were also both historians, specializing in Native American tribes of California. 'Could Dr. Brighton have assembled a more *perfect* group of professionals than these four?' he mused excitedly to himself.

"What time is the chopper getting here?" Brennan asked Dr. Brighton nonchalantly.

"It should get here at any moment now."

"Where will it land?" Stan asked curiously.

"In the backyard on the helipad," Dr. Brighton smiled, "about 100 feet beyond the racks."

Stan nodded appreciatively.

"I'm so ready!" Brennan declared. "Let's get this show on the road!"

"It's all he's talked about since you called, Robert," Kirra piped-in.

"I *am* curious about one thing though," Glen added. "Why the rush? I'll bet you haven't even come close to cataloging all of the artifacts we brought back from the dig we had there last month?"

"I was a little curious about that myself?" Teresa added.

Dr. Brighton's expression became much more thoughtful. "Well, let me just say that there is something very compelling about that site that seems to be calling me back."

The four nodded as if there was really *nothing* in what Dr. Brighton had said that warranted an argument or even a discussion? Although Stan really *wanted* to ask Dr. Brighton questions about his very *cryptic* response, he *didn't*! Moments later, they all moved into the backyard, loaded their gear onto the roomy helicopter and strapped themselves into their seats. Soon they were effortlessly lifted into the clear, blue sky with Stan feeling awe, excitement and of course gratitude, as their *adventure began*!

The distance from Berkeley, California to their exact destination in the San Gabriel Mountains, according to their young and friendly pilot named *Chris*, was about 350 total miles. The trip was scheduled to take three hours (*more or less*) depending upon the wind currents and any 'unforeseen problems,' a term which didn't exactly *thrill* Stan to think about while he was riding *ten thousand feet* off the ground in a helicopter! But, on a related topic, he was not surprised at all to learn that Chris was the same pilot who had flown Dr. Brighton and his team to their dig site a month ago, so thankfully, he *knew* where he was going! But this being Stan's first ride in a helicopter, he *was* surprised to learn that the engine was noticeably *quieter* than he had expected? In the war movies he had watched over the years, helicopters or '*choppers*' were always depicted as being obnoxiously noisy! So, *this* unexpected gift was very much appreciated. Even so, along with everyone else on board, he *still* wore a headset complete with noise eliminators to protect his ears from possible damage. Fortunately, these headsets were also equipped with built-in walkie-talkies. This enabled him to speak with *everyone* on the flight simultaneously, or to select *one or more* individual people on the flight simply by pushing the buttons linking his set to theirs! This resulted in a series of polite and private conversations during the flight *without* bothering everyone else with extraneous chatter.

"So, what drew you into archeology in the first place, Stan?" Dr. Brighton asked in a friendly tone, apparently as a conversation starter from the seat beside his.

Smiling, Stan replied, "Oh, that's easy. Traveling around the world, working in a lot of different dig sites sounded pretty exciting, and I have always been drawn to the idea of uncovering *proof* about how people lived and thought in the past." Suddenly growing excited, he added, "Maybe someday I'll even find out more about my *own* ancestors?"

"Oh yeah? What part of the world were your ancestors from?" Brighton asked curiously.

"*Every part*!" Stan laughed. "I'm a bit of a mutt!"

"Aren't we all!" Brighton chuckled. Then growing more thoughtful, he said, "I liked your reasons for pursuing archaeology. I for one, can't imagine doing anything else with my life. But what about… other more abstract reasons?"

"More *abstract* reasons?" Stan repeated, seeking clarification.

"Well," Brighton hesitated and then grinned, "For example, in my own experience every dig site has been uniquely different, and to me, that keeps my life in archeology always hopping!"

Stan smiled. "Oh yes! I'm sure you never get bored with all of the different sites you have explored."

Wearing an odd expression, Brighton replied mysteriously, "That's very true, Stan. But every once in a while, *one* of those sites seems to have a way of calling me back for more."

"Do you mean like *this* San Gabriel Mountains dig site urging you to return after only one month away?" Stan suggested astutely, remembering Brighton's *telling* comment to Teresa and Glen, earlier in the day.

"Exactly!" Dr. Brighton replied with a muted sense of excitement. "I just had this overwhelmingly strong feeling a couple of days ago that I *had* to return there for some unfinished business."

"A *couple* of days ago?" Stan repeated in surprise.

Brighton smiled at him in a fatherly way. "Yes. I believe this feeling made its presence known to me soon after we'd first met and I felt *compelled* to hire you."

"What?" Stan gasped in surprise.

Growing more serious, Brighton added, "In a strange way, I believe that *you* are supposed to guide me toward whatever truth it is that I am meant to be discovering?" Smiling, he added, "No pressure, Stan."

Stan laughed nervously.

Brighton continued, "Don't you believe that sometimes people may, for no apparent reason at all, receive *compelling mental messages*?"

"Do you mean like *hearing voices*?" Stan asked with obvious concern.

"No, not exactly. I'm *not* talking about being *crazy*," Brighton laughed. "At least I don't think I am?" he joked. Immediately becoming more serious he continued, "The question is, '*Why* would a seemingly intelligent scientist, like myself, drop everything to do this illogical dig… on a *hunch*?'"

Now it was Stan's turn to laugh. "Do you mean to tell me that this entire trip has *no* designated scientific purpose whatsoever, but is based solely on a hunch that you *might* find a worthwhile reason to justify it happening once we leave there in five days?"

"Pretty much," Brighton admitted. Lowering his voice, he added, "But I must tell you, Stan. I have experienced some pretty strange dreams about this dig site almost every night since I first left it? I believe *that* contributed a great deal toward convincing me that I needed to return so quickly." He paused, before asking with sincerity, "Do you think my dreams could be messages from God?"

Wow! Stan immediately realized that *this* moment effectively explained the odd feelings he'd experienced at Dr. Brighton's house earlier today! He understood now that they had been *spiritual* in nature. Was it possible that his senses had quietly picked-up those unsettling feelings *directly* from Dr. Brighton himself? Did the two of them share some kind of *connection*? Regardless, something about his question further assured him that this would be *much more* than your average run-of-the-mill dig! In fact, he felt cold shivers running throughout his entire body as he grew more excited about it! Quickly, he considered Dr. Brighton's deeply profound, and yet to his way of thinking, *unanswerable* spiritual question. To begin with, *Stan* had always believed in God as far back as he could remember… but God had *never* to his knowledge sent him a compelling message in the form of a dream as Dr. Brighton was suggesting *he* may have received? "Do you *believe* in God?" he asked the man gently.

Dr. Brighton grew an *uncertain* expression on his face as he responded, "I don't *not* believe in God. The question just hasn't come up lately."

"Then what makes you believe that you may be receiving *messages from him*?" Stan asked pointedly.

Very uncharacteristically, Dr. Brighton paused to think about the question, and then he replied very slowly, "I don't know?"

There was really nothing Stan could say to *that*! Dr. Brighton was obviously confused, and confusion is generally a very personal thing. Apparently, with both men understanding that, they amicably ended their conversation without another word being spoken, and closed their eyes for a little rest before landing.

Stan was abruptly awakened by a slight thump, as in spite of Chris's best efforts, the helicopter hit ground a little roughly some three and a half hours later. Once the blades had stopped spinning, everyone immediately set to work removing everything from the chopper they had packed for their five-day expedition. Next, they took it all over to a distinct place a good twenty feet away, which same as last time, had been designated as the '*unloading*' spot. Hypothetically speaking, once the unloading had been completed and the chopper had gone, if it were later discovered that something essential to this dig had been *accidentally* left at home, replacing it, even at this early juncture, could still set them back a half-day or more! Luckily, *everything* was accounted for according to Kirra, who Dr. Brighton trusted *implicitly* due to her excellent track record doing this same job for a number of his expeditions in the past. Next, at Dr. Brighton's request, they all gathered at the unloading spot to go over the day's itinerary. Brighton flashed the 'thumbs-up' sign to Chris and the helicopter immediately flew off, not scheduled to return again for another *five days*. Following the chopper's departure, the first order of business was setting-up camp. Brennan, Kirra, Teresa and Glen took the lead on this, while Stan was placed in charge of setting-up his own tent, as well as assisting Dr. Brighton with his more complicated (*meaning much larger and more comfortable*) shelter.

Stan quickly completed his own tent set-up and was helping Dr. Brighton with his, when he spied a very unusual rock formation that was sitting atop the hill closest to them *inexplicably* resembling the shape of a man? He casually pointed this out as a simple matter-of-fact to Dr. Brighton, who beyond acknowledging him, didn't seem to show much interest? 'Maybe when you are such a well-traveled archeologist as he is,' Stan thought logically, 'once you've seen *one* rock formation, as they say, *you've seen them all*?'

Stan didn't physically do much with the remainder of his day, because let's be honest, he was *completely new* to this. Instead, he watched and listened to everything going on around him as he very *wisely* considered himself to be in '*learning mode.*' He particularly focused on closely observing the other four members of Dr. Brighton's team as they spent the remaining hours of daylight efficiently setting-up for the beginning of the next day's excavation. Curiously, just as Dr. Brighton had mentioned, tomorrow's dig was scheduled to take place in the same general vicinity as the one they had so *exhaustingly* searched for meaningful artifacts a month earlier? Although they still *might* discover something new that they had missed the first time around, there were certainly *no* guarantees. But of course, *that's* what made these digs so exciting, or if God forbid, nothing significant was found… so *disappointing*!

Dr. Brighton and Stan were talking in the former's tent after supper while the others had retreated to their own desired destinations. For some unknown reason, he clearly seemed a bit distracted?

"You know what, Stan?" Brighton began slowly. "The reason I didn't comment on that odd rock formation you saw today was because… well… I *couldn't* see it."

"Oh? I'm sorry," Stan replied apologetically. "I probably didn't make it clear enough to you where I was looking."

"No, it wasn't that," Brighton replied quickly. "I *saw* the place that you were pointing to, but I *didn't* see even a hint of a rock formation? In fact, to my eyes there was absolutely nothing there but flat hilltop?"

Stan didn't risk insulting him by asking if he had visited his *optometrist* lately, but Dr. Brighton addressed that question anyway with a slight laugh. "In answer to what you are *probably* thinking, no! I *don't* need glasses! The last time I had my vision checked, my eyesight was *perfect*."

"Then what exactly *are* you suggesting?" Stan asked him, with more than a hint of confusion.

"I'm not suggesting anything at all," Dr. Brighton responded gently, without the slightest hint of sarcasm or frustration. "I'm *saying* that you can definitely see things out there that *I can't*." Stan uncomfortably stammered a bit while trying to respond, before Dr. Brighton mercifully continued, "That rock formation in the shape of a man can absolutely *only* be seen by you." Pausing and softening his voice, he added with a sparkle in his eyes, "I know, because I already *asked* everyone else in camp earlier today if they could see it? And unanimously… they *could not*!"

"What's going on here?" Stan demanded, obviously a bit shaken-up.

"Don't worry, Stan. There's absolutely no reason for you to be concerned," Brighton began calmly. "I told you I felt strongly that *you* were going to guide me somewhere, and I suppose *this* confirms the location we're going to first!"

"But how can you possibly know that?" Stan asked anxiously.

Dr. Brighton was quiet a moment as if he were considering what Stan's reaction might be once he spoke. "Someone or *something* inside my head has been sporadically communicating with me ever since I returned from my last dig at this site. They don't speak in words, mind you… yet I understand their meanings *perfectly*!" he replied calmly.

Stan felt dizzy as he realized the sheer magnitude of what Dr. Brighton was saying. "Did they suggest that you bring *me* along?" he asked hesitantly.

"*Yes*," Dr. Brighton confirmed solemnly. "And now I think we both know *why*!" With a decidedly gentler tone he added, "I was wrong about you, Stan. You *do* have the credentials to go on this dig. You obviously have something very special that I lack."

Stan was dumbfounded. "And what could *that* possibly be? My collection of '*Indiana Jones*' comic books?" he asked humorously.

Brighton laughed, "No." Then he replied meaningfully, "You share the same *wavelength* with whatever I am communicating with. *That* is why I believe you are able to see this rock formation whereas *no one else* on this trip can! So, if I want to find out exactly *where* it is that I'm supposed to go, it appears that *you* must be the key to getting me there."

Stan had to laugh, although he really did *try* to stifle it as he replied, "Are you telling me that on my very first dig, I am actually playing an integral part?"

Dr. Brighton laughed right back. "Yep! You are *most integral*! Now go to that little bitty tent of yours and get some sleep, my friend. Tomorrow morning, right after breakfast… we set off to find that *invisible* rock formation!"

The next morning, Dr. Brighton's team was up bright and early. After breakfast, they began the preliminary work for the day's upcoming dig. Stan got up a little later, while Dr. Brighton was up at *precisely* 8:00 o'clock, as was his normal routine. (*Stan made sure to check his watch to confirm it.*)

After Dr. Brighton had spoken for a sufficient time with his team and given them his go ahead to start the excavation without him, he briskly walked over to Stan. With a boyish grin, which he had *never* up to this point revealed to him, he excitedly asked, "Shall we go?"

Stan smiled and nodded affirmatively. Dr. Brighton then offered him a pair of sturdy hiking poles, while keeping another set for himself. Next, he handed him a yellow backpack to put on which was *identical* to the one he himself was already wearing. Between them, the backpacks held a very limited number of archaeology tools including a small shovel, a pickaxe, several different sized chisels, a trowel, a variety of small excavation brushes, and several strong bags for the carrying of artifacts (*just in case they needed them*). In addition, *each* backpack carried a small first-aid kit, a small roll of toilet paper, a box of matches, a flashlight (*with extra batteries*), a few energy bars, a light blanket, a flare gun, a knife and of course, six bottles of drinking water. And why were these backpacks colored bright yellow you ask? To make it easier for them to be *spotted*, should Dr. Brighton and/or Stan become lost and a helicopter had to be dispatched to search the mountains for them. With that, they immediately set off toward the man-shaped rock formation. It actually looked to be less than a mile away, Stan guessed. But to reach it, they first had to navigate the steep and potentially dangerous hillside, while simultaneously *each* carrying what felt like a *twenty-pound backpack*! He would soon find out if his experiences hiking the hilly streets of San Francisco every day as a tour guide last summer, while carrying a backpack full of water bottles and a first-aid kit for his tourists, had *inadvertently* prepared him for this?

"This is sure a *great* way of keeping in shape," Stan shared humorously after they had been climbing up a gradually steeper and more challenging incline for nearly half an hour with the thankful help of their poles.

"How do you think we archeologists stay so trim?" Dr. Brighton chuckled. Then with a more serious tone, he asked, "How much further do we have to go, Stan?"

Stan had momentarily *forgotten* that *he* was the guide here, but he quickly reclaimed his responsibility. "Not too much further," he assured him. "It's just up at the top of this hill and over there," he clearly pointed to his left.

"I must say, I have *not* been in this situation for quite some time," Dr. Brighton confessed.

"What situation is that?" Stan asked.

"*Not* being in-charge," Brighton admitted. "Not being in control of my own destiny."

Stan carefully listened to his words, and heard the unmistakable sound of *uncertainty* emanating from his voice, although he was very carefully attempting to mask it by keeping his demeanor positive. "I agree," Stan replied. "It's definitely harder to follow when you're used to leading. But *not* leading certainly does not reflect badly on you."

Brighton smiled at Stan's well-meaning comment.

"It's just that sometimes passing that leadership torch on to someone else simply feels like the *right thing to do*, don't you think?" Stan grinned. "Especially if that *someone else* can *see* the rock formation and *you can't*!" he teased.

Dr. Brighton let out a loud and cheerful laugh, "Of course it does! And I have *complete faith* in you, Stan!"

Stan smiled. "Well, thanks for trusting me. I'll try my best not to let you down."

"I'm sure you won't," Dr. Brighton replied graciously.

Their conversation ceased at that point as both men concentrated fully on their endurance. They determinedly continued climbing toward the top of the hill in hopes that they could reach it *before* they became utterly and completely exhausted! Unfortunately, considering how drained they were both feeling already, especially while being weighed down by their backpacks, that outcome was *not* the least bit farfetched! Suddenly, Stan froze in his tracks as he saw and heard the terrifying rattle of a coiled diamondback directly in his path!

"Take it easy, Stan," Brighton said calmly. "I'm sure it's more afraid of you than you are of it."

"That's *not* very helpful!" Stan quipped, while trembling.

Brighton gently instructed, "Slowly step backwards, then go five paces to your left before walking forward again."

Stan very carefully did exactly as he was told. As as he moved forward again, there was no longer any sign of the snake? He let out a big sigh of relief.

Brighton smiled. "Remember Stan, we are traipsing all over *his* home. *We* are the trespassers here. He was just letting you know that!"

"I understand," Stan agreed. "Thanks for the help!" he shared appreciatively. "How did you know that the snake wouldn't chase after me once I'd moved to the left? Experience?"

Brighton smiled. "No, Stan. Believe it or not, this is the *first time* I've ever encountered a rattlesnake in my life! In general, I just find that the best way to diffuse an angry aggressor is to calmly and without fear or anger, give them a little sincere respect, like you did when you walked around him. When I do that, I often find that they *return* the favor."

"Does that always work for you?" Stan asked curiously.

"Well, I wouldn't say *always*."

"What do you do when it doesn't?" Stan asked.

"*I run like hell* in the opposite direction!" Brighton laughed.

Stan laughed too.

Thankfully, it wasn't long before they finally reached the top of the hill. Both men immediately shed their backpacks and *collapsed* as they completely succumbed to their weariness. Every last muscle in their bodies *ached*! Curiously though, Stan noticed that Dr. Brighton seemed to be feeling much more exhausted than he did? He even appeared to be having trouble initially catching his breath? But then he rationalized that fit or not, the man was probably *twice* his age! In any case, they immediately rewarded themselves with a long fifteen-minute break to rest, along with both of them thirstily *draining* one of their valuable bottles of water from their backpacks.

As they ended their break, Stan noticed that the rock formation in the 'shape of a man,' was definitely close, only about twenty feet to their left. Leaving their hiking poles behind as markers to show them where to begin climbing back down the hill again (*assuming that they returned*), they began determinedly walking in the direction of the formation. As they drew nearer, with surprise, Stan noticed that the creature was derived from *pure white* rock? Possibly *marble*? This was especially odd because he was not aware of deposits of pure white marble being especially prevalent in these mountains? The most common rock type found here was of course, granite. From this closer proximity, he was also shocked to realize that the rock formation looked *remarkably* even more like a real person than it had from a distance?

As the two men finally reached the rock formation, Stan noticed a thin, smooth, stone tablet, about the size of an oversized coffee-table book grasped in the 'rock creature's' right hand? Things grew *stranger yet* as he suddenly heard a voice inside his head telling him, even *compelling him* to take the tablet from the rock creature and *deliver* it to Dr. Brighton! Stan oddly realized that the voice had *not* used words, and yet… just as Dr. Brighton had experienced, he had *understood* the meaning of *everything* it had said? In any case, he didn't argue. He promptly accepted the tablet from the right hand of the rock creature and proceeded to offer it to Dr. Brighton, as directed.

"*Yes*?" Dr. Brighton asked, with an outpouring of curiosity.

"I'm supposed to give you this stone tablet," Stan explained uncomfortably. "You know that *wordless voice* you were talking about? The one *inside* your head? It decided to pay me a visit… and it *insisted* that I give this to you!"

Dr. Brighton chuckled. "Well, be that as it may, you know very well that I *can't* see it, right?"

As soon as Dr. Brighton had finished talking, the rock creature suddenly turned toward them, and although it *didn't* speak in the normal fashion through its *mouth*, Stan distinctly heard its voice inside his head declaring, "Hecula tombre!"

"That stone creature just *spoke* to us!" Stan exclaimed with excitement.

"It did?" Dr. Brighton replied with heightened curiosity. "What did it say?"

"It said, 'Hecula tombre?'" Stan gushed. "I should be scared to death that a stack of rocks just *spoke* to us? But I'm way too busy feeling *fascinated*?"

"*Hecula tombre*?" Dr. Brighton whispered. "Oh my God!"

"What does it mean?" Stan asked excitedly.

Dr. Brighton grew strangely quiet for a few moments before finally returning to normal and responding to Stan's question. "Hecula tombre," he began slowly, "is part of an ancient Native American language that has only recently begun to be understood. To the best of my knowledge, it means, '*God be with you*!'" And then Dr. Brighton gasped! Inexplicably and all at once, he suddenly *saw* the stone tablet that Stan was holding! And then looking up, he very quickly found himself in a *state of shock* as he was finally able to see the *rock creature*! "My God! This is *fantastic*!" Brighton exclaimed, quickly accepting the tablet from Stan. Then with the excitement of a child, he immediately began studying the writing on it very carefully. "This is written in the *same* language as that rock creature was speaking!" he declared. But then he quickly frowned. "However, this looks to be far more *complicated* than the written examples of this language that I have come across in the past. At best, I'm afraid this could take me *years* to translate! And even then, I can't be 100% certain that my translation will be accurate?"

"Maybe *you* won't need to translate it at all?" Stan suggested slyly. "Maybe whomever you are meeting will translate it *for* you?"

"I *like* the way you think, Stan Kelly! If that's to be, it would certainly make my job a whole lot easier!" Dr. Brighton beamed. And then processing what he was actually seeing, his demeanor again grew childlike as he proclaimed, "It's simply *incredible*, Stan? Why do you suppose that I am suddenly able to see all of this now?"

Stan didn't really have a definitive answer to that question, but after quickly thinking about it, he suggested, "Maybe it's because you have *increased* your faith that this is truly possible?"

Both men suddenly heard strange scraping noises coming from the rock creature, prompting them to quickly turn around to face it.

The creature, which did not speak this time, but was still *obviously* alive, clearly raised an arm and pointed them toward a nearby hiking trail, and then just like that, the arm returned to its side, and the rock creature's life was *gone*? It inexplicably returned to being just a very curious looking rock formation made of pure white marble in the San Gabriel Mountains?

"Is there something up here that causes *hallucinations*?" Stan asked, half in jest.

Brighton laughed and said, "Oh sure! *Plenty* of things! But I've got a funny feeling that everything we've seen so far is 100% *real*!" Then, suddenly growing inspired, he declared, "I say we follow this path like our '*rock friend*' suggested, and see where it leads?"

With not a small amount of trepidation, Stan obediently nodded and followed Dr. Brighton, who was now carefully cradling the stone tablet in his arms as he determinedly marched down the path! As they walked, to their surprise and delight, they found that the path now featured *small rock formations* along the outside of it every ten feet or so, which they had certainly not noticed before? Stan shook his head and smiled as he realized that whatever was guiding them was not allowing them even the *remotest chance* of getting lost! However, after a short while, Stan's fears got the better of him as he couldn't help but feel a gnawing sense of dread? He even began to imagine that they were being led straight into some sort of *supernatural trap* from which they might *never return*? But when he glanced over at Dr. Brighton and felt his muted but clear sense of excitement and curiosity, that sense of dread completely deserted him.

After ten minutes of walking, without warning, the small rock formations along the outside of the trail completely *disappeared*? They were now met by a *gigantic granite double-door*, which appeared to lead into the side of the hill? Stan was stunned! He had never seen a door this large in his life, much less one that was hidden here in the mountains?

"It's so strange," Dr. Brighton said, genuinely perplexed. "I *know* that I studied this entire area very thoroughly from the helicopter on my last dig, and believe me Stan... there was *no door here*! I certainly would have noticed something this large!"

"Perhaps you just *couldn't* see it?" Stan suggested gently.

Dr. Brighton smiled. "Of course. Just like when I *couldn't* see that rock man!" His playfulness returned, "But it's sure nice to know that both of us are in the *same world* now, isn't it?"

Stan frowned. "Well, when you put it that way, it makes me feel as if we've just fallen down the rabbit hole in '*Alice in Wonderland*' and are about to enter the most *bizarre* place imaginable!" he laughed nervously.

"And there's every reason to believe that *we are*!" Brighton contemplated thoughtfully. Growing more urgent, he added, "And we must consider the possibility that *should* we decide to go through that door, there is every chance that whatever we find in there may turn out to be *completely incomprehensible* to us, in *spite* of our brilliant minds!" he smiled impishly. "That would seem to make this entire trip *pointless*, wouldn't it?" He paused for a moment and then shared determinedly, "But even so, as scientists, I believe we owe it to mankind to go the distance, *regardless*! Don't you agree?" he suggested strongly.

Stan instinctively nodded his head in agreement, although his heart was not completely sold on the plan. Unfortunately, his general lack of enthusiasm in moving forward, along with his sickly expression were *more* than enough to very clearly transmit his paralyzing indecision.

"Don't worry, Stan," Brighton caught the doubt he harbored as he gently placed his free arm across his shoulders and sought to reassure him. "I know that we will both come out of this adventure alive."

"How can you *possibly* know that?" Stan asked urgently.

Dr. Brighton smiled thoughtfully, and replied, "Well? Actually… I *can't*."

These were *not* the reassuring words that Stan had hoped for. However, once again for some unknown reason he *found* the courage from Dr. Brighton to continue on!

Both men now gazed in astonishment at the magnificent double-door before them. It looked to be at least forty feet high and twenty feet wide? And just as they had ascertained earlier, each side of it appeared to be made of *solid granite*. Opening the door was their first challenge. As unlikely as it seemed, they even considered the possibility that opening this door might require a *secret password* like in the Aladdin stories? But if that were the case, they were unfortunately *clueless* as to what that powerful word might be? And then as if there was something that was sympathetic toward their difficult quandary, and as a result had decided to *help them*, there suddenly appeared a new detail on the door which they had apparently neglected to notice before… or that perhaps had *only just materialized*? On the far-left side of the massive door to their right, just off center of the two doors, now appeared a small square indentation, about three feet up from the ground?

"Robert! Look!" Stan astonishingly pointed at the indentation in the door. "That looks to me like it could be some sort of odd *keyhole*?"

Brighton was equally shocked, but calmly nodded in agreement.

"I wish I knew what to do next?" Stan shared hopelessly.

Dr. Brighton meditated briefly before an honest look of excitement suddenly crossed his face. "Would you mind holding this, please?" he asked, not waiting for a response, but immediately handing the invaluable stone tablet to Stan.

"Sure," Stan replied in surprise, pulling the tablet close to his chest while simultaneously praying that he *didn't* drop it!

It was then that Dr. Brighton carefully pulled a square rock with a cross on it from deep inside his pants pocket. The *very same* artifact that he had discovered while on his trip here a month ago. "I'll bet *this* will do the trick!" he said, confidently displaying the rock to Stan. "Something just *told* me to bring it along?"

Stan stared at the square rock in awe, *not missing* the sight of the curious cross carved into the top?

"Would you care to do the honors?" Dr. Brighton asked politely, while offering the rock to Stan.

"No, thanks," he stammered nervously while holding tightly to the stone tablet. "I've kind of got my hands full."

Nodding, with an understanding smile, Dr. Brighton approached the double-doors and confidently inserted the rock into the indentation, while the two of them listened and watched with wild anticipation! Momentarily, they heard the deafening sound of rock scraping rock, as the two sides of the huge granite door slowly crept open, away from them, toward the inside. As they gazed, the now open doors revealed an incredible, even *unearthly* sight? They stood at the doorway to what appeared to be an enormous cave, *mysteriously lit* by thousands of different glowing rocks of all colors, shapes and sizes, which were *magnificently and completely* covering every square inch of space on the walls and ceiling! Along with the *usual* colors, there were just as many *unusual* ones? These 'new' colors, in addition to being bright and beautiful, *did not* so much as resemble *any color* of the human color spectrum? But regardless, their eyes were somehow able to see them?

"Shall we?" Dr. Brighton excitedly asked Stan, not hiding his delight in the least. Stan, even with his ever-growing list of misgivings and with his courage running dangerously low, forced himself to *hesitantly* follow Dr. Brighton through the doors and into the cave.

In vintage adventure and horror films, just as soon as the two had entered the cave, the doors would have inexplicably *slammed shut* behind them; leaving them trapped with absolutely *no way out*! But no such abrupt and dramatic event occurred here. In fact, it was just the opposite. The doors remained open, seemingly assuring them that they could leave whenever they wanted to; which was of course, a *great* relief to Stan! But as he looked at the open doors, very curiously he immediately noticed that the door they had inserted the key into on their right, now appearing on their left, showed absolutely *no sign* of any keyhole now? Quickly checking the backside of the door, he was relieved to find the keyhole *there*! But he also realized that it had *miraculously changed* its location? Dr. Brighton had *also* noticed this incredible phenomenon, and without explanation, casually turned back around and *removed* the key. His action immediately caused both granite doors to slowly begin closing. As Stan watched in horror, the massive doors eventually *shut tight*, while the keyhole *completely disappeared*! Frighteningly, this appeared to permanently block their only exit, effectively *trapping* them inside the cave!

"I thought that might happen," Dr. Brighton matter-of-factly mumbled to himself once the door had completely closed.

"Then *why* did you take the key out?" Stan asked him, in shock.

"Curiosity," Brighton smiled.

Stan politely forced a return smile, although he felt like *screaming*!

"Don't worry, Stan," Dr. Brighton said warmly. "I have every confidence that this journey will leave us both in one piece."

"Yes, but *in one piece of what*!" Stan replied dryly.

Dr. Brighton laughed loudly. "I do love a bit of humor whenever the situation has unexpectedly grown so dire!"

Just then, a piercingly loud and strident plethora of pitches *blasted and buzzed* its way through the cave, seemingly engulfing every inch of it! This ghastly dissonance was the result of an infinite number of clashing musical tones, each desperately seeking to be heard over the other ones as *loudly and harshly* as possible! This frightful rivalry resulted in a hideous *cacophony from hell*! The terrible abomination was even more disconcerted by what sounded like the frenzied grating of a rusty chainsaw or even a mad dentist's drill grinding away, made *wholly intolerable* by the unstable intensity of the volume erratically changing every few seconds!

"*Run*!" Dr. Brighton ordered, as he quickly darted away from the door toward the center of the cave. He was followed closely behind by a mightily confused Stan? When they momentarily reached the center of the cave, they stopped, while the ghastly noise surprisingly *stopped* as well?

"Well done!" Stan exclaimed in relief. "But now would you *please* explain to me what just happened?"

"It's incredible!" Dr. Brighton beamed.

"*What's* incredible?" Stan asked, in utter confusion.

"That we, as archeologists, study physical remnants of long dead civilizations, while being completely unprepared to study the remaining parts that are hidden, but *still alive*?"

"*What*?" Stan exclaimed, *not close* to understanding him.

Dr. Brighton smiled like someone who had just discovered that the moon *really was* made of green cheese. "It's positively *wonderful* to be able to see and hear all of this!" he declared. "Stan, the fact that we both now believe something supernatural is going on inside this cave, probably means that as a result we will be seeing and hearing *incredible things* from here on out!" He grew more serious as he strove to make young Stan further understand his great epiphany. "I believe that the sounds we were hearing so loudly in this cave belong to thousands of *living spirits* whose bodies have long since died." Still not smiling, Dr. Brighton continued, "Although I'm quite certain that these spirits would *never* intentionally try to harm us, I'm guessing they all coexist in this cave like electric current, so I am just hoping that won't *inadvertently* become a problem for us."

"A *problem*?" Stan asked intently.

"The possibility of accidentally *electrocuting* us," Brighton explained somberly. "Between the spirits, and the light radiating from the walls and ceiling, there appears to be an *incredible* amount of energy existing in this cave!"

After briefly considering Dr. Brighton's statement, Stan gently replied, "I mean no disrespect, Robert, and I really haven't a clue about any of this… but personally, I *don't* believe we need to worry about these spirits being dangerous *at all*. I mean, why would they have called you back here, and *why* would we have been shown the way to this cave and been allowed to enter it if the experience of being here was in any way dangerous for us?" he questioned logically. "And even though that noise we heard at the mouth of this cave *was* completely unexpected, and I'll admit that it was pretty *unbearable* to listen to… it still didn't sound *dangerous* to me?" he shared. "It sounded more like a raucous party where everyone is excitedly speaking over one another. I think maybe they are just happy to see us?"

Brighton laughed. "That is quite a *creative* observation!" he smiled admiringly. "If it's true, *nothing* would make me happier!"

Stan smiled at the compliment and then suddenly noticing a starry-eyed gaze consuming Dr. Brighton's face, he asked curiously, "What are you thinking about?"

"Hmm? Oh. I was just trying to make scientific sense of this cave? I'm guessing that since the spirits were uncomfortably loud by the door but strikingly silent here at the center, they *may* be spinning around circularly in this cave much like a tornado, but without the powerful wind to cause havoc and destruction. That could explain how the energy is created to run the lights all around us."

Stan nodded thoughtfully, but then suggested, "Or then again, there may just be *no logical human explanation for any of this*?"

Brighton cracked a smile. "That was *my* first thought too," he confessed. "But I just couldn't resist taking a good old-fashioned *scientific stab* at it!"

Stan chuckled, but his attention was immediately drawn to the unusual sight of a single *light-giving rock*? It had apparently fallen off the wall or ceiling, and was now resting a mere two feet in front of him? Dr. Brighton was also intently staring at it. The clear rock glowed beautifully like a huge polished diamond in all its glory, made even brighter by a mysterious *inner light*?

"Look at that!" Stan exclaimed. "Do you think we should take that with us? It's *beautiful*!"

Dr. Brighton, studying it very carefully, replied with controlled passion, "You're right! And I'm all for collecting unique samples, but we don't know *exactly* what it is yet? It could somehow be dangerous? Let me perform a few simple tests on it." He quickly removed a small shovel from his backpack and gently picked-up the rock with it. *Nothing* happened. No movement, no dimming of its light and no sound. He returned the shovel to his backpack, and took a bottle of water out, unscrewed the top and gently sprinkled a few drops onto the rock. But just like before… *nothing* happened? Finally, he very bravely picked up the rock in his own hand and gazed intently at it. Suddenly, Dr. Brighton became very calm, and simultaneously his eyes *did not* appear to be moving? It was as if he were in a *trance*?

Growing a little scared after a few moments, Stan gently shook his shoulder and asked with concern, "Are you okay?"

Dr. Brighton's eyelids momentarily fluttered, and he replied as if *nothing* abnormal had happened, "Yes, I'm fine, Stan. Thank you for asking."

"But you were so still, and your eyes *weren't* moving? I didn't know what was going on?" Stan shared with concern.

"Well, I can't really explain what was '*going on*,' myself!" Brighton chuckled. "But regarding your question as to whether or not we should take that rock with us? The answer would be a definite, *no*. I'm afraid that *this* rock belongs right here in the cave."

"What makes you think that?" Stan asked in surprise.

"Well," Brighton replied honestly. "This might sound a little odd to you, but as soon as I touched it, that was just the *impression* that it gave me."

Regardless of the fact that Dr. Brighton seemed to be treating the rock as if it were '*a living thing*,' Stan still accepted his explanation without argument. A moment later, the rock *disappeared*? "Hey? What's going on here?" he gasped.

Dr. Brighton began to laugh.

"What's so funny?" Stan demanded.

"We thought the *front* of this cave was weird!" Brighton exclaimed.

Stan smiled, acknowledging the humor of the situation and their utter *lack* of a viable reason to explain it? And then momentarily forgetting about the valuable tablet he was holding, it slowly and silently began slipping through his fingers until finally free of his grasp, it horrifyingly began *falling to the ground*! Dr. Brighton and Stan, with expressions of *immense shock*, suddenly held their breath, anticipating the *terrible crash* that would surely greet them when the tablet *smashed* into a thousand tiny pieces upon hitting the ground! But *that* never happened? Instead, the tablet gently changed direction in the air and returned to Stan's awaiting arms as if *nothing* had ever happened?

After watching this inexplicable spectacle, both Stan and Dr. Brighton immediately turned toward each other in disbelief, trying very hard to find some *logical explanation* to explain what had just occurred, but ultimately *finding none*? For the first time on this adventure, they were *both speechless*! Suddenly, without explanation, Brighton smiled and said, "Well, I believe *that's* our signal to begin conversing with our hosts!"

Stan was still in a state of shock at seeing the *flying tablet*, but he still managed to ask, "But if everyone here is a bodiless spirit, then how will they possibly speak with us? Do you think they'll communicate *inside* our heads like they've done before?"

"Perhaps," Brighton replied doubtfully, "but that would make it impossible for them to answer any questions we chose to ask them."

"How do you know that?" Stan asked.

"They shared that information with my mind the moment we entered this cave," Brighton explained. "Their method of head messaging *doesn't* have the ability to work in a conversational setting. Their messages only travel *out*. No thoughts or spoken words from us can be received by them."

"Then what do we do?" Stan asked, even more puzzled.

"Well, Stan, I think it's clear that their voices need a *human medium* to let their thoughts be clearly and fully expressed and understood. Hypothetically, this would also give them the ability to hear and answer *our* questions… like at a *séance*."

"Really?" Stan responded in surprise.

"Yes," Dr. Brighton continued cautiously. "And if I'm right, due to your apparent *sharing* of their wavelength, I believe *you* possess the ability to *act as their voice*!"

"Who, *me*?" Stan exclaimed in disbelief.

"Who else?" Dr. Brighton responded encouragingly. "The fact that you have had the ability to see their world since the beginning of this trip, *probably* means that your brain has the ability to also translate to English when they speak through you in their native language. I'll bet my life on it!"

"But I've never translated anything for anyone before in my life!" Stan protested.

"Well, we'll never know if you can do it until you try, will we!" Brighton shared with an abundance of positiveness. "So, Stan. Are you in?"

Stan considered everything for a short moment before unenthusiastically replying, "Yes, I'm in." Then he met Brighton's eyes and somberly added, "But just remember that even though

I'm willing to help… I draw the line at experiencing a *slow, gruesome* and *disgusting* death!"

Dr. Brighton laughed, "Don't worry, Stan. You're in no danger."

"Are you sure?" Stan asked pointedly. But the only answer he received was a reassuring smile from the man.

Regardless of his misgivings at this point, Stan was prepared to move forward! Faith has a wonderful way of giving a person confidence even under the most uncertain of circumstances… and it certainly *did* here! Somehow, regardless of whatever *might* happen next, Stan felt absolutely no need to worry. Immediately, something in his mind seemed to gently *guide* him through his preparation. He carefully placed the tablet on the ground in front of him, took off his backpack and laid it behind him. Next, he sat down on the ground, closed his eyes and cleared his mind of all his thoughts. Then he calmly awaited the imminent arrival of the visiting spirits. Suddenly, he felt very groggy, much like he'd felt while having his wisdom teeth taken out as a teenager, only moments before succumbing to unconsciousness as the anesthesia quickly took hold. A few moments later, his conscious mind was *gone*!

"Greetings!" the spirit occupying Stan's body shared warmly.

"Greetings!" Dr. Brighton reciprocated, as he slowly removed his backpack and sat down on the floor facing him. "Who am I speaking with?"

"I am *Cukse*. I was chief of my tribe many years ago."

"Hello, Cukse. I am *Robert Brighton*," he replied calmly. "Was there a special reason you had for calling me back here? In fact, *how* were you able to contact me at all?"

Stan's face smiled. "You possess the *key* to the cave," he replied. "With your consent, that makes *you* the next Chosen One."

"Chosen for *what* exactly?" Brighton asked curiously.

Stan's face grew thoughtful as he purposely avoided answering that question. "All of the spirits in this cave are here by choice. Each one of us is an *angel*."

"An *angel*?" Brighton exclaimed in surprise.

"When called upon, we share hope wherever it is needed," the spirit expounded.

"Are the rocks on the ceiling and walls that light-up this cave *each* an angel too?" Brighton asked curiously.

Cukse laughed. "Not *exactly*. The spirits of thousands of angels have *illuminated* the rocks in the cave walls to create that light for you to see."

"Wow!" Brighton gasped. "But why are the rocks so many different colors?"

"Because each angel and the spirit that fills them is *unique*, as are all living creatures. The color of each rock very clearly exemplifies *only* them," Cukse explained.

"Then what color are *you*?" Brighton asked.

"Myself, I am *not* any color. But *every* color can be seen through me," Cukse shared cryptically.

Brighton nodded. "Then you are the *clear* rock that disappeared?"

"Yes," Cukse replied. "I was there to greet you."

Brighton smiled. "That was quite an *unusual* welcome!" Then growing more serious, he asked, "But how did you make the rock *disappear*?"

Cukse laughed. "You are thinking like a being with limitations. Although this feat may seem *impossible* to you as a mortal, we angels are capable of doing many many things which you do not *yet* understand," he replied pleasantly.

Brighton smiled broadly, "I really like how you *laugh* a lot!"

"Thank you, Robert Brighton. To laugh is to feel the essence of spontaneous joy, is it not?" Cukse smiled.

"It certainly is," Brighton agreed. "*Now*, would you please explain to me how the 'Chosen One' fits-in with all of you?" Dr. Brighton asked a little impatiently.

Cukse, through Stan, hesitated before replying gently, "I *will* answer that question completely, but first I wish to answer any *other* questions you may have."

"Alright," Dr. Brighton agreed. "Why was Stan, the man you are now speaking through, able to see the rock creature that led us to this cave from the very beginning, while everyone else in my group, including me, was not?"

"That question is quite simple to answer. Stan is an *unwavering* believer in God. *We* are of God. So, Stan could *always* see our world," Cukse replied.

"Are you implying that the rest of us *don't* believe in God?" Brighton asked curiously.

Cukse laughed. "This is *not* a question of belief, my friend, but *faith* in that belief! Beliefs alone are without roots and may be easily washed away and replaced by others, or even by *nothing* at all. But when a person has true faith in their belief, it becomes *immovable.*"

"Okay. But if I *lacked* faith, then why was I suddenly able to see all of *this*?" Brighton's curiosity quickly piqued, completely getting the better of him.

Cukse smiled. "Just as Stan suggested," he shared calmly. "It is because you had '*increased your faith.*' Because of that, it became obvious to us that your fledgling belief in the existence of God had grown *exponentially*! That is why we happily allowed you to enter our world."

"You *heard* what Stan said *before* we came into this cave?" Brighton gasped in surprise.

Stan laughed. "The ability of angels to hear and see is not so limited as human beings," Cukse explained. "It is not unusual for our essence to cover a broad area at one time if we wish it to. We *chose* to listen from the moment the two of you began your trek up the hill."

"But I was under the impression that you could *not* hear us when we spoke to you?" Brighton said in shock. "Were you lying to me?"

Cukse laughed. "No, Robert Brighton. Lying is an *Earthly vice* which angels find no profit in. What you are speaking of only applies to *head messaging*. But that is only one of the many ways we can communicate. We hear and understand *everything* you say whenever we are focused on it *regardless* of what language you are speaking. Different languages are an earthly thing and are of no consequence to us."

"Then *why* was it so important to you that I bring Stan along for this meeting?" Brighton asked in confusion. "I thought his role was always to serve as my interpreter?"

Cukse smiled. "We only led you to believe that, so Stan's presence here would make more sense to you."

"Well then what was your *real* reason for bringing him here?" Brighton asked in bewilderment.

"To *guide* you here, and to enjoy your journey accompanied by a friendly companion," Cukse explained. "In addition, I believed you would feel much more comfortable conversing with a good friend *like Stan*, rather than speaking directly to a stranger like me in this cave."

"Why are you saying that Stan is my 'good friend?'" Brighton asked in surprise. "We only just met two days ago?"

Cukse looked thoughtful. "*That* is of no consequence! Good friends benefit and learn from each other regardless of *how long* they have been acquainted. A good friendship, like the one the two of you share, was *mutually appreciated* from the very beginning."

"Did Stan *help me* to see and believe in your world then?" Brighton asked intently.

"Only *you* can answer that question, Robert Brighton," Cukse said sincerely.

Brighton seemed to be greatly puzzled by this, and as a result, he found himself gazing far off into the distance.

Appearing to guess his quandary, Cukse added, "Don't worry, Robert Brighton. *Friendship* is just something that you are *not yet* able to fully understand."

"Will the time come when I *will* understand it fully?" Brighton asked hopefully.

"I hope so. But *that* will depend on *you*," Cukse said, without explaining his meaning. Surprisingly, Brighton seemed to understand it right away, and gently smiled.

"What is the significance of the *cross* on the key?" Brighton asked intently.

"Is it not obvious?" Cukse asked warmly. "We are eternally inspired by the story of the Christ."

"When did you first hear this story?" Brighton asked gently.

"It was shared with us by *angels*, just as we are now, while we lived our lives here on Earth, many, many, years ago," Cukse explained.

"What became of these angels?" Brighton asked mesmerized.

"After a time, their jobs were done. And it is the *same* for each of us. *When your job is done... God will bring you home*," Stan's face smiled warmly.

"Remember when you told me that the spirits inside this cave were *of* God? Where exactly *is* God?" Brighton found himself growing more and more fascinated.

Cukse laughed. "God is *not* a single entity like you or me. Understanding that *first* will make it much easier for you to comprehend that we are *all of God*! He is everywhere and a part of everything, even if you do not yet realize it. For you, God is the oxygen you breathe, the food and water you consume, and the love, passion and inspiration that often drives you in life!"

Suddenly, Robert Brighton realized that everything Cukse was so carefully explaining to him… was *absolutely* true! He had never been one for trusting the validity of mere emotions, but he felt a gentle warmth gradually sweeping throughout his entire being that he had *never known* before? He believed *this* to be his confirmation!

"Soon I am going to share a secret with you, Robert Brighton. A secret which we *only* share with the Chosen One. Although you have not yet accepted this path, I want to share this secret because I *know* that you will profit much by it."

Brighton nodded appreciatively.

"In time, this secret will bring peace to all the world. Please *do not* share this with anyone else, no matter how much you may want to. Doing that would only impede their progress. They must each learn it for themselves out of desire."

"Why must people learn it *at all*?" Brighton asked.

"Because the future of mankind *depends* upon it!" the spirit replied passionately. "And to live without it will only continue to make life confusing and unsatisfying for more and more people."

"What is the reason they must each learn it *for themselves* then?" Brighton continued his questioning.

"Because *nothing* is stronger in a person's mind than a belief which they have acquired and accepted for themselves."

"Was it just a coincidence that I came to this site in the San Gabriel Mountains a month ago and found the key?" Brighton asked, like a small child searching for the truth.

"If it pleases you to believe that," the spirit replied, "then let it be so."

"But that *doesn't* answer my question?" Brighton insisted, feeling distressed, as if Cukse were purposely avoiding sharing the answer with him.

Stan's face gently smiled as the spirit replied, "There are countless times in human history when people *unknowingly* do things which turn out to be lifechanging. Are all of these coincidences?"

"I don't know?" Brighton replied.

"Nor does *anyone else* on Earth," the spirit confirmed. "Part of the beautiful mystery of life is understanding that we *aren't meant* to know everything! Many things happen every day, seemingly without reason or explanation. Sometimes they may even appear to be *impossible*? Part of having faith is *believing* that it's sometimes necessary to be patient instead of obsessed with immediately understanding every underlying reason for every single action that takes place throughout our lives. If your faith grows unshakable, with patience replacing your former impatience, then I promise you that there will come a time when you may ask to have your questions answered… and they *will be*!"

Over the next several hours, the spirit spoke to Robert Brighton in great depth about many wonderful things. Brighton was overcome by the goodwill that he was so freely receiving through the wise words of Cukse. The spirit continued to speak through Stan until it became apparent that his body was finally tiring and his voice was beginning to grow hoarse.

"Robert Brighton? Do you understand what *choice* you must now make?" Cukse gently asked as they neared the end of their conversation together.

"I do," Brighton replied. "But please allow me to ask you one *final question* if I may?"

"Yes?" the spirit asked.

"Are you and the other spirits happy?"

Without delay, the spirit (*through Stan*) replied, "Yes, Robert Brighton. We are *most* happy!"

"Then thank you for all you have taught me, and I *gratefully accept* your invitation to become the Chosen One!" Brighton declared with a smile. "I am actually very excited about it!"

With a happy laugh, Cukse shared, "Hecula tombre, Robert Brighton!"

"Hecula tombre, Cukse!" Brighton reciprocated with a smile.

Moments later, Stan awoke, not remembering *anything at all* about the monumental conversation that had just transpired. "Did you get to speak with the spirits?" he asked Brighton excitedly, as he pulled himself up from the floor and put on his backpack.

"I spoke with only *one* spirit who called himself *Cukse*. But that conversation was *lifechanging*!" Brighton shared with clear excitement illuminating his voice.

"Your life?" Stan asked curiously.

Brighton smiled. "*All* of our lives."

"Hey? Where's the tablet?" Stan asked, suddenly realizing that it was gone.

"It's where it *should* be," Brighton replied calmly.

Stan accepted that cryptic explanation and didn't ask any more questions as they walked through the buzzing cave to the granite doors. The keyhole *inexplicably* returned, and Brighton confidently inserted the rock key into the indentation. Just like before, with a loud scraping noise, the doors opened. But this time, they opened *outwardly*! Walking outside, although the key and keyhole had once again changed their locations, *this time* they were prepared for it! Brighton gently removed the key from the *outside* of the door, and they watched their fantastic adventure slowly come to a close. Both big granite doors unmistakably snapped shut and any evidence that the doors, the keyhole, the cave, or the spirits had ever existed, *completely vanished*? They were now left standing beside an ordinary looking hill. Dr. Brighton was beaming, obviously feeling very *enlightened* by his experience, while Stan unfortunately... felt a little *left out*?

The late afternoon sun was about an hour from setting as Stan and Dr. Brighton approached the spot where they had left their poles. After each appreciatively draining a bottle of water and eating an energy bar, they picked-up their hiking poles and began their long and careful descent down the steep hillside that led back to their campsite.

"I have so many questions to ask you about what you learned through speaking with that spirit!" Stan exclaimed. "*Where* is God in all of this?"

Brighton smiled. "The real question, Stan, is where *isn't* God!"

Stan smiled back. He now realized that this experience had completely filled Dr. Brighton with *joy*! That knowledge made him feel very happy for him, but on the other hand, he disappointedly found himself increasingly feeling cheated! Why was he *unable* to remember anything at all about that life-altering encounter, he wondered? Somehow, it just didn't seem fair?

When they reached the campsite at dusk, they were greeted like rock stars! Glen pulled Stan aside just as soon as he saw him, and asked *how* they had survived for three days without food? *Three days*? Stan began to explain to Glen that they could *not* have possibly been gone for three days, but thinking better of it after a moment, he directed him to speak with Dr. Brighton instead. Due to his role as medium, he *didn't* know in days, hours and minutes exactly *how much time* they had actually spent inside that cave? But, he was *not* going to worry about it either. If Glen told him that it had been three days, then what possible reason could he have to lie about it?

The rest of the dig was pretty much a bland affair as very few new artifacts of any significance were uncovered. That is, aside from the *human skeleton* that surprisingly appeared to be in near pristine condition of an ancient 'Native American mountain inhabitant!' They uncovered it on the final working day of the dig. When they found it, it was wrapped in fragments of some kind of cloth, enclosed in what appeared to have been a *granite and mud* coffin? The coffin, however, completely fell apart as the mud disintegrated into dirt soon after exposing it to the sun and the air? But it had done its job preserving these human remains for a *very* long time! Stan was just as thrilled as everyone else at the spectacular find, and he even wondered if those could possibly be the remains of one of the spirits in the cave? Perhaps even *Cukse*? Dr. Brighton estimated the bones to be at least eight hundred years old, which was, as he had told Stan, approximately the *same age* as the granite key to the cave? A coincidence? Well, when it came right down to it, it didn't really matter to Stan *whose* bones those were or if they were even related to the key at all! The important thing was that the bones would soon be studied, eventually telling their *own* story about life in the mountains eight hundred years ago! Thinking about it, he was now *certain* that he loved being an archaeologist! Just like Dr. Brighton, he couldn't imagine a better or more fulfilling way of spending his life! Thankfully, the discovery of the well-preserved bones made this dig *officially* successful. Because of that find, everyone on this expedition would now have a reason to feel that their time spent up in these mountains over the past five days had turned out to be completely worthwhile! Only Dr. Brighton *didn't need* those bones to make him feel satisfied. In his mind, this trip had *already* achieved that status due to his incredible conversation with Cukse. And as a result, he had found this trip to be monumentally *life-changing*!

With Robert Brighton seemingly in a permanent state of bliss, and the discovery of the ancient human remains, the mood in the camp was predictably joyous! But that didn't help Stan much. He was dying to find out more about the conversation that Dr. Brighton had shared with Cukse, which he was curiously *unable* to remember at all? And the problem was that every time he tried to speak with Dr. Brighton about it, the man always seemed to find a polite excuse *not* to oblige him? Stan *was* able to speak with Brennan and Glen however. He learned that during their time away at the cave, a vicious wildcat had brazenly entered the campsite. Apparently it was scrounging for food and unfortunately *did not* appear to be afraid of people? In fact, with a vicious growl and a *murderous* intent it had nearly cornered Teresa! It was not until Glen ran onto the scene, yelling and firing his rifle into the air that the cat finally ran off. To be honest… Stan was actually *glad* he had missed that!

On the final night of the trip, it grew unseasonably cold as Stan sat alone by the campfire trying to keep warm. Momentarily, Brennan walked up and casually sat down beside him. "Do you feel like talking?" he asked hopefully.

"Sure," Stan replied. "I would love to hear about what you guys were doing while we were away."

Brennan grew serious. "Yeh. About those *three days*," he questioned. "Robert told me before you two left that you would be back exactly three days later, at the *exact time* you arrived? Now I know Robert's special, but how did you two possibly make that happen?"

This was Stan's chance to come clean, and he took it! He proceeded to share the entire story (*as he recalled it*) to Brennan, including the fact that what had seemed like a couple of hours to Dr. Brighton and him, had somehow miraculously turned into *three days* to everyone at camp? He ended his story by confessing that their predestined arrival time was surely only a coincidence.

Brennan burst-out laughing. "Robert told us you would cook-up some *kooky* explanation like that! Sorry, pal. The cat's out of the bag! We all know about your secret helicopter ride into L.A. and your two-day vacation at the Westin Bonaventure Hotel, just because Robert felt like pulling off the '*practical joke of a lifetime*! I sure hope you *enjoyed yourselves* while the rest of us were left here *working*!" he laughed. "What will that crazy man come up with next? Kudos for your very *creative* story though!"

Brennan laughed all the way back to his tent, while Stan just sat there *stunned*! Never before during his entire lifetime had he found himself so confused? He felt *completely lost*! And then he began questioning his own eyes, his own memories… and most of all, his *own sanity*? As a dismal consequence, he really didn't know who or what to believe anymore? Breaking his intense concentration, he suddenly became aware of a soft but distinct and unsettling rustling noise behind him? Fearfully, he imagined it to be a good-sized animal with very sharp teeth, inadvertently rubbing a canvas tent as it quietly and methodically passed by it on its determined path toward its *dinner*. The *wildcat*! Stan was terrified! He quickly turned around, making a weak defensive gesture with his arms crossed in front of his face, and was about to scream, when with a huge sigh of relief, he spied a smiling Dr. Brighton silently approaching him.

"Hello, Stan," Brighton greeted him warmly as he sat down next to him. "Did you think I was that *wildcat* behind you?"

"That thought *had* crossed my mind," Stan admitted, with an embarrassed grin.

Dr. Brighton laughed. "I'm sorry. I'm afraid the gang has played a little joke on you by telling you that ridiculous story. To begin with, there are *no wildcats* out here anymore, and even if there were, as a rule they always tend to avoid contact with humans."

Stan laughed with relief. "Well, true or not, that story sure had *me* going!"

Brighton smiled. "Yes. I guess the story did its job!" he chuckled. "The gang *always* tries, quite successfully I might add, to frighten our rookies with that tall tale!" Then growing more serious, he added, "But you know, the *wildcat* really was an important symbol to the ancient people living in these parts."

"It was? Why?" Stan asked curiously.

"Because it served as a simple metaphor for *the uncertainties of life and the frightening unknown.* Anyone who came across a wildcat *knew* that their reaction to it could very well dictate whether they lived or they died. And if they *died…* they were often frightened of what they might find on the *other side.*"

"What did they see as being the *best* reaction to facing a wildcat then?" Stan asked curiously.

Brighton thought for a moment, and then replied, "I couldn't really say with any certainty, but I would *guess*, by showing confidence, an absence of fear or anger, and with a sincere *respect* for it."

"Hey!" Stan laughed. "That's *exactly* what you said about dealing with that *rattlesnake*?"

"Oh, is it?" Brighton said, feigning surprise. And then he added sincerely, "I would think *that plan* would work most of the time with *any* semi-intelligent living creature."

Stan smiled. "While you are here, Robert," he began, with obvious concern. "Do you know that I have been trying *unsuccessfully* to speak with you ever since we got back from the cave? What's wrong?"

"Absolutely *nothing*!" Brighton assured him. "I just had to think about what I was going to say to you, that's all."

"You mean about the cave?" he guessed.

"For starters," Brighton replied. "But also, about why neither of us should probably speak in much detail about any of this to anyone but our closest loved ones right now."

"Is that why you told Brennan that I would probably tell a '*tall tale*' about our three days gone?" Stan shrewdly suggested.

Brighton laughed, "Right! Sorry about that, but the time we were gone and the time that we were in that cave... well, they didn't even *come close* to matching-up, did they. And we had *no* explanation for it? So, I just thought the trip to L.A. sounded like a good cover," he explained with a grin.

"It was a *great* cover," Stan agreed. "But wasn't it also a *lie*?"

"Not necessarily. It depends how you look at it, Stan. Why don't we just call it... a *creatively altered interpretation* of the truth," Brighton smiled impishly.

Stan smiled back at him. "But won't the *mystery* of how we did that be impossible for us to ever explain or prove?" he asked with concern.

Brighton laughed, "Great mysteries *never* need to be fully explained or proven because the best mysteries, the ones that are *remembered* the longest, are always the ones that *no one* can ever seem to figure out?" Brighton smiled as he expounded, "But people sure enjoy *trying* to solve them, don't they? So, I ask myself, who are we to *take* all of that fun away from them?"

"But there's *no mystery* and *no solution* at all to this!" Stan insisted. "That trip to L.A. *never* happened!"

"Exactly!" Brighton exclaimed. "And *that* is the solution!"

Stan laughed. Then growing more serious, he asked, "But will there *ever* come a time when we *can* share that story with others?"

"Of course, there will!" Brighton assured him. "And I'm sure that one way or another we'll *know* when that time comes."

Stan nodded, and somehow he understood. "So, what actually *did* happen to us in that cave that took away three days of our lives?"

"That cave, as I'm sure you will agree, was very obviously *not* of this world," Brighton explained calmly. "As you told me earlier, while attempting to explain your take on the phenomenon of the spirits and the lights on the walls and ceiling of the cave, you said, '*There may be no logical human explanation for any of this.*'

Bravo! That is one simple and concise answer, and I think it applies to the time differences found inside and outside the cave, as well. It is just something that needs to be accepted and then we move on. That's why I don't relish talking to anyone else about it. The *truth* would undoubtedly come across to anyone hearing it as lies, sheer lunacy, or the wild ravings of a couple of guys in the mountains who spent way too much time with their good friend, *Cannabis*!" he laughed.

Stan laughed too, before gently saying, "There's something else I need to ask you."

"Yes?" Dr. Brighton patiently acknowledged him.

"Brennan shared with me tonight that before we left, you told him the day and time that we would return?" he began. After a short pause, he continued. "And it matched-up *exactly* to the day and time that we actually *did* return? *Three days later*! How could you have possibly known that?"

Dr. Brighton met his eyes sincerely, and began, "Honestly, Stan, I can understand how *impressive* that feat must sound to you, but I really *didn't know* what time, or even *if ever* we would be returning?" he calmly admitted. "I was told to share that story with everyone at camp by whomever was communicating with me just as soon as I had woken-up that morning. I was merely the messenger."

"Then *why* did you share it?" Stan asked.

"Because I was determined to follow that adventure, *whatever* it was, as far as it would take us!"

"Why?" Stan implored.

"Because it was exciting, so I really *wanted to*!" Brighton admitted with an impish smile.

"I *completely* understand," Stan chuckled, and then he asked seriously, "What happened with the writing on the stone tablet? Did you ever decipher what it meant?"

"I certainly did! Just as you suggested, Cukse translated every word of it for me."

"Was it important?" Stan asked excitedly.

"Were Moses' *Ten Commandments* important?" Brighton shared teasingly.

"What?" Stan grew excited.

Brighton laughed. "No. This tablet may not have had the Ten Commandments inscribed on it, but similarly, it *did* have a foundation of principles which when followed, outlined a clear path toward attaining happiness and contentment in this life. The spirit and I discussed it together, and afterwards he saw to it that it was immediately buried somewhere in the mountains to be *rediscovered* by future generations when they needed it, like ours needs it now."

"Wow!" Stan exclaimed before eagerly asking, "What *exactly* does the tablet say?"

Brighton grew very serious as he disappointedly replied, "I'm sorry, Stan. I *truly* am! But I'm not at liberty to share that with you or anybody else… although I really wish I could."

"Okay," Stan quietly accepted his words with more than a little disappointment. "Was there anything else you wanted to talk with me about?"

"I wanted to level with you."

"*Level* with me?" Stan repeated in surprise.

"Yes," Brighton answered. "Do you know why I came back here so soon after my last expedition?"

"Sure. You already explained that to me. You told me that you were urged to return by something that was talking inside your head. Is that *not* true?" Stan asked.

Brighton looked amused, but then grew thoughtful, as he replied, "That was certainly *part* of the reason I returned here so quickly. But my other much more pressing reason was the phone call I received from my doctor only two days before we left. He warned me that my genetic heart condition had gotten worse. As a result, he advised me *not* to participate in anymore archeological expeditions, because he was afraid that the stress and excitement would probably, more likely sooner than later, *kill me*! I realized at that moment that I was being told to *change* my life forever, and to stop doing the one thing I truly loved in life!"

Suddenly, Stan had an epiphany, as he gently asked, "Isn't dealing with your heart condition kind of like dealing with the *wildcat*?"

Brighton abruptly turned toward Stan, and smiled. "You are very sharp, Stan! I've never thought of it that way before, but yes!

I *am* dealing with a potential life-or-death situation here, so I believe that I *am* staring that wildcat directly in the face!"

As he watched him reply, Stan thought of how *tired* Dr. Brighton had seemed after initially climbing the hill. With a strong sense of empathy and concern he asked, "Didn't you take a great risk by allowing yourself to make that strenuous climb to the top of the hill? That must have really taxed your heart!"

"Yes. I imagine it did," Brighton confirmed. "But I *didn't* feel sick after the climb, only fatigued. More fatigued than I can *ever* remember feeling in my entire life!" Growing more passionate, he added, "But I *don't care*! There was simply no way I was going to miss all of the exciting adventures that I *knew* we would be sharing up here! If you had been in my shoes, would you seriously have done anything differently?"

Stan laughed, "*Not* a thing!" And then meeting his eyes, he added, "That news about your heart must have really turned your world upside down."

Dr. Brighton laughed wistfully. "It did. I suppose a person never fully understands how much they love living their life a certain way, until *after* they are threatened with losing it."

"If you don't mind me asking, how long has your heart really been a problem for you?" Stan asked gently.

"A long time," Brighton confessed. "Even as a child I always had to be careful of overexerting it. But it began to behave more erratically about six years ago," he explained. "That's when I made myself sleep more, and avoided using watches, alarm clocks and cell phones."

Stan chuckled, in spite of himself. Now he understood *why* Dr. Brighton, as a rule, slept ten hours a night and didn't embrace cell phones, watches, alarm clocks or any other *stress inducing* devices. "Have you told anyone else about your condition?"

"What?" Brighton smiled, feigning shock. "And *ruin* my hard-earned reputation for acting *irrationally fastidious*? Never!"

Stan laughed. "Then why are you telling *me*?"

"Because, Stan," he shared calmly. "I don't know how much more time I have left in this world and I want *someone* to know the truth." Then with a very defiant tone, he added, "And I'll be damned if I'll let a little heart problem stop me from going out on future archeology expeditions!"

"Aren't you at least a little bit worried about your heart going out?" Stan asked him with renewed concern.

"I've survived this long with a faulty ticker, and when I do finally breathe my last breath… I want to do it as an *archaeologist*!" Brighton declared, and then quickly added, "And anyway, I'm *not* afraid of dying anymore, Stan."

"Really? Why is that?" Stan asked with heightened curiosity.

Brighton looked caringly at him, and with a soft smile and a mischievous gleam in his eyes, he replied, "Because although my life feels so much more meaningful now, and I'll continue to look forward to waking-up every morning, as I always have… I find peace in the words the spirit shared with me, "*And when your job is done, God will bring you home*!"

"You sound as if you've really learned a lot on this trip!" Stan marveled.

"I have, Stan," he replied with a thoughtful smile. "Most of all, I've learned not to worry too much about not making scientific sense out of things that appear to be impossible."

"Really?" Stan asked very inquisitively.

"Yes. Because now I believe that something that appears to be *impossible* is probably nothing more than something *beyond* our comprehension. So, to my way of thinking, *nothing* is truly impossible, and if God wishes us to *understand* the truth about something that appears that way, then in time, *we will*!"

(*Two Years Later*)

"Two years ago, I had the eye-opening experience of accompanying Dr. Robert Brighton on an unforgettable journey into the San Gabriel Mountains. As I later discovered, others, perhaps even some of you, secretly *laughed* at him. Please don't feel badly though. After all, you're only human and couldn't have possibly understood the overwhelming compulsion that was drawing Dr. Brighton back to those particular mountains. You only knew that the mountains he was digging in for the *second time* in a month had already been tirelessly studied and well-documented a number of times before. The truth was that Dr. Brighton was not only excited about his return there, but he also believed it to be his *destiny*! I cannot go into any further detail regarding what he and I discovered while up there, but I *will* tell you that it was uncanny and changed both of our lives forever! Curiously, here I am the *assistant* speaking to you about it while he, the great archeologist behind this expedition… lies *dead*. May God rest his soul. But my theory is that before he died, in his own mysterious way, Dr. Brighton was attempting to *enlighten* us through his speech at the convention. About what, you ask? Well, there lies the real mystery? But in listening to his speech, I would have to believe that it concerned *our* wellbeing and happiness. In fact, he seemed to be very *passionate* about that, which I personally found to be very touching."

"I can still remember that afternoon when Dr. Brighton presented the findings from his most recent expedition in the lecture hall at UC Berkeley. He was uncharacteristically giddy. He smiled throughout much of his presentation, almost laughing at times as though he had something *truly wonderful* he wanted to share with us? And unlike other presentations of his which I had personally attended in the past, he made *eye contact* with all of us throughout his entire lecture? In my opinion, he was trying desperately to speak directly to our souls! There is absolutely no doubt in my mind that knowing the secret *he* possessed, would have contributed greatly toward improving each and every one of our lives. It certainly seemed to *improve his*? In time, perhaps the whole world would have reaped the benefits? And he *wanted* to share that secret with us, I *know* he did! But for some unknown reason, he just couldn't? Sadly, now that he's dead, it becomes obvious that short of a miracle, he never will! But we mustn't blame him for not saying more. Knowing him as well as I did, I'm convinced that he had his reasons, and they were undoubtedly *very good* ones! As for me? My soul will not rest until I discover and understand his secret! And I hope all of you feel the same way! Someday, God willing, maybe we'll actually *succeed*! In the meantime, let's hear it for Dr. Robert Brighton! The greatest archaeologist and friend I have ever known!"

Following Dr. Brighton's passing, it was soon discovered that he had left *everything* he possessed in the world to Stan and his wife, Stephanie. They were initially overwhelmed... but also *overjoyed*! They have lived happily in his former house with the two-acre backyard for almost a year now. And not a moment passed when they didn't appreciate all that Dr. Brighton had done for them.

It had been many hours now since Stan had given his speech at UC Berkeley, and being quite late, Stephanie had already gone to bed. Stan, however, was quietly sitting on the porch-swing, gently gliding forward and back, facing his front yard and admiring the beautiful night sky. For some reason, he was *not* tired in the least.

"How goes it, old friend?"

Stan nearly jumped out of his shoes upon *shockingly* hearing that very familiar voice! He abruptly turned to his left to incredibly see *Dr. Robert Brighton* sitting right there on the swing beside him?

"Please don't be afraid, Stan," Brighton chuckled, sensing Stan's fear. "Believe me, I'm no scarier now than I was while I was alive. In fact, I may even be a little *more* normal now?"

Stan couldn't help but smile at that last comment. He *knew* that Robert Brighton could never be normal no matter how hard he tried! His '*coming back from the dead*' only strengthened that opinion! So, believing the unbelievable, Stan smiled broadly as he gently asked, "How are you, Robert?"

"*Dead*, of course," Brighton laughed, rising from the swing and casually strolling out into the front yard.

"But how is it that I can see you then?" Stan whispered in confusion, getting up from the swing and following him into the yard.

Brighton laughed. "You *know* the answer to that, Stan! As you once so *profoundly* educated me on these matters, 'It's because of your *faith* that this is truly possible!'"

Stan could not help but laugh. "To be honest, it would be unimaginable that either one of us could believe this *wasn't* possible after all that we've been through together."

Still smiling, Brighton said, "I heard your speech tonight at the University and thought it was wonderful, but… you never did tell those folks what my secret was?"

"That's because I *didn't know*, did I!" Stan laughed. "You never told me, remember? All I know is that it has something to do with principles that help people to find happiness and contentment."

"Very good, Stan!" Brighton complimented him. "You have got an excellent memory!"

Stan looked at him oddly. "Is *that* why you came back here to see me tonight?" he asked incredulously. "To tell me *that*?"

"Came back?" Brighton feigned shock. "Stan, I *never left*! I've been here for almost a year now! When I wasn't in Berkeley, I was out scouring the world for wisdom. Most recently, I was at a ranch in Arizona, learning valuable life lessons from a rancher there who raises donkeys of all things? He demonstrated to me that a truly kind person *cannot* just pick and choose who they are kind and understanding to, but must show it to everyone and every other living creature, *including donkeys*!"

Stan laughed. "Wow!" he exclaimed in surprise. "You know, my father raises donkeys too!" he shared excitedly. "Come to think of it, I learned a *lot* about treating others with kindness and understanding from him."

"I think we *both* did," Brighton smiled mysteriously. "From my experiences on that ranch watching your father, I learned that the deepest kind of understanding and kindness cannot be fully comprehended by simply living what you *perceive* to be a 'good life.' You've got to watch someone else living *their* life, and regardless of what they do for a living, spending it being kind and understanding to those around them. Seeing that, can't help but *inspire* those of us who are searching to acquire those very same virtues!"

Stan could not believe it! And his shocked expression was certainly proof of that. "I don't understand?"

Brighton smiled. "During my lifetime, the fact that I spent most of my time alone, convinced me that I still had a lot to learn! I not only wanted to grow wiser in the ways of living a happy and contented life myself, but I also *needed* to learn how to help others to achieve the very same thing."

Stan was glued to every word.

"To begin with, I was very curious to find out where *you* had first learned about and embraced kindness and understanding?" he continued.

Stan laughed uncomfortably. "Wait a minute! I'm not *exceptionally* kind or understanding. Just ask my *students*!"

Dr. Brighton chuckled. "I beg to differ! You *very clearly* displayed those two wonderful traits during the short time I have known you. I had a hunch and decided to secretly watch your father work. As it turned out, my hunch had been absolutely on target! Now, first hand, I understand the meaning of, '*The apple doesn't fall far from the tree*.'"

Stan was momentarily speechless. "Thank you, Robert! Both of us learning from my father makes me feel as if we are now somehow brothers."

"Well, actually in a way we are. I am your '*brother*' as one of God's angels now," Brighton confessed.

Stan feigned shock as he quipped, "An *angel*, huh? Aren't you supposed to have wings and a halo?"

"Hey! Give me time to *earn them*!" Brighton laughed facetiously.

Stan laughed too, and then growing more serious, he asked, "So why *did* you come to see me tonight?"

"Actually," he confessed, "to be perfectly honest, in addition to *harassing* you," he chuckled, "I came by tonight to give you *this*." He reached down deeply inside his pants pocket and retrieved the square piece of granite with the chiseled cross which had opened the door to their unforgettable adventure in the cave. He smiled as he gently offered it to Stan.

Stan was completely taken by surprise as he graciously accepted the gift. "Thank you, Robert. Is this meant to be a souvenir of our *adventure*?"

"It is," Brighton replied. "But it's also something more than that… *much more*! With this key, I am inviting you to become the next Chosen One!"

"*Chosen One*?" Stan repeated in surprise. "What exactly is *that*?"

Brighton smiled. "As Cukse explained it to me, the holder of the key, the Chosen One, is invited to look *beyond* all problems, travel the world and learn the proven principles to attaining true happiness and contentment here on Earth. All of those principles are basically written down on the stone tablet you gave me, but they can *also* be learned through personal experience for those of us who are *astute enough* to realize it," he chuckled. Then with a more serious tone, he continued, "Once learned, the Chosen One is tasked with the challenge of secretly helping others who seek happiness and contentment, to find and learn the principles of attaining them for themselves. Forcing or scaring people into following these principles will only work temporarily, if at all. That point has been proven repeatedly by watching the unsuccessful efforts of heavy-handed governments, individuals and organizations trying to *force-feed* long-term beliefs into their constituents, predominantly using force and fear as their most *common* tools!" Brighton met Stan's eyes warmly. "The only lasting way for someone to learn and believe these principles, or anything else for that matter, is for that person's heart to be *fully open* and their mind consciously *searching* for it. Once they have purposely found and embraced these principles, for all intents and purposes, they become a living embodiment of the very things they have been seeking... *happiness and contentment*." Brighton gazed warmly at Stan, and asked, "Now, do you understand why I couldn't tell you my secret?"

"Yes, of course I do!" Stan assured him, and then added thoughtfully, "You know, that's so simple, and yet it makes so much sense?"

"I know. God *likes* to work that way," Brighton smiled meaningfully.

"And you are quite certain that was your *entire* secret?" Stan asked suspiciously.

Dr. Brighton laughed. "Yes, Stan, it *was*. But I'm hoping now that it will become *yours*?"

Stan suddenly felt overwhelmed! But he quickly evaluated those meaningful last words that Dr. Robert Brighton had so sincerely shared with him, and replied, "I appreciate that you would even consider me for this *great honor*, but how could I possibly learn all of those principles without the translation of what was written on the tablet? Aside from your telling me that I already have a '*handle*' on kindness and understanding, I don't even know where to *begin*?" he said, inadvertently growing more anxious. "And you know what? When it comes to learning things from experience, *I'm really not that astute*!"

Brighton laughed. "Don't you *dare* sell yourself short, Stan! I think, and the other spirits agree with me, that you probably *already know* many of the important principles to achieving happiness and contentment if you only think about it," he smiled. "And anyway, you will have the *key* now! Just call Chris and his helicopter anytime you like, and he will return you to the cave where you will have all your questions answered."

"Do you mean that the spirits would actually be able to speak with me… *directly*?" Stan asked excitedly.

"Of course!" Brighton winked. "You would be the *Chosen One*! There would be no need for a medium and *no limits* on your ability to converse with them. They would appear to you every bit as alive as I look to you now! And I've got to tell you, conversing with *some* of those spirits has been an absolute *hoot*!"

Stan was nearly in tears! He was so incredibly happy at hearing this sudden revelation, that he *would* be conversing with the spirits after all! That was something he'd longed to do ever since he and Dr. Brighton had left the cave! Aggressively thrusting his right hand forward and meeting Brighton's halfway, he shook it vigorously and replied with a smile, "Of course I accept!"

"Hecula tombre," Brighton offered sincerely.

"Hecula tombre," Stan replied in like fashion, before adding, "Thank you Robert!"

"No, *thank you*, Stan! And feel free to share *everything* I've told you with Stephanie. I just *assumed* that you would want this arrangement to include her."

"Thank you for that," Stan shared gratefully. "But before you go, I do have *one* final question to ask you."

"Oh?" Brighton replied. "And what would that be?"

"Well, although I have my theories, what *exactly* is the meaning of, '*And when your job is done, God will bring you home*?'"

Robert Brighton *did not* smile, but his eyes twinkled thoughtfully. "Well, Stan, those words really *do* say it all without any further explanation being needed, once of course you understand the concept of what your '*job*' is."

"*My* job?" Stan asked curiously. "Do you mean what I do for a living?"

"*Possibly*," Brighton replied hesitantly. "But in this case, *your job* does not need to be the same as your *occupation*."

"What type of *job* are you talking about then?" Stan asked in confusion.

Dr. Brighton smiled. "Well, in this life *each* of us has the exciting opportunity of finding or creating an activity which uniquely suits us. One that will hopefully lead us to happiness and contentment. But we must first discover what it is we would be *happiest* spending our time doing, however large or small, and *regardless* of whether we make any money at it!" he chuckled. "Once we find it, *that* becomes *part of our job*!"

"Only *part*?" Stan asked.

"Yes," Brighton replied. "An *equally important* part rests on monitoring the welfare of others, and making ourselves available to *helping them* whenever the need arises. I'm especially talking about our extended families, friends and loved ones, but when we hear a cry for help from other people *outside* of that small circle, we must always be open to assisting them as well. You see, both *our* journey and the journeys of the people we come in contact with *can be* intimately intertwined."

"In what way?" Stan asked.

"In a *lot* of ways," Brighton laughed. "During our short lifetimes on Earth, inevitably *everyone* we come in contact with experiences times when they feel lost, alone and in need of help. Anytime we hear their cries, each of us have the remarkable abilities of offering sincere *comfort, hope* and *inspiration* to them. These are three of the *greatest* of all gifts God has bestowed upon us. And they are created to be *shared freely* with others!" Brighton replied with a smile. "Sometimes we may even be unaware that we are helping someone? We may find ourselves simply doing it *instinctively*. Like when you opened my eyes to seeing that '*other*' world. You probably had no idea that you were doing anything special… but you were helping to *guide me* toward my destiny!"

Stan was thoroughly mesmerized by his words.

Brighton smiled. "And in time, our helping others will hopefully turn into genuine *empathy* for them as we watch and feel them experience the ups and downs of their lives over the years. Sometimes, this creates opportunities for *us* to help them or for *them* to help us. To me, *that* brings us the most satisfaction in life that I can imagine, and brings us a little closer to feeling genuinely happy and contented!" Quickly adding, "Life invariably becomes an exciting journey *with* others. Our lives just wouldn't feel complete without them!" Smiling broadly, he added, "And for everyone who we get to know, we must *never* forget about the possibility of building a lasting *friendship*! Since leaving this earthly domain, I have come to really appreciate the amazing friendships that I see between people every day! A good friendship should *always* be highly valued."

Stan smiled, and replied, "Like ours?"

"*Like ours*!" Brighton smiled back. "And at some point in our lives, when our jobs are done to ours and God's satisfaction, at a time that none of us can possibly predict, he will call us home. Hence, "*And when your job is done, God will bring you home*!"

Stan beamed at his new understanding, before growing a little concerned. "But what if we know that we could have done better at our job, and helped and inspired more people, but we just *didn't* work hard enough and died before we were finished?" he confronted him passionately.

"Not to worry," Brighton calmly assured him. "Then God will give you a way to achieve it *after* death. Why do you think I'm an angel?" he winked.

"But Robert," Stan shared with sincerity, "As much as I'd like to, I *know* that I can't possibly comfort and inspire *everyone* in need?"

Brighton smiled. "Not *by yourself*, certainly. But for everyone you *do* comfort, give hope to, or inspire, they'll likely give that same gift to somebody else in need, and so it goes," Brighton shared gently. "Remember, during his brief life on Earth, Jesus spent his days living in a very small geographical area and *did not* create a church to share his teachings. It was those he had *inspired* who did that, often *years later*, eventually spreading his story and teachings all over the world!"

Suddenly, Stan *understood.*

Again, Brighton smiled. "And regardless of how much of your day it takes to help others, *never* neglect the first part of your job. Dedicate an ample portion of your life to something, *anything*, that will henceforth make you wake-up each morning *looking forward* to the day!"

"Like being an archaeologist?" Stan offered honestly.

"Like being a *wonderful* archaeologist," Dr. Brighton smiled reassuringly. "There is still so much of the past that's just waiting to be discovered!"

Growing excited, Stan asked passionately, "But how do we *know* that what we have decided to do would be considered worthy to God?"

"Well, Stan," Brighton gently replied, "in each of us there lives a *unique part* of God, and as such, we are each given an exclusive collection of natural talents, weaknesses, and desires to work with during this lifetime. Passionately and determinedly using those talents to overcome our weaknesses and *achieve* our goals, while also comforting and inspiring others in the process, will *surely* make us happy!" Brighton smiled broadly. "And it will make *God happy too*! It's as *simple* as that!" he shared warmly.

Stan gratefully took-in his words and smiled. "You know, Robert?"

"Yes?" Brighton replied curiously.

"While we were on that dig to the mountains, all of that stuff you said about me *guiding you*?" Stan began.

Brighton nodded curiously.

"Maybe it was actually *you* who were guiding *me*?" he suggested passionately. "I would never have had the courage to *embrace the unknown* over and over again by myself, or to learn all that I did without my being inspired by your determination and blind faith that everything would work out fine in the end?"

Brighton smiled appreciatively and said, "Thank you, Stan, but do you know what? I would *never* have even found that cave if it hadn't been for you! Face it! We *complemented* each other, didn't we? Just like *friends* do. So, why not just keep it simple and say that we were both *inspired by* and *appreciative* of each other, and God willing, we *always* will be! Okay?" Then he paused, and looking at Stan warmly, he added, "Incidentally, I heard what you said about me in your speech tonight. Just so we're clear, you are also the *best friend I've ever had*!"

And with that, Dr. Robert Brighton turned and slowly began walking away from the house, down the sidewalk, momentarily disappearing from view. The new *Chosen One* glanced thoughtfully at the granite key that he was so carefully cradling in his hand, smiled and whispered softly, "I'll be seeing you later, *my friend*." As he reached the front door to his house, he distinctly heard Brighton's gentle voice in his head reply, "Whenever you need me, I'll *always* be with you." And *that*… proved to be the *happy truth*.

Whiskey
THEATER

The Adventures of Horace Black!

(2016)

THE STORY I AM ABOUT TO SHARE WITH YOU is definitely *not* for the faint of heart or for those of you who don't believe in the supernatural. In fact, I am not completely sure that this story is appropriate for *anyone at all*? But I'll share it with you anyway. Regardless of your probable difficulty in believing that this story is true, I swear by everything I have experienced that it *is*! Honestly, I could never in a million years have imagined such a strange and twisted tale as this one? As I relate this fantastic story to you, if I sometimes appear to be drifting off into the realm of fantasy, let me assure you that as much as it may seem so, and as much as I may even *wish* it were so… I most definitely *am not*! My name is Horace Black, certainly as dull and ordinary a name as you or I have ever heard or imagined. But as much as it grieves me to say… the name *fits me* like a glove! What happened to me defies all logic, and unlike me, was in *no way* ordinary. So, why was I selected to play the lead role in this incredible story? I'm afraid you'll have to wait a bit to find out about that.

To most accurately describe myself, I am probably a great example of an uninteresting *(bordering on boring)* retired man of sixty-two, who used to be an aerospace engineer. Aside from having had a great job and being fortunate enough to have been married to Anne for the past forty years, I have never really viewed myself as being *special* in any way? As far as my looks go, although I try to occasionally exercise, I must admit that I am still a bit paunchy. I am about five foot seven with thinning gray hair, and although I possess a face that has all of the God-given components it should, very honestly, it has often been compared (*with absolutely no disrespect intended as far as I know*) to the face of a loyal *Saint Bernard*. So, it is *very unlikely* that I will ever win a beauty contest, at least a *human* one! I live a happy, albeit *ordinary* life with Anne, whom I simply adore. To me, through the years she has *never* lost even one speck of her inner and outer beauty, but has actually *increased* it! We had both saved and invested throughout our lives, so financially we were quite well off as we entered retirement. We didn't have any children, close friends or relatives living nearby, so we spent our days and nights happily alone together in a great big house in Jefferson City, Missouri, just a phone-call away from our loved ones! It is said that *this* house had once been owned by our 33rd President of the United States, who happened to be *born* in Missouri... *Harry S. Truman*! I can't confirm that of course, but I like to think it's true. Then one fateful night, *everything changed*! That evening I went to bed as usual, but when I woke-up later, I found myself in the midst of a *very serious stroke*! I will not depress you with the graphic details, but when I finally came home from the hospital almost a *month* later, I was still mostly paralyzed on the entire right side of my body! And although I was mentally alert... I could *not* speak a word; only *grunt*!

My wife, of course, had come to visit me in the hospital every day that I had been there, often spending the night beside me, usually sleeping in a very *uncomfortable* chair she'd find somewhere in the building. Our love knew *no* bounds! I believe that it was her care, along with her positivity that eventually allowed me to get well enough to finally return home, believing strongly that I *would* improve! But when I arrived home, things weren't exactly *hunky-dory*. Improvement came very slowly, so both of us had a lot of changes to get used to. To begin with, I pretty much *lived* in my wheel chair now, and although I had adequately learned to dress and undress myself as well as getting to and from the bathroom, those simple tasks pretty much *exhausted* me! My wife *never* complained of course, but I could see that she was being *overwhelmed* by the extra work she had to do for me. Well, one day while she was out grocery shopping, she *fortuitously* made the acquaintance of a charming young woman who happened to be a nurse and a homecare worker named Gretchen. Lucky for us, she was also looking for work at the time as she had only recently moved to Jefferson City following an ugly divorce. So, after consulting with my doctors, my wife decided that I *should* have a helper in the house during the week! Her jobs would include assisting me as well as helping Anne with the daily household chores such as cleaning the house and preparing meals. About two days later, we *hired* Gretchen.

Gretchen arrived that morning, a friendly woman with an 'actress smile' (*probably in her early thirties*), sporting long red hair and predictably dressed like a nurse. She gave me a very sincere, "Hello," and quickly got to work helping my wife with her chores. Gretchen immediately became a very valued part of our household, and we both liked her very much!

Things went swimmingly for a while as Gretchen proved herself to be an excellent cook, housekeeper and caregiver. But it was during her third week in this capacity I believe, that everything took a very *strange turn*? On that day Gretchen effortlessly helped me move from my wheelchair into my favorite easy-chair in the family room, as *was* our normal routine. After doing this, she gave me a pill with a glass of water, which was *also* an integral part of our normal routine. Then she kissed me lightly on the forehead, looked me firmly in the eyes and smiling impishly, said, "*Good luck*," which was definitely *not* a part of our normal routine? Still, we exchanged smiles, I swallowed the pill and five minutes later, I was sound asleep in my chair.

When I awoke sometime later, strangely enough, I was no longer in my chair at home but in an unfamiliar bed, dressed in red polka-dot pajamas? I immediately wondered if I had suffered a *second* stroke and as a result had been returned to the hospital?

"Get out of bed, Horace! You'll be late for work!" a sweet female voice called out from another room. That sweet female voice, I *swear* I did *not* recognize at all? I wished to God that I could speak and tell her that I was retired and didn't work anymore. But sadly, in the area of speech, I knew that all I was capable of doing right now was to *grunt*!

"I know, I'll hurry," I replied nonchalantly. *Did I just speak?*

Next, I proceeded to *effortlessly* get up, get dressed and get ready for work without so much as even thinking about it? When I looked at myself in the mirror for the first time, I was bowled over by the realization that I was a *young man again*, probably in my late twenties or early thirties? But I didn't look anything like myself at that age? I was tall, well over six feet, had a full head of red hair, and looked as though I worked out regularly? The biggest difference from the real me of course (*aside from the part about working out regularly*), was the fact that I had four working limbs and could *speak* again?

Automatically, I walked out of the bedroom and into the kitchen, where I sat down in a chair at a small table. "Umm… that food sure smells delicious, Caroline!" I said with a smile, surprising myself once again by actually *knowing* this stranger's name?

"Thanks, Horace," she responded gratefully, while carrying two plates of bacon, eggs and toast to the table. "Eat fast. It's already 7:30, and remember, your bus *leaves* at 7:45!"

Caroline looked to be a few years my junior. She was tall and thin, had long brunette hair and was very pretty, possessing a simply *captivating* smile.

"I will," I confirmed, as I voraciously consumed the food on my plate. Surprisingly, and very quickly, important information began *pouring through my brain*. First of all, I learned that *Caroline was my sister*! She shared this little house with me while she was finishing up her master's degree at Westminster College in Fulton, Missouri, which was not far from where we were living now, in Hannibal. I was the producer and director for a small theatre, also in Fulton, and I supplemented that income by teaching a couple of theatre classes each week at my sister's college. Oh, and for some crazy reason… I *did not* own a car?

I hugged Caroline goodbye (*which felt like my proper daily ritual*), closed the door behind me and caught the bus at 7:45, just as I *apparently* did on most days. I arrived at Westminster College at 8:15 and immediately walked over to the school's Little Theatre. After unlocking the door and turning on the lights, I patiently waited for my first class to begin at 8:30. I had no idea what the date was or what this class's current lesson was, but it *didn't* seem to matter? I somehow *knew* that just before I opened my mouth to speak, *everything* I would need to understand about teaching this class today would *magically* come to me!

Twenty-two young college students soon walked through the door and took their seats in the house (*the audience portion of the theatre*) only moments before the bell rang. I immediately flashed them a great big smile. I could hardly believe it? I was literally *filled* with energy and confidence, so much so that I nearly *scared myself*! But, I proceeded to speak to the class and teach today's lesson at an *exhilarating* pace! I had *never* had so much fun during my entire life! It was as if I were performing a monologue which I had flawlessly memorized, while all of my students were showing their gratitude throughout via their constant smiles and laughter? It felt as if the ninety-minute class period was over almost as quickly as it had begun? I knew that this was only a dream of course, and I was *actually* a 'wheelchair-bound stroke survivor,' but surprisingly, that didn't take away a thing from the immense joy I felt being an energetic young man again! It was at that very moment that I first noticed my classroom was empty *except* for a very young-looking male student (*probably a freshman*), who appeared to be patiently waiting to speak with me.

I immediately turned to face him and very professionally asked, "Hello. How may I help you?"

The boy offered absolutely *no* facial expression as he appeared to be carefully looking me over? And then with a very self-satisfied tone, he announced, "You're *not* the former Mr. Black, are you!"

"I'm not?" I replied jokingly, as I expected him to laugh (*and be thoroughly impressed by my well-timed punch-line*), but that laugh *never* came? The young man simply turned around and walked *straight out the door* without another word?

You know what? There was absolutely *no* information this time explaining to me what the hell had just happened? That alone struck me as odd? However, my next drama class came and went just as quickly as the first one had, so I really didn't have much time to think about anything else.

Before I knew it, it was almost noon. And while most of the students and teachers at the college were probably busy eating their lunches, I had unexpectedly received an urgent phone message to meet with the Dean of Performing Arts... *Miss Weasel*. Her office was clear across campus (*I'm not sure how I knew that*), but with my finely tuned and chiseled body, I actually found the walk there to be most invigorating!

Less than five minutes later, I reached her office. I gently knocked on her closed door and waited patiently for a response.

"*Come in*," she hissed breathily in a deep contralto voice, as I slowly turned the knob and entered her office. Miss Weasel was a woman of medium height and build, with short dark hair and a dark complexion. She looked to be somewhere in her early thirties. But I must admit, just as soon as I laid eyes on her for the first time and saw how she was dressed, I became just a little bit *unnerved*? Although I *knew* that she was a woman, it was still as if I were looking at a *leather-clad transvestite*, complete with exotic eye make-up and six-inch stilettos? She would have given *Frank N. Furter* of the '*Rocky Horror Show*' a run for his money!

"Hello, Horace," she breathed sexily.

"Hi, Frank," I responded in a friendly manner. I had just been *mentally* informed that Miss Weasel's first name was actually *Francesca*, but for some unknown reason she preferred to have her friends call her 'Frank,' so I did.

"Thank you for coming in on such *short* notice," she sighed.

"No problem. I was only going to *eat my lunch*!" I replied humorously.

Apparently Frank did not understand humor... or at least *mine*, as she completely ignored my attempt to be funny and continued dramatically, "Do you know *why* I called you here to see me?"

"Not really?" I replied honestly.

"No?" Frank asked in surprise.

There was a pregnant pause at that point before I finally felt compelled to say, with a bright theatrical smile, "Okay then. I'll see you later."

"You *bet* you will, big boy!" she winked. "You're taking me out tonight! Remember?"

Instantly, I felt a fresh rush of information invading my brain! I was taking Frank out tonight because she wasn't able to procure another date and today was *her birthday*! I chuckled and exclaimed, "*Gotcha*! Of course, I remembered! Looking forward to it Frank! What number is this birthday for you?"

"I'm twenty-nine… *again*!" she smiled. With that, she blew me a kiss, tapped her stilettos and I was *out* the door.

With both of my classes done for the day, I was now off to the local *Fulton Theatre*. It was there that I ran my little theatre group which was comprised mainly of… well, actually *entirely of* students from the college. I didn't have a rehearsal today, but apparently there were a number of loose ends for me to take care of. I suddenly learned that the expenses for my theatre were being subsidized by the college. This was due to the fact that Westminster College had *no* full-sized theatre of its own for its students to perform in. Although this appeared to be a monetary godsend for me, this arrangement gave them the power to *cancel* any of my shows which included their students *if* in their opinion, some valid reason strongly compelled them to do so! But as of today, they had thankfully *not* canceled a single Fulton Theatre performance! Suddenly feeling hungry, I stopped for lunch at a quaint, little hamburger joint called *Greasy's.* This place was charmingly made to look like an authentic 'Auto Repair Shop,' complete with plenty of *grease on the food*! It was a great 'burger and fries' joint that I had apparently been frequenting for years, due to their delicious and mouth-watering *veggie-burgers*, creatively called, 'The Soil Change!' This was a very clever title which sounded like 'oil change,' but substituted the word 'soil,' for oil, since vegetables for veggie-burgers are normally *grown* in it! **Okay**, I know *that* description of a veggie-burger sounded pretty lame, and probably belonged on a local cable channel being broadcast from someone's *garage* at three o'clock in the morning! But surprisingly, that *schlock writing* was actually earning money! The younger Horace (*whose body I was currently residing in*), had written and recorded a promo with *that* information on it for Greasy's, and it was earning him *fifty bucks* each time it was aired on a local radio station specializing in food, called KYUM! This tasty tidbit of news was proof positive that I had unreservedly *no* *filter* controlling the *quality* of the information that randomly appeared in my head! Suddenly, my brain received another important update. The Fulton Theatre, as well as my little house in nearby Hannibal, were *both mine*! My outrageously wealthy and unpredictable parents had recently sold their mansion and moved to Europe. They had left *both* of those buildings to me as an early inheritance present, since they had absolutely *no intention* of ever moving back! They left my only sibling, Caroline, our family's much larger summer house in Newport Beach, California (*overlooking the ocean*)! She excitedly planned on occupying it just as soon as she completed her Master's thesis on 'Lifestyles of the Rich and Famous,' and received her degree from the college. Then she planned on immediately becoming a '*home decorator to the stars*,' basing herself right there in Newport Beach, the hub of Southern California's *wealthiest* citizens! My parents had also seen fit to bequeath each of us an allowance of *two million dollars* a year, coming by way of our family trust. I suppose that's why I was enjoying a life in community theatre instead of something more lucrative, like *almost anything else*! Yes, it was indisputably obvious that above personal wealth, I absolutely *loved* producing and directing amateur play productions! And just as soon as I finished this scrumptious but healthy veggie-burger, I would be off to see my very own, 'Fulton Theatre!'

I soon learned, just as I had *expected*, that my theatre was located within easy walking distance of Greasy's. Although I had never been to this place before, I seemed to know *exactly* how to get there? On the one hand, this ability to suddenly *know* things that I had never known before, was *not* surprising anymore. But on the other hand, it never ceased feeling *incredible*? I had never in my life experienced anything like it, whether awake or dreaming! But although this dream did feel very lifelike, I was coherent enough to know that it *was* only a dream, and at this point I just planned on enjoying the ride until I eventually woke-up.

The Fulton Theatre was located in an older part of town, as evidenced by the abundance of smaller houses sporting 1950s and 60s architecture which surrounded it. Many of them were very noticeably in need of *cosmetic* repair, begging for a fresh coat of paint, new landscaping or *both*. In addition, there were severely cracked sidewalks lining both sides of the street that had obviously seen better days. But honestly? I thought they gave the area character and charm! As I perused the exterior of the moderately-sized wooden structure that *was* the Fulton Theatre, I was genuinely impressed! From the outside, it looked to be very well kept-up. To support this thinking, I noticed that it had been recently painted white with black trim, which looked rather classy for an older theatre like this one. I also spied a large marquee attached to the front wall of the building with the following words displayed in bold black letters, **The Adventures of Horace Black!**

What? I owned a theatre that was putting on a play about *me*? What a complete *egomaniac* I must be? It was then that a nearby poster caught my eye, advertising the upcoming play. In three short sentences the story was *concisely* explained with no frills whatsoever!

This is the story of a state treasure.
Horace Black, born in Missouri, died in Missouri.
The man who invented 'Missouri State Whiskey!'

After a long moment of *shock*, I thought, 'What the hell is *Missouri State Whiskey*?' And then, just as it always did, the information I needed suddenly *whooshed* through my brain like magic! Horace Black had lived in Missouri during the early part of the 20th century and had invented a very *unique* tasting whiskey made mostly from boiled asparagus and broccoli? Was *that* even possible? It was not exceptionally popular outside of Missouri, but citizens of the state couldn't get enough of the stuff, while Missouri's state government *featured* it at all state-sponsored events! In fact, the government was so enamored with it that they even sent cases out as gifts to political leaders in other states and countries. They felt that this move effectively *one-upped* them by flaunting a uniquely *Missouri* product in their faces! It also *guaranteed* that Horace Black's brand of whiskey would *never* go out of business!

Horace Black, the whiskey's inventor, had apparently been *his* great-grandfather. He was putting on this play as a tribute or a *homage* to him, whether crowds flocked to see it or not. This play, it seems, had actually been written by the elder Mr. Black about a year before his death. He stipulated in his will that it *had* to be performed in *this theatre* at least *once* every year, and it *had* been. He had also insisted that this theatre was *always* to be passed on to the eldest son in his extended Black family, who *had* to be named *Horace* in order to inherit the theatre and the money that apparently went along with it. In the event that the play was *not* presented, Horace Black had prophesized in his will that *bad luck* of the most severe kind would befall whoever owned the theatre at the time. In regards to the bad luck, although he *didn't* actually define 'severe,' it certainly sounded *apocalyptic*! And if the theatre were ever sold, or no Horace Black took over… the *entire* extended Black family would meet with *dire consequences*!

'*Wow*!' I thought. 'That is a mighty hefty curse!'

"Yes, it is, isn't it!" I was *shocked* to immediately recognize the voice of Calvin Offenbach, the young freshman I had spoken to in class earlier today, as he surprisingly replied from behind me.

"I don't recall saying anything *out loud*?" I stammered, as I turned to face him.

"You didn't. I *read* your mind," Calvin replied arrogantly.

I jumped and stuttered, "Whe… Whe… Where did you come from?"

"I followed you here from Greasy's," he replied calmly, without expression. "I wanted to speak with you."

Listening to Calvin I had the eerie sensation that I was about to converse with someone much older than he looked. Someone who *knew* what he wanted, like an artist, a great chef, or a *serial killer*!

"Let's go inside the theatre, shall we?" Calvin suggested mysteriously. "Perhaps you wouldn't mind *opening* the door for us?"

I hesitantly decided to oblige him as I instantly found the correct key on the ring of them that I apparently *always* carried. As soon as I had unlocked the front door, we walked through the lobby into the house, and *somehow* I knew to go inside the tech booth next, and turn on the house lights? Then we took adjoining seats five rows back from the stage. I took a moment to peruse the interior of theatre I had apparently inherited. Even though I was an engineer with *no* prior knowledge of theatres, to *my* eyes it looked efficiently designed and *beautiful*! The house sported almost 400 seats which were all meticulously covered in red velvet, all in good repair. And while the stage was a good size, with the smaller number of seats in the house, the theatre felt pleasingly intimate. I liked what I saw. I liked it *very much*!

"I realize that you are *not* the Horace Black you are supposed to be," Calvin began.

"What do you mean by that?" I asked him curiously.

"I mean that you are in a *different body*, are you not?" Calvin replied leadingly.

"Yes, I am?" I replied suspiciously. "*Why* is that?" I demanded.

"Let me explain," Calvin said calmly. "The *real* director of this theatre, as I'm sure you have already figured out, is the body you are now wearing, young Horace Black. Although he *was* prepared to present the play, '*The Adventures of Horace Black*,' this weekend, he apparently had a change of heart and was planning on *canceling* the performance instead!"

"Why?" I asked.

"Because he hadn't sold enough tickets to make it worthwhile for him, I suppose," Calvin replied dismissively. "Well, actually… he hadn't sold *any* tickets!"

"That's too bad," I shared honestly. "But what ever happened to, '*The show must go on*?'"

"Precisely!" Calvin suddenly showed a spark of life. "I completely agree with you!"

"But of course, that *doesn't* change the fact that he refuses to put on the show, now does it," I deftly pointed out.

"You *would* be correct except for the fact that he is *no longer* in charge of it," Calvin smiled wickedly. "*You* are!"

I was momentarily taken aback. "Well sure, I'm the Horace Black you might prefer at the moment," I said, "but just as soon as I wake-up…"

"You *are* awake!" Calvin boldly interjected. "As I told you, you're merely *occupying* a different body, that's all."

"*Huh*?" I shouted in confusion.

Calvin laughed for several moments before continuing. "Now just *who* do you think I am?" He waited for my answer and when I *didn't* offer one, he proceeded to answer his own question. "I am *the original* Horace Black!" he bragged. "Just like you, I am now occupying the body of someone else! Since being dead, I make it a point of coming back every year to watch my play being performed. I routinely occupy the body of a random student for a few days just so I can enjoy watching it like the living do. Call this my *little vacation* from death."

"But, how in the world did you ever get the power to do that, instead of… well… *staying dead* like everyone else who dies?" I asked incredulously.

Calvin laughed once again. "To tell you the truth, I haven't the *foggiest*? And I have always been rather perplexed about that myself? It was like this. I was alive, I died, and I lost my old body." Becoming much more animated, he continued, "*But*, for some odd reason which I cannot even begin to explain, I *never* lost the awareness of who I *had* been… and I soon discovered my power over the living!"

"What *power* is that?" I asked hesitantly.

Horace smiled mysteriously and said, "Well, let's just say that *the world is my plaything*!"

I stared at him in disbelief, before visualizing something awful! "When you switched bodies with Calvin Offenbach, did he *enter yours*?"

The young man did not reply, but looked rather pleased with himself.

I was aghast! "But your body is probably buried somewhere in a coffin with worms crawling all through your *dead and rotting carcass*!" I blurted out in disgust. "Poor *Calvin*!"

The young man laughed. "Very *amusing*, but actually I was cremated and my ashes were scattered all around the perimeter of this theatre," he said calmly. "Relax. Calvin's conscious mind is asleep inside his body, and he is suffering from no discomfort."

Suddenly, I had a big question concerning my own predicament. "Why am I taking the place of this younger Horace Black, who as far as I know is absolutely *no relation* to me?"

The young man, who upon closer examination looked to be no older than seventeen, took on a fatherly air. "Because there were no other Horace Blacks that I could find on such short notice!" he explained. "So, I decided that *you* would just have to do."

"But I don't know the *first thing* about directing a play!" I insisted. "I'm a retired aerospace engineer!"

"Neither of those two trivial concerns matter to me at all," the young man replied calmly. "The cast has already learned the play, and it is all set to go!"

"Now see here, I am under *no* moral or lawful obligation to do your bidding! I never signed a contract or took money from you," I professed testily.

"Well..." he began in a decidedly more *sinister* tone, "let's just say that if you don't cooperate, bad luck *might* befall your lovely wife Anne. And surely you would not want *that* to happen, now would you?"

I felt a decidedly *cold chill* as I inadvertently shuddered! I don't know how, but with great effort I managed to hold myself together. "If I go along with your plan and put this play on... do you *promise* to return me to my rightful body and put *everyone else* back in their bodies as well?"

"Of course," he agreed condescendingly. "You have my word that I will return you to your '*old crippled body*' if that is truly what you want me to do," the man replied with more than a little 'snarky-ness' in his voice.

"Why am I constantly having *new information* delivered to my mind?" I felt compelled to ask him.

"Because you are simultaneously *both* Horace Blacks; yourself and the body and mind of the man you currently inhabit. You are a man with two different brains working in *perfect* harmony," the man answered proudly.

"Is young Horace aware that I have *highjacked* his mind and body?" I blurted out.

Calvin chuckled. "You certainly ask a lot of questions!"

"Well, *is he*?" I insisted.

"*Of course not*!" Calvin assured me. "In reality, your mind has simply been *added* to his, so that you know what he knows, but he is *never* aware that you are in there... *visiting*."

"Does my nurse, Gretchen, work for you too?" I asked the man suspiciously.

"Oh yes!" he bragged. "She is not only on the Black payroll, but she's also one of my favorite *descendants*! Her full name is Gretchen *Black*!"

"I should have known something was fishy when my wife met her *so conveniently* at the grocery store!" I exclaimed.

The man laughed loudly. "Come on Horace, get with the program! I am just a very good businessman. I send Gretchen out to *ingratiate* herself to a select *Black* family that includes a 'Horace' about a month before the play is set to be performed every year. I do this on the off-chance that I might need *that* Horace Black to replace the director, who is also named Horace Black, as I did this year."

"How many of your descendants know about you and your power?" I asked.

"Not many. Although most of them will always remain oblivious, I consider them all to be on a *need-to-know* contract," he said cryptically.

"What in the world does *that* mean?" I asked in confusion.

Calvin slowly smiled, and explained, "It means that I contact them whenever I *need* them. For example, whenever a Horace decides to retire from the theatre, I contact their replacement. Understand?"

"Yes, I get it," I replied without smiling back. "You told me that you use Gretchen every year? What makes her so special?" I insisted.

Again, Calvin smiled. "The truth is, I like her *loyalty*! She's always willing to help me out. Why, she's been doing "odd-jobs' for me ever since she was a teenager!"

"Is she *really* a nurse and a caregiver?" I asked dubiously.

"Of course *not*!" the young man laughed. "She's an '*out of work actress*' most of the time, but nurse and caregiver are certainly part of her performance repertoire."

"But she seemed like such a nice person? *Why* would she go along with you and I assume, drug me?" I asked.

"I'd like to think it was because of her *fierce loyalty* to me, but I *do* pay her rather handsomely!" he laughed. "And don't worry about your actual body. Even now, you are perceived by your wife and doctors to be in a *temporary* non-life-threatening coma… resting comfortably… at home."

"This *coma*…" I asked. "How long will it last?"

"Until your job here is finished, or if you refuse… until you *die* of natural causes."

"Can I at least go back home to *visit* my wife?" I pleaded.

"*Absolutely not*!" old Horace proclaimed in horror. "If you leave young Horace's life by going back to your real one, even by so much as phoning your wife or sending her a letter, you will not only kill yourself… but *him* as well!"

"You have all of this pretty well planned out," I conceded disappointedly.

"Not *pretty* well," the young man chided me. "I have *all* of this *perfectly* planned out!"

"Okay," I agreed. "So, one performance without an audience. Will that do it?"

"*Certainly not*!" he gasped. "I want to see at least *one* ticket sold for this performance in order to make your part of this contract valid. And there will be *no* freebees or people coerced to watch it," he warned. "As the creator of this play, if no one comes to see it out of desire… then I may as well *kill myself*!"

"But you're *already* dead?" I reminded him.

The young man laughed. "It's just a figure of speech, Horace!"

Suddenly, I felt a *rush* of new information flowing through my mind, allowing me to instantly understand this entire situation. "So," I shared excitedly, "your great grandnephew, the director, *couldn't* sell a single ticket to this play, and you discovered that he was *using* that fact to put an end to *all* future performances! In short, if he had his way, your play would *never again* be performed… *ever*, and your story would soon be forgotten! Am I right?"

"*Bingo*!" the man masquerading as Calvin Offenbach passionately agreed. "Horace was intending to destroy my play and with it, the noble *Black family tradition*, by not caring a whit about either one of them! So, I took *decisive* action."

"You certainly did," I agreed helplessly. Then suddenly thinking of a simple alternative to his plan that would result in *me* instantly being returned home to my own body, I excitedly suggested, "Why don't *you* just possess young Horace's body instead of having me do it? Then you would have complete control over every aspect of this entire production!"

"What? Direct a *homage to myself*?" he said, flabbergasted. "What do you think I am? A *raving narcissist*?"

I didn't feel the need to answer that.

"Good luck, Mr. Black. I want this production to be a celebration of *my* life!" he announced triumphantly. "And I expect at least one person in the audience to give it a *heartfelt standing ovation*."

"Hey! That's not fair! How can I guarantee that?" I asked, exasperated.

The young man laughed. "You'll find a way. Or maybe you'll just get *lucky*? At least I didn't make it *two people*," he smiled impishly.

At 6:30 that night, I found myself driving over to Frank's house to pick her up for our '*date*.' I was driving my sister's white Ford Ranger because for some stupid reason, as I had learned this morning, I did *not* own a car? I ask you, what guy who has at least *two million bucks* in the bank *doesn't* own their own car? While driving, I kept thinking about the conversation I had earlier at the Fulton Theatre with old Horace Black. He had talked a good game, but who was to say that he, Frank, Caroline and the *new me* weren't *all* just figments of my '*newly discovered imagination*,' meticulously woven together into this crazy dream? I must admit… I *was* hoping!

Upon arriving at Frank's house, I picked-up her wrapped gift from the passenger seat and started walking toward the front door. I had 'casually' dressed-up for this date by wearing a light blue blazer with a white dress shirt that *did not* include a tie, and a nearly brand-new pair of tight-legged blue jeans. This ensemble would *not* have been my personal choice for dressing-up tonight, but I yielded to the preference of young Horace (*my other brain*), because not having been on a date for about a *zillion* years, I realized that my own fashion sense was probably just a wee bit out of date. Even so, I had absolutely *no* idea what Frank would be wearing and I fervently hoped that I was not underdressed? I knocked lightly on her door and almost immediately (*as if she had been anxiously waiting for me*), Frank appeared?

"Hi, sexy," she articulated through a harsh whisper. I let out a big sigh of relief as I realized that I was *not underdressed*! Frank was wearing her white '*home*' baseball uniform from years before, when she had actually been a student-athlete at Westminster College. I had no doubt that it was *completely authentic* too, as across the front of her white jersey in bold black lettering was written, ***The Westminster College Blue Jays***, while on the back was her last name, ***Weasel***! The entire ensemble consisted of a white jersey and pants, with a pair of black shoes that gave the *illusion* of being cleats, but in truth, were simply cool looking tennis shoes! It was truly amazing how something like *that* could look so *good* on her after all these years? But honestly, *it did*! (*That was my other brain's opinion, of course.*) "Come in, darling."

I obliged her, and once inside the house, we immediately sat down together on the couch in the living room, surprisingly made of a colorful tweed fabric of *psychedelic paisley*? The walls, floor and ceiling of the room were all painted *jet-black*, probably due to her obvious love of anything and everything *gothic*. The couch and the rest of the colorful furniture that the room was filled with, including four *rainbow-colored* chairs in the shape of Fender Stratocaster electric guitars surrounding a table that looked like a bass drum turned on its side, were highlighted nicely by the all-encompassing *black* surrounding everything! In fact, the interior of the house actually had a kind of '*nightmarish sixties-vibe*,' and I personally found it to be quite exhilarating! (*Please be advised, that last opinion once again came from the 'more flamboyant' young drama director's side of my mind.*)

"Hey, Frank!" I exclaimed with a smile. "*Happy birthday*!"

"Aww, you remembered!" she gushed. At that point, she hugged me tightly… a little *too tightly*… and planted a great big kiss smack dab on my lips.

Just as soon as she had released me, I held out her gift and said, "I brought you a present!"

Well, Frank immediately grew weepy, excitedly accepted the gift, and hugged me once again, murmuring, "You're the only one who *remembered* my birthday! Thank you *so* much!"

After she had calmed herself down and wiped away her tears of joy, she unwrapped the gift I had brought her. It was an extra-large bottle of *Horace Black's Missouri State Whiskey*, which unsurprisingly, I had just *happened* to find at my house. Once again, she grew very emotional.

"How did you know that *this* was my absolute favorite kind of whiskey?" she exclaimed, planting a series of little kisses all over my face. Then, after opening the bottle and taking a long swig from it, she offered it to me, but I politely declined. Next, she closed the bottle and placed it very carefully on her bass drum table, we left her house, climbed into my sister's truck and drove off.

My plan was to wine and dine her at *Hank's Grille*, since I somehow *knew* that we both liked it there. However, only moments before we arrived, Frank dramatically asked me to stop the car, so of course, I did? I was very concerned about her, so I didn't even park in the lot, but opted instead to park just outside of it, where it would be more private.

"Is something wrong?" I asked her innocently.

"No, Horace. I just wanted to stop for a little while… and *talk*," she replied, completely '*over-the-top*,' like someone you'd watched on a television soap opera from the 1980s! "This is my first date since the beginning of last term, and I just want you to know how *very much* I am enjoying it."

"Thank you, Frank. I'm enjoying it too!" I assured her. "The most important thing to me tonight is that *you* have a really nice time."

"*Yeah*?" Frank asked excitedly.

"Of course," I responded in the kindest and most sincere tone I could muster.

It was then, like an *oversexed hyena*, that Frank sprang on top of me and began to kiss me passionately! Within moments, we were both lying across the front bench seat of my sister's Ford Ranger, and *somehow* she had already taken off my coat and shirt, with my *pants not far behind*!

"Whoa!" I yelled as loudly as I could. "I was thinking more like *dinner and a movie*?"

Frank immediately grew embarrassed, stopped what she was doing, slowly sat up and began dispassionately rebuttoning her baseball jersey which she had apparently *also* begun taking off? I quickly followed suit by getting dressed, myself.

"You said that you wanted me to have '*a really good time*?'" she declared *salaciously*.

"Not like *that*!" I corrected her with a laugh to cover my own embarrassment. "I meant that we could have a really good time '*talking and laughing*' together over dinner!" I had intended my words to clear away any lingering confusion she had concerning my '*intentions*.' But disappointingly, she grew even *more* sullen once I had finished speaking?

Within a few minutes, we were both completely dressed and awkwardly sitting in the truck, with Frank sporting an uncomfortably *tight and erect* posture. I kept imagining that if she had been made of glass, her brittle-looking body would have surely *shattered* into a million pieces the moment anyone *touched* her! She was silently staring directly ahead of her, making sure to avoid *any* eye contact with me. I had absolutely *no idea* what to say following her misread of my feelings and her completely unexpected sexual advances? I have to say with all honesty, except for Anne, I have *never understood women*!

Finally, *she* got the courage to speak first, as she dramatically turned toward me and asked, "Why are you such a *stick in the mud*, anyway? Hmm? You'd think you were seventy years old by the way you were acting?" she pouted.

I thought hard about it before I spoke, ultimately deciding to tell her the truth. After all, honesty *is* the best policy. "Actually, I'm only 62 years old, Frank."

"I'm serious!" she insisted, with no shortage of irritation.

"So am I," I replied gently.

Well, for the next five minutes, I briefly explained everything to Frank, just the way I remembered it. Starting with my life as a retiree, my stroke, followed by my incredible transformation into someone else's body, and ultimately, what I *had* to achieve as my only way of getting home. I knew that this story sounded crazy, but I also had a strong gut feeling that somehow Frank *would* believe me!

She listened patiently without commenting. But once I had finished talking, Frank looked me straight in the eyes with the most *terrifying expression* I had seen on the face of a human being since watching the shower scene of the film, '*Psycho*,' and yelled, "If you *aren't* interested in me, there are much easier ways to tell me than by *lying to my face* with that ridiculous story of yours!"

Apparently my '*gut feeling*'... had been *way off*! So, I scrambled to think of a lie explaining my lack of physical attraction to her that she might accept as being more reasonable. "Okay, sorry. The truth is, I'm preparing for the priesthood."

"That's what you told me the *last time* we went out!" she screamed.

Just as I was about to give-up and join Frank in a no-holds-barred verbal brawl, the intensity of which the world has *never seen before*, a tall, handsome man of about thirty, with thick and glorious blonde hair as well as bulging 'Mr. America' type muscles, knocked on the passenger-side window of the truck. Frank promptly turned the crank and rolled it down (*because my sister hadn't seen fit to buy a truck with automatic windows*), and was instantly overcome with joy by the man's very *pleasing* physical appearance.

"Howdy folks! I'm sorry to bother you," he said politely, in a deeply resonant baritone voice. "The name's Calvin Offenbach. I was just sitting in the restaurant noticing that your truck, with *you* in it, had been sitting here for quite some time? Are you having car trouble? I can call a tow truck for ya if you need one?"

"Oh no, everything's fine!" Frank gushed. "Tonight's my birthday. Do you care to have *dinner* with me?"

Suddenly the man's face lit-up. "Sure, honey!" he replied excitedly. "But what about this fella here?" he added, curiously, pointing directly at me.

"Oh, him. He was *just leaving*!" Frank made a point of frowning at me.

"Uh, 'Calvin Offenbach' *is* your name, right?" I asked him.

"Yeh. What of it?" the man asked politely.

"Well, I have a student with that exact name in my drama class at Westminster College," I continued. "Are you two related?"

The man laughed. "Yeh, sure! He's my cousin! In my family you *can't* swing a dead cat around without hitting a *Calvin Offenbach*!"

Frank was simply delighted with the man's answer, and began giggling like a giddy school girl. "Shall we go, *Calvin*?"

The man nodded as he very politely opened Frank's door and she excitedly exited the truck. In truth, during the short time I had known her, I had *never* seen Frank acting *this* happy? She was smiling so big, that to me, when you combined that with her intensely focused eyes, she strongly resembled an *underfed vampire* who had been desperately searching for food and just happened upon a big and muscley *main course*! And to be honest, her gothic makeup made her face sort of *look like one* too? I considered warning Calvin about the strong possibility of a bloodletting in his near future, but I was so happy that tonight's problem between Frank and me had been *painlessly* resolved, that I very quickly decided against it. As they glided away, I heard them talking through the truck's still open passenger-side window.

"Are you driving me home tonight after dinner?" Frank asked him coyly.

"Sorry, sweetheart. I rode my *bicycle* here and it only has one seat," the man replied apologetically. "Unless of course, you don't mind riding on the handlebars?"

"That's okay. I'll just call a cab," Frank replied dryly.

As I drove the truck home, I couldn't help thinking about Frank and the good-looking man she was seeing tonight. It certainly *was* a coincidence that his name was 'Calvin Offenbach'... but nothing normal seemed to *ever* happen in this dream? Oh well. I sure looked forward to waking-up tomorrow morning in my *own bed*!

Can you say, *disappointment*? As soon as the next morning rolled around, I once again woke-up in the body and bed of *young Horace Black*! To say that I was frustrated, barely scratched the surface! I still had to survive another predictably *difficult* day. But I suppose anything was all right as long as it ultimately led to my reunion with Anne.

My 'sister' Caroline and I went through the same morning ritual as yesterday, until I thought I would break it up by asking her what day of the week this was? She matter-of-factly advised me that it was Thursday. *Yikes*! That meant that I only had *one day* left before Friday, when the performance of 'The Adventures of Horace Black,' was due to *light-up the town*! And unfortunately, it would *not* mean I'd be returning to Anne unless I sold at least *one* ticket? Surely I could do that?

I hurriedly ate my breakfast, caught the bus and arrived to teach my first class in plenty of time. As I walked into the college's little theatre and checked my daily roll sheets, I was shocked to discover that Calvin Offenbach's name was *not there anymore*? A separate memo told me that he had been officially removed from school by his parents for earning bad grades. My experiences here were getting *stranger and stranger*? If old Horace Black was *not* possessing Calvin Offenbach's body anymore… then *where* the hell was he? That really concerned me for a few moments, but then it was time for teaching.

Both classes went splendidly, just as they had gone the day before. It was certainly fun for me to be an *expert* in a field I had never so much as *thought about* before? But I really couldn't take *any* credit for this great knowledge and teaching skill I had inherited from the younger Horace Black. On the other hand, perhaps my own great understanding of engineering *may* have discreetly contributed in some *small* way to my successful teaching style? It *was* possible? Okay. *Probably not*.

Immediately after my classes had finished, I set off to see Frank. She hadn't called me into her office today, but she had acted so crazy last night that I just wanted to make sure things were still okay between us. When I arrived at her office, there was a torn sheet of butcher paper with a note written on it taped across her door, accented by a '*St. Louis Cardinals*' poster strategically placed above it. Her note read, '*Out to lunch with my new boyfriend.*' I had to laugh. Well, at least *her* day was going well.

Next, it was off to Greasy's for some lunch. All I could think about as I heartily downed my healthy and meatless Soil Change, was *how* I was going to manage this final rehearsal? I hoped the cast was on time so that we could actually run-through the entire play *just once*! That wasn't too much to ask, was it? With that in mind, I finished up my delicious lunch and quickly headed off toward the theatre. But once I arrived there, I was taken *completely* by surprise as I found myself immediately surrounded by a very *hostile* looking group of young actors. By that I mean *not one* of them was smiling?

"What seems to be the problem?" I asked in my most nonconfrontational and sincere teacher voice, accompanied by an expression that would have warmed hearts in Siberia.

A tall, lean young man who appeared pleasant enough, approached me. By his confident manner, I gathered that he was probably playing the lead role in this play. Without a moment's hesitation, he announced, "We're sorry, Mr. Black, but seeing as not even *one* ticket has been sold to watch this performance, we, the cast, have voted to chalk this up to a bad experience and quit!"

"*Quit*? But actors don't quit the day before their performance?" I lectured him.

"They do when everyone at school is *laughing* at them!" a girl dressed in purple paisley bloomers, glittery white cowboy boots, yellow full-bodied long-johns and a red bomber's jacket cried out with sincere anguish. Her face fully emoting the pain and agony she must have endured when someone in one of her classes had heinously told her that the play she was in (*and undoubtedly her 'choice of clothes'*) sucked!

"*Yeah*!" the rest of the actors vehemently added, for lack of a stronger word in their common vocabularies, *dramatically* displaying their solidarity.

"You know that you will be letting a lot of good people down if the play doesn't go on tomorrow," I tried to make my begging sound more like a heartfelt plea… but unfortunately, it *still* sounded a lot like begging.

"We're sorry, Mr. Black," the young man once again spoke for the entire group. "Nothing personal, but maybe if we had gotten class credit or pay for being in this play, it would have been worth staying. Goodbye and good luck."

"*Class credit* or *pay* for being in an *extracurricular* school play?" I repeated in disbelief. "Where's this cast's *theatrical integrity*?" As I pleaded to deaf ears, they all left… the *whole* cast… one by one… making sure that they each had a very good exit scene for me to watch just in case they ever auditioned for another one of my plays again.

It seemed that I may have just hit rock bottom in my quest to perform this play, get one person to buy a ticket and see the show receive the *minimum* number of standing ovations before being allowed to return home to my sweet Anne. To be honest, I didn't have a clue what to do next? But oddly enough, often it's these overwhelmingly hopeless situations that lead us to *sudden insight*, right? "Wait, I've got it!" I found myself spontaneously shouting to the world. I would find the original Horace Black, in *whosever* body he was currently residing in, explain this dire situation to him and just as my cast had done… *quit* this show! Consequently, waking-up in my own body and bed tomorrow! Surely old Horace would listen to reason? But then my rational mind quickly discarded that *pipedream* of a possibility as I disappointedly realized, 'No, *he wouldn't*!' When it rains, it pours! My impossible situation was suddenly made far worse just a few moments later when Frank's car came to a screeching halt in the theatre's parking lot. She angrily disembarked from her vintage, shiny-black, fully restored, 1971 *Ford Pinto*, that she was so very proud of, and determinedly began striding toward me. Her expression told me right away that I had been *completely wrong* about her? She was *not* having a good day after all!

"*Mr. Black*," she announced icily.

"Miss Weasel," I replied cordially, *oddly* feeling as though I were addressing an antagonist from Kenneth Grahame's book, '*The Wind in the Willows*?'

"I have just finished confirming that your production of 'The Adventures of Horace Black,' although scheduled to be performed tomorrow night, has not sold even *one* ticket. So, being that *you* are the director of this play, I thought you might like to know that in order to save the college from great embarrassment… this production has been *officially canceled*!"

"*What*? But you *can't* do that Frank, I mean Miss Weasel! So many people are counting on it!"

"Who?" she asked sarcastically. "Your entire cast dropped by to see me this morning in order to get my approval for *every last one of them* to quit! Once they shared with me that you neither paid them nor allowed them to earn class credit, well of course I had no choice but to *give* them my blessing."

"What?" I screamed. "So, it was you! YOU *sabotaged* my show!"

"So, what if I did?" Frank confessed indignantly. "It was *you* who sabotaged my love life by *leading me on* for all of that time!"

"What? I *never* led you on for even a moment!" I insisted. "I never pretended that we were anything more than just friends?"

"*Just friends*?" Frank repeated, overly aghast and dramatic with '*Academy Award*' written all over her performance! "What about last night when you came on to me, *lover boy*?" she fervently declared. "I really thought for one sizzling second that I had found *Mr. Right*!"

"Huh?" I exclaimed at the seemingly *insane* woman before me.

"Of course, I instantly forgot all about *you* just as soon as I met *Calvin*!" she smiled dreamily. And then suddenly her expression grew miserable, even pitiful? "But he *stood me up* for lunch, and now he's *disappeared*!" she shared, almost crying. "The truth is, I don't think he loves me anymore?"

"He actually told you that he '*loved you*' after sharing only *one* dinner?" I asked incredulously.

"Not in *those* words," she admitted awkwardly.

"In *what* words then?" I insisted curiously.

"He said, and I quote, '*Frankie, you fit into that baseball jersey real nice*.'"

"Frank, isn't there some way you would *reconsider* canceling this show?" I found myself begging once again.

"Well," she began slyly. "If you were to *find* Calvin, and he told you that he really *did* love me, and then you made him the *star* of your play… *then* I think it might be worth my while to keep your little show open."

"Would you accept *two* out of three?" I asked (*bordering on begging, once again.*) The mere fact that the ice *didn't* melt one bit on Frank's frosty face, confirmed to me that her answer was a definite, '*No*!'

"So, you had better *run* as fast as you can and *find* my Calvin by tonight, Horace Black!" she gloated, like a poker player who knew that her hand was better than mine, because *I hadn't even been dealt any cards*? "If you *don't*, then your precious little play will be history!"

"Along with *my life*," I muttered dejectedly.

With that, Frank arrogantly strutted back toward her car, with her attitude reminding me just a little *too much* of Cruella Deville. Then, just like her apparent mentor, she tore out of that parking lot like a *bat outa hell*!

I was deeper in the pit of *no hope* than I had been for the whole of this absurdly *irrational* misadventure! No cast, no audience, no performance, no Calvin and no old *Horace Black*? Where *was* that scary old guy anyway? Something just felt *very* wrong? But I had no time to worry about that now. My most pressing job at the moment was *finding* Calvin Offenbach… the big *muscley* one!

After six long and frustrating hours of tirelessly searching for big Calvin, with absolutely *no* success… I finally found myself at the public library, *frantically* going through phone books that with any luck, *might* give me a clue as to where Calvin lived? I had tried the Internet first, but since *neither* of my two brains appeared to be very computer savvy, I soon embraced the now outdated *phonebook* method. Calvin was right, and I didn't even need to *swing a dead cat around* to realize it. I found *thirty-nine* people named Calvin Offenbach within the general vicinity of Fulton, Missouri, and that was not even counting the probable multitude of Calvin Offenbachs who *weren't listed*! I knew that I couldn't possibly reach all of them in time, and this was only the *first* of three tasks that Frank had given me with the seemingly impossible deadline of *tonight*!

I was hopelessly feeling like I might as well give-up, when out of nowhere, I miraculously spied the *perfect book* to remedy my dire situation! It seemed so very odd? It was as if I had been *meant* to find it, as it was open to the very page I needed? Maybe I had a guardian angel? If I did, they certainly picked the right time to help me! The book was an overview of Westminster College, and the open page listed some of the staff members names, along with their pictures, addresses and *phone numbers*. Right there on the list, clearly circled so that I *wouldn't* miss it, was *Calvin Offenbach*! Wow! *This* was an incredible coincidence? Calvin Offenbach taught Physical Education at the *same college* that I taught at? Although the small black and white picture didn't do him justice, the muscles almost bursting through his shirt very clearly *confirmed* that it was him! A phone call later, and I was off in my sister's truck to Calvin's house at the other end of town.

Calvin lived in an older, single-story house, that like most of the homes in the area, had been built of wood and stucco, with a traditional *red-brick* chimney. Matching the chimney, the house itself was also painted in a cardinal red. The wood strip trimming the roof, accented the red with alternating stripes of navy blue, yellow and white. All four of those colors were very curiously official colors of the *St. Louis Cardinals* baseball team! Unfortunately, the part of Fulton that Calvin lived in was considered by many to be a borderline '*bad*' part of town due to its extremely high number of police visits that took place there every day. Fortunately, there were no murders or muggings, just plain old-fashioned break-ins and robberies of unoccupied houses, graffiti and stolen cars; the usual mid-level crimes one would expect in a gang-infested but *not* lethal neighborhood like this one. However, Calvin's house looked cute and well kept-up from the outside, and that certainly didn't cry HELP! I was still feeling very uneasy about leaving the truck unattended here as I carefully perused the area for any signs that would lend credence to my hopefully *unfounded* worry? I think the *biggest* reason for my overt concern was that the last thing I wanted to deal with on top of everything else, was my sister's truck being *stolen*! Caroline had been awfully sweet for allowing me to use it whenever I needed to, so I really *didn't* want to create any unnecessary headaches for her. You know what? This was so odd? Caroline was *not really* my sister, but I suppose it was due to my current *double-brain* situation that I was feeling this deep concern for her from one *half* of it? So, more precisely, I guess from now on I should refer to her as being my '*half-sister*!'

Ultimately, I felt okay parking the truck *directly* in front of Calvin's house under a streetlight. Logically, I could *not* imagine any 'mischief makers' risking jail time attempting to steal this truck at night while it was under a bright light, surely? Besides, it was a *Ford*, which I've been told has a very embarrassing reputation for breaking down on the road. Ever hear the saying, '**F**ound **O**n **R**oad **D**ead?' Except for Frank and her Pinto and Caroline and her Ranger, I really haven't known a lot of Ford owners, so I couldn't tell you if that saying is true or not? But I did hear from a local Toyota salesman that a lot of *former* Ford owners swear by that saying! He also told me that sometimes, with absolutely *no* warning at all, Ford cars will suddenly *refuse to start*? That got me imagining that it would be such a 'confidence killer' for some self-respecting hooligan to successfully break into my half-sister's truck, only to shockingly find that the engine would *not start*, while the car alarm *did*, broadcasting their *failure* all over the neighborhood! I was banking on the fact that every savvy criminal in town *knew* the blatant dangers of stealing a Ford, just like that honest and friendly Toyota salesman had shared with me, and as a result, would *gladly* look elsewhere!

Satisfied with my quick, albeit *questionable* rationalization, I walked about ten feet from where I had carefully parked the truck to the front door. I knocked and almost immediately to my *enormous* relief, Calvin answered the door.

"What's up?" he greeted me with the friendliest of smiles before inviting me inside. Once inside, he graciously offered me a chair in what I believed to be his living room. It was a little difficult to tell for sure because *all* of the upholstered furniture in the room was surprisingly covered in the 'St. Louis Cardinals' *logo*, making the room look more like a Cardinals' *shrine* than anything else?

But, in addition to his obvious love of the Cardinals, the interior of his house was also very tidy and furnished with decent, although not exceptional (*that means a man on a teacher's salary picked it out*) furniture. The rooms were small but welcoming. The walls had been painted in the same four Cardinals colors as the outside. His choice of pictures on the walls was decidedly masculine. I actually recognized a signed print on the wall facing us of '*Dogs Playing Poker*.' Looking at it carefully, I smiled as I noticed that it had been *signed* by the artist in the bottom right corner, *not* with initials or a traditional signature as one would expect, but by using the *imprint* of a dog's paw. Clever! I knew there was some reason that picture had *always* been one of my personal favorites!

"Frank is very worried about you. She says that you just *disappeared*, so she sent me out to find you," I said feigning great concern.

"Yeah?" Calvin suddenly appeared to be very nervous. "She's great and all…"

"But she's just *not* your type?" I suggested, putting myself in his shoes.

"*No*!" Calvin aggressively corrected me. "Frankie is a goddess!"

"A *goddess*?" I repeated, with more than a minor amount of surprise.

"Oh yes!" he continued vehemently. "While *I'm* just a simple P.E. teacher from Missouri. Don't you get it?"

"Get what?" my confusion multiplied every time he spoke.

"That she's *way too good* for me!" he exclaimed passionately. "That's why I decided *not* to meet her for lunch today, and stopped our relationship so early, *before* it got too serious."

"Calvin, you only went out with her on one *accidental* date!" I insisted. "You only just met her?"

"Yeah, but she must have a hundred other suiters. In time, she would only get bored with me," Calvin expounded with a sincere and deep sadness permeating every word he spoke.

If we had been talking about a lot of women who worked at the college, who had other suiters and *did not* happen to be big St. Louis Cardinals fans, I would probably have agreed with him in a second. But Frank had *no* other suiters, hadn't dated anyone else in months, and had put up a *St. Louis Cardinals* poster outside her office at school this morning to obviously *please* Calvin when he picked her up for lunch! There was no hiding the fact that she was '*head over heels*' in love with him! "She loves you, Calvin!"

"She does?" his clear blue eyes suddenly grew big, bright and mopey.

"Yes!" I confirmed strongly. "Do you love her?"

"Does a calf love its mama's *teat*?" he responded with enthusiasm.

As a retired aerospace engineer, I really had no experience with farm animals. But I assumed he was looking for a little *he-man* support here, so I yelled, "*Hell Yeah*!"

That immediately brought a smile to his face, but remembering my original question, he then replied defiantly, "Of course, I love Frankie! She's the best!" Then he made a point of looking at me with animated disbelief, thinking that the answer to my question should have been obvious. And judging by the sparkle in his eyes, it *certainly was*!

"Good! I'm sorry for coming here so late," I finally began explaining my *real* purpose behind this visit. "There is one very important question I have to ask you. Given the right answer, it would really make my life a *whole lot better*!"

"Sounds intriguing," a much happier Calvin said with amusement. "Shoot!"

"Okay," I agreed. "First I want to say how great it is to meet a fellow teacher from Westminster College. It's so rare I get the chance to socialize."

"Glad to meet you too… *again*," Calvin smiled.

From that polite and completely innocuous introduction, my half of the conversation proceeded to get much more *interesting*, as I laid out Frank's demands for reopening Friday's performance of the play.

Calvin listened politely to each and every word, and as soon as I had finished, he replied firmly, "That Frankie is some *hot babe*, huh?"

"Excuse me?" I asked, feeling as if we had just taken a sharp turn from somewhere to the extreme depths of *nowhere*?

"What I mean is… Frankie is so hot she could probably set-off a whole box of firecrackers *without* using a match!" he clarified proudly.

"Okay, I *get* that," I said gently. "But *what* are the chances of you performing in my play?"

Calvin's silence and deeply furrowed brow immediately told me that he had gone into *thinking mode*. "Well, I never have done anything like that before," he mused, "but if the love of my life is that *excited* about it… then by golly, *I'm in*!"

At that, I let out a great big Missouri sigh of relief! I quickly shook hands with my reason for hope, and was soon driving home with an enormous smile plastered across my face!

When I arrived at my house it was late and my half-sister was already asleep in bed. So, I very quietly closed the front door and walked out into the kitchen. This was the room farthest away from where she was sleeping, and I believed it was where I was *least* likely to disturb her. Next, I picked up the phone and called Frank, just as I had promised to do.

The phone barely started its first ring before she picked-up. "Hello," I said very softly.

"Hello," Frank answered, with a thinly veiled sense of urgency that clearly exposed her hyper-anxiety. "Well? What do you have to tell me?"

"I found him, he loves you, and he has *agreed* to star in my play!" I blurted out as quickly and softly as I could.

For the next thirty seconds all I heard was *screaming* on the other end of the line! Frank had apparently *not* been overly confident in my ability to grant her three wishes. After her screaming had stopped (*mostly*), there was a slight delay as she pulled herself together, and then said in her typically loud and abrasive voice, "Well done, Horace! *Let's get drunk*! I know a nice little bar that's open until four o'clock in the morning!"

I wasn't real keen on her idea of a *victory celebration*. Visiting a late-night bar with Frank sounded *dangerous* at best! But, if this would further cement her allowing the play to go on, then I really saw *no* other choice. Fifteen minutes later, I arrived at the little hole in the wall or *dive* if you prefer, called *Killer's*. This bar sat alone, just off highway 54 in the outskirts of Fulton. I already had a pretty good idea how the place had gotten its name. According to a sign I saw while driving there, Killer's was not far from a hospital for the *criminally insane*! I wasn't even sure if I should risk going inside because *outside* there were a couple dozen enormous motorcycles (*choppers*) that might mean this bar catered to a much tougher crowd than *either* of my brains was used to? My fears were *not* alleviated one bit when I tepidly walked inside the door and immediately spied Frank clinging to a huge tattooed body-builder on each arm! Rather than saying, 'Hi,' to me, each of them gave me a rather long and intense look of *silent biker disdain*!

Nevertheless, the mood at the bar was jovial, with Frank buying drinks for *everyone*! I can't say that I was immediately accepted by the other patrons, but at least they didn't tie me to the flagpole outside in my underwear! Time passed quickly as I watched Frank and her fellas play pool, throw darts and have so many drinks that I lost count! Unfortunately, they *generously* made sure that *I* was drinking right along with them, handing me one drink after another. I was so drunk at closing time that Frank, who somehow didn't seem to be even the *least* bit affected by her excessive drinking, walked me out to my truck and told me with the utmost understanding, to just '*sleep it off*.' She even insisted on covering my two morning classes on Friday, and assured me that she would contact Calvin first thing in the morning regarding the very important afternoon play rehearsal. That's all I can remember before passing out.

When I awoke, the sun was already shining brightly from its vantage point high in the sky, and curiously, the first thing I noticed was that both doors of my truck had been *locked*? I didn't remember doing that myself, but with all of the dangers that this bar had represented to me last night, it reassuringly told me that *no one* had broken-in, and I had been *safe and secure all night*! Looking around to confirm this, *nothing* in the truck's cab seemed to have been disturbed at all. I sighed with relief. *That* was certainly good news! But then I noticed something that would have certainly caught my attention much earlier had I not still been feeling the effects of being drunk last night. Someone had written in bright red lipstick all across the outside of my windshield? Not having the patience to try to read what it said *backwards*, I quickly opened my door and walked to the front of the truck. Gazing at the message, I chuckled. It read, '*Wake this man up at your own risk*!' That had to be a *big* deterrent from having anyone even *thinking* about throwing me out and stealing my half-sister's truck. Considering that Frank was the only woman in that bar last night, I'll bet that bright red lipstick was her *usual* calling card, and reading her words must have instantly *brought terror to* every man at that bar! Me, surviving the night in my half-sister's truck proved that even the *biggest and baddest* of those bikers must have been scared to death of getting on Frank's bad side! Next, I went back inside the truck and pulled out a bottle of nail polish remover and a box of Kleenex from the glove box that I somehow *knew* Caroline always kept there. I then got right to work making sure to *completely* clean off every last bit of that threatening and extremely *bright* message. It wasn't that it bothered me so much, but due to her natural *shyness*, I just thought that Caroline would absolutely *hate* that show-off shade of *red* lipstick covering her windshield. She is much more comfortable you see, wearing those completely *invisible* shades of lipstick that *no one* ever notices!

As I became more coherent, I suddenly looked at my watch and realized that it was already 12:30! I immediately hightailed it out of there as fast as I could drive, on a beeline to my house! I had a rehearsal to make at 2:00 o'clock, but first I had to return the truck to Caroline and make-up some *lame* excuse for why I'd kept it out all night. Then I had to change my clothes and catch the bus. All of that made a tall order to execute in such a short time, but I was *determined* to make that rehearsal, even *with* my hangover and splitting headache still firing on all cylinders!

Let me bring you up to date. Caroline *was* pretty steamed at me for having her truck out *all night* and into the morning. This had unfortunately caused her to miss a couple of her classes. But thankfully, *lame* excuse or not, she quickly forgave me. I got the feeling that she had a lot of *experience doing that*! She undoubtedly understood better than most, that I *wasn't* the most responsible person in the world. I got cleaned up, took a couple of aspirin for my headache, and caught the next bus to Fulton. As luck would have it, I even had time to down a *delicious* Soil Change at Greasy's, while still arriving at the theatre by two o'clock! When I got there, Calvin was already standing outside, anxiously waiting for me.

"Your *star* has arrived!" he proclaimed humorously, with sincere excitement. And then looking around with a confused expression on his face, he asked logically, "Where's everybody else?"

I had rather *conveniently* neglected to tell him about the *mass exodus* of my cast members yesterday. As he looked to me for answers, I smiled knowingly and after handing him a script, I explained confidently, “I thought I would take this play in a *whole new direction* this year by making it a *two man show*! You will play the lead character, Horace Black, while I will have the *fun* of changing costumes and playing all of the other parts!”

“Even the *girl* parts?” Calvin asked with obvious concern.

“Of course! I am an *actor*! But don’t worry, Calvin,” I assured him. “We don’t have any *romantic* scenes in this play.”

Calvin looked relieved, but after perusing his script for several moments, he asked with concern, “How will I learn *all of this* by tonight’s show?”

“No problem,” I tried to downplay the *impossibility* of the situation. “You will carry that script with you on stage at all times. The stage directions are written right there on the script in red ink.”

Calvin nodded, but immediately looking confused again, he asked, “What are *stage directions*?”

It was all I could do to *gently* explain their meaning to Calvin *without* getting just a wee bit annoyed. Not because he didn’t understand what they were, because never having been involved in theatre before, how could he have? No, it was just my nagging headache that seemed to have a very tough time with patience, even though I *knew* that for me, without Calvin in the play, *all was lost*! So, I was somehow able to maintain my professional calm and *considerable* personal charm.

Soon we entered the theatre, with Calvin excitedly running up on the stage. This marked the very first time he had *ever* stood on a theatrical stage in his life! He was noticeably *thrilled* about that, so I let him jump all over it and touch every set and prop to his heart’s content for the next five minutes! It was actually heartwarming to see him so excited about it. It reminded me of when I was a little boy watching my puppy excitedly running through our new house for the first time! Although I later found out that he was just hungry, and wanted to find out where my parents had hidden his kibble?

Once Calvin had his fill of exploring, we were able to begin ‘staging’ the show, placing him where he needed to be in each scene. Due to his being a physical education teacher, and undoubtedly being used to coaching teams and being *coached himself* before that, he effortlessly took to my instructions and had *memorized* all of his spots in the show, as well as their sequence, within a half an hour! This made me begin to feel *hopeful*, like maybe we could actually pull this thing off? But that was before we got to the *speaking* parts. Calvin had no problem reading his lines, but his inflection and timing were apparently *not invited to the party*!

"Good reading," I lied to him, trying to sound encouraging. "But let's try it again with more feeling."

"What *kind* of feeling?" Calvin asked honestly.

I won't lie. Once again I nearly lost it! Calvin was trying so hard and was getting to all of the right spots on stage and saying all of the right words… but the poor guy didn't seem to have *even one iota* of natural performing talent in his entire being? Watching him perform was very painful, like eating an omelet with all of the broken shells *mixed-in* with the eggs! The silver lining was that he had *no idea* how bad he was, and with no audience yet to make him feel nervous, I was pretty sure that he would go through with the performance. I couldn't recall if old Horace Black had insisted on a *quality* performance, but he *had* demanded an unprovoked standing ovation from at least one audience member. The way things looked right now, that would only be happening if someone stood up to *leave* the theatre! That was of course, assuming that somebody *actually attended* the performance to begin with! Hey! If somebody *did* stand up at the end of the performance, for any number of reasons (*I can't be too picky, here*!), I wonder if *that* would count as a standing ovation? Perhaps I had unknowingly discovered a *loophole* in my contract? *Fat chance of that*! Who was I trying to kid? There were still *no tickets* sold, so there would be *no one in the theatre* even if getting up for any old reason *did* count as a standing ovation!

"Super rehearsal, Calvin!" I exclaimed with my great big stage smile.

"Are you sure?" he asked with honest concern. "I don't want to hurt your show or nuthin'?"

I put my arm across his big broad Scandinavian shoulders and said reassuringly, "The only way you will hurt this show is if you *don't* show up at seven o'clock tonight to get ready for our eight o'clock performance."

"Don't you worry, Mr. Black. You bet I'll be here!" Calvin assured me. "I can't wait!"

"Me either," I lied.

Calvin smiled and shook my hand vigorously before leaving the theatre (*by bicycle of course*) to wherever he was going to prepare for his soon to be, *oh so memorable* stage debut. I felt sick! And this time it was *not* the hangover. I suppose that living a few days in the mind and body of a talented, young theatre director had made a much greater impression on me than I had originally thought? I knew that this performance in just a few hours was my ticket home to Anne, and that was *still* the most important thing to me. But now I somehow understood more clearly *why* the Horace Black I had replaced had decided to cancel this performance in the first place. You see, if a show is performed for *nobody*, is it really a performance? And might I add, if the guy playing the lead role has *no* talent and *no* experience, can he really be expected to carry the show with less than two hours of rehearsal time? I felt like getting drunk, but then I remembered just *how well* that had gone the last time! So, I hoofed it back to my office at the college to review my lines for the performance. Although to be honest, as the director, I was pretty confident that I already knew both my lines and blocking *to perfection*!

When I reached my office, the first thing I did was to check my recent voicemails for an *improbable* message from old Horace Black, but unfortunately… no such luck. The old guy had not contacted me in two days now? But of course, I was foolishly *assuming* that he knew *how* to leave a voicemail. It *wasn't even invented* until well after his death! So, what could have possibly happened to him that prevented him from contacting me *in person*? I must admit that I was feeling stumped? Next, I listened to the only message that was there. It was from Frank, and it left me feeling *devastated*! She sincerely wished me luck with tonight's performance because unfortunately, due to a just scheduled meeting, she would *not be able to attend*!

No! I had secretly been banking on Frank attending the show to see Calvin in the lead role, which was *why* he was playing it in the first place! She was my ace in the hole, my trapeze artist's net, and it had *never* occurred to me as even the *remotest* of possibilities that she would *not* be attending? The grim fact was that if she didn't attend, there would be *no* standing ovation. If there was no standing ovation… I would *never* be able to return to my own body or to see *Anne* again! This was beyond horrific! For the next few hours until call-time at 7:00 o'clock when Calvin was scheduled to arrive (*reminding me that this nightmare was actually going to happen*), I returned to the theatre and opened up the box-office for the ticket seller and me. I was hoping beyond hope that we would sell just *one ticket*! It was actually very peaceful there. Like the calm before the storm, or the final moments before *my execution*! When the clock finally struck 7:00, without having sold a single ticket… I knew that the end was frighteningly near! Tonight's show was going to look and sound like an unmitigated disaster that *no one* would watch except for the crew and me. I managed to hide my deep feelings of anguish and dread as Calvin came over to see me ten minutes before the curtain was due to go up. He couldn't hide the first-time *jitters* he felt. He was like a child who was about to jump into ice-cold water to take his first swim lesson. I only hoped he *didn't drown*!

"I'll try very hard not to embarrass you," Calvin said sincerely. "I promise that I will do my very best tonight!"

I smiled understandingly as I replied, "I know you will, Calvin. Thanks again for agreeing to do this. And don't worry! I'll be there on stage to get you back on track if you should ever lose your place in the script."

"Actually, Mr. Black, I've decided *not* to use the script at all tonight."

"*What*?" I replied in unadulterated shock.

Calvin laughed, and then said, "I studied the script really hard over the past three hours… and I believe that *I'm ready*!"

I must have sported a facial expression that resembled something between *disbelief and hysteria* as I took-in Calvin's words. But hey, there would not be a damn audience in the house tonight, so why should I care *what* Calvin chose to do? He could change all of his lines into *Transylvanian duck calls* for all I cared! If this was to be the worst night of my life, I might as well allow the play to be completely *godawful*! "Great!" I said cheerfully, while *attempting* to make my facial expression less scary. "I can't wait!"

In a few minutes, the curtain rose, the stage lights came-up, and our play began. There was no one in the house to watch it, but because I was an eternal optimist, I was still holding out completely unwarranted hope that this apparent 'lost cause' would somehow find a way to get me home. Calvin slowly walked out to the center of the stage to begin his opening monologue. Honestly? I was shocked and possibly even a little awed. He actually *looked* like a real actor?

"Tonight, you are all very privileged to watch and hear my incredible story, '*The Adventures of Horace Black*!' I was the inventor of the original, world-famous, 'Missouri State Whiskey,' as I'm sure you all know," Calvin began charmingly, and I was in double awe… because he also *sounded* like a real actor! Next, he walked toward the invisible audience and gracefully sat down on the edge of the stage. "Yessir, I started out as a poor dirt-farmer, until one day I had an epiphany! Broccoli and asparagus boiled and aged just right, would create a *glorious* whiskey that takes you higher than a kite! So, pull out that shot glass and once you've downed seven, you'll be *flyin' to heaven*!"

That was my cue to be flown down (*on ropes*) from the ceiling dressed in an all-white angel's costume. I was even playing a harp that was curiously built into the shape of a bottle of Missouri State Whiskey! My *first* of many cameos went great of course, but with no audience to applaud, I had long since checked my ego at the door. I found myself much more focused on Calvin, who was delivering an *unbelievable* performance of a lifetime!

Unfortunately, this play *did not* include an Intermission. This apparent oversight kept us performing for *two straight hours*! During that final half-hour, I was personally feeling pretty fatigued, so I can only wonder what Calvin was feeling? But, miraculously, he never seemed to lose his high-powered performance energy? Suddenly, my thoughts were broken by the *unmistakable* sound of laughter? I incredulously peeked out into the house from behind the curtain where I was awaiting my next cue at stage right, and I was simply *thrilled* to see a person in the audience… in fact… *it was Frank*? I was so euphoric beyond belief that I nearly missed my next cue! I played a minister marrying an eight-foot-high stage representation of a piece of broccoli (*to my left*) to an eight-foot-high stage representation of a piece of asparagus (*to my right*). All the while Calvin was singing a delightful song (*without accompaniment*) about this lovely marriage between the two vegetables that became the whiskey family… the '*Missouri State Whiskey*' family, to be exact! The only problem was that there was *no song* appearing anywhere in the script? Calvin was completely *adlibbing*! But I must admit, he *sang beautifully*! Was there anything this kid couldn't do?

The play moved along very quickly to the end, primarily motivated by the constant stream of laughter and applause coming from the extremely supportive audience of *one*! When the curtain call arrived and Calvin and I took our final bows, it was a sight of pure magic as I watched Frank give the show (*but mostly Calvin*) a much-coveted *standing ovation*! As the curtain closed and I began to walk-off stage, I suddenly remembered something very important. Old Horace had very clearly *required* me to sell at least *one ticket* in order to make my part of this contract valid! So, I rushed into the house, still dressed in my sexy saloon girl costume (*don't ask*) to catch Frank before she left and find out if she had indeed *bought* a ticket? As it turned out, she was not only still in the house, but she was locked in a hot and steamy make-out session with Calvin that simply showed *no signs* of ever letting up!

"Ticket, Miss?" I softly whispered into Frank's right ear, just like an old-fashioned train conductor. She responded by pulling out a ticket stub that was hidden inside her jersey and making sure that I saw it while never once breaking the embrace.

"Well," I thought out loud as I giddily retreated into my dressing room. "My contract with the devil is *now complete*, and as soon as I find him… I can finally go home!"

"Hi, Horace," Calvin *surprisingly* greeted me from my make-up chair as I closed the dressing room door behind me.

"What?" I uttered in shock. "How did you get here so fast? Just a moment ago you were in the house kissing Frank?"

"I just told her, '*Nature calls*,'" he laughed. "People fall for that old line every time!"

"Is that *you*, Horace?" I asked, in complete shock.

Calvin laughed like there was no tomorrow. "Yep! I just dropped-in to help you out with the play. I was pretty *good* too, if I do say so myself."

"How long have you been possessing Calvin's body?" I asked curiously.

"I've only been here since telling you that 'I *wasn't* using a script tonight,'" Old Horace winked.

"So where did you go after leaving the *other* Calvin's body?" I insisted.

"Well, let's see," he began mysteriously. "When that boy's parents came for him, I left his body and just ghosted around for a while."

"*Ghosted around*?" I asked curiously.

"Yep," he replied, very seriously. "That's what we *dead people* do."

"Were you following me around all of that time?" I asked intently, already guessing the answer.

"Pretty much," Old Horace confirmed gleefully. "Remember that listing of everyone who worked at Westminster College in the library? I possessed the librarian to find that for you."

"I wondered about that," I confessed.

He nodded graciously, and then added, "But you really should learn to hold your liquor better, fella. I think I may have saved your life at that bar last night."

"Really?" I asked with great concern.

"Well, I may be *exaggerating* a bit," he chuckled, "but after you became 'three sheets to the wind,'" he shared, and then seeing my look of confusion, clarified, "you know, *drunk,* I knew that at least one of those 'biker beasts' in the bar would probably prove to be *less than honest* if given half a chance. So, rather than watching you get mugged and robbed, I decided to take some action."

"What *action* did you take?" I asked anxiously.

"Well, I suppose I didn't *actually* do anything," he smiled playfully. "I *possessed* Frank, and then *she* kicked a few butts and left them all a warning written with her red lipstick across your windshield!"

"Then it was actually *you* who told me not to worry last night?" I exclaimed in shock.

"Afraid so," he admitted calmly. "Frank was as drunk as a skunk, so I stayed with her until this morning so that she would do all of those things she promised she'd do for ya."

"You know? You're really *not* such a bad guy after all," I admitted, *drastically* improving my previously low estimation of the man.

"Sure, I am!" old Horace retorted. "I'm a *sombitch*! I was just protecting my investment."

I laughed, and then asked a question that had just come to me. "Horace? What did you look like when you were *alive*?" It had suddenly occurred to me that I really had *no* idea? "You don't have a picture of yourself do you? Just for fun?"

Calvin, currently possessed by old Horace, shrugged his shoulders nonchalantly and smiled before getting up and leaving the room. He returned a minute later with what appeared to be an old, dusty photo album in his hand, and offered it to me "Take a look at this if you like," he said. "It's the only pictures I have of myself and my family."

I thanked him and accepted the book. As I looked over the first page, I noticed that Horace was a pretty good-looking young man, with *very* determined eyes as he posed with his pitchfork in his farmer days. As I turned the page, I saw him standing in a group with two much younger boys and a girl, as well as a man and a woman who appeared to be slightly older than he was.

"Is this your family?" I asked.

"Yep. I had an older brother who had a wife and three kids. When our parents died, he was kind enough to take me in and let me live with them on his farm."

"Did you like it there?" I asked.

"I *loved* it!" he exclaimed. "My brother and his family were very kind to me." Then smiling, he added, "Even though I couldn't farm *worth a damn*!"

Once again I laughed. "When did you get the idea of creating '*Missouri State Whiskey*'" I asked curiously.

Old Horace Black paused, and then hesitantly replied, "Well, after my brother died of pneumonia one winter, his wife and kids were pretty worried about their futures? Considering everything that family had done for me, I *knew* that I had to find a way to support them? Since my own future as a farmer didn't look too promising," he smiled, "I decided to sit down and get creative." He paused once again, and then proudly proclaimed, "And the creation of '*Missouri State Whiskey*' was the result! It became an *instant success*!"

"But why *broccoli* and *asparagus*?" I asked.

Old Horace laughed. "Because those were the *only two crops* that survived on the farm after I took over!"

I chuckled. "What was your brother's name?"

"His name was *Horace*," he said.

"But *your* name is Horace?" I replied in confusion.

He smiled. "Not until I *changed* it. My name used to be JJ, or *Jonathan James*, but I legally changed it to my brother's name after he died, as a sort of *tribute*," he explained gently. "I never married, but made it my life's work to take care of my brother's family. I made sure that once I died, *all* of the profits from 'Missouri State Whiskey' would go directly to them and their descendants."

I found his words to be *surprisingly* touching. "Was the play a homage to your brother, as well?" I asked with moist eyes.

"*Hell no*!" Old Horace exclaimed loudly. "Are you kidding? It's a homage to *me*!" he replied with a grin. "I created some damn good whiskey and *deserve* to be remembered for it!"

I laughed and then I had a sudden thought, "Was your oldest nephew *also* named, Horace?"

Old Horace Black smiled impishly and nodded confirmation.

"So that's when this whole, 'eldest son named Horace thing,' began?"

"Yep. That way there would *always* be a Horace in the family to honor my brother's name, while hopefully also takin' pride in putting on my play!" he confessed. "I think that idea was a real *humdinger*, myself!"

I chuckled. Well, although the man *was* a bit of a narcissist, his history gave me a new and *better* understanding of who he really was. I stood by that improved view of the man *until* he said, "You know, that Frankie wants to *marry me*, and I think I'm gonna take the plunge!"

"You mean *as Calvin*?" I exclaimed in horror.

"Who else?" the man inside Calvin's body replied with gusto.

"But you *can't* do that!" I found myself yelling.

"And why the hell not?" old Horace hollered just as loudly.

I tried to reason with him by replying softly, "Because you are *dead* and Calvin still has a full life ahead of him. You wouldn't want to take something so special as that away from him, would you?"

"Darn-tootin' I want to take *that* away from him!" old Horace bellowed.

"But Calvin truly loves Frank," I insisted. "Yesterday he told me so! And from what little I know of her she is really *not* an easy person to get along with!"

"Well hell, *neither am I*!" Horace argued hotly. "We'd make the *perfect* couple!"

"You're not even giving Calvin a *chance* to compete with you?" I exclaimed.

"No need!" he proclaimed arrogantly. "She loves *me*! The better man won!"

"*What man*?" I replied pointedly. "You are nothing more than a selfish and bullying *ghost*!"

Suddenly, old Horace fell silent. All of his inspired bravado *completely* vanished. Even when I tried to restart our conversation several times, he would always wave me off. A few minutes later, he quietly stood-up, opened the door of my dressing room… and silently walked off. I *knew* I had made him so upset that this would probably be the last time I would ever see him again. I finished looking through his photograph album and soon noticed that the admirable '*determination*' apparent in his eyes as a young man had gradually disintegrated as he grew older and been replaced with increasingly more severe stages of '*cuckoo*!' To illustrate that point, in his final pictures in the book, after he had grown very old, he looked like a '*crazy old gold miner*' from the 1800s, complete with wild eyes, a fuzzy face and the buckled posture of an old man!' And unfortunately, *that* was how I would always remember him.

Eventually, after I had changed my clothes, I left the dressing room and returned to the theatre, which by now was dark and empty except for the 'ghost light' on the stage. Exhausted, I sat down in a seat near the center of the house and let out a great big sigh. If I had learned anything from this wild and ludicrous adventure, I'd learned that it was way too easy to get self-absorbed and forget about how much *other* people's lives mattered too. I was way too focused on getting home to realize that there were *other* people around me who were just as bad off as I was? But my mind was *right* now! To begin with, Calvin and Frank deserved the chance to build a life together, while old Horace had no business interfering just because he *could*! Not to mention the Horace Black whose body I was currently possessing. He was a *hell of a director*, and I actually felt ashamed for having taken-over his life for these past few days. I really couldn't stand being a part of old Horace's selfish charade any longer! That is why we had argued tonight, and that is why… I was pretty sure that deal or no deal, he was *never* going to return me to Anne in Jefferson City! But, as much as that hurt me… *so be it*! I had said my piece, and I felt much better for it! Old Horace had acted like it was far better to live a lie in someone else's healthy body than to return to an old crippled one like mine… but I have got to strongly *disagree*. You see, even as a crippled stroke survivor, I was still very happy in Jefferson City… *with Anne*. Although at times during this recent adventure I had truly enjoyed being young again, and a rich and talented stage director to boot… *that* experience just didn't hold a candle to the perfect love and companionship I knew every day of my adult life as Anne's husband. I missed her terribly… I *really* did!

That night, before going to bed, I did a couple of unusual but *necessary* things. First, I wrote a letter to young Horace Black (*the theatre teacher and director)*, leaving it right there on the nightstand by his bed. He was sure to find it there, *if and when* I was ever released from his body, thereby returning him to his rightful place. In the letter, among other things, I suggested that he make old Horace the star of the play *every* year because that's what I believed he truly wanted, *regardless* of that ridiculous rant he had made about tickets sold and standing ovations. After considering it, I think he had only made those demands as a result of his very odd and need I add 'crazy' *sense of humor*? And in defense of my suggestion to let him permanently perform the lead role in the play, I would have to say that as an actor, old Horace was actually *quite good*… especially at *playing himself*! Next, I wrote a letter to Frank, congratulating her on her new relationship with Calvin and wishing them both the best. I addressed it to the college, stamped it, and put it outside in the mailbox to be picked up tomorrow morning. Finally, I took the time to *personally* thank my half-sister Caroline, for taking such good care of me, and then I *also* felt compelled to congratulate her on how well she was doing in her classes. Finally, I thanked her profusely for the use of her truck and then asked her the *one* question that had been bothering me since I had first arrived here? While pretending to be such a *dingbat* that I had actually forgotten the answer, I asked, "*Why* don't I own a car?"

She replied with a spontaneous giggle and a sweet smile, "Because you *don't want the responsibility* of caring for it! Remember, Horace? That's also why you've never had a *cat*!"

I had to chuckle at that. This fella obviously had *theatre* on his brain every waking moment of the day! Well, there were worse things than that to obsess over… like *Missouri State Whiskey*, for example! I snickered at that, before finally going to bed. I knew that if it was up to old Horace, I would probably be stuck here until the end of my days. But I was equally convinced that the two powerful brains cohabitating in my head would eventually think of something… and hopefully *very soon*!

It was morning before I knew it, only something seemed *very different*? Oh, I know… I was waking up in *my own bed* in Jefferson City with my wife, Anne, lying right there beside me! I was so happy that I wanted to kiss her all over her sleeping face… *so I did*!

"Horace! What's gotten into you?" she laughed as she slowly began waking-up.

"I missed you," I replied honestly, "and it seemed like the best way of saying, *I love you.*"

Anne kissed me on the lips, and then rolled back to sleep after replying, "I love you too, Horace."

'Hey,' I thought with excitement. 'I'm *not crippled* anymore, and I can *talk*?' But due to the lack of an *explanation*, I began to worry that something was *terribly wrong*? It was right then that I discovered the *letter* from old Horace Black that was neatly folded over, sitting there on the nightstand beside my bed. I felt very nervous at that moment, coupled with the curiosity of not knowing what he might have possibly written? I spent several anxious moments deliberating as to whether or not I should read it? I didn't even want to *think* about the possibility that Horace might actually be attempting to *spoil* my perfect homecoming? But I finally gave-in to my *overwhelming* curiosity. I picked up the letter, walked out of the bedroom and into the kitchen, where I sat down at the table. Then I opened the letter and begin to silently read it.

Dear Horace,

> *I've got to say that our last talk left me feeling quite wounded as you more than reminded me that I was no longer alive! In fact, I was even considering cooking-up some sly form of revenge against you! But, as you have probably already guessed... I didn't. I thought it better to explain myself through this letter. In regards to your words, you straight out said that I had no body of my own! You even called me a ghost! And unfortunately, as much as I try to forget that, you are exactly right. But as far as my being alive, every year when this play is performed, I hear my thoughts and words shared on that stage and I can't help but feel as if I am every bit as alive as you are! This year, for the first time, I performed myself in the play and at the end, Frank told me over and over again how wonderful she thought my performance had been! I guess I probably got so caught up in her kind words that I actually fell in love with her. Well, after thinking long and hard about it, I must say that although your words were just about as hurtful as being trampled by a horse wearing high heels... you were right! Thank you for having the guts to*

share them with me. I have returned you to your old life, one day before you had that pesky stroke. It is my sincere wish that you will now go to the hospital and change your fate. Here's hoping that you will live a happy and healthy life for many years to come, as you so richly deserve. I also departed from Calvin, so that he and Frank could give their feelings for each other a chance. If it doesn't work-out for them... well, then I plan on leaving my options open! I have seen the inside of 'Frank's house,' and I don't believe that having a ghost as her boyfriend would bother her one bit! As for young Horace, he read your letter and has agreed to let me star in my play every year! Many thanks for that suggestion. Finally, I believe that in our short time together, we have become... ***almost*** *friends. I would welcome us getting together once in a while for old times' sake. Think it over, and again, thank you! Horace Black*

Wow! I could hardly believe it! Old Horace Black had not only returned me to my life *before* the stroke, but he had also made everything right again in Fulton. I always knew that he was a good man... *deep down.*

After my wife and I had enjoyed a great breakfast together, I complained about recently experiencing bouts of sudden dizziness and loss of balance without provocation, which she agreed I should have checked-out immediately. So, she drove me to the hospital and after telling the doctor that I suspected I was experiencing mini-strokes, I was quickly admitted and placed in a private room to await tests that would be administered later that evening. Anne stayed with me until sometime after we had shared our dinner together in my room. It was at this point that I grew a little concerned that she was looking fatigued, so I gently suggested (*against her wishes, of course*) that she go home for a while to rest. Begrudgingly, but smiling appreciatively as she kissed me... she left.

As I was lying in bed, feeling so *grateful* for getting this second chance, a young doctor suddenly burst into my room and swiftly approached me.

"Yes, Doctor?" I asked.

"Hello, Horace," the doctor replied with a jovial spirit. "I just thought I would stop by to make sure they *caught* that damn stroke in time!"

"*Horace*?" I asked incredulously.

"Of course, it's me! Who else would it be? The *Easter Bunny*?!" Old Horace Black declared with a boisterous laugh and a playful smile via the handsome young doctor he was possessing.

Immediately, I clearly saw the *odd resemblance* between Horace and the young doctor! Except for his younger age, the doctor eerily began to remind me of that *crazy old gold miner* I'd seen in Horace's final pictures! But that didn't bother me one bit! In fact, I chuckled happily to myself as I thought about it. You know? I was probably in for a very long night because Horace had proven that he could be a real handful! But he *also* had a *great big heart*, which explained why both of us were now here together in the first place! Honestly? Aside from Anne, I couldn't think of *anyone* who I would rather have watching out for me tonight!

"Mind Over Mind"

(The unofficial prequel to the novel, 'Dimensions: The Wheat Field')

(1984)

TO BEGIN OUR STORY, IT WAS 1984, and several months had passed since Alan Dunkirk had first visited his old college professor from Reeves University, and later good friend, Dr. Joe Davis. Alan, was a good-looking man of thirty, standing nearly six feet tall, with dirty blonde hair and warm brown eyes. Joe may not have possessed Alan's youthful *good looks* being fifteen years his elder, a little shorter, heavier and with a rapidly disappearing hairline, but his personality was truly exciting, while his intellect was off the charts! According to all of the normal testing measures for IQ, he was a *bonified genius*! Perhaps that was why Alan had grown so interested in his most current endeavor? In any case, as summer had recently arrived, Alan and his wife Mary (*former high school sweethearts*), who were now both high-school teachers, were currently enjoying a well-deserved hiatus from the daily rigors of the classroom. Happily, this gave Alan *all* of the free-time he needed to participate in Joe's current project. Since the beginning, when Joe Davis had first begun working on it, Alan had been meeting with him once, sometimes twice a week, learning the results of his research fully. In fact, he was preparing to eventually *test out* his incredible theory *himself*! He had never told Mary anything *specific* about the time he spent with Joe, including his theory, the upcoming experiment *or* that he himself was slated to be the *human guinea pig* who would be finding out if it worked or not? For some reason, he wasn't convinced that she would *understand*?

Finally, *tonight* was when Joe and he would test it out at last. After much practice with hypnosis and the use of special pills (*which happened to be pink*), everything seemed to be ready. In short, Joe's theory hypothesized that a person could travel back into their own past and enjoy reliving their memories or even *changing* them if they so desired. Everything they experienced would be confined to their *own minds*, of course. But most importantly, Joe's theory suggested that as a result of taking a mind journey, when conscious in the future, the recipient would henceforth feel better about any 'bad' memories they had opted to *fix* while visiting their past! A sort of *instant* psychotherapy treatment. And all of this would happen while the person stayed *completely coherent* and aware that they were only dreaming, meaning of course that they always had the ability to return from that mind world to reality whenever they wanted to. This was the escape hatch or '*failsafe*' that Joe was convinced would make a mind journey safe for its participants. But was a *mind journey* even possible? Well, tonight they'd surely find out... *one way or another*.

Alan was like a young child at his *very first* school-aged birthday party, surrounded by all of his classmates, where seeing all of the beautifully wrapped gifts at his feet gave him a *supercharge* of excitement! He felt *no* sense of worry whatsoever about any possible adverse effects which kept him relaxed. Still, Joe was determined to keep a sharp eye on everything that happened tonight. This experiment was being done for the *very first time*, and the last thing he wanted was for any harm to befall his friend.

"Shouldn't you clamp me down to a table or attach electrodes to my brain before we start?" Alan joked.

Davis smiled guardedly. "You've been watching the *wrong* movies, my friend. Clamps and electrodes went out with 'Frankenstein's Monster.'"

In a way, Alan felt as if he was, or rather would soon become *Frankenstein's Monster*. What he was going to experience tonight was something that no other human being had ever experienced before! He was going back in time and returning to tell about it... he *hoped*!

"Okay Alan, we're all set!" Joe announced excitedly, as he watched him take his place in a very comfortable reclining chair, just as they had practiced doing multiple times before. The next step was for Alan to swallow a couple of the special pills, which he *did*. As Alan closed his eyes, Joe took out a small red notebook from his inside coat pocket and immediately began scribbling notes while simultaneously starting his seemingly endless drone of hypnotic chant.

Alan knew that his mind was *drifting* away. He clearly felt it. He could barely hear Joe's incessant droning anymore. He was floating off to explore lands he had known in the past or technically, to *reexplore them*! In any case, he was fast approaching high school in the year 1971... his senior year.

"*Shit*! What the hell are you doing, Williams?"

Alan regained awareness as his seventeen-year-old self, appropriately dressed in red P.E. shorts and a white tee shirt. He immediately found himself playing volleyball on the outdoor courts of the blacktop with his class. That *not-so subtle* comment had come from a teammate as a result of the ball bouncing off Terry William's head, going out of bounds, and ultimately costing their team a point.

Terry Williams had been Alan's best friend during most of high school. He remembered him being a wonderful athlete and a hell of a pal. The attacking voice, on the other hand, belonged to *Jeff Carter*. Alan remembered *him* very well too. Jeff Carter was the kid who had always picked on him and *anyone else* in sight throughout all of their many years of public school together. He was a very big kid with a *very big mouth* to match! Alan's immediate impulse was to ignore the comment just as he had done thirteen years earlier. Anyway, it was directed at Terry Williams, *not* at him. But wait. Why in the hell should he do that? This was a second chance, right? No more *bowing* to bullies!

"Why don't you just shut-up and play the game!" Alan heard himself yell back at Carter.

"You gonna make me?" Carter threatened, as he aggressively pushed his way toward Alan, undoubtedly *hoping* for a fight!

Alan had never fought at school during his entire life. He had always been a well-behaved student who followed every school rule… *what the hell.* He promptly threw a right hook directly into Carter's chin which knocked him *flat*! Before he had the chance to retaliate however, Coach Ferguson quickly ran up to Alan and pulled him away.

"That'll cost you a *week of detention*, Dunkirk!" Ferguson announced sternly. But then he smiled and his tone became softer. "Nice *hit* though. Have you ever thought about going out for the baseball team? You've got a *helluva* right arm! Might make a damn good pitcher for us?"

'*Me*, in sports? Hah! Since when?' Alan thought humorously.

"Hey, coach," Jeff Carter pleaded as he slowly pulled himself up from the ground, while simultaneously making a dramatic '*ouch*' expression on his face as he rubbed his chin. "You ought to *suspend* that guy for hitting me!"

"Nice try, Carter," Coach Ferguson retorted, shaking his head at the unhappy boy. "I'm afraid you were asking for that one. You've been asking for it for a *very long time*."

The bell rang and as usual, it sent Alan and the other boys racing into the locker room to get cleaned-up. After taking his shower, as he dressed in front of his locker, Alan suddenly felt someone slap his back. Turning around quickly, he discovered a smiling Terry Williams.

"Thanks, Alan!" the boy offered, very sincerely. "You really stood up for me out there. I hope I get the chance to do the same for you someday."

Alan smiled back at Terry and felt very good about how things had turned out. Jeff Carter was a bully and an *obnoxious* one at that! Today, he, Alan Dunkirk, had stood his ground and taught him a lesson in the process. *That* was well worth earning a few hours of detention!

English class was next on his schedule. So, after finishing getting dressed (*his clothes were in locker 257, combination left 2*

- right 13 - left 6), Alan bade Terry goodbye, and headed off toward his next class. On the way there, he was met by Terry's older sister, Mary… *his* Mary! He could tell that they were friends, but they had *not yet* started dating.

"Hi, Alan," she smiled warmly at him. Mary was a tall and good-looking brunette with *beautiful* blue eyes. She was dressed in a cute red skirt and white blouse which perfectly matched her bright personality.

"Hi, Mary," Alan *clearly* remembered this moment when thirteen years before, he had spontaneously met Mary here and asked her out for the first time. He knew what wonderfulness had come of that. But just for fun, what if that conversation had *never* taken place? There was a brief pause where it felt strangely like something was *supposed* to happen… but *didn't*? Alan knew that he had just shirked his very important role as the instigator of this magical historical moment… but then again, he was just so *curious* to find out what *would have happened* if he had acted differently? After all, this was only in his mind… like a game… Right?

"Well, I guess I'll see you later," Mary sighed as she finally walked off, following a very *uncomfortable* silence. To be clear, she walked off a lot *less* cheerfully than she had walked up.

Alan had really wanted to ask Mary out just as he had thirteen years earlier… but that would have been the *safe* move. After what had happened in P.E. today with Jeff Carter, he was in the mood for *rolling the dice* and experiencing a lot more adventure!

When he reached his English class, he took a seat at the extreme back of the room, where he *always* sat. From there, he joined the rest of the class in waiting for Mrs. Hud, a very sweet, but *energy-challenged* teacher who had already announced that she was retiring at the end of the schoolyear. Due to her predictably long and boring lectures, which she delivered so quietly that many students sitting in the back, like Alan, had trouble even hearing her, the class had secretly nicknamed her, Mrs. '*Huh*?'

"I heard that you and Mary Williams *might* be going out?" a low and breathy female voice whispered from his left. He immediately turned to face Dora Leoni, cheerleader, partier, and all-around popular girl on campus. She looked exceptionally cute with her long blonde hair and sporty cheerleading outfit. Although

Alan had never known her very well, she had always made a point of acting friendly toward him. He remembered Dora asking him this *exact* question thirteen years before, and of course, he had replied with an emphatic, '*Yes*!' But this time history would *not* be repeating itself!

"No, Dora. Who told you that?"

The girl smiled broadly like the star of a toothpaste commercial. "Somebody," she flirted shamelessly. "Say, are you free tonight? I really need help studying for our English exam tomorrow. Maybe we could *study together*?"

Hey! This story was *all new material*? There was absolutely *nothing* that he remembered from his past in Dora's last monologue? "Sure, Dora," he replied quickly. "I'll come over at 7:30, if that's okay?"

Dora instantly agreed with a coy, little smile, and then the class began.

The rest of the day continued exactly as it had thirteen years before, so Alan simply relaxed and enjoyed the retro-ride. All he could really think about was his big date with Dora tonight! It wasn't so much that he exceptionally liked her or was even infatuated with her? The truth was, he was just so excited about his ability to create this spontaneously new adventure! His power to change *his* history, at least in his mind, was becoming a lot of fun, and maybe even… a bit *addictive*?

The school day ended and as Alan was walking home, he suddenly heard the rush of determined feet racing-up behind him. When he turned around, he surprisingly faced a very angry Jeff Carter?

"Why'd you hit me today, *shithead*?" Carter mumbled, as he menacingly grabbed Alan's shirt by the collar.

"Because you're a *prick* and I'm sick of you shooting your mouth off!" Alan fired back at his oppressor with absolutely *no idea* what would happen next.

It only took a fraction of a second for the crazed Carter to roughly remove his hands from Alan's collar and follow-up with a nasty punch! Alan was quick enough to veer his head, thus taking the brunt of the hit on his shoulder. Although as previously mentioned, he had *never* fought in school, Alan had enough experience breaking fights up as a teacher, to know *exactly* what he had to do next. He shouted, "Hey!" During that quick moment following, when Carter looked up, temporarily distracted, Alan's right arm very effectively incapacitated the boy in a secure headlock. Carter was *shocked* by Alan's uncanny ability to instantly render him helpless? He quit resisting just as soon as he figured out that struggling was utterly pointless.

"Look Carter," Alan announced in his toughest voice, "I don't want to be enemies, but I don't want to take any more of your crap either. How about from now on you stay out of my way and I'll stay out of yours?"

Alan gently released the boy and patiently awaited his answer. Jeff Carter stared at him, completely *void* of expression for a few seconds. But in the next telling moment, he gave Alan a *warm smile* along with a friendly nod of his head before turning and walking off whistling, as if nothing at all had happened?

'Wait a second?' Alan thought incredulously. '*What was that*?' He had absolutely *hated* Jeff Carter the entire time they had been in school together? The boy had a garbage mouth, was overbearing and completely unsympathetic toward anyone's feelings but his *own*! He didn't believe that Jeff Carter was even *capable* of smiling at anyone unless it came in the form of a *sinister sneer*! But he saw what he saw… *right*? This mind journey was very quickly *turning odd*?

When he arrived home, he was actually *relieved* to find his room exactly as he remembered it. But of course, *that* is the premise behind a mind journey like this one. Even so, it left him feeling simply amazed! There were dirty clothes hastily shoved under his bed and a number of record albums, including Led Zeppelin and the Beatles, haphazardly strewn across the floor near his stereo. But most importantly, he knew (*without even looking*) that a risqué magazine predictably titled, *Buxom Beach Bunnies*, was hidden somewhere between his mattresses! But there was also something *else*? Something seemed different? His sister had seemed the same, as did his parents… it was *him*! *He* was different? Instead of thinking about Mary, as he had done during this same moment thirteen years before, here he was thinking about *Dora*? He unreservedly loved Mary! But perhaps there had always been a very small part of him during high school that had wondered what it would have been like to go out with Dora Leoni? Anyway, this wasn't real, right? It was all in his head? In any case, *tonight* he'd find out what spending a little time with Dora was really like. That's when Alan suddenly realized that he didn't even know where she lived? He chuckled. They had *never* really been friends, although he had known who she was ever since elementary school. In truth, they had *barely* even been acquaintances! But maybe that would change? He quickly looked up her number in the local phone book, and gave her a call.

"Hello," a woman answered politely.

"Hi," Alan began with an unexpected air of uncertainty. "May I please speak with Dora?"

"Certainly," the woman replied politely. "May I say who's calling?"

"Uh, sure. This is Alan Dunkirk." For the first time in years, Alan felt extremely unsure of himself and *very* nervous. More specifically, he felt like an *acne-faced adolescent* at age thirty!

A few very long moments later, Dora came on the line. "Hi, Alan!"

"Hi, Dora," he stuttered. "You're probably going to find this funny, but I just realized that I *can't* remember where you live? Would you mind refreshing my memory?"

She laughed. "That's totally understandable. You probably haven't been to my house since my *second-grade* birthday party. Remember?" Next, she happily gave him the directions he needed. After that, for the next ten minutes or so she went on a one-sided '*conversation*' involving cheerleading, who wore *what* at school today and other very *vital* topics of her school day. It was truly the *longest* monologue he had ever heard one person spontaneously deliver in his life! As soon as she had finished, she paused dramatically before resuming their conversation, albeit with a *hushed* and secretive tone. "Tell your parents that you'll be here… kind of *late* tonight," she whispered cryptically. "We've got a *lot* of studying to do."

Alan quickly agreed, said his goodbyes, and then hung-up the phone feeling more excited than ever! But having no real way of speeding-up time, regardless of the fact that he really *wanted* to, he was forced to *distract himself* by doing homework and listening to music until dinnertime. When that time finally arrived, hiding his impatience behind a smile, he eagerly sat down to eat dinner with his family.

The meal was actually quite tasty as it had always been. Tonight, featured chicken and stuffing; his favorites! As he ate, he momentarily forgot about his date with Dora. He was thinking instead about just how much he'd *loved* his family. That memory made him feel simply wonderful! He knew that his father had actually passed away several years ago, his mother was currently living in Florida with his Aunt Tessie, while his younger sister Sarah, was happily married and living with her husband and baby in Alaska. So, he really *cherished* this opportunity of seeing his family all together again just *one more time*... even if it *was* just a memory.

"Great meal, Mom!" Alan shared as he was finishing up.

"What is Alan after?" Sarah laughed. "He's acting *way too nice*?"

"Thank you, Alan," his mother beamed, while also chuckling at Sarah's remarks. "Thank you very much!"

Once dinner had ended, and he had assisted his sister and mother in clearing the dirty dishes from the table, Alan felt like 'shooting the breeze' with his father. He invited him outside to the chairs on the porch where they sat down together to watch the beautiful star-filled sky, just as they had done countless times before, while he was growing-up.

"Thanks for helping me with that math homework yesterday, Dad. I don't think I'll ever understand advanced Algebra!" Alan chuckled.

His father laughed. "No problem, son! Anytime!"

"Don't you ever get tired of helping me?" Alan asked.

His father turned to him and smiled warmly, "Far from it! Once you *stop* asking me for help, I don't think I'll know what to do with myself?"

They both laughed, and then Alan and his father leaned back together and resumed studying the stars. At the same time, they found themselves being gently serenaded by the wonderful cacophony of multiple crickets and a single toad. Believe it or not, this was actually one of Alan's favorite childhood memories. A little while later, when his watch showed 7:15, he excitedly got up, hugged his dad, said goodbye to his mother and sister, collected his English book, and *resumed* his adventure by heading straight for Dora's house... *on foot*! According to her directions, she couldn't live more than a half-mile away.

"Hi, Alan!" a boy riding a bright yellow Schwinn Stingray bicycle (*exactly like the one he remembered riding when he was a kid*), suddenly rode-up alongside of him and stopped. "What're you doing out here?"

It was his friend and Mary's younger brother, Terry Williams. "Oh, I'm just going over to Dora Leoni's house to do some studying," Alan replied calmly.

Terry let out a loud *wolf's whistle* as his eyes bulged wide-open, "Dora Leoni? She's sure one *hot-looking babe*! Popular too!" he exclaimed. "Have you seen her dressed in that *skimpy* cheerleader getup?"

"Where are *you* headed, Terry?" Alan asked, without responding to his friend's last question.

"Oh, I'm meeting my sister, Mary, for dinner on her first date with Larry Peters at the Lynwood Cafe," he explained. "I guess she wants me there for protection!" he laughed. After that, Terry waved goodbye, and rode off.

For *protection*? Alan was suddenly feeling very jealous of this *Larry Peters*, whoever *he* was! How dare he go out with his wife! Although technically, Mary and he hadn't even started dating yet, so what right did he actually have to be jealous? All the same… *he was*! Alan continued to walk briskly down the street, deeply in thought. He had already changed his history *significantly* by merely doing a few things differently. But unfortunately, the results had *not* turned out as well as he'd hoped. The bottom line seemed to be the fact that Mary going out with somebody else… *really bothered him*?

It wasn't long before Alan reached Dora's house. It was a very nicely landscaped two-story brick dwelling with a fancy looking red speedboat neatly parked on the right side of the driveway as he walked up. It was the type of house that screamed, *RICH FAMILY*, to anyone looking at it. As Alan approached the front door, knowing that he was still five minutes early, he initially hesitated. But bravery won out in the end as he finally mustered up the courage to *ring* the doorbell.

"Hi, Alan," Dora smiled *mysteriously* as she opened the door and met him at the doorway. After he politely returned her, 'Hi,' she gently took his hand and ushered him inside the house. The interior of the place was every bit as impressive as the exterior. There were an abundance of interesting wallpapers, beautiful furniture and even dynamic seven-foot Roman, Grecian and Nordic statues depicting their gods, *similar* to the ones he had been studying in art class. The interior of this house looked absolutely *amazing*!

"Would you like to go into the living room to *study* now?" Dora suggested, with a secretive tone impatiently illuminating her voice. "We can even watch TV if you like?"

"Won't the noise bother your family?" he asked politely.

"*No one else* is home," Dora whispered boldly into his ear. "Not until late."

Alan was stunned! Was Dora suggesting something *other* than studying? No, surely not. He was probably just misunderstanding her? Dora had asked him over to study, and *that* was undoubtedly what she intended for them to do.

"Would you like a drink?" Dora politely asked her guest as he sat down on the black leather couch.

"Sure," Alan quickly agreed.

"Coke or 7up?" she brightly asked for clarification.

"Coke, please," he replied with a smile. He was really impressed by what a great hostess she was.

Moments later, Dora returned from the kitchen carrying two highball glasses. She immediately offered one to Alan, which he politely accepted. "My parents gave a party last night and all they have left is *rum*? I hope rum and coke is okay with you?"

Alan was not shocked… *exactly*. He was well aware that some of the kids at his high school hosted parties with alcohol, but he and his own little circle of friends had just *never* attended one? Much less, *been invited*! Once again, he was experiencing something that had *never* actually happened to him during high school?

"Do you *like* me, Alan?" Dora was suddenly sitting on the couch beside him so closely that he could feel the *exciting tingle* of her long, beautiful leg barely touching his.

Alan was shaken a bit by her bluntness, but replied, "Sure," since this was only a dream, and then he asked her, "Do you like me?"

The girl giggled with glee. "What do *you* think?" she teased. "I was so happy today when you told me you weren't going out with Mary Williams. I didn't want to say anything… but that girl is such a slut!"

Alan was furious! Who was this girl to call Mary a *slut*?

"You deserve better than Mary Williams, Alan!" Dora told him fervently. "I hope that you and I become really *close* friends tonight so that I can *show* you."

"What do you mean by that… *exactly*?" Alan was once again confused.

In answer to his question, Dora gently turned down the lights, seductively pulled him very close to her and the next thing you know, the two of them were locked in a *passionate* kiss!

Shockingly, at that exact instant, the *hideous* sound of a thousand gigantic eggshells loudly *cracking open* at the same moment quickly usurped his attention? This immediately caused him to stop kissing Dora and frighteningly turn toward the source of the noise. As he watched in horror, something *terrible* came bursting out from the dark recesses of what *had* been a dynamic statue of the Nordic god, *Thor*! As the former piece of art crumbled to dust, out stepped *Dora's father*! He was a tall, husky man with thick and fiery-red hair that stuck-out below his warrior's helmet with clear abandon! Visibly angry and showing a Viking's bravado, he bellowed some sort of loud and abrasive war cry as he abruptly made his dominating presence felt! Next, he very threateningly pulled out a very large and noticeably *sharp knife* from his leather scabbard, which appeared to come straight out of a classic *'slasher'* movie! Unmitigated *terror* was instantly emblazoned upon Alan's face as he saw that the man had hideously filed down each and every one of his front teeth into a *deadly sharp point*! Together, he imagined they could easily tear a man's throat out! In fact, he realized with a shudder, they could easily tear *his throat out*! The incredibly fearsome man suddenly turned toward him and looking him over with fierce contempt, he yelled, "So this is how you *study*? I'll make you *pay* dearly for messing around with my sweet daughter!"

As soon as Alan realized that the man was directing his rage expressly at *him*, he instantly grew paralyzed with fear! But as the crazed man was nearly upon him, his butcher knife reflecting wickedly off the pale moonlight which was eerily creeping through the window, the sharp blade menacingly pointed on a collision course with his *manhood*, Alan suddenly felt his current consciousness growing distant? Dora, her father and all of his immediate problems quickly dissolved into nothingness, as tranquility began to override the unmitigated terror that had completely consumed him only moments before.

"Alan? Alan? Easy boy, you're okay! It was only a dream. Relax, son," Joe Davis, was quickly entering the conscious mind of Alan Dunkirk with calming words to ease the tension he visibly saw on his face and throughout his *entire body*, as he abruptly left his mind journey behind him.

A feeling of great relief quickly spread throughout Alan's entire sweat-soaked body as he took refuge in the fact that he had indeed *returned safely* from the journey. And as far as he knew, he was both physically and mentally *intact*! "Am I really okay, Joe?" Alan begged for assurances as he slowly opened his eyes to see his old college professor standing caringly over him.

"Joe Davis was half-smiling and half in shock as he voraciously replied, "Of course you are! Hell, you're looking great, kid!"

The professor spent the next hour or so helping Alan to relax as he gently probed his memory about his recent adventures. Once Joe was satisfied that he had gotten all of the information he was likely to get from Alan tonight, he drew a real look of earned pride and satisfaction on his face, and settled back into his chair with his hands gently clasped together behind his head.

Alan caught that *smug* expression on Davis' face and began to feel proud too. Well, hadn't he done as much as the first astronaut to walk on the moon or the first European to ever set foot on the shores of the new world? He was an explorer, a trailblazer… a *damn fool*! He had nearly been *castrated*!

"What's wrong, Alan?" Davis asked alertly, as he *clearly* observed his prized pupil wince?

"Remember when I told you about my journey?" Alan began hesitantly.

"Yes," Davis confirmed curiously.

"Well, do you remember how I mentioned Dora's father's *great big knife*?" Alan shared anxiously. "Right before I woke-up, I think he was going to use it to seriously affect my *ability to procreate*!"

Joe burst out laughing.

"What's so funny?" Alan asked, feeling very insulted by his lack of empathy.

Davis walked over to Alan, compassionately laid a hand on his shoulder and gently said, "Alan, I know it must be hard to think rationally after such an intense experience as the one you have just endured. But I ask you, how could a man born of and living *exclusively* in your imagination… hurt you?"

Alan smiled and then laughed too, as he quickly comprehended the truth that Joe was so *clearly* illuminating for him.

"As you know," Joe explained calmly, "*everything* you experienced tonight was either based on what opinion of the truth your mind had stored-up from past experiences or what it could *invent* on the fly to fill-in the gaps when you *changed* the truth. Because you purposely *altered* your history, you forced your mind to alter your *reality* as well. For that reason, although *portions* of what you experienced tonight were probably authentic memories, *none* of what you experienced should be accepted in its entirety as the truth… especially that damn *chiseled tooth Viking slasher*!"

Alan chuckled. "I should have realized that."

"Have you ever *really* met Dora's father before?" Davis asked suspiciously.

Alan took a moment to think. "No," he admitted hesitantly. "Not that I can recall?" And then after thinking again for just a moment, he unreservedly admitted, "*No*, I definitely *never have*!"

Davis laughed. “I didn’t think so. I don’t think you could easily forget *teeth* like those!”

Alan chuckled.

“But the person you *wanted* him to be materialized just as soon as you needed him to,” Davis explained more seriously.

“Wait a minute. Do you mean to say that I *wanted* him to appear like a terrifying Viking and attack me?” Alan exclaimed in disbelief.

Davis smiled. “Sure, you did! Your conscious mind was in love with Mary and felt guilty for what was going on, so it devised a handy little *escape hatch* for you.”

“Amazing!” Alan declared. And as the realization soaked-in further, he declared, “So I did it! *I controlled everything*!”

“As you were *meant* to do,” Joe confirmed.

“Then it couldn’t have possibly gone wrong, could it?” Alan queried.

Joe thought carefully for a moment and then replied, “Well, not *this time* anyway. Everything seemed to go exactly as planned!”

“By the way, Joe. How long was I actually gone?” Alan asked.

Davis looked deep in thought as he replied, “Well, I would calculate that you experienced about twelve hours of life during your visit, while in *reality*, you were only asleep for about *one hour* of real time. That means for every hour spent in your subconscious, it only took about five minutes of real time.”

Alan was floored! He had only been in his subconscious mind for one hour, and yet so *very much* had transpired during that time?

“Don’t act so surprised, Alan,” Joe laughed. “I’m sure you already knew that dreams *often* slow real time down by a factor of twelve to one.”

“No! It’s not that. It’s just that my dreams are generally *eclectic* scenes and moments that don’t normally well fit together,” Alan responded. “But I have *never* had a dream that was as continuous and lifelike as this one was?”

Joe Davis fell silent. He *knew* that what Alan had just described was truly *remarkable*, and yet he had *no* explanation for it? How could a person’s mind possibly come up with twelve hours of believable and continuous memories and illusions in only *one hour* of real time? "It's far too early to draw any concrete conclusions from your journey tonight, Alan. But you went, you created and experienced *new versions* of your history, and you came back to tell me about it. I think I would call that a *success*, wouldn't you? Congratulations!"

Alan graciously acknowledged Joe's compliment, before a very curious thought suddenly forced its way to his conscious mind. "Joe, I spent twelve waking hours in my subconscious today. That means that I could conceivably spend *four* '24 hour' days there during just *one* actual eight-hour sleeping cycle, am I right?"

"Possibly, if your mind didn't *explode* first!" Davis replied hesitantly.

"What?" Alan asked, baffled.

"During these experiments," Davis carefully explained, "your mind is being asked not only to retain your *real memories*, but also the *new storylines* that you continue to spontaneously create. I don't believe a person's mind was ever built to work that hard over an extended period of time? We need to tread very cautiously here, Alan. Honestly? I would be very fearful of the immense fatigue and possible mental damage that placing you in that situation for too long might very well cause!"

"Noted!" Alan agreed. "But suppose I was to stay for… let's say only *one* 24-hour period? That would conceivably compute to only two hours of real time, right? What would happen *after* I ended the day on that journey and actually went to sleep, while literally *already* being asleep in this chair? Would I wake up the next morning *here*… or *there*?"

Joe cracked a slight smile as he considered that exciting question. After a few moments he attempted to answer it as best he could. "You know, Alan, when you're involved with something as new and unpredictable as this is, there are really no easy answers… only theories. The only *confirmed* knowledge we have right now is what you have personally experienced and shared with me in this red book. Based on what little we know so far, I honestly *haven't any idea* how to answer your question?" Joe admitted honestly, before gently adding, "But I really do think it has great potential for future studies!"

"Then why don't we?" Alan enthusiastically challenged him.

"Why don't we *what*?" Davis asked in confusion.

"Why don't we find out what happens when I fall asleep during my next journey?" Alan strongly urged him.

"*No*! It's too dangerous!" Joe shot back quickly. "You could go crazy for all I know! Maybe even slip into a *permanent coma*?"

Alan immediately blew-off Joe's fears and laughed, "But what if I *survived* and lived to tell the tale? Imagine the valuable knowledge we could gain?"

Joe smiled thoughtfully. He appreciated Alan's tenacious enthusiasm, he always had. But, he also clearly realized that it was premature and foolhardy to discuss such an extreme challenge as this one at such an early point in the testing of his theory. They still had so very much to learn! "C'mon kid. You made history tonight! Be happy with that! You know, Rome wasn't built in a day? Let's just enjoy our success for a while and worry about the *new questions* when we feel more prepared to answer them. What do ya say?"

After a slight pause, Alan smiled and conceded, "Oh, all right. But just for *now*!"

That night while Alan was driving home, he thought about everything that had transpired during his first mind journey. Had he really controlled the action? Damn right! It was a clear case of *mind over mind*!

Mary, Alan's wife of seven years, was just as pretty as the day he had first started dating her back in high school. Graced with a beautiful face that was perfectly framed by her long dark-brown hair and equipped with a mind as *sharp* as a tack, she found herself baffled? Things had been going so well between Alan and her, when suddenly out of nowhere she had noticed the *subtle* change in him almost immediately following his return home from his meeting with Joe Davis yesterday? Although he had been acting mysterious about this project for a while now, *this* was different? She still didn't possess a single clue as to what was going on during their sessions together, but she clearly felt herself growing more *keenly* interested every time he returned? To her, it appeared that he had become infatuated with something perhaps *related* to those sessions, and it was causing him to forget all about everything else in his life?

On this particular day while Alan was away, as he recently was more and more, Mary decided to find out for herself what it was that had become so very important to him? He had always spent a great deal of 'alone time' in his den, and even referred to it more than once in comic book vernacular as his own, personal *Bat Cave*! But over these past few days… he *never* seemed to leave it? Mary hadn't the foggiest idea what she was looking for, but she intuitively knew that the answer *had* to be in that room!

As his wife, Mary certainly knew Alan well enough to predict many of his recurring behaviors. For example, he never left anything of importance lying around in plain sight. He had a tendency to *hide* those personal items that were most important to him. Only last year, for example, Mary had discovered a small batch of letters he had archived since high school. He had admitted to her that he hadn't read any of them in years, but hated to part with anything that reminded him of his fun and exciting years of high school, as those letters did! Of course, *most* of the letters were written to him by 'female acquaintances' (*as he put it*), and he did very poorly in trying to explain away *why* he had specifically chosen to keep *them*? In the end however, Alan had agreed to dispose of those letters, in part because Mary had convincingly explained to him, "*It's never healthy for anyone to hang-on to the past for too long*." Apparently, she felt that was *exactly* what he had been doing. Mary truly believed that those letters had represented Alan's final secret, but lately, she had good reason to suspect that there *might* be yet another one?

She spent a good hour carefully sifting through her husband's desk and files, but discovered nothing to satisfy her curiosity? At long last, she became discouraged and dejectedly began to walk out of the room. It was then with a *smile* that she spied Alan's high school yearbooks neatly stacked in a pile near the door. She honestly didn't think they would shed any new light on the mystery at hand, but she needed a break so she slowly sat down on the floor and began casually flipping through each one.

The exercise of perusing through one's old yearbooks has a definite tendency to evoke pleasant memories from the reader's past. Curiously, those pleasant memories may appear *more* fondly in a person's mind than what actually transpired, while former friendships may appear to be *stronger* than they actually were? Probably due to these reasons, Mary was enjoying her *high school nostalgia* very much. That is, until she came across a picture that was curiously *circled* inside one of the yearbooks? It was the senior picture of a girl... *Dora Leoni*? An address and phone number were scribbled below it, with yet *another* name written beneath that... *Mrs. Jeff Carter*?

What in the world was this? Mary had been through these exact yearbooks many times before, but had *never* noticed this writing before? It *had* to be recent, she reasoned... but why?

"What a *bitch*!" she inadvertently hissed under her breath. All that Mary could think about now was *Dora Leoni*, the cheerleader in high school who she had only known well enough to *dislike*! Phony smile, irritating laugh, cheap as a two-week-old loaf of bread and worst of all, apparently a *very secret* acquaintance of Alan's!

But why on Earth was Dora Leoni's picture circled *now*, after all of these years? And was she to assume that '*Mrs. Jeff Carter*' meant she was married to Jeff Carter from high school?" The longer Mary thought about all of this, the more confused, and angry she became? She even considered the shocking possibility that the two of them might actually be having a *clandestine love affair* right under Jeff and her noses? Maybe Alan *wasn't* spending time with Joe Davis at all? That could actually make sense?! But, in reality, she had to honestly admit... she didn't really know *anything* at all. At least it was clear what her next move would be. She was going to find out *very quickly* what this mystery was all about just as soon as Alan returned home. In the meantime, she just couldn't resist adding a little facial artwork to Dora's picture while she waited. It was either that or the *scissors*!

Alan felt just a little bit guilty about what he had chosen to do today, but unfortunately, it could not be helped. He *had* to know the truth! Ever since his return from his mind journey, he had become *obsessed* with everything that had happened to him there, which if memory serves, was quite a lot! It had all felt so real to him at the time, so of course, it was becoming increasingly more difficult for him to separate *those* events from the events that had *actually happened* to him all of those years ago? This situation clearly made his search for the truth even harder!

Thanks to Dora's mother, Alan had gotten *all* of the information he needed to successfully execute today's quest, or at least get him to the *right house*! He had called her last night, posing as an old high school friend of Dora and Jeff's. When he politely asked for her current information, he immediately received Dora's phone number and address, which he quickly jotted down near her picture in one of his old high school yearbooks he had been looking at. He then transferred that information to a handy scrap of paper and he was on his way! This compulsion to know the answers, regardless of the fact that he *didn't* yet know the *questions*, had been gradually increasing since the beginning of his work with Joe Davis on his mind project, and it seemed to have culminated right after his return from the recent mind journey? *Why* it had become so important to him to find-out the truth about some obscure and forgotten event in his past… he really had *no idea*? But deep down, he knew for sure that Dora and Jeff Carter somehow figured prominently in the answer!

Alan arrived at his old hometown of Lynwood about noon. Eerily, the place looked nearly exactly the same as it had when he had spent his youth here. Lynwood could probably best be described as pleasant, peaceful, well kept-up… and *hopelessly lost* in 1955! But that wasn't such a bad thing, was it? Although he had only been two at the time, he imagined that 1955 must have certainly been a much more peaceful time to live in than today. 1955 was when *Disneyland* had first opened its doors, for heaven's sake! How could any other year even *hope* to compete with that? Alan was quite anxious to visit Dora and her husband Jeff today, but he didn't quite know how to go about doing that? Popping-in was rude enough when it involved friends, but unexpectedly visiting a mere acquaintance and her *psychopathic husband* after not seeing them for over a decade? Now *that* sounded just plain *ludicrous*!

He stopped at the first gas station he found. Alan slowly got out of his car, and even more slowly made his way to the pay telephone booth. Once there, he somehow rallied the courage to make the call. He carefully dialed Dora's number and then anxiously waited for her to pick-up. After five or six long rings… someone's voice *finally* appeared on the line.

"Hello?" the voice belonged to a very high-spirited young child.

"Hello," Alan replied cautiously.

"Huh?" the voice questioned him, as though they *hadn't* been able to understand his last reply.

"I said, *hello*," Alan repeated a little louder, trying very hard not to sound nervous. "I wonder if I might speak to Mrs. Dora Carter?"

Alan involuntarily *winced* for just a moment as the thump of the telephone receiver hitting something solid, shocked his ear. He could faintly distinguish a bright little voice in the background calling out, "Mom? Mommy?!"

A few moments later, a woman's voice came on the line. "Hello?" she sounded both cheerful and curious.

"Hello," Alan announced politely (*for the third time in the past thirty seconds*). Emotionally unprepared for this moment to actually happen, he now found himself embarrassingly feeling as if he were talking to her in the high school quad at lunchtime in 1971, with his *pants pulled down* and a piece of paper taped to to the back of his shirt which read, '*Kick Me*!' Still, he somehow managed to act as normal and friendly as his *uncomfortable* mental state allowed. "Hi, Dora? I don't know if you remember me? I'm Alan Dunkirk… from high school?"

There was a noticeably awkward pause before the voice hesitantly replied, "Oh yes! Hi, Alan! How are you? What brings you into my little life today?"

Alan frighteningly realized that his response to her question would surely dictate the success or failure of his having a meeting with her *at all*! He couldn't risk losing any more of his nerve, so he quickly got right to the point. "Well, just for fun I'd really like to talk with you about old times. Is this a convenient time to drop-by?"

Dora laughed softly, and quickly replied, "Well? Oh, why not! Just give me five minutes to tidy things up, okay? Do you know how to get here, Alan?"

After assuring her that he did, he hung up the phone and walked back to his car. He could hardly believe what *great* luck he was having! Everything so far was going *exactly* to plan! He excitedly feasted on that thought as he drove the short distance to her house.

A mere five minutes later, he arrived. But as he looked at the house, he felt *strangely disappointed*? This was *not* the big rich-looking mansion that he had imagined she lived in? Instead, it was a rather average looking tract-home, similar to his own, painted yellow with white trim. The house was surrounded by what was surely supposed to be a nice, big yard. However, at the moment, it was quite obviously in need of a little *TLC*, as evidenced by the tall weeds growing throughout! There were two young girls (*probably four or five years old*) with long blonde hair, identically dressed in pink shorts and matching pink tee shirts, sitting on the steps leading up to the porch, animatedly playing with their dolls. Alan chuckled to himself as he quickly surmised that one of them was *obviously* the young child of limited vocabulary who he had just spoken with on the telephone.

He left his car and slowly began making his way toward the front door. The two children only paused from their play long enough to give him a *serious* looking-over as he passed them on the steps. Alan suddenly felt a little embarrassed for being here in the first place, but since he'd made it this far… he was *determined* to go through with his plan. He confidently pushed the doorbell.

Momentarily, the door swung open. "Hello, *Alan Dunkirk*!" He immediately came face to face with a little fuller, a little older version of Dora Leoni! And she came complete with that great-big *cheerleader smile* that he'd gotten to know so very intimately during his recent mind journey. Her face was still very cute, although her brown hair was cut short, unlike the long curly locks she had possessed in high school. This drastic change in her appearance *almost* made her look like a different person to him? But her high energy and electric smile quickly convinced him that she was definitely the former *Dora Leoni*!

"Won't you come in?" Dora asked sweetly, neatly dressed in an olive-colored sundress.

Alan smiled and replied graciously, "Thank you," as he entered the house. Once inside, he looked around and immediately noticed that the living-room was quite roomy. It was well-furnished too, beginning with a leather couch that had a solid mahogany coffee table set directly in front of it. Adjacent to the coffee table and to its right sat a matching chair. There were also two child-sized bean bags (*that were undoubtedly there for the girls*) to the right of the couch in the center of the room. They were facing what looked like a pretty new television set which sat ten feet in front of them. On the wall, directly above the television, hung a very large picture of '*George Washington Crossing the Delaware*.' The surrounding walls were painted Navajo white, the carpet was a dark tan, and in general he found the room to be very welcoming.

Dora led Alan to the couch, motioned for him to sit down and then gracefully sat down next to him. "Well?" she began straightforwardly. "You wanted to talk with *me*, Alan? After all of this time? *What about*?"

"I'm sorry," Alan began hesitantly. "It probably sounds stupid, I know, but I just felt like looking up a few of my friends and acquaintances from high school today."

Dora immediately smiled very oddly at him? Suddenly growing very somber, she dramatically began shaking her head knowingly. "*Disappointed*, aren't you, Alan!"

Alan was immediately perplexed? He had absolutely no idea what she was talking about? "Disappointed about *what*?"

Her large brown eyes suddenly grew a size larger. "Disappointed that I *married* Jeff Carter instead of *you*, of course!"

As Alan sat there, *dumbfounded*, his face clearly conveying his tortured confusion, Dora suddenly burst into what initially felt like a never-ending fit of *giggles*? Desperate to salvage the conversation, he replied awkwardly, "How did you ever guess?" Then he joined her in the laughter, although he still had *no idea* what he was laughing at?

"It wasn't hard," Dora suddenly became deathly serious again. "When you called, I couldn't imagine what could possibly bring *you* here to see *me* after all of these years? And then it *hit* me! You're hoping to convince me to drop everything and *travel the world* with you! Am I right?" Again, she giggled, waving her large wedding ring in his face, "Well, you are way too late, buster! I'm a *married* woman!"

Alan was beside himself! He felt as though he were conversing with a person who'd taken this conversation so far *south* that he'd never find *north* again, even if it bit him on the nose! And then just as quickly as her '*insanity*' had manifested itself… Dora suddenly appeared to be acting *normal* again?

"Forgive me for acting so whacky, Alan," she said apologetically. "My girls had trouble falling asleep last night, so I didn't get much sleep myself. Add that to my dramatic and extravert nature, and ta-da! *That's* why I'm so extra *silly* today!" she laughed. "Sorry. I'm not really a *psycho*!"

Alan chuckled.

She smiled back at him, and asked, "Now seriously, *what* did you want to talk with me about?"

Ignoring her question, Alan replied excitedly, "You *really* had me going there! I must say, that was a *very funny bit*!"

"Thanks, Alan!" she beamed. "I'm glad you understand my weirdness!"

"Are you kidding?" he exclaimed. "I *live* in the land of weird! Your *weirdness* is a gift, believe me!"

"A *gift*? Well thanks for that!" she laughed gratefully. "Actually, I use a little bit of humor every day! On particularly tough days I use it just to keep me from going *insane*," she laughed. "Ideally, the day I lose my sense of humor will be the day *after* I pass away."

Alan laughed. "That's a *wonderful* saying! Did you come up with that one yourself?"

"Thanks," Dora smiled. "Well, actually that was just a spontaneous little 'spur-of-the-moment' answer to your question. But I *suppose* I did? I'm not really a trained writer, though."

"It made *me* laugh!" Alan chuckled.

"Thank you again," Dora said appreciatively. And then growing more thoughtful, she said, "You know, as a *hobby*… definitely for my eyes only, I like to write humorous short stories at night after my twin girls, Margaret and Katie, have gone to sleep. It's a way for me to repackage my problems each day into jokes and funny situations that I can laugh at later. That way, I can *always* go to bed happy!"

After hearing Dora's inspiring thoughts, unfortunately, all that Alan could feel was *envy*. Lately, he *never* enjoyed having a good night's sleep anymore. He wished *he* could package his problems into jokes… but first he had to find out exactly *what* his problems were? "That's great!" he responded with a grin. "*Not* being a particularly funny person myself, I sure appreciate someone who *is*."

Dora smiled warmly, and replied, "Thank you, Alan! Thanks a lot!"

"Sure!" Alan smiled back. Then changing the subject, he asked, "What does Jeff do for a living?"

"Well, not to *brag*," she smiled playfully, "but once he agreed to take-over the family trucking business after his father had officially retired, we 'inherited' a large fleet of trucks as well as the sales office and a large vehicle repair and storage area in downtown Lynwood."

"Wow!" Alan exclaimed. "Then Jeff must be pretty busy I'll bet?"

"You would think," she agreed, "but actually, no." Then she explained with a smile, "He's the *boss*, so he hires the drivers, mechanics, and office staff, and spends most of his time just sitting down in a big, comfy chair in his office." Then she added, "Although, there are times when he gets *very busy* negotiating truck rates with his customers or trying to drum-up more business"

"That sounds very stressful!" Alan retorted. "Does he *like* doing that?"

"Oh yes!" Dora laughed. "You must know Jeff well enough to know that he's firmly in his *wheelhouse* when it comes to arguing with other people! He finds it *stimulating*!"

Suddenly both daughters came bursting through the front door gleefully announcing, "Daddy's home!" before *immediately* rushing back outside to no doubt, *resume* playing with their dolls.

Dora shook her head at Alan, and said, “Buckle-up, pardner. Jeff is not always the *most charming* person when he first comes home from work.”

Alan immediately had recollections of two *completely different* Jeff Carters. First, there was the obnoxious, self-centered bully that he had the displeasure of knowing throughout all of his years in public school. Secondly, there was that oddly *friendly* and *smiling* boy from his mind journey who seemed to appear out of nowhere? A moment later, there was little doubt as to *which* of the two men walked through the door!

“Can’t you keep those damn kids off the lawn?” he hollered at the room without making eye contact with anyone.

“*What lawn*?” Dora quipped, without a smile. “All I see out there are a bunch of *celebratory weeds*!”

“Haha!” Jeff replied sarcastically. “I’ll get to it *when* I get to it, okay?” It was then, that he first noticed Alan sitting uncomfortably on the couch beside Dora. His face grew a curious expression of *bewilderment* as he first eyed his guest. Then his expression quickly evolved into a broad grin as he walked over to him, offering his hand in greeting.

Alan stood up and shook hands with the man before feigning a similar grin. That’s when he noticed that except for being a few pounds heavier, Jeff Carter *didn’t* look much different than he had back in high school? After the handshake, Jeff went to the wingback chair and sat down, while Alan returned to the couch.

“You’ll never guess who came-by to see us today?” Dora informed her very curious husband. “This is *Alan Dunkirk*, from high school, remember?”

Suddenly Jeff looked slightly amused. “Yes!” he began, “So Alan Dunkirk returns to Lynwood to reminisce with his old classmates, eh?”

“Exactly!” Alan smiled. “On a *whim*, I decided to find out what you guys were up to?” Then he added, “Dora already told me about the trucking company you own. Very nice!”

“Thanks. What do *you* do for a living?” Jeff inquired suspiciously. “You aren’t a *salesman* or a *lawyer*, are ya?”

“Hardly,” Alan chuckled. “I’m a teacher.”

Jeff's expression grew incredulous as he immediately let out an emphatic burst of laughter, "Just couldn't get enough of '*going to school*,' could you, old buddy? Personally, I had my fill with high school!"

"So, Alan, what have *you* been doing with yourself since high school?" Dora quickly interrupted Jeff's misplaced laughter, giving him an *evil glare* in the process.

"Let's see," Alan began slowly, "Well, I married Mary Williams just as soon as we graduated from college about eight years ago." He paused momentarily, but with no one else offering a comment, he quickly continued. "Right now, we live in San Diego where we both teach high school." With still *no sign* of either of them relieving him as they listened attentively, he added, "Uh, we don't have any kids yet like the two of you do, but we *are* seriously thinking about starting-up a family before too long."

Alan's last comment stirred something in Jeff, causing him to grow noticeably more thoughtful. He appeared to have a response that he wanted to deliver, although he hesitated before finally deciding to speak. "I don't know if my opinion matters to you in that department," he shared gently, looking very sincere. "And I never thought that I would feel this way, believe me. But I just *adore* my kids, Alan! Along with Dora, they bring out the best in me. *I mean it*!"

Alan was absolutely *shocked* at hearing Jeff's beautiful words? His wife and kids '*brought out the best in him*?' Where in the hell did *that* come from?

"I'm sure that when the time comes, you and Mary won't be able to get enough of your kids either," Jeff smiled. "Even if like me, you *don't* always show it."

"I'm sure you're right," Alan smiled awkwardly. "On *both* counts!"

Dora chuckled. "In our family, even when we yell, we tell our girls that it's filled with love," Dora and Jeff smiled at each other. "We call it *Yove*!"

Alan laughed, even though in actuality… he was *dumfounded*? Somehow, he had expected these two to always fight like cats and dogs, just as he had witnessed earlier. And he had honestly expected them to both be *miserable* as a result! But the

Carters had genuinely surprised him by sincerely appearing to be happily in love? This little epiphany unnerved him so much that it caused him to *completely forget* what it was he had come to talk with them about in the first place?

"Hey, Alan," Jeff hesitatingly began, "I'd like to apologize for sometimes bullying you and *everyone else* in school," he laughed nervously, and then immediately offered him a sincerely penitent expression. This was obviously difficult for him, and was probably why he kept looking at Dora for reassurance. "Dora made me go to therapy for all of my 'issues' a long time ago. I can still be a bully at work sometimes when things get too hectic… but I try very hard to control that part of me whenever I'm at home." Then meeting Alan's eyes, he added, "Sorry about laughing at you earlier. Old habits *do* die hard. I suppose I backslid a bit, huh?" he chuckled.

"No offense taken," Alan smiled warmly.

"So, what are you and Mary doing this summer?" Jeff suddenly asked.

"I imagine that we'll probably just be hanging around the house," Alan mused. "We don't really have anything else planned."

"Well, if you're ever around here again," Jeff continued, "give us a call and we can fire-up the barbeque or something!"

"Yes," Dora piped in. "That would be fun!"

Alan was blown away by the goodwill he was receiving from both of them, and replied, "I'll speak with Mary about it, but I think that sounds *wonderful*!" Smiling broadly, he added, "Thanks for meeting with me today, you two. This has truly been a pleasure!"

Dora wouldn't let Alan leave without 'officially' meeting their twin daughters, who in addition to playing dolls, were *both* very sweet. And by watching how effortlessly they hugged their parents it quickly became even *more* apparent to him that the Carters were genuinely just *one big happy family*!

As he drove back to San Diego that day, Alan had mixed feelings about his visit with the Carters. Most of all he was of course, *happy* for them. But deep down he was clearly disappointed that they had changed so much from what he remembered? *Especially Jeff*? He was no longer a relentless bully and Alan now found it *impossible* to hate him anymore? Jeff's remarkable transformation had undoubtedly come with a little more maturity and a few years of therapy. There was really nothing strange about that at all. Nevertheless, he found that for some completely unknown and seemingly irrational reason, he was *not at all happy about it*?

Alan arrived home at four o'clock that afternoon. He was feeling pretty good about his investigation today… but *not* great. He still didn't know exactly what he was looking for? But he rationalized that at least he had gotten the ball rolling.

"Where have *you* been?" Mary asked her husband coldly, void of any facial expression, as Alan unsuspectingly walked through the front door and into the house.

"Oh, I thought I'd drive out to Lynwood," he replied nonchalantly, "to see the old place."

"*Why*?" Mary prodded him icily.

Alan would have to have been deaf, blind and exceedingly *dense* to have missed the very oppressive tone that was emanating from his wife. "What's wrong, Mary?"

"Just *answer* my question!" she demanded in no uncertain terms.

Alan was completely taken aback, and found himself growing increasingly more irritated by her seemingly unprovoked attack? "What the *hell* is the matter with you?" he barked.

Mary could no longer contain her emotions as she confessed, "It's your high school yearbook, Alan! You circled Dora Leoni's picture and wrote her address and phone number right next to it. Would you mind *explaining that* to me?"

Alan immediately processed what had just happened and couldn't help but laugh. "Is this the 'jealous wife' routine, Mary?"

Mary in *no way* appreciated her husband's flippant response to this potentially very explosive situation. She had spent the entire day stewing over it, and would *not* be put off so lightly! "I just want to know what you're up to, Alan?" Mary chose her words very carefully, being mindful to keep control of her temper. "You've been acting awfully secretive for a while now."

Alan abruptly paused the conversation in order to weigh his options. As always, he knew that his only *real* option was to tell Mary the truth. Anything less, meant disaster at a later date. "Okay Mary," he began in his most sincere tone, "I'll tell you exactly what's been going on."

"Please do," Mary urged him, with most of her anger still in check.

Alan proceeded to explain everything from his interest in Joe Davis' theory, to his recent mind journey, and finally to his actual meeting with Dora and Jeff. At the conclusion of his lengthy and detailed explanation, Mary first appeared to be more shocked than angry… but it *didn't* remain that way for long.

"You've been doing all of this *behind my back*?" Mary accused him, enraged.

"I'm sorry, Mary," he stammered. "I… uh… I… just wasn't sure how well you would take it."

"Take *what*?" Mary exploded. "You traveling back in time to see old 'sexy *girlfriends*?' Now *why* should I get angry about that?"

Alan simply could not believe what he was hearing? His own wife was belittling his part in the groundbreaking mind journey he had just taken! She was overlooking the extremely complex things that had happened to him, and reduced *everything* into an emotional tirade of petty jealousy. "Look, Mary!" he made no attempt to disguise his irritation. "I've told you the truth. I've completely leveled with you, and damnit, I was right! You won't even *try* to understand!"

Mary had little trouble matching his intensity. "Oh, I understand all right! You just *can't* deal with being a grown-up, can you!" Mary shouted angrily. "Alan Dunkirk is just another name for *Peter Pan*!"

"Why don't you just *shut-up*!" Alan responded angrily.

Exactly one second after Alan had delivered that simple but highly confrontational request, Mary's emotions got the better of her! She truly felt like *slapping him* as hard as she could across his face, because at *that* moment, she felt nothing but *anger*! But, thinking better of it after glaring at him for a long moment, she determinedly stormed off into their bedroom, slamming the door shut behind her.

Alan hesitated. As he saw it, he had two choices. He could follow her into the bedroom and attempt to continue this emotionally-charged sparring of words, wherever it might lead, or... he could leave.

He left! Alan jumped into his car and promptly headed for Reeves University, where Joe Davis was a professor. He didn't know if Joe was at the University, away or at his nearby home, but he knew for certain that he *would* find him. He *had* to! Joe Davis was the only soul on Earth who could understand him now!

As luck would have it, Joe Davis *was* in town! Alan found him relaxing at his home near the University. As they sat together in his living room, Alan lost little time getting right to the point, "I drove to Lynwood and visited the *real* Dora and Jeff today, and now Mary's mad as hell at me, Joe! She doesn't understand what I'm doing?"

Joe chuckled. "Well honestly, Alan... *do you*?" he retorted calmly. "I certainly *don't*!"

Alan cracked the faintest of smiles and replied, "To tell you the truth, no! I don't have a clue why it was so important for me to visit Dora and Jeff?" Then growing more anxious, he added, "But on top of that, even though they both seemed to be very happy, and Jeff even *apologized* to me for being such a bully in school... I felt strangely *disappointed* after I'd left them? Like that scenario was *completely* wrong? It's been really bothering me ever since?"

"Perhaps you thought they were *only pretending* to be happy?" Joe suggested.

"No, that's not it. The crazy thing is, I *know* they were being sincere and that Jeff's apology was on the level. But for some reason I just *can't* seem to accept it?"

Joe instantly grew a concerned look on his face. "Really? You know, what you are describing might very well be raising a red flag?" he shared.

"A *red flag*?" Alan repeated curiously.

"Yes," Joe confirmed, and then explained, "I'm thinking that you may have *a conflict* going on between your conscious and subconscious minds."

"What? Why?" Alan asked in surprise.

Joe laughed uncomfortably. "Your guess is as good as mine? It could be *anything*?"

Alan looked a little anxious as he asked, "Well, what do you think I should do about it?"

"I think the sooner you get some professional help, the sooner you'll discover what this problem is and how to treat it," Joe shared honestly. "But don't wait too long. Get with a good psychiatrist as soon as you can!"

"*You* studied psychiatry in college," Alan suddenly reminded him. "Why can't *you* help me?"

Joe looked even more uncomfortable. "Alan, there is no telling how serious this condition of yours is and as you must be aware, *most* of my training and experience is in psychology… *not* psychiatry!"

"I know," Alan admitted anxiously. "But couldn't you at least take a *preliminary look* at it? Just to help me understand it a little bit better?"

Joe looked very conflicted, but after a moment he hesitantly agreed. "Okay. I'll do my best. But just this *once*! Starting tomorrow, you've got to find yourself a *real* psychiatrist!"

"Thanks, Joe! This means a lot to me!" Alan shared with relief.

"My *bill* is in the mail," he quipped.

Alan smiled.

"Now, to begin with," Davis said, "why do you think you feel so compelled to relive a part of your past?"

"What makes you think that I do?" Alan asked defensively.

Davis chuckled. "C'mon, Alan! It's *obvious*! You told me the exact date and location you wanted to go before taking your mind journey."

"Thursday, January 14th, 1971, Lynwood High School," Alan quickly shared.

"That's right!" Joe exclaimed, proving his point. "Now tell me *why* that date and location are so important to you?"

"I haven't the foggiest idea?" Alan confessed sincerely.

Joe smiled encouragingly. "Perhaps you have just temporarily forgotten? Think about it."

"Okay," Alan agreed.

A long minute later, Joe politely asked, "Well?"

"I *want* to remember, Joe. I really do! But nothing is coming up?"

"*Nothing*?" Joe repeated in disbelief. "Do you mean to tell me that you just chose that date and location at *random*?" he asked incredulously.

"No, of course not!" Alan stuttered nervously. "They *must* be important to me somehow, but I just don't seem to remember *why*?" he replied in frustration.

Joe Davis gently nodded. "Okay, let's look at this another way," he suggested calmly. "What *exactly* seems to be driving you so strongly to revisit your past?"

Alan grew thoughtful. "I think that I may need to *change* something," he confessed. "I don't have any idea what that '*something*' is, but I just know that by going back into my past it will somehow be made clear to me." He paused, as he pulled a folded paper out of his pocket. "Incidentally, I had a very *vivid* dream last night that frankly didn't make a whole lot of sense to me? But it was so unusual, like *nothing* I've ever dreamt before? I think it may be important? Anyway, I wrote down the gist of it right after I woke-up. It should give you a little more to ponder," Alan smiled, while placing the document on the end-table next to the couch.

"Thanks, Alan," Joe smiled back.

"Hey? What do you say we send me back *right now*?" Alan excitedly suggested. "It just feels right!"

"I'm sure it does," Joe replied understandingly. "But Alan, when a person *blindly* does anything, like you are suggesting we do right now, they never really know what their next step is? They have to *guess*. And you can probably imagine what the dismal odds are for being successful *strictly* through guessing? Ask any gambling addict who's lost everything?" After a slight pause, he continued, "Why don't we take our time figuring this thing out first before sending you back again? We could formulate a workable plan? It would be *much safer* for you. Don't you agree?"

Alan instantly looked very disappointed as he made one final emotional plea to his mentor. "But, Joe, every part of my being is *screaming* that if I go back into my past again, I will *definitely* figure this nightmare out once and for all!"

"I'm sorry, Alan," Joe shared gently. "We need to get a better handle on what it is we're looking at first *before* taking any more risks with your mind. If this problem of yours turns-out *not* to be too serious, we could probably send you out on another mind journey in just a few months following the completion of your therapy. What do you say?"

After an *uncomfortable* pause, Alan glumly conceded, "Okay." Then a moment later he perked up a bit and added, "Maybe I'll do what you suggested and see that psychiatrist later this week?"

"That sounds great! The sooner the better!" Davis reiterated, obviously relieved that Alan was accepting his diagnosis. "Now, how about a beer?"

"Great!" Alan exclaimed. "I'll go get a couple from your fridge."

"I'm afraid *that* would be a waste of time," Davis quickly shared impishly. "They *were* in the fridge, but… okay I *already drank* the last one!" he chuckled. "However, as you know, I always keep a spare sixpack in the mini-fridge in the garage. I'll be right back!" he promised, as he rose from his chair and resolutely traveled through the kitchen, which conveniently connected with the door leading into the garage.

The moment Alan heard the door close, he jumped up and very quietly opened the top drawer of the only filing cabinet in the room. He recalled seeing Joe taking the pink pills out of it *prior* to his recent mind journey. He quickly sighted and grabbed them, stuffed the small bottle deep into his pants pocket, while also retrieving Joe's valuable *red book*. After securely placing it inside his inner jacket pocket, he calmly closed the file drawer and returned to the couch. He rationalized this as *borrowing* since he had every intention of returning both the notebook and bottle just as soon as he was done using them. Soon, Joe returned with the beers.

The two men did not discuss 'mind journeys' for the remainder of the visit. Davis didn't bring them up for fear of intensifying the powerful compulsion that was already beginning to control Alan's mind, while Alan didn't touch the subject because... well... frankly, there *didn't* seem to be a need to anymore? He had procured the drug and the notebook, so as far as he was concerned, everything was going to be just fine. It would not be long now before he would once again have the incredible opportunity of revisiting his past! Only this time, he'd make sure to stay as long as it took... *to face the dragon.*

Alan had not returned home to San Diego that night at all? But to Mary, there was little mystery as to *where* he had probably gone! The next morning, she jumped into her car with a vengeance! She had been driving now for well over an hour but still felt undaunted. She was determined to give Alan's friend and mentor, Joe Davis, a great big piece of her mind! In truth, she didn't actually know the man very well. She had only spoken with him during those rare times when Alan had taken her to his house for some eclectic *psychological* discussions. This had sporadically occurred while they had been dating and simultaneously attending the University of Reeves together almost a *decade* ago. She didn't understand much about any of this, but she *did* know that things didn't really begin to go haywire between Alan and her until *after* the good professor rudely '*stuck his nose*' into their lives!

When she finally arrived in front of Davis' house, Mary momentarily found herself losing her nerve. She seriously wondered how she could have even *considered* attacking a man who she knew so very little about? To be honest, she knew even less about the role he had played, *if any*, in this whole mess?

During the very next moment, she witnessed a frantic Joe Davis bursting through his front door and running to the sidewalk in front of his house? He appeared to be extremely stressed as he kept looking wildly up and down the street as if his life depended on it! She immediately felt a terrible hollowness in the pit of her stomach as she just *knew* that the professor's terror had something awful to do with *Alan*!

"Professor Davis!" Mary shouted, as she jumped out of her car.

The distraught and distracted man abruptly turned to look at her. Miraculously, it only took a few moments for him to recognize her. "Mary? Mary Dunkirk?" he whispered, in surprise.

Mary nodded, as she quickly ran up to face him. Davis looked to be even more nervous now as he slowly bowed his head, *noticeably* having difficulty meeting her eyes.

"Mary, Alan was here yesterday. He shared with me that he'd told you *everything*," he began. "Is that true? Do you really understand what's been going on?" he asked her gently.

Mary began to feel sick once again as she anxiously replied, "I… I think so?"

"It was obviously *never* my intention to hurt Alan in any way," Davis continued, "and I certainly didn't wish to create any problems between the two of you."

"What exactly are you trying to tell me?" Mary abruptly questioned him, trying hard not to expect the worst.

"What I'm *trying* to tell you, Mary, is that I successfully used an experimental drug to help induce Alan into his subconscious mind just before he began his mind journey." He paused for one anxious moment before continuing. "I believe that Alan has *taken* my only bottle of that drug with him!"

"Is the drug safe?" Mary demanded.

"I truly believe it to be," Davis calmly assured her, "but like any drug, only when taken in *controlled* amounts." Looking more pressed, he continued, "He also took my notebook that has all of the notes I've accumulated since the *beginning* of this project. I ran outside just as soon as I discovered that they were both gone, *in hopes* that Alan might still be here… maybe sitting in his car having second thoughts? But he's *definitely* gone!"

"*Second thoughts* about what?" Mary insisted.

"Attempting a mind journey by *himself*!" Davis declared with both fear and curiosity in his voice.

"Is that even possible?" Mary asked anxiously.

"Oh, it's possible to *attempt* it," Joe confirmed. "But being *successful*? I really have *no* idea?"

"You said you saw him yesterday?" Mary recalled, trying very hard not to scream.

"Yes, in the late afternoon," he replied as calmly as he could.

"Well, what makes you so sure that it was *him* who took your pills and notebook?" she asked intently.

Davis replied grimly. "I only just discovered that they were both gone, but I'm certain that Alan took them because I had *no other visitors* yesterday or today!"

"Well, maybe someone took them *another* day, or you simply misplaced them?" Mary suggested hopefully.

Davis shook his head sadly. "I'm sorry Mary, but those two possibilities are *impossible*. You see, as a rule I *always* check to make sure that the pills and notebook are there *every* morning, just as I did today." And then he added seriously, "You should have seen how *desperate* Alan was to return to his past! I *know* he took them!"

Although she was very much afraid of hearing the wrong answer, Mary forced herself to ask, "Are there any physical or mental dangers that Alan might face as a result of taking too many of those pills?"

Davis met Mary's eyes as he replied, "Possibly. But I think it's very unlikely that Alan would *not* realize the inherent dangers in taking too many pills. I guess it all depends on how rational his mind is right now."

Mary was immediately thrown into *utter terror*! She completely forgot the hurt and anger that had possessed her earlier, and replaced it instead with a desperate need to be with her husband. "Oh, Professor Davis," she pleaded, nearly in tears. "We have got to save him!"

Davis gazed helplessly at Mary *without* any reassuring words to offer her as he stated the obvious, "I'm afraid we've got to *find him* first!" Then suddenly coming to life, he added, "I just remembered. Alan had a recent dream that he had written down and wanted me to look at? He thought it might help me to figure out the source of this compulsion of his? He left the paper on a table in my living room."

"Well then what are we waiting for? Let's go get it!" Mary screamed, as she aggressively nudged Joe back toward his front door. Once inside, Joe retrieved the paper, and with Mary anxiously standing close beside him, he began reading it aloud:

"*Fear struck me to the core as the dragon downed my dear comrade.*

He had fought with honor, but proved to be no match for this all-consuming fiery fiend from hell.

A heavenly damsel ran up to help him, only to be mercilessly taunted by the dragon for her kind intentions.

And off in the distance was a lady so pure and fair, that simple words cannot describe.

She silently watched... as I turned to stone by the dragon's breath."

"Can you make anything out of that?" Mary tried to *will* Joe to magically come up with a spontaneous and accurate answer.

"I wish I could," he muttered. "But I *do* know that Alan asked me to program his mind journey for January 14th, 1971 at Lynwood High School. Does that ring any bells?"

"*January 14th, 1971*? Are you sure?" she asked Joe, excitedly.

"Positive."

"I've got to call my brother!" she screamed. "I hope to God he's home!"

Joe instantly pointed her the way to his telephone, and moments later she was conversing with her brother, Terry Williams. The conversation took several minutes, and then Mary excitedly hung-up.

"Well? What did he say?" Joe asked intently.

"Never mind *that*!" she replied anxiously. "Right now, we've got to get to Lynwood as fast as we can!"

Joe did not ask Mary any further questions. Instead, feeling her insatiable sense of urgency, he quickly followed her out the door. Momentarily, the two jumped into Mary's car and sped off.

Once they were on the freeway, Joe asked excitedly, "Is it something about Alan's dream?"

"Yes, it's *exactly* about his dream!" Mary confirmed.

"Well? What did your brother say?" Joe impatiently prodded her.

"Apparently, Alan drove to our hometown of Lynwood, right after he'd left your place. My brother, Terry, who still lives there, was just leaving the high school when he saw Alan standing alone in the parking lot?"

"Why was your brother at the school in the first place?" Joe asked her curiously.

"He was playing handball, like he does on most days," she replied. "He has *always* been a stickler for staying in shape and looking his best."

Joe Davis nodded.

"Anyway," Mary continued, "my brother of course, invited Alan to stay the night."

"Go on!" Joe urged excitedly.

"Alan accepted his invitation, and Terry says they spent the entire evening just chatting about high school? The strangest part though," she added, "was when Alan asked him, 'how his *arm* was doing?"'

"What's *wrong* with his arm?" Joe asked.

"Nothing *now*," Mary began. "But on January 14th, 1971, Terry had his arm *broken* while in a fight with Jeff Carter."

Joe quickly pulled out the paper with Alan's dream written on it and began to read it once again. With this unexpected wealth of insight, he hoped it might somehow create a '*eureka experience*' for them. They could certainly use one! "'*Fear struck me to the core as the dragon downed my dear comrade.*' How did Alan know so much about this incident?" Joe asked.

"Because *he* was there! It was about four o'clock, right after Terry was done with baseball practice and Alan and I were sitting nearby talking. Suddenly, Alan noticed Terry and Jeff arguing in front of the student store and he raced over there," she recalled excitedly.

"Wait a minute," Joe uttered in surprise. "*You* were there too?"

"Yes, I watched most of it from about one hundred feet away," she explained.

Joe continued reading, '"*He had fought with honor, but proved to be no match for this all-consuming fiery fiend from hell.*"'

"Yes!" Joe shouted. "This part is *obviously* about the aftermath of the fight between Terry and Jeff!"

He continued on, "*A heavenly damsel ran up to help him, only to be mercilessly taunted by the dragon for her kind intentions.*" Joe appeared to be a little puzzled? "Who was this '*heavenly damsel*?'"

"I'm not really sure? I wasn't paying much attention to who all may have been there, aside from Alan and my brother. I was actually running down to help just as soon as Terry hit the ground!" Mary recalled anxiously. "But I do remember that there *was* a girl who ran to help him when he first fell and broke his arm. She may have been talking with Jeff too?"

"Could that girl have possibly been *Dora Leoni*?" Joe hypothesized excitedly.

"I suppose it *could* have been?" Mary agreed hesitantly.

"Great! We'll stop by her house in Lynwood to find out for sure!" Joe declared.

Joe continued reading, "*And off in the distance was a lady so pure and fair, that simple words cannot describe.*"

"Oh my God! He must be talking about *me*?" Mary shouted in alarm, as she inadvertently swerved the car.

"How do you know that?" Joe asked in surprise and anticipation.

"Because that was the day that Alan asked me out for the *very first time*," she shared. "I will *never* forget that day!" she insisted. "He had told me that morning how much he liked me! And then later that same day, Jeff broke Terry's arm… and no one did a *thing* to stop him!" she added icily.

"By '*no one*,' do you mean *Alan*?" Joe prodded intuitively.

"I guess I do," she admitted. "But I was more concerned about Terry during and after that fight. I drew *that* conclusion much later."

"But obviously your relationship with Alan survived," Joe surmised.

Mary was silent. "It did," she began slowly. "I didn't blame him *directly* for not helping Terry. But in those days, he was like an older brother to him. They were *best friends*! I guess I always wondered *why* he hadn't stepped up to protect him? He just stood there?"

"I'm sure he had his reasons, Mary," Joe offered. "Besides, *you* were a hundred feet away. Are you *sure* you know exactly what happened?"

"Well, I couldn't actually *hear* them, but I thought I figured everything out pretty well by watching," she shared.

"By watching *without* hearing?" Joe exclaimed in shock. "Then aside from what you *think* you saw, you can't possibly know for sure *what happened*, can you?"

"No. When you put it that way, I guess I can't," Mary agreed uncomfortably. Then suddenly growing panicky she shared, "You don't suppose that my jumping to conclusions about this had anything to do with Alan's preoccupation with it, do you? I mean, I never *really* told him how I felt about it?"

"But Alan is very perceptive," Joe reminded her.

"Then *you* believe that what I thought about his lack of action bothered him this much?" Mary asked incredulously.

Joe continued to read aloud, "'*She silently watched... as I turned to stone by the dragon's breath.*'" Joe looked at her intently after reading that final line and gently replied, "Is there really any *other* viable conclusion to come to?"

"Then this was all *my* fault!" Mary cried out in shock.

"No, it wasn't!" Joe quickly corrected her. "This is something that Alan has had hidden away in his subconscious for years now, until the experiment apparently *released* all of those terrible feelings all at once."

"Do you think he's even aware of why he's so miserable then?" Mary asked.

"Deep down, perhaps," Joe surmised. "I strongly believe that his subconscious mind, through trying to help is determinedly telling him to go back to 1971 to *fix something* at all costs! Hence, his compulsion."

Mary didn't comment. She felt terrible. But she also realized that keeping Alan alive was far more important than crying at the moment… so she didn't.

"Did Terry share anything else with you?" Joe asked.

"Just that Alan wanted to hang-out at Lynwood High School all day today," she recalled. "He told Terry that he really missed it."

"What time did he leave Terry's house?" Joe quizzed her.

"I think he had just left when I called," she said.

"And just one more question. Do you have Dora's address?" Joe asked.

"Yes, I do. I copied it out of Alan's yearbook... *don't ask*!" she almost smiled.

"Okay," Joe nodded understandingly. "*Dora* will be our first stop in Lynwood!"

Although *he* obviously felt hopeful, Mary only felt anxious. To her, they couldn't get to Lynwood *soon enough*!

When they arrived, just as she had said, Mary had *no* problem finding Dora's house. She and Joe immediately jumped out of the car and quickly raced toward the front door. Mary rang the doorbell and Dora soon answered it, showing very *obvious* surprise?

"Hi, Dora," Mary said politely. "We're very sorry for intruding like this. I'm Mary Dunkirk, Alan's wife, and this is our friend, Joe Davis. Would you mind if we came in and talked with you a bit?"

"I guess not," Dora replied with a bewildered expression on her face. The three moved swiftly to the living room and sat down.

"Is Jeff here?" Mary asked on impulse. "We would love to speak with him too."

"Sorry. He took the girls to the movie theatre about half an hour ago," Dora shared hesitantly. "What's this all about?"

"Oh, it's nothing serious," Mary assured her with a smile. "It's about *Alan*."

"Oh yeah?" Dora laughed. "As you probably know, he was just here yesterday. He wanted to ask Jeff and me some questions too, but our conversation never really got past the small talk and catching-up? I'm afraid that was probably my fault. I acted *pretty goofy*," she confessed with a laugh. "I probably *terrified* him!" Quickly growing more serious, she added, "To be honest, I really have *no idea* what it was he drove all this way to ask us?"

"He probably wanted to ask you about the *fight* that your husband had with Mary's brother, Terry, on January 14th, 1971, at Lynwood High School," Joe efficiently bypassed the small talk.

"*God*!" Dora exclaimed with absolute shock in her voice and a facial expression to match. "That was thirteen years and *two kids* ago!"

"I know it happened while we were all still in high school," Mary pressed her, "but do you remember anything at all about that fight? Were you there? I have a bet with Alan."

"Oh, this is for *wifely superiority* eh? I'm all for that!" she laughed. "Yes, I was there alright!" she confirmed. "Jeff and I were supposed to meet in front of the student store after cheerleading practice. I got there and the first thing I saw and heard was the beginning of a *fight*! I couldn't believe it! Terry and Jeff were starting to really go at it!"

"Who started the fight?" Mary probed.

"I wasn't too sure at the time," Dora admitted, "but Jeff told me later that it was Terry picking a fight with him."

"Why on Earth would he do that?" Mary demanded.

"Because… he thought that Jeff was *stealing me away* from him," Dora confessed uncomfortably. "Terry had already asked me to go steady that morning, but I had turned him down… *for Jeff*."

"Would you read this story please?" Joe asked Dora while handing her the paper. "We think it's a highly symbolic version of Alan's account of the events that happened that afternoon."

"Where did you get this?" Dora asked curiously.

"It was a dream that Alan had the other night that he thought was important enough to write down," Mary explained.

Dora nodded, accepted the paper and promptly began to peruse it. The next thing she did was to laugh with abandon. "Alan always was a creative sort, eh? Dreaming that this fight was a poem about a battle with a *dragon*?"

"Do you understand who each character in his poem represents?" Joe asked.

"I'm just beginning to," Dora replied playfully. "Oops! I'm afraid that Alan got part of his facts wrong."

"How could he have?" Mary questioned. "He watched the whole fight from no more than ten feet away?"

"Yes, but I watched it from even *closer*!" Dora insisted. "I don't doubt any of his personal feelings, but *factually*, from the viewpoint of 'the heavenly damsel,' whom I assume that I am," she smiled, "although I *did* run up to help Terry after the fight was over, the dragon, who I assume is Jeff, *never* yelled at me! As a matter of fact, I yelled at *him* to call for help! If it hadn't happened that way, I promise you that our marriage would *never* have even come close to happening!"

Joe laughed. "Are there any other discrepancies in Alan's story?"

Looking over the paper one last time, Dora suddenly noticed something else. "Aha!" she announced. "Assuming once again that Jeff is the dragon, Alan *did not* turn to stone because he was afraid of him as he describes at the end of this story. During this entire fight, at least the part that I saw of it, Alan and Jeff *never* made eye contact or spoke to each other even once! Alan just kept talking to Terry, trying to get him to stop."

"So, how *exactly* did Terry break his arm?" Mary asked curiously.

"I'm not entirely sure? But I would guess that after Jeff pushed him back, Terry must have fallen on his arm and broken it."

"So, you think it was an accident?" Mary suggested with relief.

"Oh definitely!" she replied. Suddenly changing her expression to a very *impish* one, she added, "Or I suppose you could blame *me* for that fight, for having too much *sex appeal* for those two to handle!" she laughed loudly.

Both Mary and Joe laughed too, before they thanked her and departed. They saw no reason to share their *real purpose* for coming to see her today. As far as Dora was concerned, they were just double-checking Alan's story to prove him *wrong* in a simple family bet. *If only*!

"We've got one more stop to make before we go to the school, Professor," Mary announced as they left Dora's house.

"Am I right in assuming that this stop will be to see *your brother*?" Davis asked slyly.

"You *are* correct," she confirmed.

When they arrived at Terry's apartment complex, they got out of the car and couldn't help but admire the *beautiful building* that it was housed in. It was very obviously built for the wealthy and more sophisticated residents of Lynwood, which as a successful banker, Terry *certainly* qualified. Upon entering the building, after first marveling at the breathtaking art deco style of decor throughout the lobby, which clearly said *luxury*, they took the elevator up to the top floor where Terry rented the largest apartment in the building… taking up the *entire* seventh floor! In a city that was larger than Lynwood, his apartment would definitely have been considered the *Penthouse*. As they traveled upward, each of them in their own way considered how much they had already learned by speaking with Dora. But they also felt an intense burst of *anticipation* at how much *more* enlightenment they would undoubtedly gain from talking with Terry, in guiding them closer to the truth! Unfortunately, they couldn't help but also feel very scared and concerned for Alan. They had absolutely *no idea* how long he had been on his current mind journey *or* if he had even been able to make it happen? But knowing Alan as well as he did, Joe believed that he *had* been successful, and was on his mind journey at that very moment! That being said, he was determined to find him *before* he chose to fall asleep during his journey. That was because just as he'd warned Alan, if he *did* fall asleep while still in his dream state, there was absolutely no telling *where* he'd wake-up? Or *if* he'd wake-up at all?

Mary aggressively knocked on the front door of Terry's apartment and after a short moment, he answered.

"May we come in?" Mary asked abruptly. "We need to speak with you!"

"Uh-oh!" Terry laughed charmingly, as he ushered them inside. "What have I done *this* time?"

Terry, Mary's younger brother by one year, had an athletic body and like his sister, was blessed with *stunningly* good looks! He was the type of guy seen in movies that *every girl* dreamed of marrying. He was six feet tall, with brooding brown eyes and a dark, thick mane of hair which was perfectly combed. He was also spontaneous and energetic, but for some odd reason he had decided to become a *banker*? But apparently, this had been a *very good* career choice for him because as mentioned, he was a *very successful* one! He lived alone in this beautiful apartment, but that didn't stop him from also being the most *eligible bachelor* in the building! Everyone sat down in the well-appointed sitting room; Mary and Joe on the couch and Terry in a chair facing them. The room was strikingly decorated *all in white*, including the walls, ceiling, furniture, lamps, carpet and curtains. Joe smiled as he imagined for a brief moment that after he died, he could see himself sitting in a pure white waiting room just like this one, *waiting to see the boss*!

After Joe and Terry were introduced to each other by Mary, she began an extremely urgent interview with her brother. "Okay, Terry," she said, taking charge of the conversation. "What *really* happened on January 14th, 1971? You know, when you and Jeff Carter were fighting and you wound up breaking your arm?"

Terry laughed. "Are you serious? That's *ancient* history! It's water under the bridge."

"You would think so," Mary replied, "but I realize now that you never fully explained what happened? I just assumed that I understood everything. Alan *needs you* to tell us the truth!"

"What about Alan?" Terry asked with sudden concern manifesting in his voice.

At that point, Joe and Mary brought him completely up to speed. Then Joe read Alan's dream to him. Terry exhaustedly drooped forward, placing his head in his hands at the conclusion of being exposed to that *avalanche* of information. He sighed deeply.

"Well?" Mary impatiently prompted him.

"Alan's and Dora's stories don't really sound much different from whatever I can remember?" he confessed slowly. "Dora *did* turn me down when I asked her to go steady," he admitted, "and I was pretty angry, especially when I discovered that I had lost out to *Jeff Carter*!"

"I can see why he appealed to her," Mary explained. "After all, he *was* one of the stars of our football and wrestling teams."

"*Big deal*!" Terry shouted. "I was on the baseball team!"

"But Dora *chose* Jeff," Mary continued stubbornly. "Why couldn't you just accept that?"

"Because I *hated* to lose!" Terry replied emotionally. "So, after baseball practice, I saw him out in front of the student store and told him just what I thought about him stealing my girl."

"Who shoved who first?" Mary asked.

"Aren't you really asking me, '*Who started the fight*?'" Terry corrected her very intuitively, but suspiciously.

"Yes. Okay," Mary quickly agreed. "So, who *did* start the fight?"

Terry paused for a long moment and then replied with a noticeable lack of any emotion, "I really *can't* remember?"

Although Mary believed that he was *hiding* something, she continued, "Dora thought that the two of you were intensely going at it? Was she right?"

"Probably," Terry conjectured passively. "Who knows?"

"*Who knows*?" Mary replied skeptically. "You *broke* your arm in a fight, Terry! Can't you clearly remember *anything* about that day?"

"No. I suppose I can't," Terry quickly agreed, showing some slight irritation. "Like I said before, sis, this is *ancient* history."

Mary grew emotional, as she said, "Maybe for *you*, but we still don't know what happened to Alan that day that was so traumatic and devastating that *thirteen years later* it drove him to go back and try to change it!"

"Some truths are just *meant* to be forgotten," Terry replied flippantly. "Anyway, this all happened a very long time ago when we were just kids, so *who cares*?" he didn't even attempt to hide his annoyance as he raised his voice and said, "Can't you see? None of this, *matters* anymore?"

"It *does* to Alan!" Mary yelled back, thoroughly disgusted by his lack of cooperation. "Did he try to stop the fight?" she demanded. "Dora seems to think that he did."

Terry hesitated for a moment, before finally declaring tersely, "I *can't* remember, okay? But think about it, Mary. Does that *honestly* sound like *mild-mannered Alan* to you?" he said very sarcastically. "C'mon!"

Mary didn't comment, but she was steaming.

"Okay, Terry. Thanks for helping us out," Joe interjected, effectively breaking the awkward moment of silence. "We hate to leave so abruptly, but it's high time we went to find Alan at Lynwood High School. We haven't a moment to lose!"

"Why don't you come along with us?" Mary begrudgingly invited her brother, without smiling. "You *do* want to help us find Alan, don't you?"

"Of course, I do!" Terry replied with a newfound positiveness. "I wouldn't miss helping Alan for the world!"

"Okay," Joe proclaimed. "Are we done chitchatting? Good. Now, let's get our keisters out of here!"

As they headed down the elevator, Joe did *not* feel at all satisfied. Oh, it was true that some of the smaller pieces of the puzzle were just beginning to fit together… but the *biggest* piece was still missing? What happened on January 14th, 1971, that had left Alan, even after all of these years, feeling so *desperately* driven to return?

Alan smiled as he found himself in the special hideout he had frequented during all of his years of high school, *completely* hidden from view. This was the spot where he had found solace after the school day had ended whenever he needed it, and *this* was certainly *one* of those times! He had just completed reading everything in Joe Davis' red notebook… *again*… and now he felt completely up-to-date. In fact, he believed that he was as ready as he'd ever be to send himself off on a mind journey! Understandably, he was a little nervous about it though, especially not having Joe's brilliant mind to supervise the trip, but he was determined, even *compelled* to try it anyway! He thought hard about everything that had happened to him over these past few days, especially his meeting with Dora and Jeff Carter. Puzzled, he realized that although he should be feeling better after that meeting, in reality, he felt even *more* confused? He was now convinced more than ever that the *only way* he would ever get to the truth behind what he had done and what he had to change, was by going back to his past once again… to *January 14th, 1971*. The answer *had* to be there!

He determinedly opened the bottle of pink pills and swallowed a small handful of them, *definitely* more than the two he had taken the last time. He was well aware of the possible dangers of overdosing, but he was *willing* to take that risk in order to make certain that he saw this quest *all the way through* to the end! He knew that he would not know peace again until he did! Next, he closed his eyes and began to chant, just as Joe Davis had done the last time, "*Lynwood High School, January 14th, 1971*," over and over again. True, there was no guarantee that this *do-it-yourself* method would work, but he had nearly memorized all of the notes in Joe's red book, so he strongly believed… that it *would*! It just *had to*! Soon, he felt himself gently drifting off.

Mary, Joe and Terry arrived at Lynwood High School about four o'clock in the afternoon. There was no school in session, the buildings were all locked-up tight, but fortunately, the gate connected to the chain-link fence that surrounded the school was *still* unlocked and open. Mary recalled that while she had attended here, the school was *never* locked before 10:00 p.m., and sometimes even 11:00? That, of course, was *great* news for them!

"Hey look! Over there!" Mary excitedly pointed at one of the few cars in the main school parking lot they were entering. It was Alan's silver Mustang convertible.

"Thank goodness!" Joe exclaimed. "Now we just need to find him."

Mary parked her beige Camry next to the Mustang, and the three of them immediately disembarked.

"Here's the plan," Mary immediately took charge. "Terry, you and I will split-up and look for Alan on campus, because we know this school forward and backward." Turning to Joe, she added, "You should probably wait here, just in case Alan returns before we find him, okay?"

Joe appeared to be a little disappointed by his seemingly *menial* role in Mary's masterplan, but he readily agreed. He knew that the job he had been assigned certainly made sense, given that he had *never* even set foot on this campus before, while Mary and her brother had spent four years as students here. So, as Mary and Terry set off to scour different parts of the campus, Joe sat in the car trying very hard to think like Alan would have thought when he had first arrived here today. But the Lynwood High School campus was large, and he soon realized that the possibilities for where Alan could be hiding seemed *endless*, and just too diverse? What he really needed now was a good, old-fashioned *epiphany*!

Just as soon as Alan became coherent, he breathed a great big sigh of relief to find himself back at Lynwood High School, in what certainly *appeared* to be 1971. Success! He was once again in his first period P.E. class, but *wait a second*? Something was very different from last time? He shockingly observed that instead of his class taking place *outdoors* on the volleyball courts as it had on his last journey, everyone was *inside* the gymnasium taking a written test on 'how to play the game correctly?' He looked around at everyone else who was taking the test and on their papers under *date*, they were writing, 'January ***13***, 1971!' Alan felt like *screaming*! But he didn't. He remembered how Joe had repeatedly coached him, essentially telling him, '*Every change you make will probably create a ripple effect of changes as long as you are there. But if you are very careful to let things play out exactly as they originally happened... then nothing is likely to divert from the truth.*'

He grimaced as he remembered what mayhem had resulted on his *first* journey, which he had foolishly opted to spontaneously change. So, in order to avoid that same disastrous fate, he resolved to let his subconscious memory *dictate* every one of his actions today! That would hopefully mean that tomorrow would *not* be altered in any way. His search for the truth *depended* on it! He would deal with successfully getting to tomorrow... later.

It wasn't at all difficult keeping things the same as they had originally happened thirteen years before. As planned, he simply *didn't* make any new decisions. He talked to people, answered questions, laughed at jokes and occasionally even felt embarrassed... but he *never* thought about it. Curiously, he felt as though his very existence while in high school had demonstrated a combination of autopilot and *immaturity*. He really had no idea that he had been so *juvenile-acting* back in those days? He actually remembered himself being a pretty smart and mature guy, much like he saw himself as an *adult*? He inadvertently smiled as he realized that his *real* adult life's history would certainly *disprove* that glowing description of himself! In truth, he probably had *not* changed much at all! Wasn't that one of the things that Mary said she *loved* about him? He thought about her fondly for a moment, but then quickly returned to his '*present time*.'

As far as he knew, up to this point he had *not* changed a thing, and in addition he was paying very close attention to everything that was going on around him. His hope was that this might lead him to some clues as to what it was that he needed so badly to change? The first event that he found to be odd, happened during this P.E. class. First, once they had both finished taking their tests, Dora was talking and laughing with Jeff Carter. Next, he curiously spied Terry giving Jeff the *evil eye*? If this was some teenage act of petty jealousy, the funny thing was that Alan could not remember Terry *ever* having a thing for Dora Leoni? He must have *forgotten* that since his eyes had obviously witnessed this exact scene some 13 years earlier? In any case, simply being *reminded* of this event greatly bothered him for the rest of the day?

When school ended, he met up with Terry on a bench outside the student store. Here, they were destined to have a very telling conversation that he had also completely forgotten about?

"Do you think Mary likes me?" Alan asked Terry, nervously.

"Who, *my sister*?" Terry replied, taken a bit off-guard. "She always says nice things about you whenever you come up."

"Oh," Alan responded hopefully. "Well, *how often* do I come up?" he tried not to sound too anxious.

"*Whenever* you come up," Terry laughed.

"I think I'll ask her out tomorrow," Alan shared excitedly.

"Really?" Terry replied oddly.

"Yeah. Why?" Alan asked curiously.

"Because I was going to ask Dora Leoni to *go steady* with me tomorrow too."

"Wow!" Alan honestly sounded surprised. "That's an awfully big step from just being *casual friends*, don't you think?"

Terry laughed. "You don't know how she looks at me whenever I glance her way!"

"She's a *cheerleader*, Terry! That's what cheerleaders *do*!" Alan humorously chided him.

"Well, I think it's great that tomorrow we'll *both* have girlfriends," Terry beamed.

"Now wait a second, Terry," Alan backtracked a bit, "I'm just going to *ask* Mary out."

"That's where it *always begins*, my friend," Terry laughed. "Your days as a carefree bachelor are definitely numbered!"

Alan laughed, and then becoming more serious, he asked, "Have you and Dora actually ever spent time together?"

"We *shared* a bench seat on the bus during the ride home from a couple of my away-games last year," Terry replied proudly. "We also *worked together* in a small group on a science project."

"Well then I'll bet she's *definitely* ready to go steady with you!" Alan replied with humorous sarcasm.

"Don't *mock me*, knave!" Terry playfully said with reproach. "The worst thing she could do is say, no, and I *certainly* think I could handle that!"

Alan smiled while nodding his acknowledgement as the two friends got up from the bench and began walking home together, animatedly conversing the whole time. Their talk finally ended when they predictably reached a fork in the road, and parted ways as they each continued on in opposite directions toward their homes, but only after Alan had wished Terry, *luck* tomorrow! When Alan arrived at his house, he was tired. So, after doing his homework and eating dinner with his family, he went straight upstairs to his room, played some music on his stereo for a while and then got ready for bed. As he tried to sleep, he suddenly remembered about tomorrow. He had been *perfect* today. Perhaps even *better* than perfect by not changing a thing! This meant of course, that tomorrow *should* playout in an historically accurate manner. The critical question *was*; would young Alan *be there* to experience it, or would older Alan completely miss it by waking-up to his adult life? There was really no way he knew of controlling his fate. All he could do was concentrate very hard on 'Lynwood

High School, January 14th, 1971,' and *hopefully* that was exactly where he would find himself in the morning!

Mary was investigating all of the spots that she and Alan had hung-out in while they had been students here; beside a tree, on a bench in front of the choir room (*where they both had a lot of friends*) and of course, at the tables outside of the cafeteria where absolutely *everybody* hung-out! Regardless of the disappointing fact that there was *no* sign of Alan, these locations succeeded in bringing back a lot of happy memories. She laughed out loud without meaning to. Alan was definitely her soulmate, even if he sometimes did appear to act '*strangely*?' Regardless, she really *did* understand him after so many years together. He didn't just *think* outside of the box, he *lived* there! Now the million-dollar-question; where would he have gone to evade notice? Every place that she had checked so far was out in the open where *anyone* could find him, even if they *weren't* looking for him? So, with all of the buildings closed-up for summer, where could he be?

Meanwhile, Terry was checking the special places where he and Alan used to hang-out together, although honestly, he could only think of *one*. Since Terry had been a school athlete while Alan had *not even been close*, after his baseball practice, they had often met in front of the student store which was located in front of the gymnasium. This was near the locker room for Terry, while easy to get to for Alan since it was located at the center of the school. Terry puzzled over the possibility that he might be forgetting a *second* place that Alan had briefly mentioned to him as kids, although he had personally *never* actually been there? But, he soon stopped thinking about that and sat down on a bench to consider if there was anything else he might be missing? The surprising thought that immediately popped into his head was the very *disturbing* question of *why* their friendship had seriously drifted apart ever since Alan had begun dating his sister Mary? In fact, when Alan and he had met, entirely by chance yesterday, it had marked the *first time* they'd been together, face to face, in *years*? Oh, they usually shared Christmas and birthday phone calls, but whatever happened to that great friendship they had shared throughout their youth? For years they had been inseparable… and suddenly… they *weren't*?

Being a bright person who loved solving riddles, sitting in the car while Mary and Terry walked around looking for Alan, felt like nothing short of *a waste of time* for Joe Davis. For a desperately needed change, he had recently gotten out of the car to check on Mary and her brother, to disappointingly find them both *sitting*? Apparently, they were contemplating their next moves, having thus far found *absolutely nothing*! So, he returned to Mary's car, sighted Alan's Mustang still parked there beside it (*assuring him that he had not returned*), and decided that he would somehow *make himself useful*. From his vantage point in the front seat of Mary's car, he could really only see the school's administration building, some tall oak trees and the front gate. His mind nevertheless, took that meager amount of information and began to formulate any seemingly *likely* possibilities of where Alan might be hiding? He speculated that he may have broken into a locked room somewhere on campus, or he could be sitting against the fence in a dark corner of an athletic field, or he might even be up in a tree somewhere, where absolutely *nobody* could see him? It was then that he decided to *seriously* begin his quest for solving the mystery of where Alan was most likely hiding, by carefully *analyzing* everything in front of him. In this case, it was the administration building. But he also looked *beyond* that. And then like a bolt of lightning had suddenly illuminated his mind, he found himself thinking *like a teenage boy*!

As Alan slept, he experienced some *very odd dreams*? Dreams that involved his future perhaps? In these dreams he was a grown man with a beautiful wife who looked *a lot* like Mary? When he woke-up, he was lying in his *own bed*… in 1971! *Unfortunately*, he no longer had the advantage of *two* minds. Unlike yesterday, today his sole reality was completely embedded in the youthful mind of a seventeen-year-old boy experiencing his senior year of high school! Today was January 14th, and he was *very* excited! This was the day when he would *attempt* to convince Mary to go out with him on a date! He and Terry had already discussed this. They were going to meet in front of the student store at four o'clock to *hopefully* celebrate their new lives with girlfriends! Alan had decided that he would pop the important question to Mary just as soon as he saw her. He was very anxious, and for the sake of his nerves, he wanted to get it done *quickly*. Terry, on the other hand, preferred to make his special moment with Dora, more public… and much more *dramatic*! He decided to ask her right after school ended, while plenty of other people were still around to witness the *frontpage event* unfold. Alan got dressed, ate breakfast, and was off before he knew it.

School for him, as usual, started with P.E. class. Before long, the teams had been chosen and everyone was outside on the courts playing volleyball. Suddenly, Jeff Carter set-up a perfect ball for Terry to spike, but instead of spiking it, Terry allowed the ball to bounce off his head and go out of bounds, *glaring* at Carter the whole time?

"Shit! What the hell are you doing, Williams?" Jeff Carter asked humorously. "I set-up a homerun for you, baseball boy!"

A few guys sniggered, but the game went on and the incident was soon forgotten.

Long after the shower bell had rung, after everyone had dressed and were impatiently waiting outside for the passing bell to ring, Alan pulled a *seething* Terry aside. "Hey, what's going on?"

"I asked Dora to go steady with me first thing this morning," he shared angrily.

"I thought you were going to wait until *after* school?" Alan replied in surprise.

"I was too excited to wait that long," Terry confessed. "Anyway, she *turned me down*!"

Alan could only imagine how badly Terry must be feeling. He had *never* personally asked anyone to go steady, but he instinctively knew that Terry had to be feeling completely *devastated*! So, he was very careful in what he said next.

"I'm sorry. It's her loss!"

"You would think," Terry began angrily *seething* again, "but she chose *Jeff Carter* over me? Can you believe that?"

Alan was initially stunned by that revelation. Jeff Carter and Dora Leoni? But on the other hand, they were both popular seniors on campus? Perhaps they had more things in common than met the eye? He left it at that. "I'm sorry, Terry," he repeated.

Suddenly, Terry turned toward Alan like a crazy man and maniacally insisted, "Don't you *dare* ever discuss my getting rejected by Dora with anyone!"

"Okay," Alan quickly agreed, a little shaken by his aggressive manner.

"And another thing," Terry shared emotionally. "I'm going to *fight* Jeff Carter after practice today at four o'clock! Don't go telling *my sister* or anyone else about it! You can watch, but no matter how it's going, you let the fight *finish*. Got it?"

Alan had *no idea* how to react? This was *not* the Terry Williams he had known for most of his high school life? One part of him wanted to tell him what an *idiot* he was being, while another part… just felt *sorry* for him. Due to being best friends, the *latter* part won out. "Got it," Alan promised, less than enthusiastically.

Suddenly Terry relaxed. "Okay, buddy. This will be *our* little secret until we *die*."

The bell rang, and a very *conflicted* Alan Dunkirk dragged himself off toward his English class. As he reached his destination, he immediately felt a whole lot better just as soon as he caught sight of the very pretty, *Mary Williams*.

"Hi, Alan," she smiled warmly at him. Mary was a tall and good-looking brunette with *beautiful* blue eyes. She was dressed in a cute red skirt and white blouse which perfectly matched her bright personality.

"Hi, Mary," Alan replied shyly. "Um… would you like to go out with me on Saturday night? There's a great movie playing downtown, I hear?"

Mary's face turned instantly aglow! "Sure, Alan. That sounds like fun."

"There is just *one small problem* though. I don't have my license yet," he awkwardly explained, with a sizeable degree of embarrassment.

"No big deal." Mary smiled kindly. "I'll just pick *you* up then!"

They both laughed, and Alan felt the urge to *hug* her. Fortunately, she was feeling the same way. When they parted, both kids were all smiles. In fact, Alan was completely *obsessed* with thinking only about Mary for as long as he could.

"Any luck?" Joe asked Mary and Terry, after yelling for them to meet him in front of the gymnasium.

"No," Mary confessed disappointedly.

"Not yet," Terry added, "but I do seem to recall Alan mentioning *another place* where he'd hang out alone? I just can't seem to remember *specifically* where it was? Maybe he never actually told me?"

"Can you think of anything at all *about it*?" Mary asked anxiously.

Terry paused a long moment in thought. "Well, I think I remember him telling me that this place was like a treehouse, where he could *see* all over the school if he wanted to, without anyone else *ever* seeing him?"

"Could this treehouse actually be a *rooftop*?" Joe confidently suggested.

Terry gasped. "Why didn't I think of that?" he exclaimed excitedly.

"A treehouse has a *ladder* leading up to it," Joe surmised. "Are there any rooftops on this campus that have an exceptionally good view of the school, as well as *outside* ladder access?"

The three of them immediately focused on the roof of the gymnasium, now directly in front of them.

"I'll bet there is a view of this whole campus from up there," Mary suggested enthusiastically. "And I'm also quite sure that workmen need *outdoor* ladder access to reach the roof when the school is closed!"

"My thoughts exactly!" Terry exclaimed.

"Okay, you two," Joe quickly instructed. "Start tearing the outside of this building apart to *find* that ladder!" He paused and then added tensely, "I would guess that Alan could likely be on his *third* hour by now."

"How long do the pills last?" Mary asked with concern.

"I really don't know for *certain*, Mary," Joe confessed. "But if I'm right, Alan has already been on this mind journey more than *twice as long* as he was the last time!"

"Do you still believe that he took more pills this time than last?" Mary implored him.

"*Definitely*!" Davis shared somberly. "I would guess that he is prepared to stay up there for as long as it takes!"

"For as long as *what* takes?" Mary repeated, confused.

"For as long as it takes for him to make things *right* for himself," Joe replied with empathy.

"How many pills are *too* many?" Mary couldn't hide her fear.

"That's impossible for me to say," Davis admitted. "We only used two last time, and he was asleep for one hour, our time, or twelve hours, dream time. Although, I have a sneaky suspicion that if he hadn't been scared on that journey, he probably could have stayed there at least *twice* that long!"

"Yes, but in *your opinion*, how many pills are too many?" Mary repeated urgently.

After considering her question, Davis replied calmly, "Well, Mary, if he felt that he needed to stay there longer this time in order to sort out this problem of his, and he decided to take a couple of additional pills, it probably means his brain will be working twice as hard as last time, which might still be okay. But if he took *more* than that," he paused, "then I guess it just comes down to how many pills his brain can *tolerate* at one time. Unfortunately, I'm as much in the dark about that as you are."

"Do you think he'll be okay?" Mary pleaded.

But before Joe Davis had the chance to deliver a response, Mary quickly turned away, effectively retracting her question. She realized that no amount of speculation could help Alan now. *Hope* was all they had! She quickly ran off in search of the all-important ladder.

Being at school today oddly alternated between going very fast and *painfully* slow. It depended upon whether Alan was thinking about his upcoming date with Mary, or the fact that Terry was planning on fighting Jeff Carter after school! He had promised Terry not to tell anyone about it, and worse… not to *interfere* no matter what happened! He wasn't a snitch when it came to dumb things like when a friend lied to keep from getting in trouble, but *this*? In no universe was Terry or any other student at this school *ever* going to beat Jeff Carter in a fight! Alan knew that if Terry got hurt as a result, it would be entirely *his* fault for not stopping it! But he had given his word that he would not interfere? If he broke it, he realized that his friendship with Terry would come crashing down to a quick and permanent end! This created an impossible quandary?

Alan decided to wait around at school until 4:00 0'clock to watch the fight. He wasn't absolutely sure that he could keep his promises to Terry if things got too out of hand, but for the sake of their friendship, he was *determined* to try. He slowly walked over to a bench sitting atop a small hill directly facing the gymnasium and sat down. He was as miserable as he had ever been. Time continued to drag on until sometime later, Mary noticed him, he noticed her, and the next thing you know they were sitting on the bench *together* immersed in friendly conversation.

Although Alan was very obviously pleased to see her, he wondered what she was doing at school an *hour* after it was over? "Hey, Mary, why are you at school so late today?" he asked, as cheerfully as he could muster.

"I was taking a make-up test in Trig," she replied. "What's *your* excuse?"

"I'm working on an assignment for Art class," he lied. "Mr. Bates told us to study a building in detail for at least an hour and tell the class about it tomorrow."

Mary smiled. "That sounds like an easy way to improve your observation skills and attention to detail, I guess? What have you noticed about the gym so far?"

Their conversation went on for about half an hour, but neither of them was complaining. It seemed the more they talked together… the more *fun* it became. Regardless, feeling a little guilty, Alan decided to steer the conversation to a topic that was *not* a lie.

"How is Terry doing on the varsity baseball team?" Alan began. "He hasn't talked much about that lately?"

"That's probably because he doesn't want to *jinx* his chances," Mary said quietly.

"Jinx his chances for *what*?" Alan asked uneasily.

"He's up to be the team's number one starting pitcher!" she bragged. "But don't tell anyone just yet. The coach won't be announcing his final decision until tomorrow." Suddenly looking around, making sure that she was not being overheard and then lowering her voice even more, she added with an excited smile, "Terry told me yesterday that the coach secretly told him *he's* the odds-on favorite! Isn't that great news?"

Alan suddenly felt *very sick*! But somehow he managed to hold it together and *not* reveal his extreme discomfort to Mary. What a terrible day for Terry to pick a fight, especially against *Jeff Carter*! His great opportunity to become the star of the Lynwood High School Baseball Team was suddenly becoming *severely* compromised! Hearing shouting, Alan abruptly looked out toward the student store and was immediately struck by the sight he had been dreading; Terry and Jeff were already intently facing each other, *arguing*! Thankfully, he had not yet seen any punches thrown, but nevertheless, he knew that for his friend, short of a miracle, *disaster was imminent*! He quickly excused himself to Mary and ran as quickly as he could toward the student store. By the time he arrived, the verbal attacks from Terry had intensified, but *strangely*, Jeff stayed calm? He appeared to be trying very hard to *diffuse* Terry's anger? Unfortunately, Jeff's cool demeanor seemed to incense Terry all the more! It enraged him so much, in fact, that he became determined to hurry the fight along by *shoving* Jeff in the chest just as hard as he could! But Jeff refused to take the bait. He quietly absorbed Terry's shove and continued his gentle efforts to end the conflict peacefully.

"C'mon Terry! Stop the fight! Carter's not even fighting back? You've made your point!" Alan pleaded.

"Go away, Alan! I'm in this fight to the *very end*!" Terry shot back angrily.

Alan so wanted to stop the fight and bring Terry back to the person he had been *before* all of his romantic plans had gone to *hell*, but his binding promise to him *wouldn't* let him. So, the fight went on like this for several more minutes, with Alan repeatedly urging Terry to stop, but having his heartfelt requests *slammed down* every time! Finally, Terry, who was determined to *hurt* the guy that he believed had stolen his girl and was extremely *impatient* to do it, reached deep down for everything he had and *shoved* Jeff Carter one last time!

In the end, it was Terry who found the ladder. It was an unobtrusive metal one, cleverly painted the same color as the wall it was attached to at the back of the gymnasium building. In addition, the ladder was carefully hidden from everyone's view by different types of foliage planted in front of it, coming up from the ground about six feet. Terry very proudly presented his discovery to Mary and Joe. They both congratulated him before Joe immediately sent Mary up the ladder with a warning *not* to try to wake-up Alan if she found him there. The safest route, he told her, was for him to wake-up naturally. But, if he *didn't* do that… then he assured Mary that there were *safer methods* at his disposal which he'd employ if that need became apparent. After Mary had begun climbing up the ladder, Joe quietly called Terry over to talk with him.

"This little charade of yours is *over*, my friend," Joe said quietly but firmly. "I *know* that you didn't want your sister to know what *actually* happened at that fight you had in high school, so you only told us partial truths or downright *lied* when we asked you some very important questions. However, you've got to tell me the truth now or there is a real chance that I may *not* be able to bring Alan back!"

Terry suddenly grew very nervous and confessed, "Okay, I *never* actually lied about the fight to anyone! Everyone just *believed* what they wanted to believe. They assumed that Jeff Carter had picked on me and was at *fault* for my broken arm."

"But that *wasn't* true, was it," Joe calmly challenged him.

"No, it wasn't," Terry begrudgingly confirmed.

"Dora told us that *you* started the fight," Joe shared. "Was she wrong?"

"No, I started it alright… and I *finished* it too!" Terry professed bitterly. "Carter never pushed me back even once!"

"Now for the *big* question. What did you mean when you told us at your apartment that, '*Some truths are just meant to be forgotten*?'"

Terry choked-up, and then hesitantly began, "I was going to be the starting pitcher for the varsity baseball team, so I thought that I needed to get a cheerleader for my girlfriend. Dora Leoni had always caught my eye, but when she turned me down… I felt *so humiliated*! That experience was something I *never* wanted to be reminded of again! That's what I meant."

Joe nodded understandingly. "Was there any more to that story?"

"Well, yes," Terry admitted begrudgingly. "I got so angry about Dora rejecting me that I decided to *fight* Jeff Carter!" he explained passionately. "I thought that regardless of whether I won or lost, once Dora saw how much she meant to me by watching me fighting for her, I mean… she might *change her mind* about being with Jeff?"

Joe let a tiny smile sadly illuminate his face as he shook his head. "If only life were that simple," he said wistfully.

"Well, it seemed like a good idea at the time," Terry confessed sheepishly.

Growing more determined, Joe asked, "Specifically *what* did Alan do that day that he has become so *obsessed* with changing? Why is he such a wreck?"

"Hell, if I know?" Terry responded belligerently.

"*Think hard*!" Joe demanded sternly.

Terry looked very uneasy as he admitted, "Well, it *might* be that I made him promise me *not* to tell anyone about Dora turning me down. I also made him promise not to interfere with the fight, even if I were losing," he continued.

"What happened after the fight was over?" Joe asked calmly.

Terry grew very passionate. "I *threatened* him, okay! I told him that if he ever told anyone about how this fight had gone down, our friendship would be *over*!" he admitted angrily.

"*Emotional blackmail*?"

"Yes! So what? A guy does what he *has* to do!" Terry shared, with absolutely *no* remorse. "I thought I was going to be a sports star with a cheerleader as my girlfriend!" he explained. "But after I'd broken my arm, it became crystal clear to me that I was left with *nothing*!" Becoming more controlled, he added, "You know how *judgmental* people can be? Right? I couldn't take any chances! The most important thing at that moment was that my *reputation* stayed intact. After all, I was only a Junior at the time." he shared determinedly. "So, I made Alan swear to me that he would *never* talk about any of this to anyone as long as he lived! And it worked! My star was *not* tarnished! After my arm healed and I worked hard at strengthening it over the summer, I went on to have a great senior year as my baseball team's *top pitcher*! It was strangely as if that fight with Jeff Carter had *never* really happened? Absolutely *no* harm done!"

Joe's face suddenly exposed his realization of the shocking truth that had just *ambushed* him! His jaw grew slack, while his eyes went wide as he slowly exclaimed, "*No harm done*? After all of the pain you've caused Alan over the past 13 years as a result of that fight, now you tell me it's as if it *never really happened*, simply because you were *anointed* your team's best pitcher? My God! ***You are the dragon*** in Alan's story… *not* Jeff Carter!" Quickly pulling Alan's story from his back pocket, Joe began to read, "'*Fear struck me to the core as the dragon downed my dear comrade.*' *You* downed yourself, didn't you?" Joe exclaimed! "You *accidentally* broke your own arm and then to hide your embarrassment, you were replaced by a narcissistic bully of your own creation!"

Terry stared at Joe very uncomfortably.

Joe continued reading, "'*He had fought with honor, but proved to be no match for this all-consuming fiery fiend from hell.*'" Joe was beside himself with shock. "Jeff Carter had *nothing* to do with this story, did he? You were *possessed* by this monster, this dragon, and you were the *antagonist* of the entire saga!"

Terry remained uncomfortably silent, so Joe continued reading, "'*A heavenly damsel ran up to help him, only to be mercilessly taunted by the dragon for her kind intentions.*' Jeff *never* yelled at Dora… ***you did***!" Joe accused him.

"Yeah? So, what if *I did*! I was angry and in pain!" he bellowed. Then his eyes grew softer and his voice more controlled as he shared, "But after doing it, I realized that I had *ended* any chance of changing Dora's mind about leaving Jeff!"

"Did you ever apologize to her?" Joe asked.

"No. I guess I thought that would've come across as a sign of weakness," Terry admitted arrogantly. "So, we just *never* spoke again."

Joe shook his head, and continued reading, "'*And off in the distance was a lady so pure and fair, that simple words cannot describe. She silently watched... as I turned to stone by the dragon's breath.*' It was *your* unreasonable demands and coerced promises from Alan that turned him to stone while Mary watched! Your terrible words were the *dragon's breath*!"

"Okay! *Yes*! So what?" Terry admitted defiantly, through a combination of anger and humiliation. "I had *no idea* that Alan would be so messed-up by any of this, all of these years later?"

"The promises you *forced* him to make became a festering sore hidden away in his subconscious for over a decade!" Joe explained forcefully. "To a sensitive person like Alan Dunkirk, the painful memory and guilt of *not* stopping that fight and as a result, *allowing* his best friend to break his arm and miss his chance at becoming the star of his team, *does not* just go away, Terry! Especially when it is sealed by a strong-armed promise to your best friend *to never tell*!" Joe was livid. "Alan was convinced that your broken arm and shattered baseball dreams that happened as a result of that fight were *completely his fault*! So, when his subconscious saw a way to return to the scene of the crime and actually *change* his behavior that it had found so reprehensible, he ran with it!"

"*Big deal*! Don't you get it? Just because Alan changes a 'past behavior' *in his mind*, doesn't change *anything* in his real life!" Terry proclaimed arrogantly. "*Absolutely nothing*! Everybody knows that whatever you did in the past can *never* be changed! You either hide it, or accept it and learn to live with it!" he argued vehemently.

"Well, it's pretty clear to me *which* one of those two options *you took*!" Joe heatedly replied. But then growing momentarily quiet, he gazed sadly at Terry while shaking his head as he shared passionately, "Alan subconsciously *yearned* for this opportunity to make things right, even if it was only in *his* mind. *That's* what I believe he was so driven to do, Terry. You may have been his best friend at some point in your lives, but the two of you are absolutely *nothing* alike!" he continued. "Alan was so concerned about you in 1971 that he agreed to promises that have made him *emotionally sick* ever since! Today, when you have the opportunity of helping him escape that monstrous existence which you are *directly responsible* for, all you do is try to justify everything you did? Trying so hard to keep yourself blameless while continuing to throw Alan *under the bus*!"

"But we were *just kids* then! Don't you see? What if I *did* make him promise me things? Those promises certainly don't apply now!" Terry yelled, completely out of control.

"Not to *you*, perhaps," Joe explained defiantly. "But Alan agreed to keep those promises *forever…* and I'm quite certain that he has!" Growing calmer while locking eyes with Terry, he added, "That's called *integrity*!"

Terry abruptly stopped arguing. He dropped his head and sighed. "Okay. I'm so very sorry," he mumbled humbly. "You're right about *everything*. I always knew it, but I just didn't want anyone to think badly of me."

"*That* was the most important thing to you?" Joe retorted in shock. "Did you even *think* about Alan at all?"

"Yes. But I didn't know how to get our friendship back on track again without bringing Dora and that fight with Jeff up again? So, even though I didn't want to, I guess I thought it best to just move on without him and the rest of that baggage," Terry very hesitantly admitted.

"*Baggage*?" Joe exclaimed. "Why should Alan pay for everything *you* did that you want to forget?"

"*He shouldn't*, I know," Terry nodded in agreement. "I just didn't know what else to do?"

"*You coward*!" Joe declared.

"You're right!" Terry replied with his eyes beginning to moisten. "But I promise you that I *won't* be one any longer! What can I do to help?"

"Well, Terry," Joe said in a kinder voice. "For starters, you can remove those *curses* you called *promises* that your friendship forced Alan to agree to, by talking to him."

"Of course. I would be glad to do that, but what if he's not awake yet?" Terry asked gently.

"Talk to him anyway," Joe insisted gently. "I *guarantee* that he'll hear you."

"I *found* him! He's up here sleeping!" Mary yelled joyously from the rooftop of the gymnasium, completely unaware of the highly emotional conversation that had just transpired… and after tonight, neither Terry or Joe planned on *ever* bringing it up again!

"We'll be right up!" Terry yelled back to her.

Regardless of the fact that Terry had used every ounce of energy in his body and all of the *hate-filled* determination in his mind that he could possibly muster, his shove once again proved ineffective and did not move Jeff Carter *at all*! Just like before, the strong burly boy absorbed the shove fully. Unfortunately, the impact of Terry's vicious shove generated so much backlash, that after making contact with Jeff's chest, it surprisingly pushed him backwards in a very *haphazard* way. As he fell, his foot tripped over his own backpack, which he had set down a few feet behind him just before the fight had started. In slow motion, feeling strangely as if he were experiencing *déjà vu*, Alan watched in horror as Terry helplessly fell back toward his right side. As he put his right hand out to lessen the impact of his inevitable fall, his coordination completely deserted him and he landed very awkwardly on his right arm! As a result, everyone clearly heard the sickening *crack* of his bone! As Terry began screaming with pain, Dora raced over to help him, while Alan watched a very concerned-looking Jeff Carter running toward the payphone to presumably call for help. Turning back toward Dora, Alan couldn't believe his ears when Terry angrily *spurned* her attempts to comfort him? He quickly raced over to Terry's side to try to calm him down, and *that's* when the distraught boy *threatened him*! "If you tell anyone the truth about any of this, I swear I will *lie* to Mary and tell her that this fight was all *your* idea! I'll say that I wanted to back out, but you *wouldn't let me*!" Terry seethed angrily. Alan could not believe what he was hearing? But suddenly… he began hearing *something else*?

He was literally *hearing voices* inside his head? But he *knew* he wasn't crazy? Somehow he *recognized* both of the voices that were speaking to him? First, he heard adult Terry saying, "I'm so sorry, Alan. I didn't mean anything that I told you in anger before and after that fight! You don't need to promise me a thing. *Please* forgive me!" Next, he heard his wife, Mary, saying very sweetly, "Come home, Alan. I *know* everything now! I should have tried much harder to understand what you were going through. *I love you*!"

The next thing he knew, teenage Mary was standing there beside him, smiling… and it was then that he remembered *this* was only a mind journey to his past! He immediately realized who he *really was*, and what year he *actually* lived in! He also remembered *everything* that had happened to him on January 14th, 1971 as clearly as the day he had first experienced it!

Although Alan had known for the past couple of days that he was being drawn back into his past to *change* something very important that he had done, Joe Davis had erroneously believed that the thing he so desperately needed to change was his '*wrong decision*' not to break-up the fight between Terry and Jeff. That fight had of course, led to Terry's broken arm and hence his heartbreaking inability to star on the school's baseball team that year, which Davis knew that Alan completely blamed himself for! But as it turned out, although that incident had indeed weighed *heavily* on Alan's repugnant feelings toward himself… it was actually *not* the main problem? That went far deeper than the fight, and just as Joe had suggested earlier, it dealt with an *intense conflict* between his conscious and subconscious minds? As it turned out, Alan needed to *change* the fact that his conscious mind had not accepted the truth about who the *good* guy and the *bad* guy actually were in that fight? That tenacious refusal to eradicate the *severe* difference of opinion between his two minds, had eventually resulted in a dangerous *mental impasse* that had then disallowed his subconscious mind from ever entering his conscious mind with the truth about that incident! This is called *dissociative amnesia*. That became the mental 'Band-Aid' that allowed him to function 'normally' for the next 13 years of his life, up until the time following his first mind journey, when he began to feel strongly that *something was wrong*? Thankfully, the effects of the amnesia were lifted just as soon as he remembered and was finally able to *accept* the truth. As it turned out, Jeff Carter, for all of his bullying tendencies was in reality a pretty stand-up guy. Now he understood why he had given him a *friendly smile* during his first mind journey. Alan's subconscious mind had simply *tried* to remind him who Jeff Carter really was. On the other hand, Terry the '*golden boy*,' who seemed to have it all, was in reality a terribly immature kid with dashed dreams of grandeur who couldn't bear the thought of anyone ever thinking badly of him. Alan had *unwittingly* and very unhealthily done his part to preserve Terry's flawless image over the past thirteen years. Although he didn't do it consciously, he had kept his promise *not* to tell the truth and talk about his rejection by Dora or the fight to *anyone*, which of course caused his mental condition! In a nutshell, Alan's main problem was his conscious mind's tenacious *refusal* to accept the truth that Terry had *not always* been the great friend he preferred to remember him as being! Terry, had in fact *bullied* him into submission as the dragon! Alan grimaced. He realized that although Terry's actions had severely affected him, his own *regrets* about his lack of self-confidence to stand-up for himself and do the right thing, had also *contributed greatly* to his confused mindset. He smiled. He recognized that just like everybody else, Terry and he were only *human*; prone to periods of immaturity, fear and selfishness… *especially* as adolescents! He knew that he *could* accept that without a problem, and finally call this nightmare once and for all… *over*! He shook his head at the fact that this single memory had caused him so much grief! But at last, he had remembered and accepted the truth, and as they say, *the truth shall set you free*!

"I'm ready to go home now," he gently shared with Mary. "Everything is fine… it's *better* than fine!"

With that, Mary smiled and took his hand, leaving her brother, Terry, Dora Leoni and Jeff Carter behind. This event would remain in Alan's memory for as long as he lived, which was of course where it *belonged*! Happily, it no longer held sway over his present or future! That belonged *exclusively* to Mary and him! As they walked through the main gate, leaving Lynwood High School behind them, Alan inadvertently sighed. A heavy burden that his mind had unconsciously endured for so very long had finally been lifted, and at last he was *free*! He couldn't believe how good he felt! Smiling now, Alan looked so forward to his and Mary's future! And that was *exactly* what he was thinking when he woke-up on the rooftop of the Lynwood High School gymnasium, surrounded by Mary, Joe and Terry… only *moments* later.

www.ingramcontent.com/pod-product-compliance
Lightning Source LLC
Chambersburg PA
CBHW020604310726
48979CB00008B/1339/J

* 9 7 8 1 6 3 8 6 8 1 1 4 4 *